Hither Shore
Interdisciplinary Journal
on Modern Fantasy Literature

Jahrbuch der
Deutschen Tolkien Gesellschaft e. V.

Der Hobbit

Interdisziplinäres Seminar der DTG
25.-27. April 2008, Jena

Herausgegeben von:
Thomas Fornet-Ponse (Gesamtleitung),
Marcel Bülles, Thomas Honegger,
Rainer Nagel, Alexandra Velten,
Frank Weinreich

SCRIPTORIUM OXONIAE

Bibliografische Information
der Deutschen Bibliothek

Die Deutsche Bibliothek verzeichnet diese Publikation in der Deutschen Nationalbibliografie; detaillierte bibliografische Daten sind im Internet über http://dnb.ddb.de abrufbar.

ISBN 978-3-9810612-3-9

Hither Shore, DTG-Jahrbuch 2008
veröffentlicht im Verlag »Scriptorium Oxoniae«

Deutsche Tolkien Gesellschaft e. V. (DTG)
E-Mail: info@tolkiengesellschaft.de

Scriptorium Oxoniae im Atelier für Textaufgaben e. K.
Brehmstraße 50 · D-40239 Düsseldorf
E-Mail: rayermann@scriptorium-oxoniae.de

Hither Shore, Gesamtleitung: Thomas Fornet-Ponse
Graurheindorfer Straße 64 · D-53111 Bonn
E-Mail: hither-shore@tolkiengesellschaft.de

Vorschläge für Beiträge in deutscher oder englischer Sprache (inklusive Exposé von ca. 100 Wörtern) werden erbeten an o.g. Adresse.

Alle Rechte verbleiben beim Autor des jeweiligen Einzelbeitrags. Es gilt als vereinbart, dass ein Beitrag innerhalb der nächsten 18 Monate nach Erscheinen dieser Hither-Shore-Ausgabe nicht anderweitig veröffentlicht werden darf.

Abwicklung: Susanne A. Rayermann, Düsseldorf
Vorlagenherstellung: Kathrin Bondzio, Solingen
Umschlagillustration: Anke Eißmann, Herborn
Fotografien: Bo Gröper, Düsseldorf; momosu/photocase.com (S. 221)
Druck und Vertrieb: Books on Demand, Norderstedt

Alle Rechte vorbehalten.

Inhalt

Vorwort ... 6
Preface ... 7

Tolkien Seminar 2008

The Eucharistic Poetics in *The Hobbit* ... 9
Fanfan Chen (Taiwan)

Changing Perspectives: Secret Doors and Narrative
Thresholds in *The Hobbit* ... 30
Judith Klinger (Potsdam)

Wolves, Ravens, and Eagles:
A mythic Presence in *The Hobbit* ... 47
Guglielmo Spirito (Assisi)

Dreams and Dream Visions in J.R.R. Tolkien's *The Hobbit* ... 67
Doreen Triebel (Jena)

The Hobbit and Desire ... 83
Allan Turner (Marburg)

On Moral Imagination in J.R.R. Tolkien's *The Hobbit* ... 93
Blanca Grzegorczyk (Wrocław)

Vom Umgang mit Reichtum im *Hobbit* ... 106
Thomas Fornet-Ponse (Bonn)

The Arkenstone as Symbol of Kingship and
Seat of Royal Luck in *The Hobbit* ... 121
Martin G.E. Sternberg (Bonn)

The Dwarven Philharmonic Orchestra 135
Heidi Steimel (Lippstadt)

Lieder und Gedichte in J.R.R. Tolkien's *Der Hobbit* 142
Julian T.M. Eilmann (Aachen)

Augen als Schutz und Bedrohung im *Hobbit* 161
Christian Weichmann (Braunschweig)

Seeing Fire and Sword, or Refining Hobbits 174
Anna Slack (Palermo)

The Comic-Book Adaptation of *The Hobbit* 186
Dirk Vanderbeke (Jena)

Additional Essay

Eine Neubewertung der theoretischen Konzeption
von »Faërie« und »fairy-story«
auf Basis der 2008 erschienenen erweiterten Ausgabe
Tolkien On Fairy-stories 197
Heidi Krüger (Hamburg)

Note

Ist das des Hobbits Kern?
Essentielle Stellen im *Hobbit* 222
Christian Weichmann (Braunschweig)

Zusammenfassungen der englischen Beiträge 227

Summaries of the German Essays 236

Rezensionen

Judith E. Tonning, Brendan N. Wolfe (eds.): The Chronicle of the
Oxford University C.S. Lewis Society 241

Anne Besson: D'Asimov à Tolkien. Cycles et séries dans la
littérature de genre 242

Lucie Armitt: Fantasy Fiction: An Introduction. 243

Fanfan Chen: Fantasticism. Poetics of Fantastic Literature. 244

Eduardo Segura, Thomas Honegger (eds.): Myth and Magic.
Art according to the Inklings. 247

Verlyn Flieger, Douglas A. Anderson (eds.): J.R.R. Tolkien.
On Fairy-stories. 248

Lynn Forrest-Hill (ed.): The Mirror Crack'd. Fear and Horror
in J.R.R. Tolkien's Major Works. 251

Christian Kölzer: ›Fairy tales are more than true‹. Das mythische
und neomythische Weltdeutungspotential der Fantasy
am Beispiel von J.R.R. Tolkiens *The Lord of the Rings* und
Philip Pulmans *His Dark Materials.* 255

Martin Simonson: *The Lord of the Rings* and the Western
Narrative Tradition 257

Tolkien Studies. An Annual Scholarly Review. Volume V 259

Allan Turner (ed.): *The Silmarillion* – Thirty Years On. 263

Sarah Wells (ed.): The Ring Goes Ever On. Proceedings of the
2005 Tolkien Conference. 2 Vols. 264

Dimitra Fimi: Tolkien, Race, and Cultural History.
From Fairies to Hobbits. 266

Über die Autorinnen und Autoren 269
About our Authors 272

Siglen-Liste 276

Verlagsinformation: die Fotoseiten 278

Index 279

Vorwort

Im Jahr ihres zehnjährigen Jubiläums konnte die DTG schon ihr fünftes internationales Tolkien Seminar durchführen – wiederum in der bereits erprobten Kooperation mit der Friedrich-Schiller-Universität Jena (und mit freundlicher Unterstützung des Verlags Walking Tree Publishers). Diesmal stand ein Werk im Vordergrund, das erstaunlicherweise bisher sehr selten als eigenständiger Forschungsgegenstand, sondern bestenfalls als Vorgänger von The Lord of the Rings untersucht wurde: The Hobbit. Insofern war es höchste Zeit, ihm ein eigenes Seminar zu widmen – weniger wegen der in Aussicht stehenden Verfilmung, als vielmehr weil es tatsächlich ein Forschungsdesiderat darstellt.

Ein solches Desiderat kann selbstverständlich nicht in einem einzigen Seminar vollständig abgearbeitet werden, aber mit den hier dokumentierten dreizehn Beiträgen des Seminars (zwei Beiträger haben ihre Manuskripte leider nicht eingereicht) können zumindest das Feld abgesteckt und einige wichtige Markierungen gesetzt werden. Wie zudem die angeregten Diskussionen während des Seminars gezeigt haben, wurden auch zu den besprochenen Themen längst nicht alle Fragen völlig erschöpfend behandelt, sondern weitere Forschungsperspektiven aufgezeigt. Dazu hat sicherlich die – wie ich mit Befriedigung seitens unserer Gesellschaft schreiben darf – mittlerweile übliche Interdisziplinarität und Vielfalt der unterschiedlichen Perspektiven beigetragen.

Beim hohen Anteil an englischen Aufsätzen in diesem Jahr handelt es sich nicht um eine gezielte Politik des Board of Editors oder der Gesellschaft, gleichwohl könnte dies dabei helfen, die hier präsenten Forschungsergebnisse auch weit über den deutschsprachigen Raum bekannt zu machen.

Neben den dreizehn Beiträgen gibt es wiederum zahlreiche Rezensionen, zusätzlich haben Heidi Krüger einen höchst aktuellen Artikel zur neuen Edition der verschiedenen Manuskripte von *On Fairy-Stories* (hg. von Douglas A. Anderson und Verlyn Flieger) und Christian Weichmann eine meta-kritische Note zu den Seminarbeiträgen beigesteuert.

Schließlich sei noch allen am Erfolg des Seminars und dem Zustandekommen dieser Ausgabe Beteiligten herzlich gedankt: Prof. Dr. Thomas Honegger und seinen Mitarbeiterinnen vom Lehrstuhl für Mediävistik an der Friedrich-Schiller-Universität für die wiederum einwandfreie Organisation vor Ort und die Ermöglichung einer dem Jubiläum angemessenen Tagung; den *Walking Tree Publishers* für die freundliche Unterstützung vor Ort sowie natürlich wie immer allen Beitragenden, meinen Mitherausgebern und der Mitherausgeberin im Board of Editors sowie schließlich der Verlegerin Susanne A. Rayermann sowie Kathrin Bondzio für die Herstellung und die Idee einer besonderen Gestaltung dieses Jahrbuchs.   TFP

Preface

In the year of its tenth anniversary, the German Tolkien Society was able to organise its fifth international Tolkien Seminar already – again in the tried and tested cooperation with Friedrich Schiller University, Jena (and with the gracious support of *Walking Tree Publishers*). After last year's so-called small works, this Seminar centred on one particular book by Tolkien that, so far, has not been in the foreground of academic study but has only, if ever, received attention as the precursor of *The Lord of the Rings*: *The Hobbit*. Thus, it was high time to devote an entire Seminar just to that book – not so much because of the approaching film adaptation (the decision on that topic was made well before the recent film news), but because it is indeed a desideratum of research.

Such a desideratum can, of course, never be fully covered in one single Seminar. However, the thirteen papers presented here (two of the speakers unfortunately never handed in their manuscripts) are at least able to delimit the field and plant some important signposts. Furthermore, as the spirited discussions after the presentations have shown, even the topics presented during the Seminar could not manage to treat their respective subjects exhaustively, opening the floor for further perspectives for research. Indubitably, this was aided by – and I take great gratification from the point of view of our society in writing this – the by now common interdisciplinarity and multitude of the various perspectives.

The rather high percentage of English-language papers in this year is not the result of some actual policy on the part of the Board of Editors or the Society. However, it might help in making the scientific results collected here more accessible beyond the sphere of influence of German.

The thirteen papers are again complemented by a multitude of reviews. In addition, we have a very topical article by Heidi Krüger on the new edition of the various manuscripts of *On Fairy-Stories* (eds. Douglas A. Anderson and Verlyn Flieger), as well as a meta-critical note on the seminar papers by Christian Weichmann.

Finally, I would like to thank the people behind the success of the Seminar and the publication of this issue of our Annual: First of all, thanks go to Prof. Dr. Thomas Honegger and his assistants at the chair of mediaeval literature at Friedrich Schiller University for once again faultlessly organising the seminar, resulting in an event worthy of our anniversary; *Walking Tree Publishers* for their gracious support; and, of course, my colleagues on the Board of Editors, the publisher, Susanne A. Rayermann, and Kathrin Bondzio for typesetting and the idea of this annual's special layout.

TFP

Unsere Reise beginnt. Ob wir es schaffen, hin und wieder zurück? Ich verlasse meine Heimat, und plötzlich fallen mir Kleinigkeiten am Wegesrand viel bewusster ins Auge....

Fanfan Chen

The Eucharistic Poetics of *The Hobbit*
Fanfan Chen (Taiwan)

he Hobbit has long been overshadowed by *The Lord of the Rings* and the Middle-earth mythology. Treating the novel as a pre-sequel to the great ring trilogy, critics are inclined to study H as a source book. Its narrative is often characterised as being confined to the conventional fairy tales in children's literature. It is also evident that the tone of the novel appears delightful and lacks the solemnity in the ring trilogy. In similar fashion, it is treated in a light way. The novel is thus considered to embrace children readership, which the author himself also regretted. Tolkien tried to speak for the narrative poetics of H in his letters but not very effective.

If we take a second look of the book and give it a second thought, we will discover that the novel speaks for Tolkien's theory in *On Fairy-Stories* and represents the imaginary of the element earth permeating the Middle-earth mythology. H is "an important work in its own right", as Tolkien esteemed. This is a euphoriant novel that unfolds a horizon from the west to the east, with revelation of the vertical power. Bilbo is an unassuming hero yet with serendipity. His down-to-earth character resounds with the dwarves' metal predisposition, for metal is born from earth. Their attachment to the ground resonates with their language. H provides readers with an archaic picture of human mind, the labyrinth archetype, which is formed by the imaginary of element earth. Delving deep below the surface of a simple adventure story about a hobbit, I would like to bring to light the profundity of Tolkien's poetic art of narration by expounding how the novel unfolds a text world, a world of language, before our eyes. This is not a world hidden behind but realised or 'individualised' through our communion with the text and the author. This comprehension of the novel rendered by the author's art of Fantasy, I would term as the 'Eucharistic poetics'.

Then what is Eucharistic poetics? A Eucharistic reading of literary texts necessitates saturated phenomena of language. It involves passive reception in the active reading. Such passivity retrieves iconic language from its idolatry. In order to make the text world unfold before our eyes, the phenomenological reading as cosmological reverberation brings into play the communion among the author, the text, the reader. Like the Eucharistic cult as transubstantiation through flesh/bread and blood/wine, the Eucharistic poetics is consummated through the mediation of poetic substances: elements, language and story.

In what follows, I will analyse the poetics from four aspects: The imaginary text world of language unfolded with 'saturated phenomena'; the metapoetics of the element earth with Bilbo's 'down-to-earth' heroism and the dwarves' language style and character; archaism of labyrinth as the universal nostalgic image of the element earth; the mythological bridge between the past and the present – time and narrative.

The imaginary text world of language unfolded with 'saturated phenomena'

The term 'Eucharistic' as a poetical concept is borrowed from the French philosopher Jean-Luc Marion, who is also a catholic like Tolkien. In order to find a third way for philosophers and theologians to love wisdom and God, he postulates the Eucharistic hermeneutic metaphysics. In fact, the philosopher Marion finds his counterpart in literature, Tolkien. The former proposes "God without Being" and challenges the idolatry of Western metaphysics, whereas the latter creates his novels in which God is ubiquitous but 'without being'. Marion's conception of Eucharist in philosophy and theology is understood as follows:

> The Eucharist accomplishes, as its central moment, the hermeneutic. It alone allows the text to pass to its referent, recognized as the nontextual Word of the words.... The Eucharist alone completes the hermeneutic; the hermeneutic culminates in the Eucharist; the one assures the other its condition of possibility: the intervention in person of the referent of the text as center of its meaning of the Word, outside of the words, to reappropriate them to himself as "what concerns him, ta peri heautou". (*God* 149)

But how can the Eucharist be possible? Marion proposes passive reception and the gaze of icon. During the experience of ego-object perceptions, there is an ego *I*, an object of experience and a horizon within which the experience takes place. However, different from traditional phenomenology that emphasises the role of the ego, Marion sees the paradox of the infinite *I* limited to and based on two finite factors: a horizon and a defined intuition. He tries to develop a feasible hypothesis to prove that the relation between the ego and the infinite other is possible. Therefore, he proposes the concept of "saturated phenomena". Before the possibility of a saturated phenomenon, everything was reducible to the *I*. The saturated phenomenon could "allow us to experience anew what possibility means – or gives" ("Saturated" 184). The significance of "allow us to" indicates that the subject is not the one that experiences but one that is *allowed* to experience. There is something that controls the situation. Marion explains that in saturated phenomena, the passion of "amazement" ("Saturated" 199) is generated. Because of an excess of intuition beyond the ego's full comprehension, amazement is experienced. The ego, not the subjective *I* that constitutes, becomes a *me* that passively receives and is constituted.

This concept of the ego allowed to experience echoes Paul Ricoeur's dialectic of master and mastered. He recognises that religious experience and feelings are experienced only by the individual ego. Nevertheless, this ego would find himself shifted from *master* of meaning to that of *mastered*. The ego is in fact the affected not the affecter. Both Marion and Ricoeur presume that the ego is not merely as the subject that experiences but also as the object that is called or constituted by the 'Object'. The essential point is the passivity of the ego. I will apply this philosophical theory, based on religious faith, to the phenomenological reading of literary narrative, in particular, Tolkien's fairy-stories.

Marion's Eucharistic hermeneutic metaphysics is possible only through the passive reception of the perceiver in the course of reading and interpreting the Scriptures and of probably treating metaphysics in our times. It is about the text, though the referent is nontextual Word of the words. He insists on the importance of passivity in the process of reading and understanding. With the possibility of passive reception, we will experience the gaze of icon. Like Tolkien and Barfield that criticise the idolatry of language, Marion sees the danger in the idolatry of metaphysics.

Marion's 'phenomenology of religion' sometimes links with Mircea Eliade, also a Catholic mythologist. For Marion, the "object" returns as "hierophany" (manifestation of the Sacred) which he discusses in the context of the "icon" (Taylor 2). This experience is like a "mystical eucharistic encounter with the divine" (Kearney 32). The connection between Eliade and Marion further supports my hypothesis of a Eucharistic reading of Tolkien's sub-creation, correlative to myth and mythopoeia. Tolkien's "recovery" and "escapism" in fact reflect Eliade's idea of returning to mythic origin. Speaking of myth, we will refer to Ricoeur's study of Aristotle's *Poetics* and *Rhetoric*.

Ricoeur esteems the creative power of *mythos* and regards it as creative imitation. His theory of hermeneutic reading searches a text world unfolded:

> [W]hat is sought is no longer an intention hidden behind the text, but a world unfolded in front of it. The power of the text to open a dimension of reality implies in principle a recourse against any given reality and thereby the possibility of a critique of the real. It is in poetic discourse that this subversive power is most alive.
> (*Hermeneutics* 93)

In rhetorical perspective, the power of *mythos* helps 'unrealise oneself': "in reading, I 'unrealise myself'. Reading introduces me to imaginative variations of the *ego*. The metamorphosis of the world in play is also the playful metamorphosis of the *ego*" (*Hermeneutics* 94). This is all the more evident in the creative imitation of Fantasy, or sub-creation, given its double 'unreality': fictive and imaginary. In addition, Fantasy comprises well-threaded plots. For Ricoeur, mimesis is a creative imitation, a kind of metaphor of reality. There is mimesis only where there is 'doing' or 'activity', and poetic 'activity' consists precisely in the construction of plots. Moreover, what mimesis imitates is not effectivity of events but their logical structure, their meaning. This logical structure mirrors Tolkien's insistence in Reason for the composition of fairy-story. Ricoeur sees in fictional narrative an iconic augmentation of the human world of action. Furthermore, "it must be said that fiction is not an instance of reproductive imagination, but of *productive imagination*. As such, it refers to reality not in order to copy it, but in order to prescribe a new reading" (*Hermeneutics* 292). This notion of "a new reading" or "perceiving things differently" evokes Tolkien's idea of "recovery" in the narration of fairy-story.

Fantasy is significant in "un-realising ourselves to "realise" our identity, for we need "distanciation" and "alienation" to (re)appropriate to the Object. Consider the last element in Tolkien's fairy-story theory: Eucatastrophe or consolation. The prefix "euca" homophonic with "eucha" may expand the semantic horizon by sound and image. This last element is significant in the reception of luck, chance or providence. The correspondence between Tolkien's creation of fairy-stories and Marion's philosophy will further extend to readers' reception and participation in Tolkien's texts. Readers thus enter his text world of language, which may reveal "timeless truth" (Ellwood 6). Accordingly, we enter the text world of H by walking with Bilbo through his adventure and the 'saturated phenomena' of Tolkien's words.

The novel is at the same time an adventure, a myth and the manifestation of the Sacred. By imitating Bilbo's adventure, through language, readers could re-enter the mythical truth or "the Great Time" (Eliade). Tolkien insisted on the assumption that the myth is the pristine, or rather 'healthy' language, thus the statement that his novel's world is one of language may also refer to myths. As Eliade illuminates, "In *imitating* the exemplary acts of a god or of a mythical hero, or simply by recounting their adventures, the man of an archaic society detaches himself from profane time and magically re-enters the Great Time, the sacred time" (23). This concept is termed by Eliade as "eternal return". Tolkien's readers ('allowed') may easily feel this impulsion of "eternal return" while reading his works. In this literary experience, the "eternal return" is carried by language. For Tolkien, the essential is language itself:

> ... a primary 'fact' about my work, that it is all of a piece, and *fundamentally linguistic* in inspiration. The authorities of the university might well consider it an aberration an elderly professor of philology to write and publish fairy stories and romances, and call it a 'hobby', ... But it is not a 'hobby', in the sense of something

quite different from one's work, taken up as a relief-outlet. The invention of languages is the foundation. The 'stories' were made rather to provide a world for the languages than the reverse. To me a name comes first and the story follows. (L 219)

However, Tolkien's world of language existing by itself is often criticised or misunderstood as overly allegorical. In regard to this comment, Tolkien retorted by clarifying the definition of allegory. He contended that applicability is not allegory: applicability resides in the reader's freedom, allegory in the purported domination of the author. Therefore, applicability through readers' comprehension is an evidence of Eucharistic poetics, through the reading process that the text world of language becomes life. Marion's "saturated phenomena" can be applied to illustrate the "saturated language as phenomenon" that entails allegorical comprehension. In this manner, allegory can be regarded as the effect of Eucharist, achieved naturally through the mediation of 'saturated language', as Tolkien explicated:

> Of course, Allegory and Story converge, meeting somewhere in Truth. So that the only perfectly consistent allegory is a real life; and the only fully intelligible story is an allegory. And one finds, even in imperfect human 'literature', that the better and more consistent an allegory is the more easily can it be read 'just as a story'; and the better and more closely woven a story is the more easily can those so minded find allegory in it. But the two start out from opposite ends. (L 121)

In reading Tolkien's novel, I feel the enchanting power that 'allows' me to commune with the author, the words and the beyond. The Eucharistic substance here is language itself as poetic diction[1] and narrative fluidity, which make transubstantiation possible. The poetic diction, iconic not idolatrous, arouses aesthetic imagination that leads us to the state of participation. The saturation of words enables passive reception. This process empowers the fantastic text world, yet another 'reality', to 'unfold' before my eyes and thus 'unrealise myself'. In H, the communion is enacted through the metapoetics of the element earth, enhanced by the narrator's storytelling style, the discourses of/on Bilbo's and

---

1 In his *Poetic Diction*, Owen Barfield offers the following definition: "When words are selected and arranged in such a way that their meaning either arouse, or is obviously intended to arouse, aesthetic imagination, the result may be described as poetic diction. Imagination is recognizable as aesthetic, when it produces pleasure merely by its proper activity. Meaning includes the whole content of a word, or of a group of words arranged in a particular order, other than the actual sounds of which they are composed" (41).

the dwarves' languages. The imaginary profundity reverberating with our collective unconscious is the archaic image of labyrinth underlying the novel.

The metapoetics of the element earth

In the Eucharistic reading, poetic diction and the fluidity of narration are the essential substance that makes transubstantiation possible. The figures of flesh/bread and blood/wine in literature are metaphors that refer to poetic diction and narrative fluidity. The occurrence of 'saturated phenomena' in the text world hinges on the art of language. Nonetheless, the metaphor here can also imply the literal "is" if we consider Bachelard's poetics of material imagination, which supplements the poetics of form by bringing to light the particles of the four classical elements that imbue poetic images. Matters here are the elements permeating words.

This is a phenomenological reading that emphasises the communion between the author, the text, and the reader. Different from the focus of psychoanalytical reading – the subject, it studies imagination and language, which requires readers' participation that effects a kind of sublimation of words and matters. And just as specific elements may exercise dominating power over certain phenomena in the physical world, images and words of a text or an author may be characterised with a reigning element. Bachelard termed this poetics as "metapoetics", which can be crystallised through the approach of *rythmanalyse*[2] (*Eau*).

We would characterize H with the metapoetics of earth. Right from the inceptive sentence of the novel, "In a hole in the ground there lived a hobbit", the element earth penetrates into our perception through the musical rhythm of the line. The image of "hole" and "ground" leads us into the imaginary of "cave" and "earth". If we adopt the musical theory of Sidney Lanier to assign each syllable as a musical note, the line can be measured as 'quarter-note, quarter-note, half-note / quarter-note, quarter-note, half-note / half-note, half-note / quarter-note, half-note, quarter-note'. Tolkien begins his story with a tetrameter, a common meter for ballads and Norse epics. The tetrameter also reflects the four classical elements.

Tolkien's famous description of how the sentence came into being without knowing why while correcting School Certificate papers also expounds how he commences the tale: sound and image appear naturally and intuitively. The imagery associated with the sound 'hobbit' can be 'hole' (reminiscent of *Sara-*

---

2   According to Gaston Bachelard, to *rythmanalyse* literature means to realise the profound rhythm of the vibrations that animate the poetics of an author.

hole) and 'rabbit'. Readers are impressed by these images, then the semantic horizon emerges: "hob" historically refers to "rustic, clown, sprite" and "Bilbo" to "sword of fine temper" (Onions). According to Tolkien's description, this is certainly by no means purposely constructed by his conscious mind, since he "did not and do not know why" (L 215). He also mentioned that the great Author guides and inspires him throughout his sub-creation. With H, we are in fact at the core of Middle-earth, figuring 'down to earth' characters: Bilbo and his dwarf companions.

The hobbit-hole image launches the isotopic imagery of caves. In light of Bachelard, the cave is an essential image derived from the element earth. Earth symbolises life and death. It is the land that fertilises and devours lives. By the same token, the cave is a paradox of life and death because it is an embracing womb and devouring tomb. Death is inevitable but life can be sublimated. Tolkien's story, though imaginary, is a human story and about human, thus death. He emphasised the principal theme of death. The delightful story of Bilbo's adventure still ends with the death of Thorin, Fili and Kili.

Then readers, as Bilbo, experience the Eucatastrophic emotion by seeing the coming of the Eagles. The image of the hole and the cave may extend to alchemy, which treats Eschatology inversely by returning to the stage of minerals. However, Tolkien's alchemy is poetical.

The main characters of the story are Bilbo and the dwarves, the former lives in a hobbit-hole, the latter in dwarf caves. The story begins and ends with the hobbit-hole but with a process of individuation, to employ Jung's term. Their adventure can be structured by caves and tunnels, also an earth-elemental image:

The hobbit-hole – the trolls' cave – the Misty Mountain with Goblins' caves and tunnels – the Misty Mountain with Gollum's cave and tunnels – the Mirkwood with tree-constructed tunnels – the Elvenking's cave – the Lonely Mountain with tunnels and caves – Smaug's lair/cave – the main gate/hole of the Misty Mountain – the hobbit-hole.

Caves and labyrinthine tunnels can be regarded as the *mise en abyme* of the entire adventure, as the narrator describes, "That, of course, is the dangerous part about caves: you don't know how far they go back, sometimes, or where a passage behind may lead to, or what is waiting for you inside" (H 55f/54). Likewise, the shift from the dwarves' mistaken sheltering cave into a Goblins' cave illustrates the dialectic of the cave. According to Bachelard, the cave is the alchemical vision, for when we gaze into it, conversely, we are gazed by its eyes in darkness. The cave is at the same time a mouth that murmurs Nature's words. The saturation of Nature's words also reverberates with the language style and character of the two main elemental creatures: the hobbit and dwarves.

Bilbo's 'down-to-earth' heroism

Hobbits are 'down-to-earth' folks that live in hobbit-holes and lead a common and simple life. In the novel, the poetics of the element earth is embodied through Bilbo's down-to-earth character and language. His attachment to his land, hobbit-hole and food reveals the perpetuating feeling of comfort and security that the earth connotes. Bilbo, with his Baggins side, enjoys the safe and cozy life in his hobbit-hole. This character makes him miss his snug hole and often dream of it throughout his adventure, a spatial shifting from a cozy hole to a devouring dragon hole. This rustic nature demonstrates the common motif in fairy tales: serendipity. Bilbo is a decent hobbit and often granted luck. He even obtains the magic object in the story, which will be the principal object in the ring trilogy: the ring, Gollum's lost precious. The perils he encounters always have a good turn, for he never loses hope.

In fact, Tolkien deliberately avoids depicting a conventional hero and "the kind of Celtic beauty that maddened Anglo-Saxons in a large dose" (L 215). He explicitly states that the value of the hobbits he creates lies in "putting earth under the feet of 'romance', and in providing subjects for 'ennoblement' and heroes more praiseworthy than professionals: *nolo heroizari* is of course as good as start for a hero, as *nolo episcopari* for a bishop" (L 215). Through his Fantasy art of storytelling, the humble is exalted. In the case of Bilbo, a mocked 'burglar' eventually becomes, though with the residue of 'burglar', a true 'hero', as recognised by the dwarves.

However, the hobbit is not as simple as it seems, as Tolkien highlighted. Bilbo represents the archetypical mythic origin of the dialectic nature. He struggles between being a Baggins or a Took. Eliade notes that many myths present us with a "twofold revelation". The mystical experiences involve a "coincidence of opposites" or *"coincidentia oppositorum"*. Bilbo reveals to us the paradoxical personality that everyone may contain. It is noticeable that he becomes unconscious many times in the novel. His dreams or nightmares reveal his deep desire and his mystic intuition.

This unassuming hero's language, the language of hobbits, is like English, as Tolkien indicated (L 31). His character and nature is like common people, though with Tolkien's esteemed Englishness as the signature quality. His linguistic style is in standard manner, polite and educated. Nonetheless, he often speaks "crossly" with the dwarves and "grumbles" sometimes. Being down-to-earth, he is not hypocrite but faithful to his feeling while speaking. Though he gradually assumes the leadership in the group, he never boasts his schemes and courage. The narrator truly describes the state of Bilbo: "He was trembling with fear, but his little face was set and grim. Already he was a very different hobbit from the one that had run out without a pocket-handkerchief from Bag

End long ago" (H 199/192). Bilbo himself also utters his own self-comment. He really takes "burglar" literally when he is supposed to do something with the dragon Smaug:

> "What else do you suppose a burglar is to do?" asked Bilbo angrily. "I was not engaged to kill dragons, that is warrior's work, but to steal treasure... If there is any grumbling to be done, I think I might have a say. You ought to have brought five hundred burglars not one... I should want hundreds of years to bring it all up, if I was fifty times as big, and Smaug as tame as a rabbit."
> (H 205/198)

The image and sound in representing the hobbit as a rabbit enhance Bilbo's heroic image as being tame and frightened, just like a rabbit. The rabbit is a recurrent epithet attributed to Bilbo. Many characters, such as Gandalf, the dwarves and the narrator as well, associate Bilbo the hobbit with the rabbit. Even the Eagle that carries him expresses the same impression towards Bilbo: "Don't pinch!" said his eagle. "You need not be frightened like a rabbit, even if you look rather like one" (H 106/103). Different from the rabbit in Lewis Carroll's *Alice*, this is a rabbit that comes out of the hole and leads us into a fantastic journey, where Bilbo and the dwarves adventure literally 'down to earth'.

The dwarves' language style and character

The greatest difference between H and LotR is the significant role dwarves play. In the ring trilogy, dwarves appear relatively invisible in the story, though we are still impressed by Gimli's exclaims and curses by the names of tools and speech like the tool wielded, with a heavy and metallic sense (TT 195). Dwarves in H are the cause of "an unexpected party" and "dark business" that bring about Bilbo's unexpected adventure and self-evolution. Their toughness, rudeness and rush contrast with Bilbo's resilience, comfortableness and gracefulness. And yet they both are physically short and temperamentally down-to-earth. The dwarves are 'down-to-earth' because they love mining and caves. They are also materialistic: "dwarves are not heroes, but calculating folk with a great idea of the value of money" (H 199/192). Dwarves make noises throughout the story, like their beloved treasures and metals. Bilbo uses "dwarvish racket" (H 33/32; 167/162) to describe and complain about his dwarf friends' clamour and clumsiness.

A variety of verbs are employed to mark the dwarves' discourses, for example, "Thorin muttered something about supper" (H 31/30), "yammering and bleating like anything" (H 58), "The dwarves groaned" (H 107/104 and passim), "It was Bofur, and he was grumbling about it" (H 121/118), "'O good-bye and go away!' grunted the dwarves" (H 131/127). The dwarves' groaning and grumbling nature expose their boorishness and bluntness. The complaining verbs resound with the back and low vowels, which give a sense of metallic heaviness. Furthermore, this vocalic sound also echoes with the assonance that associates the dwarves' language and the moon, characterized by the rune letters.

During their stay at Elrond' house, the dwarves and Bilbo learn about the secret of the map given by Gandalf. Elrond reads and decodes rune-letters for them: "'Moon-letters are rune-letters, but you cannot see them,' said Elrond, 'not when you look straight at them. They can only be seen when the moon shines behind them … These must have been written on a midsummer's eve in a crescent moon, a long while ago'" (H 51/50). The rhyme of [un] makes the image and sound of the moon and runes merge together. This is further enhanced by the nomenclature of 'Durin', with an accentuated [u] making assonance with the above vowel sounds.

Tolkien's alliteration shows his obvious inclination for Germanic and Old-English epics. Since rune-letters are idiosyncratic Germanic and Scandinavian (Tolkien mentioned that dwarves have Scandinavian names), he reinforces the sound effect in the passage that describes the secret of the map with the alliterative [d] to connect "Durin's Day" and Dwarves. The alliterative pattern then extends to the spatial description with the alliterative [m], such as "Misty Mountain", "a midsummer's eve", "moon", and eventually expands to the temporal description: "The next morning was a midsummer's morning as fair and fresh as could be dreamed…" (H 52/50f). The image of "moon" not only rhymes with the "rune" but also alliterates with "Misty Mountain" and "midsummer's eve".

Though described as rude, coarse, brusque, blunt, ill-mannered, the dwarves love music. They play instrument and sing. Their singing also corresponds to their voice quality: "And suddenly first one and then another began to sing as they played, deep-throated singing of the dwarves in the deep places of their ancient homes; and this is like a fragment of their song, if it can be like their song without their music" (H 14). Here is the first stanza of the song sung twice in the novel, first by all the dwarves and the second by Thorin before sleep. Their song lyric also has a rhyme with the back-low vowel, like their voice:

> Far over the misty mountains cold
> To dungeons deep and caverns old
> We must away, ere break of day,
> To find our long-forgotten gold. (H 14/26)

Thorin's language style is explicitly commented by the narrator: "You are quite familiar with Thorin's style on important occasions, so I will not give you any more of it, though he went on a good deal longer than this" (H 198/191). An earlier discourse may exemplify Thorin's style, also Dwarvish style: "Now scuttle off, and come back quick, if all is well. If not, come back if you can! If you can't, hoot twice like barn-owl and once like a screech-owl, and we will do what we can" (H 33/32). However, when he is in full rage, he utters very coarse diction to charge Bilbo: "'You miserable hobbit! You undersized – burglar!" he shouted at a loss for words, and he shook poor Bilbo like a rabbit" (H 254/247).

In reality, we are unable to know the real language of Dwarvish, as Tolkien indicated that the dwarves' speeches are 'translated' into English. Nonetheless, we still perceive the Dwarvish nature: "Dwarvish was both complicated and cacophonous" (L 31).

Archaism of labyrinth as the universal nostalgic image of the element earth

The extensive caves and numerous tunnels in the story construct an archaic archetypal image of labyrinth, also the image of fissure, gliding and river. According to Bachelard, the labyrinth is the imaginary of earth embodied in underground waters: "These rivers have the same dynamic contradictions as the labyrinth's dream. They don't run regularly; they have rapids and meanders. They are fiery and coiled up, for all underground movement is bent and difficult" (*Terre* 243)[3]. The dreamer is simply carried by the underground rivers (*Terre* 243). Following Bachelard's theory of the imaginary, Siganos further studies the image of labyrinth as the most primitive one remaining in our nostalgia of archaism (41-2).

H stages a space of saturated labyrinthine caves and tunnels. From the hobbit-hole to the Lonely Mountain, the horizontal journey is perilous because the characters lack a vertical vision. They have to conquer the labyrinthine intricacy to accomplish their journey. The trolls' cave is the first landmark that menaces Bilbo and the dwarves, sometimes Gandalf. The Misty Mountain prolongs this anxiety with enigmatic mountain passes, tunnels, caves and caverns, which

---

3   My translation from French text: "Ces fleuves ont les mêmes contradictions dynamiques que le rêve du labyrinthe. Ils ne coulent pas avec régularité, ils ont des rapides et des méandres. Ils sont fougueux [fiery] et repliés, car tout mouvement souterrain est courbé et difficile" (243).

form a mountainous maze. Even the image in the Mirkwood is described as a labyrinth with tunnels:

> They walked in single file. The entrance to the path was like a sort of arch leading into a gloomy tunnel made by two great trees that leant together, too old and strangled with ivy and hung with lichen to bear more than a few blackened leaves. The path itself was narrow and wound in and out among the trunks. Soon the light at the gate was like a little bright hole far behind... (H 132/128)

In the Mirkwood, the scene of the barrels out of bond, where Bilbo rescues his dwarf friends, also offers a labyrinthine image of Elvenking's cave and underground river that flows out to the Long Lake. This archaic pattern of labyrinth structures the storyline and leads the characters and readers into a mythic voyage into the past. Along with Bilbo and the dwarves, we experience a time travel into the medieval myth: the dragon and its slayer. The real dragon slayer is not Bilbo the burglar but Bard, a descendant in long line of Girion, Lord of Dale. The archetypal motif of a bird speaking to the hero is represented here (a black thrush), but before killing the dragon.

Nature's symphony as Eucharistic substance

Tolkien's style of recovering language through mythopoeia from its 'disease' is the substance that bridges the present and the past, the visible and the invisible. This is the very substance that enables a Eucharistic reading of the author's narrative poetics. Different creatures in the story speak for Nature. This is a realisation of the style of imitation, *harmonism*[4]. Bachelard termed it as imagination's music, realised through language. Journeying with Bilbo and the dwarves, we listen to various creatures' languages that construct the musical space of the labyrinth as Nature's symphony. This murmuring linguistic music running with the underground labyrinthine rivers from the trolls to the Eagles saturated the text world.

We listen to trolls' language that carries us back to the original state of animism and the mineralisation of the magic mode – being petrified: "'Dawn take you all, and be stone to you!' ... And there they stand to this day, all alone, unless the birds perch on them" (H 40f/39). This episode of mineralisation/

---

[4] Fontanier's definition of the style: *Harmonism*, where onomatopoeia and alliteration can enter as elements, consists in a choice and a combination of words, in a texture and a layout of the sentence or of the period, so that by the tone, the sounds, the numbers, the cadences, the pauses, and all the other physical qualities, the expression is in harmony with thought or with sentiment. (my translation, 392)

petrifaction constructs a mythic past for the text world in LotR (I 169ff). The following dialogue among the trolls exemplifies the primitive linguistic form of these archaic creatures:

> "Mutton yesterday, mutton today, and blimey, if it don't look like mutton again tomorrer," said one of the trolls. "Never a blinking bit of manflesh have we had for long enough," said a second. "What the 'ell William was-a-thinkin' of to bring us into these parts at all, beats me – and the drink runnin' short, what's more..." (34/33)

After the encounter with trolls, we journey into the perilous realm of the goblins. With goblins' language, the goggling sound resounds with our collective unconscious, though menacing and cacophonic:

> "What do you mean by it?" said the Great Goblin turning to Thorin. "Up to no good, I'll warrant! Spying on the private business of my people, I guess! Thieves, I shouldn't be surprised to learn! Murderers and friends of Elves, not unlikely! Come! What have you got to say?" (H 61/59)

When the goblins sing, they "sing, or croak, keeping time with the flap of their flat feet on the stone, and shaking their prisoners as well": "Clap! Snap! the black crack! / Grip, grab! Pinch, nab! / And down down to Goblin-town / You go, my lad!" (H 58/56). And their sound is described as "truly terrifying" and their laughter "ugly" (H 58). The Great Goblin has a style when he shouts, though still accentuated by the fricative palato-alveolar sound /sh/ and the open vowel /a/: "Slash them! Beat them! Gnash them! Take them away to dark holes full of snakes, and never let them see the light again!" (H 62/60). Their clamour and rudeness are further reinforced by the narrator's vivid description, coloured with animal images: "The yells and yammering, croaking, jibbering and jabbering; howls, growls and curses; shrieking and skriking, that followed were beyond description. Several hundred wild cats and wolves being roasted slowly alive together would not have compared with it" (H 62/61).

Parallel to the mysterious figures Tom Bombadil and Ents in LotR, Beorn appears as the mythic figure in H. What is in common is their intimacy with Nature, further revealed through their somewhat ecological attitude. For example, Beorn shows a predilection for wood against metal (H 119/116). If Tom Bombadil represents time, and Ents the vitality of vegetation, Beorn embodies the animal power, in particular, his physical strength and his ability of talking to animals: "Beorn said something to them in a queer language like animal noises turned into talk" (H 118/115). Gandalf illustrates Beorn's linguistic nature by the naming of *Carrock*, which shows the relations between sound and image: "He called it the Carrock [the steps on the great rock], because carrock is his word for it. He calls things like that carrocks, and this one is the Carrock because it is the only one near his home and he knows it well" (H 109/5). Half-man half-bear, his being shape-shifter represents the universal theme of metamorphosis. Benevolent, he nevertheless frequently growls, which betrays his bestial nature. And yet, he demonstrates his involvement in human civilisation: "Hullo!" said Beorn. "You came pretty quick – where were you hiding? Come on my *jack-in-the-boxes*! (my emphasis, H 114/1). Moreover, he delivers solemn human speech like a sage: "There is one stream there, I know, black and strong which crosses the path. That you should neither drink of, nor bathe in; for I have heard that it carries enchantment and a great drowsiness and forgetfulness… That you MUST not do, for any reason" (H 125/21f).

Entering the space of the Mirkwood, the Company is faced with terrifying spiders in the middle of the suffocating 'pitch-dark' forest tunnel (H 133/129). These spiders' queer noises of scuffling and hurryings aggravate the perilous situation in the Mirkwood, a wood-labyrinth and the archetype of forest: "There were queer noises too, grunts, scufflings, and hurryings in the undergrowth" (H 132/128). The spiders "splutter" and "hiss" (H 152/147) in the darkness, which is all the more piercing with the presence of their insect eyes. From the perilous realm of the spiders' lair, the Company is not far from their ultimate spatial destiny: the dragon's lair.

The gloating and boasting dragon Smaug, vulnerable to flattering, is a rhetorician. He tries to beguile Bilbo into uncovering his identity. Different from other antagonistic characters in the novel, the arch-enemy Smaug that hinders the accomplishment of the Company's quest is a more complex figure both on the level of narrating and the narrated.

The narrator employs free indirect speech to depict the dragon's feeling and thought: "Thieves! Fire! Murder! Such a thing had not happened since first he came to the Mountains! His rage passes description …" (H 203/195). The figurative expressions further associate the element fire with the fire-spitting dragon and its rage: "as if it was an old volcano that had made up its mind to start eruptions once again" (H 202/195). Even Smaug manifests his rhetorical art through stylistic discourse, such as the use of anaphora and isocolon: "Well, thief! I smell you and I feel your air. I hear your breath. Come along! Help yourself again, there is plenty and to spare!" (H 207/199f). With Smaug and his language, readers enter into the draconic space that straddles the present and the past, which is marked by the dragon's magic power. Moreover, his spell is still at work: "Whenever Smaug's roving eye, seeking for him in the shadows, flashed across him, he trembled, and an unaccountable desire seized hold of him to rush and reveal himself and tell all the truth to Smaug. In fact he was in grievous danger of coming under the dragon-spell" (H 209/201f).

However, Smaug has his 'tragic' flaw that makes Bilbo perceive his weak point. He cannot resist Bilbo's flattering and thus gloats his armour so as to expose his vulnerable belly.

The Eagles, the temporal and vertical symbol in the story (versus the horizontal map), re-interpret the role of Daedalus's wings that carry him from the entrapment of Minotaur's labyrinth. The Eagles come to the rescue of the Company two times by their advantage of verticality. Tolkien described it as the manifestation of Eucatastrophe, which is shown by Bilbo's exclamation "The Eagles! The Eagles are coming!" (H 263/256). Style polished, the Eagles' language illustrates harmonism that resounds with their physical world and their vertical height:

> "Farewell!" they cried, "wherever you fare, till your eyries receive you at the journey's end!" That is the polite thing to say among eagles. Gandalf replies in following this linguistic harmony: "'May the wind under your wings bear you where the sun sails and the moon walks,' answered Gandalf, who knew the correct reply".
> (H 107/104)

The mythological bridge between the past and the present – time and narrative

> Roads go ever ever on,
> Over rock and under tree,
> By caves where never sun has shone,
> By streams that never find the sea... (H 276/269)

The quoted "road" where Tolkien meets with Bilbo (and later Frodo) is a long one. Verlyn Flieger, referring to Alboin in *The Lost Road* with the desire 'to go back', brings to light Tolkien's desire of travelling back through time, being dissatisfied with the present: "Tolkien himself found ways to walk that long road, ways that informed both his life and his fiction. The first way was through language" (3). The above quoted lines indicate the unending and unknown path. This is a labyrinthine space, an archaic image derived from the element earth. Unlimited spaces and archaism make time. Language was, for the philologist Tolkien, "the expression of the most profound and ancient beliefs of the human consciousness, both collective and individual. Language was for Tolkien the repository and conveyance of myth through time. He had an almost mystical belief in the relationship of language to human consciousness" (3). This indeed corresponds to Barfield's philosophy on language, which deems the evolution of language as the evolution of human consciousness. The only way of rendering language into a time machine is to regain the iconic reception of language. For Barfield it is a return to semantic unity; for Tolkien, it is the mythopoeia reflecting the splintered light.

Aside from language, Flieger states that another way into the past for Tolkien was through dream. Tolkien's dreams are not gratuitous unconscious writings; rather, they are penned with his elaborate plotting of reason, with "inner consistency of reality" (FS 139). They assume the role of enriching the metaleptic narration through dream narrative and the eventual realisation in the represented reality. His narrated dreams are significant to the analepsis and prolepsis of the plot development. Moreover, his losing consciousness that often occurs at the end of some episodes creates a temporal space where language and dreams converge. The function of dream is of temporality:

> Language and dream connect to memory, and all three connect to time past. Time, as Tolkien envisioned it, was not a simple forward progression but a complex field of experience encompassing past, present, and future, a field of experience to which dream, memory, and language all gave access". (Flieger 5)

In the cave, first taken as a shelter from the storm and eventually a Goblins' cave, Bilbo had a dream, which turned out to be reality. This is an archaic space that bridges the real and the unreal. The omniscient narrator describes this dream as a sheer staging of a scene where the boundary between the dream and reality is blurred and inter-penetrable:

> He dreamed that a crack in the wall at the back of the cave got bigger and bigger, and opened wider and wider, and he was very afraid but could not call out or do anything but lie and look. Then he dreamed that the floor of the cave was giving way, and he was slipping – beginning to fall down, down, goodness knows where to.
> At that he woke up with a horrible start, and found that part of his dream was true. A crack had opened at the back of the cave, and was already a wide passage. (H 57/55f)

The free indirect speech of "goodness knows where to" implies that the narrator/author seems to be watching the dream of Bilbo. We readers read the dream told by the narrator; the narrator seems to be the dreamer; Tolkien seems to have been writing from Bilbo's dream. We all participate in this synchronicity of story, which leads to the comprehension of identity construction: "The narrative constructs the identity of the character, what can be called his or her narrative identity, in constructing that of the story told. It is the identity of the story that makes the identity of the character" (Ricoeur, *Hermeneutics* 147-8). Tolkien's storytelling involves the identity of the story, the identity of the dream, the identity of the character, the identity of the author and the identity of the reader.

And the synchronic identity of different realms resides in the narrator's discourse. In terms of temporality, the stylistic narrating instance is crucial to the fluidity of storytelling. The narrator as the implied author tells the adventure story with stylistic figures that echo characters' style of language. The narrator's figures can be regarded as a style of recovery threading the 'maze' into 'amazement'. We are led into the historicity of the 'mythic cauldron' through Tolkien's poetic style. The majority of compound sentences (rather than complex ones) with the repetitive conjunctions such as "and", "nor", "so... that" correspond with the colloquialism in storytelling. Tolkien's frequent use of the present participles and gerunds highlights the temporal significance of the diction. In addition, the adverbial phrases such as "at times" and "then" as temporal markers of episodes redress the order of time in history amidst the eternity of mythic time. In what follows, I will list the patterns of figures (repetition and rhythm) and phonological parallelism (sound pattern) that characterise the narrator's style of discourse with examples: isocolon, anaphora, diacope, epizeuxis, etc.

Isocolon:
"Now it is a strange thing, but things that are good to have and days that are good to spend are soon told about, and not much to listen to" (H 49/48)

Isocolon and diacope or epizeuxis:
Talk and talk; down and down; deep deep dark; bigger and bigger; wider and wider; nor...nor (passim)
Fire leaped from the dragon's jaw. / Fire leaped from thatched roofs and wooden beam-ends as he hurtle down and past and round again, though all had been drenched with before he came. (230/223)
"When the tale of their journeyings was told, there were other tales, and yet more tales, tales of long ago, and tales of new things, and tales of no time at all," (274/267)

In combination with patterns of numbers – binary, ternary, quaternary, pentamerous
Here are some examples of ternary diacope / isocolon and pentamerous isocolon:
"He [Gandalf] had eaten most, talked most, and laughed most." (32/30)
"while their eyes grew bigger and bigger and bigger" (68/66)

"He was as noble as fair in face as an elf-lord, as strong as a warrior, as wise as a wizard, as venerable as a king of dwarves, and as kind as summer." (49/8)

The inceptive pattern: rhythm and inversion modelled on "In a hole/ in the ground/ there/ lived a hobbit":
"On the table/ in the light/ of a big lamp/ with a red shade/ he spread a piece of parchment rather like a map" (3/19).
"Deep down here/ by the dark water/ lived old Gollum, a small slimy creature" (69/67)
"There/ on the grey stone/ in the grass/ was an enormous thrush,/ nearly coal black, its pale yellow breast freckled with dark spots" (196/189)

Phonological parallelism: alliteration, consonance, assonance
down, howl, growl, mountain, ground, round, loud, 'old road', 'deep dell', etc. (passim)
"They were burning bright and blue." (46/5)
"They all laughed and stamped and clapped their hands." (58)
"Buttons burst off in all directions. He was through, with a torn coat and waistcoat, leaping down the steps like a goat, while bewildered goblins were picking up his nice brass buttons on the doorstep." (85/82f)
"Yellowing bracken, fallen branches, deep-piled pine needles, and here and there dead trees, were soon in flames. All round the clearing of the Wargs fire was leaping. But the wolf-guards did not leave the trees. Maddened and angry they were leaping and howling round the trunks, and cursing the dwarves in their horrible language, with their tongues hanging out, and their eyes shining as red and fierce as the flames." (98/96)
"So he sat down and wished in vain for a wash and a brush. He did not get either, nor tea nor toast nor bacon for his breakfast, only cold mutton and rabbit. And after that he had to get ready for a fresh start." (106/3)

If figures and phonological parallelism construct a musical pattern imbued with matters of elements in the novel that helps bridge the temporal gap and unfold the text world, the historicity of this text world is emblematised by the discourses about philology. Language not only illustrates synchronic features and patterns but also contains diachronic quality that reveals the integration between the figurative and the literal. The narrator explicitly comments on this philological issue as he describes the darkness in the Mirkwood:

> The night was the worst. It then became pitch-dark – not what you call pitch-dark, but really pitch: so black that you really could see nothing. Bilbo tried flapping his hand in front of his nose, but he could not see it at all. Well, perhaps it is not true to say that they could see nothing: they could see eyes. (H 133/129)

By the same token, the narrator explicitly refers to the evolution and change of language: "To say that Bilbo's breath was taken away is no description at all. There are no words left to express his staggerment, since Men changed the language that they learned of elves in the days when all the world was wonderful" (H 210/194).

With the above examples, we are guided back to the beginning of the story where the conversation between Bilbo and Gandalf touches upon figurative and literal meanings of the expression "Good morning":

> "Good morning!" said Bilbo, and he meant it. The sun was shining, and the grass was very green... "What do you mean?" he said. "Do you wish me a good morning, or mean that it is a good morning whether I want it or not; or that you feel good this morning; or that it is a morning to be good on?" / "All of them at once," said Bilbo. (H 5f)

This dialogue may be considered delightful and even tongue-in-cheek given that the readership is supposed to be children, who would simply delight in this playful questioning. Nonetheless, Tolkien, having children in his mind while writing the story, has his narrator entitled with narrative authority, who unworriedly reminds readers the distinction between the fictive and reality but at the same time recovers the literal meanings to the figurative. "Good morning" indeed raises the issue of dead and living metaphor. Language could be a linguistic monument of history, as Leibniz assumed.

Speaking of the children readership, I will make a last comment on narrative authority in H to close this section on time and narrative. H is often counted as a tale written for children. The fairy-tale style is all the more evident that the narrator is in fact the implied author that interferes throughout the story by metaleptic, analeptic and prolectic devices and explanations in parentheses. The plethora of parentheses further demonstrates the authority of the omniscient narrator. After introducing the Hobbit, the narrator's discourse is followed by prolepsis: "This is a story of how a Baggins had an adventure, and found himself doing and saying things altogether unexpected. He may have lost the neighbours' respect, but he gained – well, you will see whether he gained anything in the end" (H 3f). Throughout the storytelling, readers are guided, reminded, and even 'instructed' by the narrator about the threading of the plot. It is possible to interpret Tolkien's special style of telling this story in such a way as to remind children readers that this is not reality but a 'story'. This reminder is unnecessary for adults. Such an interpretation corresponds to Tolkien's argument in *On Fairy-Stories* that fairy-stories are not for Children, as Andrew Lang assumed. Indeed, Tolkien had children in his mind while writing H: "*The Hobbit* was intended to be one of them ['children's stories' for their private amusement]. It had no necessary connexion with the 'mythology', but naturally became attracted towards this dominant construction in my mind, causing the tale to become larger and more heroic as it proceeded (L 346). In this manner, the novel shifts from a 'children's story' to a heroic and solemn one, which comply with Tolkien's criteria for fairy-stories, not written for children.

Conclusion

The cosmic time and the lived time can only be reconciled through a third time, the narrative time. In light of Ricoeur, action, taken in the present, preserves the space of experience in a dialectical tension with the horizon of expectation. In reading Tolkien's H, the realisation and integrity of identity is effective, on the levels of characters as well as of readers. Thus the poetics of narrative responds to the aporia of temporality. Tolkien, though not oriented by a metaphysical thinking, used his concrete storytelling into a world of language to manifest the essence. His creative process is also a Eucharistic experience: "My work did not 'evolve' into a serious work... The so-called 'children's story' was a fragment, torn out of an already existing mythology" (L 218).

Tolkien's poetic diction is like magic that creates "wonder and surprise", important feature in Aristotle's mimesis. Fantasy is *per se* "surprise and wonder". It is the *mythos*, the creative imitation, the rhetorical bridge between the real and the imaginary. The wonder and surprise is essentially grounded in language and story. We experience it vicariously with Bilbo in H, effectuated through the process of Eucharistic poetics: passive reception, active reading and the gaze of iconic language through saturated phenomena.

The aporia in philosophy seems to have found a third way in poetics as Ricoeur theorises the issue and as Tolkien feels it: "Life is rather above the measure of us all (save for a very few perhaps). We all need literature that is above our measure..." (L 298). This third way is the Tolkienian Fantasy. So life is like a labyrinth, but we, like Bilbo, expect for luck and providence. The labyrinth and earth-element reverberate with our collective unconscious, which is connected with myths to link with the past culture. Mythology and fairy tales bridge the gap between generations. Tolkien's art of Fantasy conduces to the convergence of myth, legend, history and myth. This is the hierophany of 'the Tree' painted by Niggle in the story *Leaf by Niggle*.

Bibliography

Bachelard, Gaston. *L'Eau et les Rêves*. Paris: José Corti, 1942
---. *La Terre et les rêveries du repos*. Paris: Librairie José Corti, 1948
Barfield, Owen. *Poetic Diction: A Study in Meaning*. Middletown: Wesleyan UP, 1973
---. *Saving the Appearances: A Study in Idolatry*. Middletown: Wesleyan UP, 1988
Carpenter, Humphrey, Ed. with assistance of C. Tolkien. *The Letters of J.R.R. Tolkien*. London: HarperCollins, 1995
Eliade, Mircea. *Myths, Dreams and Mysteries*. Trans. Philip Mairet, New York, Harper & Row, 1967
Ellwood, Rober. *The Politics of Myth: A Study of C.G. Jung, Mircea Eliade, and Joseph Campell*. Albany: State U of New York P, 1999
Flieger, Verlyn. *A Question of Time: J.R.R. Tolkien's Road to Faërie*. Kent & London: The Kent State UP, 1997
Fontanier, Pierre. *Les Figures du discours*. Paris: Flammarion, 1968
Kearney, Richard. *The God who May be*. Bloomington: U of Indiana P, 2001
Lanier, Sidney. *Science of English Verse*. In Centennial Edition. Vol. II. Ed. Charles Anderson. Baltimore, 1945: pp. vii-xlviii
Marion, Jean-Luc. *God Without Being*. Trans. Thomas A. Carison. U of Chicago P, 1991
---. "The Saturated Phenomenon." *Phenomenology and the "Theological Turn": The French Debate*. Trans. Thomas A. Carlson. New York: Fordham UP, 2000
---. *The Idol and Distance: Five Studies*. Trans. Thomas A. Carlson. New York: Fordham UP, 2001
Onions, C. T. (ed.). *The Oxford Dictionary of English Etymology*. Oxford UP, 1996
Ricoeur, Paul. *Oneself as Another*. Trans. Kathleen Blamey. The U of Chicago P, 1992
---. "Experience and Language in Religious Discourse". *Phenomenology and the "Theological Turn": The French Debate*. Trans. Jeffrey L. Kosky. New York: Fordham UP, 2000
---. *Hermeneutics & the Human Sciences*. Trans. John B. Thompson. Cambridge UP, 2005
Taylor, Victor E. "A Conversation with Jean-Luc Marion." JCRT. 7.2. Spring 2006
Tolkien, J.R.R. *The Hobbit or There and Back again*. London: HarperCollins, 1995
---. *The Monsters and the Critics and Other Essays*. London: HarperCollins, 1997
---. "Leaf by Niggle." *Tales from the Perilous Realm*. London: HarperCollins, 1997: 121-144

Changing Perspectives
Secret Doors and Narrative Thresholds in *The Hobbit*
Judith Klinger (Potsdam)

"This is a story of how a Baggins had an adventure, and found himself doing and saying things altogether unexpected" (H 30). Delivered early in *The Hobbit*, the narrator's casual announcement seems to promise nothing more spectacular than an original tale about a humble and somewhat stolid hero. Yet by the time the book approaches its conclusion, this initial promise has been fulfilled beyond all expectations: Bilbo Baggins has entered a world of legend and epic history,[1] his 'adventure' extends to encounters with elves, the formidable Eagles, a shape-shifter and – not least – the greatest dragon of his world.

It is essential to note immediately that, instead of introducing readers to a single, coherent 'fairy-tale' universe, *The Hobbit* presents two separate spheres of existence with equally distinct connections to the readers' reality.[2] Bilbo Baggins' comfortable hobbit world, the story's point of departure, may contain "wonderful tales ... about dragons and goblins and giants" (H 35), but certainly does not embrace the full, overwhelming reality of such creatures.[3] Initially, the interference of a wizard is required to steer an unsuspecting Bilbo into the midst of these dubious contemporaries, for "[t]ales and adventures sprouted up all over the place wherever he [Gandalf] went, in the most extraordinary fashion" (H 31). The implicit analogy of 'tale' and 'adventure' draws attention to the double boundary crossed in *The Hobbit*. By the time of his return, Bilbo possesses the concrete experience of a world that previously existed only in the shape of a text (or tale).[4] Although his report is met by the general disbelief of

---

1 In his discussion of the poetological implications of Tolkien's dragons, Patrick Brückner proposes that Smaug grounds the emergence of a specifically medieval understanding of 'heroic' or 'epic history' in *The Hobbit* (103f). Historical truth, within this concept, transcends the modern division of 'factual' and 'legendary' historiography. "The dragon ... sustains the significance of the noble past" and "represents an epically historical world and its significance – not, it must be noted, as a symbol, but as a 'real' dragon" (Brückner 104).
2 For a more comprehensive treatment of this crucial aspect of the text, see Brückner.
3 While flattering the dragon, Bilbo evidently voices the truth when he tells Smaug: "Truly songs and tales fall utterly short of the reality, O Smaug the Chiefest and Greatest of Calamities" (H 279).
4 From an external perspective, Bilbo himself has entered a 'tale' ("Most of the tale he knew, for he had been in it"; H 356): a theme more fully developed in *The Lord of the Rings*, where Frodo and Sam discuss the complex implications on the Stairs of Cirith Ungol (cf. LotR 696f). On the return journey, Bilbo explicitly refers to a transition back into 'ordinary' reality: "'Merry is May-time!' said Bilbo, as the rain beat into his face. 'But our back is to legends and we are coming home. I suppose this is a first taste of it'" (H 358).

his fellow hobbits (cf. H 361), 'legendary' spaces and beings have emerged as actual reality and, in the process, the texture of the narration itself has been transformed. In other words, the transition into a different reality shapes not only Bilbo's story but the story's discourse as well.

The "major changes in the narrative voice" that occur in the latter parts of *The Hobbit* have already been noted by Paul Edmund Thomas, who concludes: "This is the narrator of a prose epic. This is a whisper from the narrator who speaks in full voice in *The Lord of the Rings*" (179).[5] It would seem, therefore, that not only Bilbo Baggins embarks on an unforeseen adventure: the narrator, too, ventures out into unfamiliar territory. Yet is it conceivable that, like Bilbo, the narrator 'finds himself doing and saying things altogether unexpected', or, in the stricter terms of literary criticism, that the story-teller explores previously inaccessible narrative strategies?

At first glance, this assumption may seem to take the analogy of 'tale' and 'adventure' one step too far. To begin with, the narrator of *The Hobbit* commands a far more comprehensive knowledge of the larger reality and its perils than the tale's woefully ignorant protagonist; the narrator orders the story, whereas Bilbo often struggles to get his bearings within it. Furthermore, the narrator's distinct voice mediates between the readers' familiar reality and the strange, sometimes bewildering spaces of Middle-earth, thereby establishing a layer of coherence that bridges a widening gap. Yet this ostensible coherence must be viewed against unexpected changes, even ruptures, within the texture of narrated space and history. At a closer look, the narrator seems to negotiate shifting grounds.

In this essay, I will trace a correlation of transitions on both levels of the text: the level of the story and the level of the narration (or discourse). Beyond the striking changes of mood and tone in the book's final chapters, abrupt shifts of tense and viewpoint surround the discoveries of Durin's Day, Bilbo's entry into Smaug's lair by means of the secret door, and Smaug's re-emergence into the outer world: transitions that promote the most dramatic events of the tale. The crossing of critical boundaries and thresholds – the spatial and temporal transitions within the story – thus coincide with marked shifts of tone and perspective within the discourse. The overall effect, I will argue, is a textual transformation of legendary into experienced reality, an "imaginative transfer into the impossible" (Fludernik 393). By examining these features of *The Hobbit*, I also hope to demonstrate that the text's specific construction of a narrative entry into 'legendary' space is indeed unique within the corpus of Tolkien's works.

With regard to narrative thresholds, two intersecting paradigms stand out: the secret door discovered on Durin's Day and the correlation of shifting

---

5 Thomas specifically refers to the 'spreading tidings' of Smaug's death.

realities with equally shifting viewpoints and perceptions in the narration. On the level of the narrated story, this essential correlation is mirrored by the gradual unriddling of Thror's Map, a process that establishes an inherent link between 'tale' and 'adventure' and subtly transforms the texture of the represented reality.

I Maps and Thresholds

In the opening chapter of *The Hobbit*, the motif of the secret door is introduced during the discussion of Thror's Map that takes place at Bag End. In fact, the map itself serves as a launching point for the transformation of legend into reality, for it initiates a progressive translation of text and image (within the story) into actual experience. This translation occurs across several stages, as the map itself possesses more than one layer of text. Significantly, the decoding of each layer manifests a new aspect of the reality that becomes accessible by means of the map.

The first, most readily comprehensible layer consists of the drawings that represent features of the landscape and the accompanying (English) captions and explanations. Even Bilbo, the uninformed hobbit, is able to relate to this layer, for he "loved maps, and in his hall there hung a large one of the Country Round with all his favourite walks marked on it in red ink" (H 52). He is therefore able to read the map as an organized representation of space, even if the depicted landscape is unfamiliar.

The second layer of Thror's Map contains visible (English) runes that require a translation, which Gandalf supplies: "'Five feet high the door and three may walk abreast' say the runes" (H 52). This specification of the door's dimensions does not provide directions, however: a 'd'-rune (ᛞ) marks its place somewhere on the western side of the Mountain, but neither Gandalf nor the dwarves are aware of its precise location.

Yet the map proves to be textually productive in another sense as well. Prior to its emergence, the dwarves' mysterious song – a condensed poetic account of their legendary history – has stimulated Bilbo's imagination, stirring his adventurous Took side.[6] However, Bilbo remains ignorant of the history behind

---

6   Cf. H 45f: "As they sang the hobbit felt the love of beautiful things made by hands and by cunning and by magic moving through him, a fierce and jealous love, the desire of the hearts of dwarves. Then something Tookish woke up inside him, and he wished to go and see the great mountains, and hear the pine-trees and the waterfalls, and explore the caves, and wear a sword instead of a walking-stick. He looked out of the window. The stars were out in a dark sky above the trees. He thought of the jewels of the dwarves shining in dark caverns. Suddenly in the wood beyond The Water a flame leapt up – probably somebody lighting a wood-fire – and he thought of plundering dragons settling on

the song as well as his guests' purpose and his own role in the larger scheme of things. Subsequent discussion of the map then produces a first coherent account of the dwarves' ancient conflict with the dragon and their plan to re-conquer their kingdom. Furthermore, studying Thror's Map – which provides at least some foothold of familiarity – engages Bilbo to the point where he envisions 'sitting on the doorstep' of the secret entrance (H 58).

At this first stage, the map thus serves as a medium that inserts the dwarves' unfamiliar history into Bilbo's perception of reality. Everything it reveals may still appear "comfortably far-off (and therefore legendary)", as Gandalf says with regard to dragons (H 53), yet it has generated a comprehensible story both Bilbo and the reader can appreciate.

However, this alignment of Bilbo's and the reader's awareness is disrupted at the next stage of decoding the map. Gandalf, Bilbo and the dwarves have crossed the 'Edge of the Wild':[7] they have left the predictable world of (and around) the Shire and proceed into the realm of 'legend', inhabited by Elves, goblins, wargs – and dragons.[8] In Rivendell, it is Elrond who, on Midsummer Eve, discovers the 'moon-letters' on the map by the light of the crescent moon and translates the previously invisible runic inscription, the third layer of the text:[9] "'Stand by the grey stone when the thrush knocks,' read Elrond, 'and the setting sun with the last light of Durin's Day will shine upon the key-hole'" (H 96).

At this juncture, the discovered runes and the process of discovery amount to a relocation of Thror's Map (and its text) within time. The moon-letters can only be read at a specific time determined by both the solar cycle (midsummer) and the phase of the moon (the crescent moon). Secondly, the secret door's opening depends on temporal coordinates more specifically defined by the dwarves' ancient (lunar) calendar: on this level, too, the simultaneous presence of sun and moon is essential.

---

his quiet Hill and kindling it all to flames. He shuddered; and very quickly he was plain Mr. Baggins of Bag-End, Under-Hill, again."

7   The 'Edge of the Wild' is clearly marked on the *Map of Wilderland* that accompanies the text, yet the story itself seems to locate it elsewhere. As Patrick Brückner has convincingly argued, this dividing line marks the difference between fairy-tale realm and the space of epic history, which the dragon inhabits (109-114).

8   Cf. H 88: "They asked him [Gandalf] where he was making for, and he answered: 'You are come to the very edge of the Wild, as some of you may know. Hidden somewhere ahead of us is the fair valley of Rivendell where Elrond lives in the Last Homely House...'" H 101f: "Even the good plans of wise wizards like Gandalf and of good friends like Elrond go astray sometimes when you are off on dangerous adventures over the Edge of the Wild; and Gandalf was a wise enough wizard to know it."

9   Once again, Bilbo's interest is immediately roused: "'What are moon-letters?' asked the hobbit full of excitement. He loved maps, as I have told you before; and he also liked runes and letters and cunning handwriting, though when he wrote himself it was a bit thin and spidery" (H 95).

The map and the door are thus aligned to specific points in time. While the secret door occupies a fixed (as yet unknown) geographical site, Thror's Map is at first mobile and may be consulted independent of time and space. The temporal relocation of the map gains significance once we consider it in terms of a text that refers to an external reality. At first, the signifier that marks the door (ᛯ) within this text appears to provide only an arbitrary reference to a place that may or may not exist – things far-off are 'legendary' after all – and that may or may not be reached. The decoding of the moon-letters, however, reveals that the relation between signifier and signified is by no means arbitrary: an objective temporal connection grounds the map-text within reality. Its meaning depends on its disclosure at a specific moment, just as the secret door will only be revealed at a specific point in time.

In addition, Bilbo's reality is unquestionably disconnected from the reader's. While the audience may still read and make sense of *The Hobbit* where- and whenever it pleases, discovery of the moon-letters establishes a radically different type of reading. Beyond the Edge of the Wild, the map-text signifies because it enters meaningful relations with its temporal environment. Evidently, this newly revealed interdependence paves the way for Bilbo's entry into the world of 'legend'. Transgression of the boundary between the map and external reality precedes and enables the crossing of a crucial threshold that divides separate realities.

With regard to the correlation of narrated and narrative thresholds, the gradual decoding of the map serves to embed its text within the space and time of the story: that is, within a context that determines and unfolds its full meaning. Rivendell, a place reached by secret paths, provides an initial connection with 'legendary' reality. However, this significant shift concerns a text within the text, and does not (immediately or necessarily) affect the narrator's position within the changing texture of the narrated reality. In the following section, I will therefore address the narrator's involvement with the transition into the 'legendary' realm.

II Shifting Focalizations

In his analysis of the narrative voice in *The Hobbit*, Paul Edmund Thomas points out four distinct traits: the narrator interprets his material, reveals and withholds his knowledge selectively, and interacts with his audience in a fully self-conscious manner (Thomas 163-66).[10] The narrator is indeed distinguished

---

10 The 'self-conscious' narrator displays an awareness of his own role and the process of storytelling, as he does in the following commentary: "'Excitable little fellow,' said Gandalf, as they sat down again. 'Gets funny queer fits, but he is one of the best, one of the best – as fierce as a dragon in a pinch.' If you have ever seen a dragon in a pinch, you will realise that *this was only poetical exaggeration* applied to any hobbit" (H 47; emphasis added).

by far-ranging insight into the histories and peculiarities of Middle-earth, yet the events of his tale are observed and presented from an external perspective. By referring to features of modern life (such as the notorious "whistle of an engine coming out of a tunnel"; H 47), the overt heterodiegetic narrator[11] maintains a connection with his audience's reality, thus straddling the gap between the textual and the extra-textual world. However, the narrator's discourse is by no means limited to this emergence of a distinct voice and the role of an intermediary. As Thomas points out, the narrator also appears as a "self-effacing reporter" in other parts of the story, where "the description, not the describer, receives the emphasis" (168). Thomas does not examine the interconnections between these traits, nor does he relate the diverging narrator strategies – especially the obvious tension between a 'self-conscious' and a 'self-effacing' approach – to the development of the story and its key events.

To achieve greater precision in the description of the narrator's discourse, I will refer to different strategies of *focalization* and to *windows of perception*.[12] The concept of focalization allows for a distinction between a speaking and a seeing agent, or between voice and perspective: we may see a certain event through a character's eyes, while the narrator voices these perceptions. In this case, a scene is focalized through the character but told by the narrator. The apparent tension between 'self-conscious' and 'self-effacing' narrator can thus be restated as a matter of shifting focalization. The second analytical category, the 'window' of perception, draws attention to the techniques by which a text suggests mental images, so that the reader may "see through language" (Jahn, *Windows* 256, quoting Roger Fowler). In *The Hobbit*, the narrator sometimes explicitly encourages imaginative perception; more importantly, shifts of focalization may serve to unclose windows on different levels of imagination.

A few brief examples may illustrate the effects. The strategy of strict focalization (through a character) is employed in the following description, relating Bilbo's (visual) perceptions: "Far, far away in the West, *where things were blue and faint*, Bilbo knew there lay his own country of safe and comfortable things, and his little hobbit-hole" (H 101; emphasis added). Here, the narrator, who

---

11 A heterodiegetic narrator relates the described events but does not experience them directly: "he is in the story but not in the plot" (Thomas 163).
12 According to Jahn's proposed model, based on modifications of Genette's theory (Jahn, *Aspects*, *Narratology*). Cf. Jahn, *Windows* 243: "Typically, F1 [focus-1] is a point at which all perceptual stimuli come together, a zero point from which all spatio-temporal and experiential coordinates start, an origo ...; in short, a point that defines the position, the literal and figurative point of view, inhabited by a thinking and experiencing I." Developing the theoretical models proposed by James and Ryan, Jahn (*Windows* 256) combines focalization with a reception-oriented approach: "Focalization theory, under this view, deals with the gradient of possibilities of a text's windows on story events and existents. A passage that presents objects and events as seen, perceived, or conceptualized from a specific focus-1 will, naturally and automatically, invoke a reader's adoption of (or transposition to) this point of view and open a window defined by the perceptual, evaluative, and affective parameters that characterize the agent providing the focus-1."

has often before delayed the unfolding of events by relating information to the audience or directly addressing the reader, not only focalizes through Bilbo but also provides a distinct spatial frame of reference.

In the following example, the employed focalization is more complex: "He [Gandalf] lit up his wand – *as he did that day in Bilbo's dining-room that seemed so long ago, if you remember* –, and by its light they explored the cave from end to end" (H 105; emphasis added). With his interjection, the narrator implicitly invites readers to embed Bilbo's subjective perception ("that day ... that seemed so long ago") within their own memory of the story as it was told ("if you remember"). The condensed phrasing suggests an intimate link between the reader's and Bilbo's memory of the event: a shared past.

Both examples come from the chapter "Over Hill and Under Hill", immediately following the company's sojourn at Rivendell. At several points in this chapter, the narrator's articulation of the tale approaches the characters' perceptions not only through his representation of visual impressions: he also adopts their style of speech and draws on their specific range of experience and knowledge.[13] The result of this variable focalization is an increasingly dialogic text.[14] As diverging voices and perspectives become more pronounced, elements of strangeness and otherness enter the narrative discourse, anticipating the transition into an unfamiliar reality. From this dialogue, too, emerges a link between the characters' entry into realms of legend and the narrator's shifting position, as an example from the same chapter may illustrate.

As the company seeks shelter in an apparently unoccupied cave, the narrator inserts a general comment: "That, of course, is the dangerous part about caves: you don't know how far they go back, sometimes, or where a passage behind may lead to, or what is waiting for you inside" (H 105). The implicit warning (addressed to the reader) can easily be read as a foreshadowing of future events (within the story). However, the narration does not simply proceed from a

---

13 For instance, in the opening chapter the narrator compares Bilbo's "shriek" to "the whistle of an engine coming out of a tunnel" (H 47). Later on, however, the goblins' "yells and yammering, croaking, jibbering and jabbering; howls, growls and curses" are likened to the noises made by "[s]everal hundred wild cats and wolves being roasted slowly alive together" (H 111). Similarly: "These [goblins] ran forward, as swift as weasels in the dark, and with hardly any more noise than bats" (H 114). While the presence of weasels and bats may have been more familiar to Tolkien's initial and contemporary audience than it is today, such knowledge of animal behaviour relates to the world Bilbo inhabits first and foremost.
14 Cf. Jahn's definition (*Narratology* N.3.1.9): "*dialogism*: The effect created when a text contains a diversity of authorial, narratorial, and characterial voices creating significant contrasts and tensions. The result is a *polyphonic* or dialogic text." – This technique may also be described as a "dual voice" effect, which "occurs when the authorial narrator voices opinions of a character, mimicking that character's diction" (Fludernik 396).

generalized prediction of danger to its concrete materialization (the goblins' following attack). In between, Bilbo dreams:

> He dreamed that a crack in the wall at the back of the cave got bigger and bigger, and opened wider and wider, and he was very afraid but could not call out or do anything but lie and look. Then he dreamed that the floor of the cave was giving way, and he was slipping – beginning to fall down, down, goodness knows where to. At that he woke up with a horrible start, and found that part of his dream was true. A crack had opened at the back of the cave, and was already a wide passage. (H 106)

Bilbo's dreaming consciousness evidently partakes of the knowledge the narrator drew on shortly before. At the same time, his dream-experience is far more dramatic than the narrator's abstract statement: it combines a concrete feature of the approaching danger – the focussed image of the widening crack – with heightened sensory perception. This scene not only focalizes an unexpected transformation of space through Bilbo's awareness, it also opens up a new window of perception:[15] the dream conveys an intense experience of profound disorientation that precedes the transition from 'over hill' to 'under hill' and into the unfamiliar realm of goblins.[16] This transition is processed through a state of altered consciousness; the 'window' introduces a different mode of perception both in terms of imagery and of the level of awareness.

A similar process can be observed in the "Queer Lodgings" chapter, where Bilbo has another clairvoyant dream. However, in this chapter the narrator's part is largely delegated to Gandalf who not only provides Bilbo and the dwarves with the necessary background information about Beorn, but also charms their grudging host with a suspenseful rendering of their previous adventures. On the second day at Beorn's house, it is Gandalf who talks about the nocturnal meeting of their 'skin-changing' host with other bears:

> There must have been a regular bears' meeting outside here last night. I soon saw that Beorn could not have made them all: there were far too many of them, and they were of various sizes too. I should say there were little bears, large bears, ordinary bears,

---

15 On shifting and stacking 'focalization windows': Jahn, *Windows* and *Aspects*, 101-04.
16 Previously, goblins belonged to the realm of stories, not to actual experience; Bilbo associates them with Gandalf's tales: "Not the fellow who used to tell such wonderful tales at parties, about dragons and goblins and giants and the rescue of princesses and the unexpected luck of widows' sons?" (H 33f). As the narrator points out later: "He [Bilbo] had read of a good many things he had never seen or done" (H 73)

and gigantic big bears, all dancing outside from dark to nearly dawn. They came from almost every direction, except from the west over the river, from the Mountains. In that direction only one set of footprints led – none coming, only ones going away from here. (H 180)

During the following night, Bilbo's dream 'translates' the reported information into an intense visual impression:

while the dwarves were still singing songs he dropped asleep, still puzzling his little head about Beorn, *till he dreamed a dream of hundreds of black bears dancing slow heavy dances round and round in the moonlight in the courtyard.* Then he woke up when everyone else was asleep, and he heard the same scraping, scuffling, snuffling, and growling as before. (H 181; emphasis added)

Complex focalization strategies are thus employed to convey the mystery of Beorn's transformation. Instead of incorporating the 'skin-changing' into the narration (either by telling – *diegesis* – or showing – *mimesis*), the narrator cedes the role of instructor and distributor of information to Gandalf. Yet the wizard merely divulges general knowledge[17] and his own deductions, based on the bear-tracks he followed. It is Bilbo's dream that visually conjures the presence of Beorn in bear-shape and, through a newly opened window of perception, provides a glimpse at a magical reality. Not surprisingly, Beorn's later appearance as a bear, as the company approaches the gate of Mirkwood, is again focalized through Bilbo: "As the light faded Bilbo thought he saw away to the right, or to the left, the shadowy form of a great bear prowling along in the same direction" (H 186).[18]

These briefly discussed examples share several important features: transitions into unfamiliar space and transformations of reality are introduced by generalized narrator statements and subsequently focalized through Bilbo's dream perceptions, only then to emerge within the narrated reality. Focalization and the successive introduction of different windows – the characters' waking and dreaming perceptions – serve to manifest this transition on the level of the narration, not merely on the level of the related events. Narrator strategies are obviously involved with the emergence of another reality within the story.

---

17 Cf. H 164f: "He is a skin-changer. He changes his skin; sometimes he is a huge black bear, sometimes he is a great strong black-haired man with huge arms and a great beard. I cannot tell you much more, though that ought to be enough."
18 Gandalf, the narratorial authority on Beorn, confirms and approves his perceptions when he admonishes the Dwarves: "Mr. Baggins' eyes are sharper than yours, if you have not seen each night after dark a great bear going along with us or sitting far off in the moon watching our camps" (H 186).

III Durin's Day

A closer look at the single most significant transition within the story – the opening of the secret entrance – can serve to further illuminate this involvement and the overall effect for the text. Durin's Day is, of course, a central plot point, as it ultimately unleashes the dragon into the tale. Once Smaug has been roused, the texture of the story changes dramatically: the most obvious feature is a marked shift in mood and tone, towards a heroic style anticipating *The Lord of the Rings* (cf. Thomas 179). As Tolkien noted in a letter: "the tone and style change with the *Hobbit's* development, passing from fairy-tale to the noble and high and relapsing with the return" (L 159). With Durin's Day, a narrative threshold has clearly been reached and a different perception of the world emerges. I will therefore begin by examining the implications of the event itself.

In Rivendell, an apparent inconsistency has already arisen. Although Durin's Day is determined by the dwarves' traditional calendar and refers to a distinct astronomical constellation, Thorin points out that his contemporaries no longer know how to calculate the exact time. The event itself indeed seems to intensify this inconsistency: when all the predicted factors finally coincide, the dwarves are not only caught by surprise, they also fail to notice the arrival of Durin's Day. Instead, it is Bilbo, who – after renewed and intense study of the map[19] – anticipates the opening of the door and alerts the dwarves to the presence of sun and moon in the sky.

> All day Bilbo sat gloomily in the grassy bay gazing at the stone, or out west through the narrow opening. He had a queer feeling that he was waiting for something... *If he lifted his head he could see* a glimpse of the distant forest. As the sun turned west there was a gleam of yellow upon its far roof, as if the light caught the last pale leaves. Soon he *saw* the orange ball of the sun sinking towards *the level of his eyes. He went to the opening and there* pale and faint was a thin new moon above the rim of Earth. *At that very moment he heard* a sharp crack behind him. There on the grey stone in the grass was an enormous thrush, nearly coal black, its pale yellow breast freckled dark spots. Crack! It had caught a snail and was knocking it on the stone. Crack! Crack! Suddenly Bilbo understood. Forgetting all danger he stood on the ledge and hailed the dwarves, shouting and waving.
> (H 264f; emphasis added)

---

[19] Cf. H 260: "Now strange to say Mr. Baggins had more [spirit] than the others. He would often borrow Thorin's map and gaze at it, pondering over the runes and the message of the moon-letters Elrond had read. It was he that made the dwarves begin the dangerous search on the western slopes for the secret door."

At this point in the text, spatial and temporal coordinates are at their most detailed and definite,[20] yet these objective (and calculable) conditions alone do not allow a crossing of the final threshold. Once again, a crucial transition is focalized through Bilbo, even though he seems the most unlikely choice among the company. Yet the narration stresses repeatedly that everything depends on Bilbo's subjective perception: what he sees and hears, the correlation of vision and movement, clearly contribute to the coincidence of all the factors.[21]

'Durin's Day' is not, in effect, a calculable calendrical event that takes place regardless of spectators – such as the midwinter sunrise, marked by a ray of light that falls into the passage tomb of Newgrange, focused through the 'roof box'. By contrast, the revelation of the secret entrance is inseparable from Bilbo's perception: time and space, the door and a specific observer position jointly enable the disclosure; cosmic conjunction and subjective experience are interdependent. The discovery reveals the true meaning of a secret that the map (and its textual layers) merely referred to: the result is a magical – or even mythical – moment.[22]

During this moment, time, space and the movement of celestial bodies no longer form a neutral, objective continuum but shape meaningful events that affect everything within the textual world: from the smallest creatures – the trush and the snails as well as Bilbo – to the fate of kingdoms. Time articulated as light points out a path that transforms Bilbo, the world around him and the texture of the story. The previously marked distinction of signifier and signified

---

[20] As the recently published notes for a reworking of *The Hobbit* after the completion of *The Lord of the Rings* demonstrate, Tolkien's efforts focussed increasingly on constructing a coherent spatio-temporal continuum for the tale: an attempt he ultimately abandoned (cf. HH II 813ff). John Rateliff proposes that the construction of a historically plausible continuum contradicted the 'fairy-tale' style of referring to time and space in *The Hobbit*.

[21] The textual emphasis is underlined by Tolkien's complementary illustrations of the bay that shelter the hidden door: one drawing gives a view of the site from an external, detached perspective (possibly correlating with the narrator's point of view), while the other represents Bilbo's perspective (cf. Hammond/Scull, no. 131 and 132: 'The Back Door' and 'View from Back Door').

[22] The 'magic' of the door is mentioned several times: "They were too eager to trouble about the runes and the moon-letters, but tried without resting to discover where exactly in the smooth face of the rock the door was hidden. They had brought picks and tools of many sorts from Lake-town, and at first they tried to use these. But when they struck the stone the handles splintered and jarred their arms cruelly, and the steel heads broke or bent like lead. Mining work, they saw clearly was no good against *the magic that had shut this door*" (H 262). – "But they found that the upper end of the tunnel had been shattered and blocked with broken rock. Neither key nor the magic it had once obeyed would ever open that door again" (H 289). – "As a matter of fact two nights and the day between had gone by (and not altogether without food) since the dragon smashed the *magic door*" (H 299).

is superseded by an immediate perceptual experience,[23] which amalgamates 'objective' and 'subjective' factors in an eruptive revelation of meaning. 'Durin's Day' thus amounts to a prime example of experienced 'myth' as Tolkien conceptualized it elsewhere.[24] In the terminology of *The Hobbit*, it is at this point that a 'magical' reality fully materializes within the text.[25]

In a letter to his publishers, Allen and Unwin, Tolkien wrote: "The presence of the sun and moon in the sky together refers to the magic attaching to the door" (L 16). But how exactly does the joint presence of sun and moon *refer* to the door's magic? The verb denotes a relation as well as a directing of attention,[26] and this double meaning indeed seems to capture the essential features of the transformative moment. Both implications point us back to the literary constituents of this moment: the coincidence of cosmic event and subjective perception is a magical event in and of the text, as it is achieved by means of focalization. The meaning of this moment is processed through the window of Bilbo's perception in the same manner that his previous dreams allowed glimpses into a magical reality. However, 'Durin's Day' is a waking experience, and it rouses not only the dragon: it also turns the narrator loose on a new level of imagination.

In the following chapters, several distinctive shifts of focalization occur. A first notable instance can be found where Bilbo is about to face Smaug:

> It was at this point that Bilbo stopped. Going on from there was the bravest thing he ever did. The tremendous things that happened afterward were as nothing compared to it. He fought the real battle in the tunnel alone, before he ever saw the vast danger that lay in wait. At any rate after a short halt go on he did; and *you can picture him* coming to the end of the tunnel, an opening of much the same size and shape as the door above. *Through it peeps the hobbit's little head.* Before him lies the great bottommost cellar or dungeon-hall of the ancient dwarves right at the Mountain's root.

---

23 An artistic expression of this transition appears among Tolkien's 'doodles' for the sleeve design of *The Hobbit*: the various emblems of Durin's Day he devised all relate the 'd'-rune (ᛞ) to the simultaneous presence of the setting sun and the rising moon (cf. Hammond/Scull no. 141).

24 The conceptions Tolkien developed most elaborately in *The Notion Club Papers* show strong affinities with Owen Barfield's theory of 'poetic diction' and his concept of an original 'semantic unity' preserved in the recorded mythologies (cf. Klinger).

25 'Magic', in Tolkien's own terminology, is inherently connected to his conception of Faërie: "Faërie itself may perhaps most nearly be translated by Magic – but it is magic of a peculiar mood and power, at the furthest pole from the vulgar devices of the laborious, scientific, magician" (FS 114).

26 Cf. the OED definitions (refer, II. intransitive senses): "to have reference or relation to a thing" (12.a); "to make reference or allusion, to give a reference, direct the attention, to something" (12.d).

It is almost dark so that its vastness can only be dimly guessed, but rising from the near side of the rocky floor there is a great glow. The glow of Smaug! (H 270; emphasis added)

Most significant is the spatial shift of perspective – the view switches from within the tunnel to a point outside it – and the grammatical shift from past to present tense.[27] The reader is encouraged to picture Bilbo from a site somewhere within the dragon's lair: to do no less, in other words, than mirror Bilbo's 'bravest' deed. In effect, the narration imaginatively joins the present of the narrator (and his audience) to the presence of Smaug, synchronizing narrated with narrating time. With this sudden shift, the narrator's established manner of referring to spatial and temporal coordinates (the deictic orientation[28]) becomes subject to transformation as well: the referenced world of 'here' and 'there', past and present, is no longer quite the same that it was before Bilbo crossed the threshold.

This transition is sharply visible where the text performs a radical referential break, that is, a sudden shift to a different location in space and time.[29] At the beginning of "Fire and Water" – the chapter that portrays the dragon's flight, his attack on Lake-town and death –, the alignment of the narration to the experiences of Bilbo and the dwarves is severed and the linear temporal continuum ruptured:[30] "Now if you wish, like the dwarves, to hear news of

---

27 In one of Tolkien's drafts, the same appellative gesture occurs in the description of Durin's Day: "You can just *picture Bilbo standing now beside the thrushes' stone*, and the dwarves with wagging beards watching excitedly by the walls. The sun sank lower and lower. Then their hopes fell. It sank into a belt of red-stained clouds and disappeared. The dwarves groaned, but still Bilbo stood almost without moving. The little moon was dipping to the [river >] horizon. Evening was coming on. Then suddenly when their hope was lowest, a red ray of the sun escaped like a finger through a rent in the bars of cloud. A gleam of light came straight through the opening in the bay and fell on the smooth rock face" (HH II 476). See also the initial draft of the quoted description: "*At last you can picture the tunnel ending in a square opening* [> *opening of much the same size as the door above*]. Through it peeps the hobbit's little head. Before him lies the great bottommost [dungeon >] cellar or dungeon-hall of the ancient dwarves right at the Mountain's root" (HH II 506).
28 Cf. Jahn, *Narratology* N.6.4: "any description of space invokes a perception of space: apart from the reader's imaginative perception, this is either a narrator's perception, or a character's perception; both can be either actual perception or imaginary perception. For this reason, fictional space is evidently strongly correlated to focalization."
29 Cf. Jahn, *Aspects* 101: "Referential breaks come in two forms: either 'the camera goes offline' and shifts to a different location, or the 'narrative clock is reset, either forward or backward' ([Ryan] 1987, 63)."
30 A metaleptic quality to this shift of scene must be noted, since the narrator proposes to enter into the story at a different point in time: "the shift becomes less a shift from scene A to scene B than a retracing of the narrative from progression to a flashback of delayed orientation" (Fludernik 390). At the same time, it must be noted that "[m]etalepsis is not necessarily an anti-illusionistic device", but can enhance "the realistic illusion in the realist novel" (Fludernik 392). – Twice before in *The Hobbit*, similar referential breaks occur. First, when the narration shifts suddenly to the Eagles in "Out of the Frying-

Smaug, *you must go back again* to the evening when he smashed the door and flew off in rage, two days before" (H 302; emphasis added).

The new mobility of focalization is best illustrated by a memorable description that follows Smaug's death:

> The waxing moon rose higher and higher and the wind grew loud and cold. It twisted the white fog into bending pillars and hurrying clouds and drove it off to the West to scatter in tattered shreds over the marshes before Mirkwood. *Then the many boats could be seen dotted dark on the surface of the lake, and down the wind came the voices of the people of Esgaroth lamenting their lost town and goods and ruined houses.*
> (H 308; emphasis added)[31]

Yet who sees and hears, and from which position?[32] The narration has leapt into the air to float above the Lake, adrift with the wind: more precisely, it flies where Smaug flew a short while ago and fills the rent torn by the dragon's fall, to record the aftermath of this dramatic event. This specific window of perception has been thrust open when the narrator, following Bilbo, passed through the secret door.

These brief remarks must suffice to demonstrate how new modes of focalization coincide with the emergence of a changed reality that takes place on many levels of the text, embracing the shift from the casually, sometimes humorously told "story of Bilbo's great adventure" (H 94) to an account of epic battles in heroic style and mood. The 'magic' that once referred to bewildering tricks[33] now points to a changed experience of the world: a world in which cosmic bodies and subjective perceptions unite to shape the full meaning of events.

Pan into the Fire": "'What is all this uproar in the forest tonight?' said the Lord of the Eagles. He was sitting, black in the moonlight, on the top of a lonely pinnacle of rock at the eastern edge of the mountains. 'I hear wolves' voices! Are the goblins at mischief in the woods?'" (H 149). The second instance introduces a brief shift to the Wood-elves' situation while Bilbo and the Dwarves stay in Lake-town (H 252f). In both cases, the narration shifts to a different location, but leaves the temporal continuum intact; they also lack the metaleptic reader-address with which "Fire and Water" opens: "*you must go back* again to the evening..." (H 302; emphasis added).

31   In the initial draft, Tolkien started to write this description in present tense as well: "The moon [rises >] rose higher and higher, and the North wind grew loud and cold" (HH II 550).

32   The description may be characterized as a case of "figuralization": "A reflector-mode representation of narrative events or existents in the absence of any internal focalizer or reflector figure, hence from the point of view of an 'empty (deictic) center'" (Jahn, Narratology N.3.2.5). However, in this particular deployment of figuralization, the 'empty deictic center' has been generated by a story event: the death of Smaug.

33   Compare Bilbo's initial characterization of Gandalf as an agent of magic: "Gandalf, Gandalf! Good gracious me! Not the wandering wizard that gave Old Took a pair of magic diamond studs that fastened themselves and never came undone till ordered?" (H 33).

IV Entry into a Different Mode of Imagination

How can this transition be conceptualized? In his discussion of *Beowulf*, Tolkien refers to the "mythical mode of imagination" (BMC 15) that shapes the textual world and its reality.[34] *On Fairy-Stories* proposes a similar notion with regard to tales of dragons: "But the world that contained even the imagination of Fáfnir was richer and more beautiful, at whatever cost of peril" (FS 135). Tolkien's remarks in the essay are particularly illuminating, because they articulate a tension that characterizes *The Hobbit* and Bilbo's role in the story as well: "I desired dragons with a profound desire. Of course, I in my timid body did not wish to have them in the neighbourhood, intruding into my relatively safe world, in which it was, for instance, possible to read stories in peace of mind, free from fear" (FS 135).

An identical division is easily recognisable in *The Hobbit*. Initially, the dwarves' song roused Bilbo's imagination to the point where he envisioned the devastating intrusion of a dragon into his quiet world (cf. H 45). Yet Bilbo successfully enters the realm where fearful imaginings give way to the actual presence of the dragon, and it is with good reason that this transition is emphasized as "the bravest thing he ever did". The narrative discourse performs an analogous movement. In the early chapters, the narrator predominantly acts as a mediator between the 'legendary' world and the 'relatively safe', contemporary environment. He occupies a position on the threshold – one might also call it 'sitting on the doorstep' – that separates the two spheres.

Over various stages, only a few of which I have discussed, the dividing threshold is negotiated and eventually crossed. With 'Durin's Day', a new mode of imagination (and signification) manifests within the text: what was 'far off, therefore legendary' has become present reality that can – and must be – subjectively perceived and experienced. Once the narrator enters this reality, placing himself somewhere inside Smaug's lair and encouraging his audience to imagine Bilbo from that site, the division has been removed – and reading the story 'free from fear' of the dragon may no longer be the desired response.

The reconfiguration of perspectives, the variable focalizations up to the point of dramatic referential breaks, all serve to promote an imaginative shift that concerned Tolkien deeply: "Fantasy, the making or the glimpsing of Otherworlds," he writes in *On Fairy-Stories*, "was the heart of the desire of Faërie" (FS 135). Indeed, successful fairy-stories induce a 'mythical effect' when "they open a door on Other Time" (FS 128f).

---

34 Cf. BMC 15: "The significance of a myth is not easily to be pinned on paper by analytical reasoning. It is at its best when it is presented by a poet who feels rather than makes explicit what his theme portends; who presents it incarnate in the world of history and geography, as our poet has done."

If we conclude that the transition to another mode of imagination – magical, legendary, or mythical – occurs not only for the characters but also within the texture of the story, a unique narrative approach can be identified as well; an approach that sets *The Hobbit* apart from Tolkien's other tales of Middle-earth. Narrative possibilities of focalization are nowhere explored quite so comprehensively, and no other narrator is as intimately engaged with both the contemporary and the 'legendary' world.

Or to put it differently, prolonged 'sitting on the doorstep' has indeed led to unexpected, enchanting results: 'the glimpsing of Other-worlds' in and through a deceptively simple story.[35]

Bibliography

Anderson, Douglas A. (ed.). *The Annotated Hobbit. Revised and Expanded Edition*. London: HarperCollins, 2003

Brückner, Patrick. "'... Until the Dragon Comes': Tolkien's Dragon-Motif as Poetological Concept". *Tolkien's Shorter Works. Essays of the Jena Conference 2007*. Ed. Margaret Hiley and Frank Weinreich. Zurich and Jena: Walking Tree, 2007, 101-133

Fludernik, Monika. "Scene Shift, Metalepsis, and the Metaleptic Mode". *Style* 37.4 (2003): 382-400

Hammond, Wayne G. and Christina Scull. *J.R.R. Tolkien, Artist and Illustrator*. London: HarperCollins, 1995

Jahn, Manfred. "Windows of Focalization: Deconstructing and Reconstructing a Narratological Concept". *Style* 30.2 (1996): 241-267

---. "More Aspects of Focalization: Refinements and Applications". *Recent Trends in Narratological Research*. Ed. John Pier. (GRAAT: Revue des Groupes de Recherches Anglo-Américaines de L'Université Francois Rabelais de Tours 21.) Tours: Université de Tours, 1999, 85-110

---. *Narratology: A Guide to the Theory of Narrative*. English Department, University of Cologne, 2005. <http://www.uni-koeln.de/~ame02/pppn.htm> Accessed 08272008

Klinger, Judith. "'More Poetical, Less Prosaic'. The Convergence of Myth and History in Tolkien's Works". *Hither Shore* 3 (2006): 53-68

Rateliff, John D., Ed. *The History of 'The Hobbit'*. 2 Vols. London: HarperCollins, 2007

Thomas, Paul Edmund. "Some Of Tolkien's Narrators". *Tolkien's Legendarium. Essays on 'The History of Middle-earth'*. Ed. Verlyn Flieger and Carl F. Hostetter. Westport: Greenwood Press, 2000, 161-181

Tolkien, J.R.R. *The Lord of the Rings*. 1954/1955. London: HarperCollins, 1995

---. "Beowulf: The Monsters and the Critics". *The Monsters and the Critics and Other Essays*. Ed. Christopher Tolkien. 1983. London: HarperCollins, 1997, 5-48

---. "On Fairy-Stories". *The Monsters and the Critics and Other Essays*. Ed. Christopher Tolkien. 1983. London: HarperCollins, 1997, 109-161

---

35 It is noteworthy that Bilbo's transition enables him to create poetry – the literary analogue to an experienced legendary reality –, once he has returned. Cf. H 361: "He took to writing poetry and visiting the elves; and though many shook their heads and touched their foreheads and said 'Poor old Baggins!' and though few believed any of his tales, he remained very happy to the end of his days, and those were extraordinarily long."

Für manche Wesen birgt das Licht der Sonne allergrößte Gefahr. Mir und meinen Gefährten hat es das Leben gerettet...

Wolves, Ravens, and Eagles
A mythic Presence in *The Hobbit*

Guglielmo Spirito (Assisi)

In *The Spell of the Sensuous*, David Abram writes:

> Late one evening I stepped out of my little hut in the rice paddies of eastern Bali and found myself falling through space. Over my head the black sky was rippling with stars, densely clustered in some regions, almost blocking out the darkness between them, and more loosely scattered in other areas, pulsing and beckoning to each other. Behind them all streamed the great river of light with its several tributaries. Yet the Milky Way churned beneath me as well, for my hut was set in the middle of a large patchwork of rice paddies, separated from each other by narrow two-foot-high dikes, and these paddies were all filled with water. The surface of these pools, by day, reflected perfectly the blue sky, a reflection broken only by the thin, bright green tips of new rice. But by night the stars themselves glimmered from the surface of the paddies, and the river of light whirled through the darkness underfoot as well as above; there seemed no ground in front of my feet, only the abyss of star-studded space falling away forever.
> I was no longer simply beneath the night sky, but also above it – the immediate impression was of weightlessness. I might have been able to reorient myself, to regain some sense of ground and gravity, were it not for a fact that confounded my senses entirely: between the constellations below and the constellations above drifted countless fireflies, their lights flickering like the stars, some drifting up to join the clusters of stars overhead, others, like graceful meteors, slipping down from above to join the constellations underfoot, and all these paths of light upward and downward were mirrored, as well, in the still surface of the paddies. I felt myself at times falling through space, at other moments floating and drifting. I simply could not dispel the profound vertigo and giddiness; the paths of the fireflies, and their reflections in the water's surface, held me in a sustained trance. Even after I crawled back to my hut and shut the door on this whirling world, I felt that now the little room in which I lay was itself floating free of the earth. (Abram 3f)

Could this have been the feeling, I wonder, that Bilbo had flying seized by the eagle, far from the threatening wolves, or later, when he was allowed to climb on the eagle's back and cling between his wings?

Indeed could have been this feeling, but nevertheless, it is better not to jump to conclusions: that would had not meant for him to agree with the (rethoric) question of his eagle: 'What is finer than flying?', for the unspoken answer he would have like to give then (we should remember) was: 'A warm bath and late breakfast on the lawn afterwards'.

Well, Bilbo was then for sure at the beginning of his adventure, and perhaps his enthusiasm at the unexpected and most welcome arrival of the eagles at the Battle of the Five Armies ('The Eagles! The Eagles!' Bilbo cried, dancing and waving his arms) may indicate a change in his mind, we may wonder. I doubt it: also for a much more mature, experienced and radically less rabbit-like hobbit *breakfast* would be always be *breakfast* and held a preferential place!

Imagination helps us to see, understand, speak about, and relate to reality – in particular, reality or realities that cannot be perceived directly through our senses – in a way beyond our rational discourse.

> Humans share their imaginations and bond with one another through the stories they tell... Myths are a special kind of story. They capture and express realities that cannot be put directly into words and shared in any other way. Mythologist Joseph Campbell maintained that what is common to all humanity is the experience of awe and wonder ... and the resulting creation of myths that help give our lives meaning and purpose. That is experiencing awe and wonder, and creating myths are cause and effect. Myths allow us to communicate about intangible realities that cannot be communicated in any other way.
> (Somerville 15; cf. Schönborn)

'The myth sovereign in the old age was that everything means everything. The myth sovereign in the new is that nothing *means* anything', wrote Thomas Howard (Chance 12).

Myths speak of another life running in us like an underground river-current, always present, never quite seen, exerting influence on us lapping quietly on our dry ground, rich soil from which things grow.

Here, animals join the scene. When I was reading the book *I heard the Owl call my name* by Margaret Craven I was surprised by the description of a fifty foot Totem by the church in a native village on the coast of British Colombia, Canada, because this Totem was holding up an Eagle, a Wolf and a Raven. I didn't expect that a native Canadian Totem would gather together the three animals in which I am interested in for this paper.

Should we call for help upon the guardian spirits of the tribe – as natives do – to help us: 'come wolf, come raven, come eagle' although we live in the other end of the world? (Craven 12.130)

In the meanwhile, from the closer picks of the High Mountains in the heart of Europe we recognize the voice and presence of the 'Beasts of Battle', i.e. the wolf, the raven, the eagle. Thomas Honegger had splendidly studied their role in the Old English heroic literature (cf. 289-298) – including obviously *Beowulf* – so that he gives us a wider insight in which to read Tolkien's re-visitation of the three animals.

Wolves, ravens and eagles had the actual habit of frequenting places of carn-age (for what they are considered, with diversified accuracy, along the 'carrion beasts' who feed on the corpses left on the battlefield). The poetic creative powers shown in the Old English (and also Old Norse) texts give a powerful and evoking association of impending doom to the theme.

If Tolkien's *wolves, ravens and eagles* follow the tracks, in his creative and personal way, of this pattern.

> 'Don't the great tales never end?', asked Sam. 'No, they never end as tales', said Frodo. 'But the people in them come, and go when their part's ended'. (LotR 697)

Are we in the same tale still? And have we a part in this tale? May we find ourselves facing (somehow) *wolves, ravens and eagles*: fighting against them; being counselled by them; hopefully being rescued and carried to safety by them? I wonder...

Let us start with the **Wolves.**

In the final scene of *King Lear*, the distraught king enters with his dead daughter Cordelia in his arms. His first words are not words. He howls. "Howl, howl, howl!"

The same Lear who earlier in the play was so afraid of becoming an animal has become a wolf. He is not *like* a wolf. He speaks *as* a wolf. Howling in unspeakable pain, Lear slides dazed into the animal, becoming a wolf.

Lear's howl is the culmination in the play of an almost obsessive interest in the ways in which humans become animals. On the heath, during the storm, Lear finds himself "comrade to the owl and wolf," living like a "belly-pinch'd wolf". Poor Gloucester, eyes gouged out, can no longer see to find his way. He must "smell his way to Dover," living like a dog. Lear and Gloucester are a brace of canines (cf. Bergmann in Wockner 111ff).

I remember once hearing a biologist say that the most important thing to know about a wolf is that, for people, it is always a symbol.

And I think about how, for me, wolves began in the realms of history, myth, and dream, of imagination, desire and apparition. How they've emerged now into actuality, inhabited real bodies, here and now.

But the wolf is not a metaphor. The question of the wolf – like the question of Lear's howl or Gloucester's sense of smell – is not what it is *like*. The question of the wolf is what it *is*. Listen carefully to Lear's howling wolf. It's the best wolf in literature, because it actually has "speaking" lines. What does it say? It says "no" to human meaning. It says "no" to representation.

Yet in *King Lear*, Shakespeare is doubtful. Lear gains a greater dignity in the play, but it is not a transcendent dignity. It is a dignity that is shared with other creatures, located in Lear's howl. It is the dignity inherent in all living, and suffering, creatures – man and beast alike.

No other animal that I know of evokes such intensity of feeling, for and against. It is the intensity of this passion that attracts me to wolves. They have helped me find myself, howling me back to myself.

One of the problems that come with trying to take a wider view of animals is that most of us have cut ourselves off from them conceptually. We do not think of ourselves as part of the animal kingdom. Indians did.

Even when we speak about wolves or other animals and their relationship to humans we aren't talking, really, about our wolf anymore. We are talking about *their* wolf. We are in a sense, in a foreign country.[1]

So, in the wolf we have not so much an animal that we have always known as one that we have consistently imagined. To the human imagination the wolf has proved at various times the appropriate symbol for greed or savagery, the exactly proper guise for the Devil, or fitting as a patron of warrior clans.

It is perhaps not an accident that the wolf, a creature of the twilight hours, came and went so frequently in the expressions of a people emerging from the Dark Ages. From classical times he had been a symbol of things in transit. He was a twilight hunter, seen at dawn and dusk.

His howl in the morning elevated the spirit. Like the crow of the cock it signalled the dawn, the end of night and the hours of the wolf. His howl at night terrified the soul: the hours of the wolf (famine, witchery, carnage) were coming on.

In times of old Loki fathered Fenris, the huge wolf of Teutonic myth whose progeny would devour the sun at the end of the world and precipitate *Götterdämmerung*, the twilight of the gods. There is a German folk rhyme invented to help children learn the hours of the day that preserves this fourth association between wolves and a return to darkness. It ends: "um elfe kommen die wölfe, um zwölfe bricht das gewölbe" – at eleven come the wolves, at twelve the tombs of the dead open (cf. Lopez 210).

---

1 Cfr. Lopez for a careful and wide range study about wolves and civilization.

The wolf as a symbol of war and lust, two very common associations throughout Western history (and psychoanalysis), became an appropriate metaphor for Shakespeare in *Troilus and Cressida*. There the parallel themes of violence and sex end in self-annihilation. The wolf is dead; the beast in man is dead. There is a promise in a fresh dawn.

Of course, there were some better views about the wolf in times of old. There is an old story about a wolf in Gubbio, Italy, involving Saint Francis. The wolf had been threatening the villagers and Saint Francis was trying to get the animal to desist. He and the wolf met one day outside the city walls and made the following agreement, witnessed by a notary: the residents of Gubbio would feed the wolf and let him wander at will through the town and the wolf, for his part, would never harm man or beast there.

Beneath the popular, anecdotal appeal of this story is a common allegory: the bestial, uncontrolled nature of the wolf is transformed by sanctity, and by extension those identified with the wolf – thieves, heretics, and outlaws – are redeemed by Saint Francis's all-embracing compassion and courtesy.

Medieval men believed that they saw in wolves a reflection of their own bestial nature; man's longing to make peace with the beast in himself is what makes this tale of the Wolf of Gubbio one of the more poignant stories of the Middle Ages. To have compassion for the wolf, whom man saw as enslaved by the same base drives as himself, was to yearn for self-forgiveness.[2]

It is curious to find the wolf as a character in children's literature, for all wolves in literature are the creations of adult minds, that is, of adult fears, adult fantasies, adult allegories, and adult perversions. So the tendency to look on animal stories as simplistic is misleading.

Most of the wolves in European literature are dangerous, cruel and bad, unlike in many of the many Native American stories (cf. Casey/Clark 3-49).

> The possibility has yet to be realized of a synthesis between the benevolent wolf of Native Americans ... and the malcontented wolf of most European fairy tales. At present we seem incapable of such a creation, unable to write about a whole wolf because, for most of us, animals are still either two-dimensional symbols or simply inconsequential, suitable only for children's stories where good and evil are clearly separated. (Lopez 270, cf. Rehnmark)

Here we find that the wolves in Tolkien's works from *The Hobbit*, *The Lord of the Rings* and *The Silmarillion* are not different from the wolves in the rest of Europe.

---

2 Cfr. Spirito 61-86; Bell 20-21, 33-35, 61-65, 119-120; Waddell 6f, and Honegger 290f.

> All of a sudden they heard a howl away down hill, a long shuddering howl. It was answered by another away on to the side right and a good deal nearer to them; then by another not far on away to the left. It was wolves, howling at the moon, wolves gathering together! There were no wolves living near Mr. Baggins' hole at home, but he knew that noise. He had had it described to him. One of his cousins among the Tooks used to do it to frighten him – he had visited the forests in the north of Bilbo's country and heard it there. To hear it out in the forest under the moon was too much for Bilbo; even magic-rings are not much use against wolves (and against probably very evil wolves, if they live under the shadow of goblin-infested mountains, in a country right on the edge of the wild and far into the unknown). Wolves of that sort smell keener than goblins, and don't need to see you to find you!
> 'What shall we do, what shall we do' he cried. 'Escaping goblins to be caught by wolves' he said – and it became a proverb, though we now say 'out of the frying pan into the fire' in the same sort of uncomfortable situations.
> 'Up the trees quick' said Bladorthin, and they ran to the trees at the edge of the glade ... (HH I 203)

Tolkien himself said:

> the episode of the 'wargs' (I believe) is in part derived from a scene in S.R. Crokett's *The Black Douglas*, probably his best romance and anyway one that deeply impressed me in school-days, though I have never looked at it again. (L 391)

Closer examination of Crokett's book shows that while there is indeed a battle with wolves in it, the scene bears little resemblance to Tolkien's in *The Hobbit* (in fact, it is far closer to the battle after the storm at the Caradhras in *The Lord of the Rings*, which it probably did inspire).

The only points in common are a wolf-attack in a forest clearing, the uncanny fire (magical but real in Tolkien's case, merely illumination from distant lightning in Crokett's), and the idea that the wolves are a lesser evil in service or allegiance to the real enemy (HH I 216f).

Tolkien's wargs owe less to literary tradition than his own imagination, stimulated as always by philology.

> The word Warg used in *The Hobbit* and the L. R. (i.e. *The Lord of the Rings*) for an evil breed of (demonic) wolves is not supposed to be A[nglo] – S[axon] specifically, and is given prim[itive] Ger-

manic form as representing the noun common to the Northmen
of these creatures. (L 381)

He reiterates this point, after distinguishing between the 'internal' history of
names within the story and their 'external' history (the sources from which I,
as an author, derived them') in a letter of 7th November 1966 to fellow fantasy
author Gene Wolfe:

> Warg ... is an old word for wolf, which also had the sense of an
> outlaw or hunted criminal. This is its usual sense in surviving texts.
> [O[ld] E[nglilsh] wearg; O[ld] High German warg; O[ld] Norse
> varg-r (also = 'wolf', espec[ially] of legendary kind.] I adopted the
> word, which had a good sound for the meaning, as a name for
> this particular brand of demonic wolf in the story.
> (HH I 217. 225)

Let us now remember the kindness of **Ravens**:

> 'I only wish he was a raven!', said Balin.
> 'I thought you did not like the ravens of these parts, when we
> came this way before', said Bilbo to him.
> 'Those were crows!', said Balin, 'nasty suspicious-looking ones
> at that, and rude as well ... But there are some ravens still about
> here, though, for I have seen them in my wanderings about, that
> remember the old friendship between us in Thror's day. They used
> to live on many many years, and their memories are long, and
> they hand their wisdom on to their children. I had many a friend
> among the Ravens of the Mountain when I was a boy – this very
> ridge we stand on was called Ravenhill.'
> Before long there was a flutter of wings ... it was a very aged
> raven of great size. It alighted stiffly on the ground, flapped its
> wings slowly and bobbed towards Thorin and Balin, and began
> to croak. – 'I am Roac son of Carc. Carc is dead, but once he was
> well known to you. It is one hundred years and three and fifty
> since I came out of the egg, but I do not forget what my father
> told me. I am the chief of the old great Ravens of the Mountain,
> who remember still the king that was of old.'
>
> Among the flocking birds are many crows and birds of carrion –
> indeed ravens are among them though they fly by themselves – for
> they espy a gathering of arms, and to our minds an army and a
> hoard means dead men ere long.   (HH II 618f; cf. H 242ff)

Helpful birds had played an important part in Tolkien's writing from the earliest days: the Eagles of Manwe, of which we will speak later, the swans of Ulmo, the birds of Melian, even New the seagull in *Roverandom*, so it is no surprise to see the wise Thrush and old Raven figure prominently in the Lonely Mountain chapters, from the discovery of the Secret Door to the revealing of Smaug's weak spot and setting in motion preparations for the Siege of the Mountain.

Tolkien's specific choice of ravens combines elements of traditional myth and real-world fact. Not only are ravens and crows traditionally associated with battles, but they are the smartest of all birds, exceptionally long-lived.

He combines their rather sinister reputation as harbingers of battle (they are, after all carrion birds, as Roac admits) with their legendary exploits as messengers: Odin's two ravens Hugin and Munin ('Thought' and 'Memory') fly forth every day and report back to him all that passes in the world. He also draws on the Biblical account of ravens feeding the prophet Elijah 'bread and meat' in the Wilderness and has the Ravens of the Mountain bring 'meat and bread' to the besieged dwarves until (even more surprisingly) they are driven away by elven archers. The scene with a raven feeding Saint Antony and Saint Paul in the desert is very common in Irish High Crosses (cf. HH II 623f, De Waal 118).

The Common Raven, *Corvus corax*, is a real bird with a very considerable amount of mythology and folklore attached to it. Ravens appear in both Celtic and Germanic cultural spheres. In both, the raven like the wolf is a symbol of the flip-side of the heroic tradition – of battles lost, heroes slain and wild beasts feasting on the bodies of those with none to bury them. Again in both sets of traditions, ravens were associated with battle. And also with saints.[3]

To the best of our knowledge, ravens appear in Tolkien's published works only in *The Hobbit*. They first occur in chapter 15. Later other ravens serve as Thorin's messengers to his fellow-Dwarf and kinsman Dain of the Iron Hills; they also spy out the movements of the various hosts in the run up to the Battle of the Five Armies which follows shortly after. These are no common ravens but rather Ravens, larger and more intelligent than any normal bird, and capable of speech. Tolkien tells us in chapter 15 of *The Hobbit* that:

> There used to be great friendship between them [the Ravens] and the people of Thror [the Dwarves of the Lonely Mountain]; and they often brought us secret news, and were rewarded with such bright tings as they coveted to hide in their dwellings ... They live many a year and their memories are long, and they hand on their wisdom to their children.

---

3 Cfr. Bell 24-25, 53-54, 90-91; Waddell 58-62; Luce 197; Honegger. For hebrew understanding of ravens: Pinney 169-170; Toperoff 199-203.

In some ways, Tolkien's image corresponds to the traditional one. His ravens are intelligent, far-sighted and wise, with a particular interest in war and politics, and they have an important part to play in the acquisition and communication of knowledge. Their liking for small, shiny things comes from natural history, not myth – ravens are just as bad if not worse than the much-maligned magpie on this front. In other ways, Tolkien departs from tradition. His Ravens have lost their role as birds of ill-omen and their anti-heroic aspect as devourers of the slain. In part, this may be because *The Hobbit* is after all a children's' book. Crows are said to be 'gathering for battle', but no reason for this is given, which would fit that idea. However, there may be more to it that that. Crows are mentioned in *The Lord of the Rings* as spies of Sauron, probably following on from their association with evil creatures in *The Hobbit*; *crebain*, a sort of large crow from Dunland (cf. Lewis/Currie, *Uncharted* 60).

The King of the Golden Hall, Théoden calls Gandalf 'Stormcrow'. Indeed Gandalf is a figure of a kind of Odinic wonderer which fits very well with the company of crows (LotR 535; Lewis/Currie, *Uncharted* 62).

By the way, "*Roac* and *Carc* are marvellously onomatopoeic invented names for birds in bird-speech" (Anderson 316).

Coming back to the wolf for a moment, we should not forget that "the most important of all the *Legendarium's* wolves, however, is Sauron himself; Tolkien even considered having it be the necromancer in wolf-form who devoured Beren's companions one by one in the dungeons beneath Tol-in-Gaurhoth, the Isle of Werewolves." Tolkien was working on *The Lay of Leithian* simultaneously with the original drafting of *The Hobbit*, and the identification with wolves is "so great that the title 'Master of Wolves' almost tends to overwhelm the identification of Thu in that work as 'the necromancer'." (HH I 218)[4]

So in Tolkien's works many of the wolves are demonic *wargs*, possessed by evil spirits; but they were delivered after the fall of Sauron, when they become again simple wolves (LotR 985). Ravens, on the contrary, are good allies and nothing bad is said about them.

But well above wolves and ravens are the eagles.

Last but not least, we come to the **Eagles.**

The atmosphere of wind has unreached realms of longing. It is a keening that no mind could ease. Wind is wild with dream. How a bird plays among the high geographies of wind-force, soaring, sliding and balancing on its invisible hills and waves, is a awesome thing to contemplate. And when it is an eagle, it seems the mind fancied that all may rushed up finally to heaven. There is

---

4 See also the interesting remark about 'waelwulfas' in The Battle of Maldon in Honegger 297f.

an epiphany of elegance, of dignity even of royalty. Eagles reveals *majesty* (although in *tono minore* in *The Hobbit* respect to LotR and *The Sillmarillion*; everyone and everything has a sort of lesser tone: but is still a *mythic* presence in a simple *hobbit tale*).

Truly we can believe that it is rightfully *The King of the Birds*, in a strict sense, although Flannery O'Connor with her unreachable humorous magnanimity and elegance applies the title to her peacocks in her homonymous story (cf. O'Connor 21).

Unlike wolves, which have played the villain in any number of folk and fairy tales, eagles appear in surprisingly few well-known myths and folktales. Of course, as John Rateliff points out

> there is the story of the eagle sent by Zeus to carry off Ganymede the Trojan to be his cup-bearer (a tale which gave its name to the Inklings' favourite pub, The Eagle and Child, 'The Bird and Baby' whose street-sign illustrates the scene). There is also the grimmer story of another eagle, also sent by Zeus, which each day rips out the liver of the bound titan Prometheus as punishment for his having helped mankind against the Olympians' wishes. Descending from the level of myth to gossip, Sir Thomas Browne reports the old story that an eagle killed the Athenian playwright Aeschylus (author of Agamemnon and Prometheus Bound, d. 456 BC) when, mistaking the great man's bald head for a rock, it dropped a turtle on it from a great height.   (HH I 219)[5]

Rateliff forgets in his list the splendid Latin novel, the *Metamorphoses* (sometimes called *The Golden Ass*) of Lucius Apuleius Platonicus, who tells within it the story of Cupid and Psiche, and how (trough the trials that Psiche endures) she is helped by the same Olimpic Eagle whom Cupid have long ago send to bring up to Zeus the 'phrygian cupbearer', Ganimede (cf. book VI, 15). We should recall that C.S. Lewis gave a magnificent reinterpretation of the old story, in a gorgeous way, in *Till we have faces. A myth retold* (cf. Apuleio, Howard, Lewis 207-259).

The *Old Testament* shows eagles (and birds of prey in general, including vultures) in a rich and polyvalent way, both as symbol of powerful enemies (cf. Ez 17,3-10; Lam 4,19; Jer 49,16) or more often , the great eagle , soaring swiftly among mountain heights, was a symbol of divine power as well as of protection (cf. Deut 32,11-12; Ex 19,4; Is 40,31).

---

5   Cf. also for the eagle in the Fathers of the Church Ciccarese 109-138; for the raven: 357-377. About Eagle & Child, cfr. Sears 6f.

Most touching is Ex 19, 4: 'You have seen what I did to the Egyptians and bore you on eagles' wings and brought you unto Myself'. In the words of Rashi, 'As an eagle which bears its fledglings upon its wings. Scripture uses this metaphor because all other birds place their young between their feet since they are afraid of other birds that fly around them, but the eagle fears non except man who may shoot arrows at it, as no bird flies above it. For this reason the eagle places its young upon its wings saying. better that the arrows and missiles strike me rather than my young'. (Toperoff 60; Pinney 28f. 147f)

Christian iconography associated the eagle with John The Evangelist, Tolkien's favourite apostle (cf. L 397; HH I 226; Winkler 10f). This association was due also to the keen sight of the eagle, for his seeing rather than looking, seeing and seeing beyond, illuminated by a steady radiance of a wonder, the source of which is beyond all reason. For his 'eagle-like' sight John is called *the Theologian* in the Christian East, title extended later as a privilege to St. Gregory of Nazianzus, *Gregory the Theologian*, the deep and sensitive great Cappadocian Father of the 4th century, who boldly christianized Hellenism.

By the way, in Rev 8,13 John heard "an eagle crying with a loud voice as it flew in midheaven, 'Woe, woe, woe to the inhabitants of the earth...'", announcing impending doom exactly as one of our 'Beast of Battle' should be expected to do.

However, as things are, Eagles carrying on their back those who are rescued are unknown in literature except for the story of Ganymede. Was it because of the *Inklings*' pub, or by the story of Ganymede itself, that eagles became important in Tolkien's work?

I should dare to focus on this for a while, making a kind of *stylistic detour*, returning later to the larger picture.

Has the Trojan Epic Cycle had some influence on Tolkien?

> It's easy to forget that Tolkien began his academic career as a classicist and only transferred his major to medieval studies in his second year at Oxford; the influence of classical literature on his work has been sadly neglected by Tolkien studies.
> (HH I 152)

Nor did he abandon interest in his former subject once he found his vocation in Gothic, Old English, Middle English, and Old Norse; as late as 1936, roughly half a decade after writing this chapter of *The Hobbit*, he compared Virgil's *Aeneid* to *Beowulf* as examples of 'greater and lesser things', respectively, clearly identifying the greatest work of Old English poetry as the lesser of the two (HH I 336, cf. Lewis/Currie, *Forsaken*).

By the way, Troy is mentioned in the first line of *Sir Gawain & the Green Knight*. Chaucer's Troy at least, we may say. There was an immense re elaboration of the Trojan Myth in Western and Northern Europe along the centuries.[6]

There are some stories in which Trojans are involved with mortals as when Aphrodite reassures Anchises that he has nothing to fear because he is dear to the gods, and she will bear a son who will rule among the Trojans and have generations of descendants. He will be called Aeneas, "because I had painful sorrow, because I fell into a mortal's bed". It is the mortality of Anchises, rather than the act of intercourse, that causes her sorrow, for he will die, and her son will die, and so will all his descendants (cf. Lefkowitz 38).

Aphrodite now explains that the Trojans were always most like the immortals in appearance. Zeus carried off one of them, Ganymede, and made him immortal, and gave immortal horses to his father, Tros, to compensate for the loss of his son. Eos, the goddess of dawn, carried off the Trojan prince Tithonus, and although she asked Zeus to grant him immortality she forgot to ask also for eternal youth.

Gods who are forever young and beautiful are particularly averse to old age, as Aphrodite makes clear to Anchises: "I would not choose to have you be immortal and live all your days like Tithonus; if you could live as you are now in looks and in stature, you might be called my husband; then grief would not cover my heart. But soon savage old age will surround you, ruthless old age that afterward accompanies mortals, dreadful wearying, which the gods despise".

Anchises is left alone, with his life forever changed. But Aphrodite too is unhappy, because of the wound to her pride and the contact with the pain and decay of mortality (cf. Lefkowitz 39; Woodford 42-44).

This reflects quite well the fear related there to mortals; the fear of the elves to have relationships with mortals as *Athrabeth Finrod an Andreth* (MR 303-366) shows poignantly.

> The story of Ganymede is one of the oldest of Greek myths, one of the oldest of the 'gay myths', and the one that has the greatest claim of any myth to central religious significance. (Davidson 170)

In getting the Greeks a reputation, Ganymede has a lot to answer for, which is ironic, since he wasn't Greek. A prince of Troy, great-uncle to Priam, who was king when the city was sacked, Ganymede disappeared in his youth and was reported to have become a cupbearer to the gods on Mount Olympus.

Zeus had sent an eagle to take him away. This particular image is vivid and has been imagined over and over again throughout the long history of European

---

6   Cfr.Chaucer; Thompson; Gerritsen/van Melle; Federico; specially the all comprehensive: *Troia. Traum und Wirklichkeit*.

art: the giant bird spreading its feathers behind the long-haired handsome youth. The Trojan prince has been seen on countless cups and vases.

Xenophon, writing around four hundred year before the Christian era, has the philosopher Socrates doing amateur etymology on Ganymede's name (*Ganytai* – delight in'; *medea* – 'thoughts'): Even in the case of Ganymede, it was not for his body but for his soul that he was elevated by Zeus to Olympus ... so he is called Ganymede not because of his physical attractions, but because of his sweetness of thought. This brief passage would eventually become one of the most popular quotes from Greek authors, but not until two thousand years later (cf. Davidson 171-174).

Sometimes the eagle grabs him from the front, sometimes we had Ganymede climb on the eagle's back. This is how he was painted on the ceiling of the immense palace Nero built on the area cleared by the Great Fire of Rome, the palace called *Domus Aurea* ,'House of Gold'. Ganymede was viewed as if through a skylight, disappearing into the blue. When shown as rider rather than as prey, he tends to look less 'enraptured' or 'transported', more triumphant and in control, a joyrider.

Ganymede was a popular subject throughout antiquity and wasn't forgotten in the Middle Ages, getting a mention in the works of Ovid, and therefore in the influential fourteenth-century allegorical version of the *Metamorphoses*, *Ovid Moralized*, as well as in Dante's *Purgatory*, in Petrarch's sonnets and in Boccaccio's *Genealogy of the Pagan Gods* (1375). He even finds his way, in the 1440's onto the doors of St. Peter's in Rome, where he remains, thanks to the neo-Platonist 'Filarete'. After the Reformation, in the High Renaissance and Baroque especially, his images multiplied. Around the middle of the sixteenth century, Niccolò Tribolo produced an image in bronze with Ganymede riding the bird like a pony, and Benvenuto Cellini, sculptor, jeweller and raff, took an antique torso and supplied it with arms, legs and eagle.

As visitors mounted the Grand Staircase in the residence of the Bishop of Würzburg, they found their gaze drawn higher and higher by Ganymede and the eagle. Doubtless many thought of the soul rising up to God, and one or two thought of Nero.

The image of uplifting in itself encapsulated movement from the worldly plane of physical attraction into the realm of pure celestial joy. This is Eros at his best, that enterprising ambitious love that shrinks the gap between heaven and earth, the pious man always reaching up to the golden apples on the top of the tree of heaven, just out of reach.

Religious emblem books, albums of inspirational talking pictures, which flourished in the first centuries of printing, rammed the message home. The first and most influential was that produced by Andrea Alciato in Augsburg in 1531 and reprinted with modifications in over 150 editions after that. In these books, Ganymede has a starring role.

The emblem of Ganymede had a prominent place near the front of Alciato's *Emblemata*, before all the images illustrating the virtues and the vices, in the preface, as it were representing 'religion' itself, and his motto was *in Deo laetandum*, 'God is for rejoicing in'.

Very often the printers included excerpts of Xenophon's etymology of Ganymede's name in the alphabet of the Greeks – 'delighting in thoughts'. It has been argued that there was a decline in the quantity and seriousness of images of Ganymede after the edicts of the counter-reformation Council of Trent, but if there were fewer new oil-paintings and frescoes and if a large proportion of those made the Trojan prince an anonymous baby, nevertheless the neo-Platonic Ganymede of Alciato's emblem-books was multiplying through the printing-press. As a celebration of the high-minded uses of the image, emblematic Ganymede, lifting off the ground, could stand as the frontispiece for the whole counter-reformational project.

> Goethe transformed Ganymede into a rapturous environmentalist, full of the joys: **Wie im Morgenglanze...** – 'How, in the flashes of morning, you wrestle...' he wrote, before trying again: **Wie im Morgenrot...** – 'How, iin the blush of dawn, you wrestles me red-faced, O Spring, beloved...' In the final stanza Ganymede feels his feet rising off the ground: **Ich komm, ich komme! Wohin? Ach, wohin? Hinauf!** 'I'm coming! Whither? ... where? Up there! ...' Franz Schubert, and Hugo Wolf, among many others, made the poem into a song. There had already been several cantatas on the subject of Ganymede...
>
> (Davidson 174f)

Virgil had made Ganymede's elevation the reason for Hera's hostility to the entire royal family of Troy, the family from which his patron Augustus claimed descent. To make matters worse, this mortal had taken a role away from her own daughter, Hebe, goddess of youthful bloom, who had previously carried the refreshments, but stumbled once.

In the fourteenth century the Latin *Ovidius moralizatus* by Pierre Bersaire compare Ganymede to St. John and talked of getting close to God . *I bore you on eagles' wings and brought you to myself*, as *Exodus* 19,4 puts it.

Ganymede's extreme youth also helps to highlight a contrast with Tithonus, his relative. Abducted Tithonus ages but never dies, lingering in eternal decrepitude in Dawn's abode on the margins between earthly and unearthly existence. Abducted Ganymede, who gets to travel right to the heart of heaven, is, by contrast, forever on the brink of maturity, always a boy... Both of them are stuck at the opposite ends of the Athenian age-class system that starts at Eighteen and finishes at Sixty.

> Indeed he is a unique figure in Greek religion, a mortal on Olympus. It was the very nectar served by Ganymede and the 'ambrosia', the food of the gods (ambrosia just means 'without mortality'), that kept the gods gods, that kept them up there. The significance of his role is revealed by the fact that it was also performed by Hebe, daughter of Zeus and Hera. Hebe is the personification of youthful 'flowering', and as we see in the case of Tithonus it is not just deathlessness but undying youthful vigour that distinguishes gods from men. Her presence on Olympus is terribly important therefore, and when Ganymede takes over her role, he too must be seen to embody the youthfulness he both possesses and dispenses, the fuels of immortality. He is what he serves. He is, precisely, the sap-filled youthfulness that his brother Tithonus, the dried-out cicada, has lost. (Davidson 196)

If we consider Ganymede, therefore, up among the gods, doing his job any Greek would start thinking about the nectar and ambrosia he serves, about immortality, libations and sacrifice. They would see in Ganymede a pure once-mortal boy mediating between earth and heaven, a resonant symbol of human and divine exchange, a uniquely remarkable figure.

What is odd is how anyone could have failed to see his importance. In the *Iliad*, on vases, in statues at Olympia beside the greatest altar in all Greece, and later featuring prominently in the imperial propaganda of the Julio-Claudians, the story of the mortal serving immortality to the immortals seems a far more central, widespread and significant myth about sacrifice and the gulf between men and gods than either the myth of Prometheus or the myth of Lycaon the cannibal man-wolf of Arcadia, myths that usually take centre-stage.

So Ganymede flying on the back of Zeus' eagle, as Manwe's eagles have carried some characters in *The Sillmarilion* , *The Lord of the Rings* and *The Hobbit* – this could be a good inspirational figure, I daresay.

Anyhow, perhaps some would also agree that, at least for the *Inklings*, olympian *ambrosia* is identified with good *ale*, and that is expectedly good news for us!

Not all those who wander are lost: after our long (and I dare to hope not totally useless) detour, here we come again to our Tolkienian eagles.

Indeed a long-established tradition in Tolkien's work going back to *The Book of Lost Tales* portrays eagles as the messengers of Manwe, guardians of Gondolin, bitter foes of Melko. We are told that Manwe created the eagles himself (cf. HH I 220f).

Eagles are depicted with the greatest levels of self-awareness, especially the lineage of Thorondor – king of the eagles (the Lord of the Eagles in *The Hobbit* and Gwaihir in *The Lord of the Rings*).

Eagles perform functions related to eschatology. In both the Battle of the Five Armies (*The Hobbit*) and the battle before the Black Gates of Mordor (*The Lord of the Rings*), Eagles arrive unexpectedly at the last moment and turn the tide, saving the heroes of the stories. As they saved Beren and Lúthien in the *Silmarillion*, or Bilbo, Gandalf and the Dwarves in *The Hobbit* and Gandalf, Frodo and Sam in *The Lord of the Rings* (cf. Drout 20f; Hammond/Scull, *Companion* 630).

Tolkien incorporates the enduring folk belief that eagles carry off lambs and even sheep directly into his text, putting it into the mouth of the Lord of the Eagles himself: 'they will think we are after their lambs – or their babies. And at other times they might be right.' Interestingly enough, this alarming statement was toned down in the revisions, with the 'Ganymede' element being taken out" said Rateliff "before the First Typescript (where it's simply the lambs they're after and the *lambs* changed to *sheep* in the page proofs. Perhaps Tolkien wanted to emphasize the size and majesty of these great birds; perhaps he wanted to give another example of the divisions between the good peoples of the story (thus laying the groundwork for the wood-elf episode and Siege of the Lonely Mountain that were to follow). Still, he makes it clear that, while not 'kindly birds' (as the published text puts it), they are nevertheless foes of evil who put a stop to the goblins' 'wickedness' whenever they can.

Later the eagles move their eyries to the Encircling Mountains surrounding Gondolin, to help guard this last elven refuge against Melko's spies. While they cannot prevent the fall of the city, the eagles do save the refugees from fallen Gondolin as they battle goblins and a balrog in a mountain pass in a scene strikingly similar to that in *The Hobbit* but predating it by more than a decade.

> Tolkien himself felt that the eagles were a dangerous device, apt to be overused as a deus ex machina; he deplored their ubiquitous appearance throughout the first movie script for a potential *Lord of the Rings* movie sent to him in 1958. Indeed, in *The Hobbit* they appear only twice and in *The Lord of the Rings* only three times, with two of those episodes being off-stage (the rescue of Gandalf from Orthanc and the retrieval of his body from atop Zirakzigil).
> Close examination of the *Silmarillion* texts shows the danger: the more times Tolkien re-wrote the stories, the more new episodes featuring the eagles worked their way in... Clearly, Tolkien was fond of his eagles and found it difficult to keep them out of each of the major stories that make up the *Silmarillion* cycle. (HH I 220)[7]

---

7 Also he painted the welknown wonderful watercolour, inspired in Thorburn *Golden Eagle (Immature)*, although has the small defect of keeping the white feathers, improper for a grown up eagle as the Lord of the Winds: cfr. Hammond and Scull (*Artist* 120-124)

Given Tolkien's continued interest in the eagles, it is odd that in The Battle of Five Armies the wargs and goblins each count as a 'people' for purposes of the tally yet the eagles do not. Perhaps there are simply too few eagles present to be described as an 'army'.

Finally, we should note the mythic resonance of the parting words to the eagles: 'May the wind under your wings bear you where the sun sails and the moon walks'.

It refers to the creation of Arda. These words "obliquely tie into the cosmology of the created world and reaffirm that the Great Eagles are indeed the eagles of Manwe, either spirits incarnated as birds or their (mortal) descendants, just as the wargs are descended from spirits of evil that had taken wolf-form. The eagles and the wargs neatly counterpoise each other, and each play in our story what had already by 1930 become their 'traditional' roles in the stories that comprised Tolkien's *Legendarium*: the one to threaten the heroes and the other to intervene when all hope had been lost and deliver them from evil, almost as a visible grace" (HH I 223f).

'The eagles are coming!' 'That came in Bilbo's tale' said Pippin. He gave a great cry, he had seen a sight that made his heart leap – dark shapes, small yet majestic against the distant glow.

Bilbo's eye was seldom wrong. The eagles were coming down the wind: line after line in such a host as must have gathered from all the eyries of the North. The eagles helped to turn the tide of battle.

In any case, it seems that eagles bring always a sense of help, rescue and regained freedom. A sense of vastness, of space, of freshness: true, clean, sharp and wild freshness. As if their feathers had a kind of *kingsfoil's* (or *Athelas*) qualities, so to speak!

For flying on the back of an eagle, free and safe (at least for Gandalf, a bit less no doubt for poor Bilbo and the dwarves), was not as to ride *a keen wind, wholly fresh and clean and young, as if it had not before been breathed by any living thing and came new-made from snowy mountains high beneath a dome of stars?*

Or in the words of John O'Donohue:

As a bird soars high
In the free holding of the wind,
Clear of the certainty of ground,
Opening the imagination of wings
Into the grace of emptiness
To fulfil new voyagings,
May your life awaken
To the call of its freedom.
(O'Donohue 48)

May we, too, receive the help of the *eagles* after hearing the good counsel of *ravens* to do our best in the battle: to escape from the threatening *wolves/wargs* and to climb high on the back of the eagles into the depth of Mystery.

Air, perfect emptiness
For the mind of birds
To map with vanishings;
Womb of forms
That shapes embraces
To hold animal presence.
(O'Donohue 55)

May we hear the call of the sense of beyondness at the heart of things; may we be brought beyond where *the sun sails and the moon walks*. Even beyond *the circles of the world.*
And may we become as Ganymede in the reshaping of Arda by Iluvatar.

'Farewell!' they cried,' wherever you fare, till your eyries receive you at the journey's end!' That is the polite thing to say among eagles.

Bibliography

Apuleio, *Metamorfosi (l'asino d'oro)*. Milano: Oscar Mondadori, 1989

Abram, David. *The spell of the sensuous perception and language in a More-Than-Human World*. New York: Vintage Books, 1996

Anderson, Douglas A. *The annotated Hobbit*. London: HarperCollins, 2003

Baroni, P./C. Isoldi/P. Lodone/E. Rialti/M. Zupo. *Uno sguardo fino al mare J.R.R. Tolkien: le parole dell'epica contemporanea*. Rimini: Il Cerchio, 2004

Bell, David N. 1992, *Wholly animals a book of beastly tales*. Kalamazoo: Cistercian Publications, 1992

Casey, Denise/Tim W. Clark. *Tales of the Wolf – fifty-one stories of wolf encounters in the wild*. Wyoming: Homestead Publishing, 1996

Chaucer, Geoffrey. *Troilus and Criseyde*, ed. John Warrington. London/New York: Dent Dutton, 1974

Ciccarese, Maria Pia. *Animali simbolici alle origini del bestiario cristiano I Agnello – Gufo*. Bologna: EDB, 2002

Craven, Margaret. *I heard the owl call my name*. London: Picador, 1974

Davidson, James. *The Greeks and Greek love a radical reappraisal of homosexuality in Ancient Greece*. London: Weiderfeld & Nicolson, 2007

De Waal, Ester. *The Celtic Way of Prayer – the Recovery of the religious Imagination*. London/Sidney/Auckland: Hodder & Stoughton, 2003

Drout, Michael D.C. (ed.). *J.R.R. Tolkien Encyclopedia. Scholarship and Critical Assessment*. New York/London: Routledge, 2007

Federico, Silvia. *New Troy Fantasies of Empire in the Late Middle Ages*. Minneapolis: University of Minnesota Press, 2003

Gerritsen, Willem P./Anthony G. van Melle. *A Directionary of Medieval Heroes Characters in Medieval Narrative Traditions and Their Afterlife in Literature Theatre and the visual Arts*. Woodbridge: the Boydell Press, 1998

Hammond, Wayne G./Christina Scull. *J.R.R. Tolkien Artist & Illustrator*. London: HarperCollins, 1995

---. *The Lord of the Rings. A Reader's Companion*. London: HarperCollins, 2005

Honegger, Thomas. "Form and function: The Beasts of Battle revisited". *English Studies* 79 (1998): 289-298

Howard, Th. *Chance or the dance. A critique of modern secularism*. San Francisco: Ignatius Press, 1969

---. *C.S. Lewis Man of Letters. A reading of his fiction*. San Francisco: Ignatius Press, 1987

Lefkowitz, Mary, *Greek Gods Human Lives. What we can learn from Myths*. New Haven/London: Yale University Press, 2003

Lewis, Alex/ Elizabeth Currie. *The Uncharted Realms of Tolkien*. London: Medea Publishing, 2002

---. *The Forsaken Realm of Tolkien*. London: Medea Publishing, 2005

Lewis, Clive Staples. *Till we have faces. A myth retold*, San Diego/New York/London: HBJ, 1985

Lobdell, Jared, *The World of the Rings – language, religion, and adventure in Tolkien*. Chicago/La Salle (IL): Open Court, 2004

Lopez, Barry. *Of Wolves and man*. New York/London/Toronto/Sydney: Scribner Classics, 2004

Luce, F. V. *Celebrating Homer's Landscapes. Troy and Ithaca Revisited*. New Haven/London: Yale University Press, 1998

O'Connor, Flannery. *Mistery and Manners. Occasional prose*, New York: The Noonday Press, 1969

O'Donohue, John. *Benedictus. A book of blessings*. London/Toronto/Sydney/Auckland/Johannesburg: Bantam Press, 2007

Pinney, R. *The animals in the Bible*. Philadelphia/New York: Chilton Books, 1964

Rateliff, John D. *The History of* The Hobbit. 2 Vols. London: HarperCollins, 2007

Rehnmark, Eva-Lena. *Neither God nor Devil rethinking our perception of Wolves*. San Francisco, Pomegranate, 2000

Schönborn, Christoph, *Weihnacht. Mythos wird Wirklichkeit. Meditationen zur Menschwerdung*. Einsiedeln-Freiburg: Johannes Verlag, 2007

Somerville, Margaret. *The Ethical Imagination Journeys of the Human Spirit*, Toronto: Anansi, 2006

Spirito, Guglielmo. "Il lupo "malvagio": un mito rivisitato". *Convivium Assisiense* VIII (2006): 61-86

Thompson, Diane P. *The Trojan War Literature and Legends from the Bronze Age to the Present*. Jefferson (NC)/London: Mc Farland & Company Inc., 2004

Tolkien, John Ronald Reuel. *The Hobbit or There and Back again*. London: HarperCollins, 1993

---. *The Lord of the Rings*. London: HarperCollins, 1995

---. *Morgoth's Ring the later Silmarillion part one the legends of Aman*, ed. Christopher Tolkien. London: HarperCollins, 1994

Toperoff, S. P. *The animal kingdom in jewish thought*. Northvale London: Jason Aronson Inc., 1995

Troia. Traum und Wirklichkeit. Stuttgart: Theiss, 2001

Waddell, Helen. *Beasts and Saints*. London: Darton Longman Todd, 1995

Winkler, J. "Winged Creatures". *Messanger of Saint Anthony. International edition* April (2008): 10-11

Wockner, Gary/Gregory McNamee/SueEllen Campbell. *Comeback Wolves. Western Writers Welcome the Wolf Home*. Boulder: Johnson Books, 2005

Woodford, Susan. *The Trojan War in Ancient Art*. Ithaca (NY): Cornell University Press, 1993

'Sing we now softly, and dreams let us weave him!': Dreams and Dream Visions in J.R.R. Tolkien's *The Hobbit*

Doreen Triebel (Jena)

The influence of medieval literature and languages on Tolkien's creative work has been widely acknowledged and investigated. Among those ancient works of art the dream vision was one of the most prevalent literary forms especially in the later Middle Ages, with numerous works by Chaucer[1], Langland's *Piers Plowman*, the Gawain poet's *Pearl*, *Sir Orfeo*, the Old English *Dream of the Rood* and tales from the *Welsh Mabinogion*[2] or Mallory's *Le Morte D'Arthur*[3] as remarkable examples. There are, however, even older occurrences of meaningful dream visions in classical literature, such as the *Aeneid* and the *Odyssey*, but also in Bede's *Historia ecclesiastica gentis Anglorum* and notably the *Bible*.

The Scriptures recount numerous meaningful instances, like Jacob's dream at Bethel in which he encounters God (Gen. 28:10-22), the dream of Pharaoh which foreshadows seven years of abundance and seven years of famine (Gen. 41:14-24), Nebuchadnezzer's foretelling dream (Dan. 4:19-37), the dream in which Joseph is instructed of the coming of Jesus (Matt. 1:20-25), and finally St John's Apocalypse.

On the one hand these and other examples have supported the notion that such nightly visions possess prophetic significance and they have led to theories like the one of Synesius of Cyrene, who saw a divine source in virtually every dream (cf. Synesius 326-359). But they have also shown the difficulties associated with the disclosure of their particular meanings. As Constance Hieatt has pointed out, it was common belief that dreams were not always sent by God and thus could not be considered as 'true'; the Devil also had such powers and, according to contemporary dream lore, he used them in order to lead people

---

1 To these works belong *The Book of the Duchess*, *The House of Fame*, *The Parliament of Fowls*, and *The Legend of Good Women* but also several stories from *The Canterbury Tales*.
2 "The Dream of Macsen Wledig" and "The Dream of Rhonabwy"
3 Notable examples are Arthur's strange dream about a dragon and a bear fighting in *The Tale of King Arthur and the Emperor Lucius* (cf. Mallory: 99) and another vision in *Le Morte D'Arthur* in which Arthur sees an apparition of Sir Gawaine's ghost who warns the King not to fight Sir Mordred the following day and advises him to make a treaty with the enemy until Sir Launcelot arrives to defeat him (cf. 498).

astray with 'false' visions (cf. Hieatt 24). This is one of the main reasons why the medieval church often expressed strong objections to dream divination and popular works such as the Somniale Danielis, a handbook for the interpretation of dreams (cf. Kruger 11). Even learned men like John of Salisbury, who was versed in dream lore and devised a classification system of dreams himself, felt that their interpretation demanded knowledge and wisdom that exceeded human capability (cf. Hieatt 29).

Nevertheless, the idea of transcendent dreams has continued to grasp the imagination of people in all époques and the preoccupation with their analysis and interpretation has resulted in very different, partly divergent dream theories.

Medieval Dream Theories

Among the most noticeable scholars in this field was Macrobius, who in his *Commentary on the Dream of Scipio* declared that all dreams may be classified under five main types so as to organise and simplify possible interpretations and to distinguish valid dreams - which are spiritual in origin and reveal the holy purposes of God - from invalid dreams of mundane origin. This classification comprises the enigmatic dream [lat. *somnium*], the prophetic vision [lat. *visio*], the oracular dream [lat. *oraculum*], the nightmare [lat. *insomnium*], and finally the apparition [lat. *visum*] (cf. Macrobius 88). Macrobius did not attribute any prophetic significance to the nightmare (a distorted vision which may be caused by "mental or physical distress, or anxiety about the future" (ibid.)) or the apparition (a delusion or hallucination resulting from mental disorder) but his classification suggests a meaningful importance of the first three kinds of dreams. Macrobius held that an oracular dream is one that foreshadows future events – often in dialogue with a parent, a revered person, or a god who offers guidance concerning the dreamer's actions.

He further explains that a prophetic vision is a visual experience of an event that will eventually come true just as it had been beheld in the vision, whereas an enigmatic dream conceals its true content by means of obscure or ambiguous forms. However, these categories are by no means mutually exclusive and hardly appear in their pure form, as Macrobius' analysis of Scipio's dream also reveals.

In this context it should also be noted that the acknowledgement of foreshadowing dreams poses a particularly interesting problem for the notion of mankind's free will – a complex and much discussed philosophical and theological issue, which we also encounter in Tolkien's fiction. However, therein it is not only reflected in prophetic dream visions but even more explicitly in passages like the final paragraph of *The Hobbit*, in which Gandalf suggests that the whole adventure and its outcome are somehow predetermined:

> "Then the prophecies of the old songs have turned out to be true, after a fashion!" said Bilbo. "Of course!" said Gandalf. "And why should not they prove true? Surely you don't disbelieve the prophecies, because you had a hand in bringing them about yourself? You don't really suppose, do you, that all your adventures and escapes were managed by mere luck, just for your sole benefit? You are a very fine person, Mr Baggins, and I am very fond of you; but you are only quite a little fellow in a wide world after all!" (H 272)

The obvious dilemma in this context is that the future cannot be easily foreseen, unless it is to a certain extent predestined, either by an omnipotent God or by some kind of fate. However, if propositions or dreams about the future were not contingent but necessarily true, it would inevitably follow that man's power to exercise control over his actions and decisions is considerably restricted, if not completely negated, because, in this case, the free choice to act otherwise is, of course, merely an illusion. But any attempt to maintain the idea of mankind's inherent free will entails the impossibility to predict future events and also the need to adjust or abandon the doctrine of God's almightiness and omniscience. Additionally, this issue has important moral implications. As it would seem, people whose actions and decisions are inevitably guided by God or fate in order to accord with a larger plan, cannot be held responsible for their deeds, whether good or bad.

However, the notion of the prophetic value of dreams did by no means go unchallenged. Hippocrates, widely regarded as the 'father of medicine', believed that the mostly visual symbolism of dreams was largely explicable in terms of physical or psychological symptoms and he even used dreams as a tool for diagnosis and treatment of illnesses (cf. Hippocrates 421-447).

Aristotle also described dreams as being brought about by an interaction of physical and psychological causes. According to the Greek philosopher, these nightly visions were based upon the movements of sensory impressions – whether derived from external objects or from causes within the body – that persisted in the human mind even after the object that evoked the perception had departed (cf. Aristotle 41). Aristotle held that this phenomenon could occur when the person was awake but even more frequently when he/she found himself/herself in the state of sleep, because then the senses and the intellect could no longer obscure these impressions. Disturbances could be evoked by the consumption of food shortly before retiring to sleep and they could either preclude or utterly distort the otherwise clear and plain images appearing to the dreamer (cf. ibid. 44). As Aristotle argued, the quality and clarity of the dream could be further influenced by physical health or illnesses, intoxicating beverages or movements of the bodily liquids, notably the blood. It is fairly obvious that in such a view, gods can hardly be held responsible for the content of dreams and therefore Aristotle's theory was a strong case against the divinatory meanings of these nightly visions.

Although somatic causes of dreams were partly recognised by medieval scholars "the twelfth- and thirteenth-century introduction of new medical and scientific texts to the Latin West gave the body and bodily processes a new prominence in European dream theory" (Kruger 55). Thus, Kruger argues, Aristotle's postulate brought about an important change in medieval dream lore by establishing a close connection between dreams and bodily processes.

We can conclude that medieval dream theories held that there were three different kinds of dreams: the 'somnium naturale', a dream of bodily causes, the 'somnium animale', a dream of psychological causes, and the 'somnium coeleste', a dream of external causes that has its origin either in God, angels or devils (cf. Spearing 55-56; Amendt-Raduege 47).

Medieval Dream Literature

These very different dream theories found their way into contemporary literature, which thus mirrored the ambiguous status of the nightly visions. Especially in the early Middle Ages, literary dream frameworks often drew on Macrobius' ideas and frequently presented the nightly visions as a means of divine intervention. However, inspired by Aristotelian dream theory and the French *Roman de la Rose*, an immensely influential secular poem incorporating the vehicle of dream, many poets of the later Middle Ages began to use this literary device in non-religious contexts, such as the romantic love experience, in order to offer insights into the characters' psyche, depict his/her motivations, and provide an impetus for action (cf. Peden 67).

These divergent ideas are nicely reflected and summarized, for instance, in Chaucer's *The Nun's Priest's Tale*, in which Chauntecleer's prophetic interpretation of his dream is significantly contrasted with Pertelote's explanation of a physical disorder as the only likely cause of the apparition. It is however remarkable that in all traditions of medieval dream literature the visions were not always depicted as particularly dreamlike in that they are often allegorical in nature. As Tolkien asserts in the introduction to his translations of *Sir Gawain and the Green Knight, Pearl,* and *Sir Orfeo*, one of the main reasons for the popularity of visions was that

they allowed marvels to be placed within the real world, linking
them with a person, a place, a time, while providing them with an
explanation in the phantasies of sleep, and a defence against critics
in the notorious deception of dreams. So even explicit allegory was
usually presented as a thing seen in sleep. (GPO 10)

Thus, the dream framework was often regarded as a device to lend credence to marvellous events or creatures. In the following literary époques the allegorical structure and the notion of prophetic dreams were progressively abandoned and nightly visions became increasingly connected to the psyche and the waking concerns of the dreamer as we can see, for example, in Shakespeare's *Macbeth* or more recently in Dostoevsky's *Crime and Punishment* [4] and even more so, of course, in the literature of the post-Freudian era.

Tolkien appreciated the use of dream visions in literature, because he believed that these phenomena were connected to the notion of Faërie. In *On Fairy-Stories* he argued that "[i]n dreams strange powers of the mind may be unlocked. In some of them a man may for a space wield the power of Faërie, that power which, even as it conceives the story, causes it to take living form and colour before the eyes" (FS 14). Yet, he was clearly averse to using dreams as a means of rationally explaining and disenchanting the occurrence of marvels in a tale, as this would "deliberately [cheat] the primal desire at the heart of Faërie: the realisation, independent of the conceiving mind, of imaged wonder" (ibid.). However, this is the main function of the dream framework in Shakespeare's *A Midsummer Night's Dream* or Lewis Caroll's *Alice* books.

Dream Visions in Tolkien's Works

Being aware of its possibilities but also of its limitations, Tolkien drew on the vast and diverse dream lore as reflected primarily in the medieval literature that dominated his professional life. The motif of the dream vision found its way into his creative writings, in particular into *The Lost Road*, *The Notion Club Papers*, *The Lord of the Rings*, and *The Hobbit*. It is furthermore notable that Tolkien had a very personal connection to dreams, since he himself was haunted by a recurrent enigmatic Atlantis vision of a great wave drowning a green land – a dream that he had even passed on to one of his sons[5], that he

---

[4] Both Lady Macbeth and Raskolnikov are haunted by troubled dreams after having committed murders.
[5] In a letter to W.H. Auden Tolkien remarks that Michael had apparently inherited the dream from him, although both of them did not know about the respective other having the same dream until Michael was about 34 years old (cf. L 213).

incorporated into the two fragmented stories and 'The Downfall of Númenor', before bequeathing it to Faramir in *The Lord of the Rings* (cf. L 213).

In the secondary world of Tolkien's *Legendarium* the borders between dreams and the experiences of the waking mind are not always clear-cut. His fiction deliberately establishes a link between the two by incorporating the conventions of medieval dream literature, which, as we have seen, often connected those visions to reality. Furthermore, the different instances of dreams in his creative works show a remarkable visual quality that was also common to dreams in medieval literature (cf. Hieatt 18 and Amendt-Raduege 45) and just as in *The Dream of the Rood*, or Dante's *Divine Comedy* the vision in Tolkien's stories offers the dreamer "oneiric access to a higher moral or eschatological realm" and very often s/he "awakens enlightened" (Kruger 124, cf. also Amendt-Raduege 46).

Dreaming in *The Hobbit*

In many respects the dream visions in *The Hobbit* resemble those we find incorporated in *The Lord of the Rings*. In both works Tolkien uses the dream motif to reach into hidden parts of the characters' minds and to transcend the borders of space and time in various degrees. The tales thus contain dreams that have somatic or psychological causes but also those that are more suggestive in nature or downright predictive. The first category could be equated with what Macrobius calls insomnium and visum, and it is also still largely in line with Aristotle's theories. These dreams may have no prophetic significance but, nevertheless, they fulfil the important function of offering valuable insights into the dreamer's state of mind. In the first instance of dreaming in *The Hobbit* we learn that Bilbo has "very uncomfortable dreams" (H 26) the night before he undertakes his adventure with the dwarves. The content of the dreams is not specified, but this is not necessary as they achieve their function of revealing the hobbit's anxiety about leaving his comfortable middle class home and getting involved with a wide world that is totally alien to him and most of his fellow halflings. Bilbo has more or less agreed to accompany the dwarves on their quest but his troubled dreams in the face of such a venture show his limited adventurousness and ultimately his lack of heroic qualities at the beginning of the tale.

After enjoying the security of Beorn's house, the company heads for the eerie forest Mirkwood, about whose dangers they have been gravely warned by their host. On the way the dwarves and Bilbo seemingly manage to forget the upcoming perils for a while. They begin to talk and sing merrily but their dreams convey a rather different message. At night "most of them slept uneasily with dreams in which there came the howl of hunting wolves and the cries of goblins" (123). Here Tolkien again uses nightmares to show the inner turmoil of the characters, which is not always visible from their behaviour. Outwardly the dwarves and Bilbo appear unafraid, even cheerful, but the dreams reveal their true state of mind and their maybe still unconscious certainty that the quest they had so optimistically undertaken has turned out to be more dangerous than they had expected. The same awareness becomes apparent in the "uncomfortable sleep full of horrible dreams" (151) the company falls into after they have fought the fearsome spiders of Mirkwood and wondered what dreadful fate has befallen Thorin.

However, the dwarves and Bilbo are not the only dreamers in *The Hobbit*. The first time Bilbo enters the dragon's lair he feels overwhelmed by the splendour and glory of the hoard that fills his heart with enchantment – a sensation that is beautifully contrasted with the malice of the worm who does not wake up when Bilbo steals the cup but "shift[s] into other dreams of greed and violence" (194). So far we have only heard others report on the viciousness of the dragon but the first insight we get into his psyche by means of the dream motif reinforces this impression.

We find another instance of non-prophetic dreams after Bilbo has handed over the Arkenstone to Bard and the Elvenking. The hobbit "was soon fast asleep forgetting all his worries till the morning. As a matter of fact he was dreaming of eggs and bacon" (245). The situation in which Bilbo finds himself at this moment is very intricate. He has just betrayed his companions by stealing what Thorin treasures above all the riches in the dragon's lair and delivering it to the alleged enemies, but even after the Elvenking has advised him not to return to the dwarves, he decides to stick by his friends. He knows that there is trouble ahead and Gandalf warns him that "[t]here is an unpleasant time just in front of you; but keep your heart up! You *may* come through all right" (245). This does not sound particularly comforting but, nevertheless, the hungry hobbit's pleasant and untroubled dream shows two things: firstly he knows very well what he has done and is convinced that it was undoubtedly the right thing to do, and secondly it proves how he has matured. He has developed from a timid little hobbit to some kind of hero and that is clearly reflected in his dreams, which are no longer haunted by inner struggles and anxieties.

These dreams can largely be classified as 'somnia animale' or, in the last case, as a conflation of 'somnium animale' and 'somnium naturale'. They possess no qualities beyond the ordinary and equivalents can be encountered numerously in *The Lord of the Rings* where they have rather similar functions and the most important dreamers are also hobbits. On the trail with the Orcs, for example, Pippin "lay in a dark and troubled dream" (LotR 434) and we learn that leaving the Orc road in Mordor, Frodo's "sleep had been uneasy, full of dreams of fire" (901).

Both tales, however, also contain several instances of dreams that go beyond insomnia or visa. These visions are more meaningful and correspond to Macrobius' notion of 'enigmatic dreams'. In the abode of the eagles Bilbo slept

> curled up on the hard rock more soundly than ever he had done on his feather-bed in his own little hole at home. But all night he dreamed of his own house and wandered in his sleep into all his different rooms looking for something that he could not find nor remember what it looked like. (H 102)

Just like the formerly discussed dreams, this vision is actually redundant to the overall plot but it is obviously indicative of Bilbo's spiritual struggles, although both its content and its source are somewhat cryptic. It is quite conceivable that the vision could refer to and indeed even have been sent by the Ring that starts to manipulate Bilbo's psyche, albeit unconsciously, in his dreams.

Yet the scene was already contained in the book before Tolkien had revised decisive parts so as to reduce several inconsistencies with *The Lord of the Rings* (cf. HH I 210) and most notably those connected to the importance of the Ring. It is therefore also possible that the dream merely reflects Bilbo's psychological journey. The unidentified thing he is looking for in his dream might be nothing less than his true self, which seems to have changed considerably since he went on the quest with the dwarves and was able to live out the adventurous, Tookish side of his personality. Having discovered that part of himself he can, as the narrator informs us, sleep more soundly on the hard rock in the Misty Mountains than ever before in his comfortable soft bed.

Just like the eagles' abode, Beorn's house inspires enigmatic dreams in the hobbit. On the second night the company spends there "he dropped asleep, still puzzling his little head about Beorn, till he dreamed a dream of hundreds of black bears dancing slow heavy dances round and round in the moonlight in the courtyard. Then he woke up and he heard the same scraping, scuffing, snuffling, and growling as before" (H 120). Comparable to the former enigmatic dream, which allowed the hobbit's mind to travel to Bag End, this vision has the power to transcend space, albeit to a lesser degree. However, it is left ambiguous as to whether the dream grants Bilbo the ability to see past events, namely the regular bears' meeting that has apparently taken place the night before, some future event that is not necessarily referred to later, or something that happens simultaneously to his dreaming (as the recurred snuffling and scraping he hears when he wakes up might suggest).

Yet what has become quite clear is that the dream reflects Bilbo's deep anxieties in the house of the shape-shifter. In this context, it is also notable that Tolkien modelled Beorn's hall directly on Heorot, King Hrothgar's monster-haunted mead-hall in *Beowulf* (cf. HH I 261). He thus increases the sense of

Bilbo's fear by paralleling the hobbit's position in the shape-shifter's house when he hears the strange and menacing noises from outside with the situation in which Beowulf and his companions wait for Grendel's attack on the seat of the Danish king.

In *The Lord of the Rings* it is Frodo in particular who has dreams that are so enigmatic and ambiguous that they sometimes seem to indicate a divine source. While still in the Shire, for example, "a strange vision of mountains that he had never seen came into his dreams" (LotR 42) and at Crickhollow he experiences a baffling and unclear dream, in which he hears strange snuffling noises and sounds of the sea (cf. 106). Yet these visions become more delusive and gloomy with every step that brings Frodo closer to Mordor (cf. Amendt-Raduege 47). In so doing they serve to mirror the hobbit's state of mind and indicate approaching evil.

Even more significant are the visions that parallel the 'oracular' and the 'prophetic dreams' of Macrobius' classification. Just like the 'somnia', they are capable of foreshadowing future events but to a greater extent and far more explicitly in their meaning. Advancing towards the Misty Mountains, the company of *The Hobbit* looks for shelter in a cave, which later turns out to be the entrance to the subterranean goblin realm. We learn that Bilbo

> could not sleep for a while; but when he did sleep, he had very nasty dreams. He dreamed that a crack in the wall at the back of the cave got bigger and bigger, and opened wider and wider and he was afraid but could not call out or do anything but lie and look. Then he dreamed that the floor of the cave was giving way, and that he was slipping – beginning to fall down, down, goodness knows where to.
> At that he woke up with a horrible start, and found that part of his dream was true. A crack had opened at the back of the cave, and was already a wide passage... Of course he gave a very loud yell...
> (H 55f)

This dream is undoubtedly prophetic and what is more it is, in contrast to the formerly discussed instances, highly relevant to the plot in that it causes Bilbo to wake up and sharpens his senses for what he sees, thus making him more capable of acting.

Yet, again the origins of the dream are left unclear. Is Bilbo's vision merely initiated by his latent fears in the face of the perilous quest that he has undertaken? Does he unconsciously perceive what is happening around him and integrate it into his dream, which then develops prophetic value? Or is the vision of divine origin and sent by a godlike or angelic being who intends to warn him? This is not altogether impossible, because it is notably the first time in the book that the hobbit is actually 'useful' to the company. He gives the yell that enables the wizard to escape, to kill the Great Goblin, and ultimately to save the whole mission.

We find similar, yet even more clearly divine visions in *The Lord of the Rings*, when, for instance, Faramir and Boromir both experience meaningful dreams which advise a clear course of action, unambiguously prophesise the proceedings of the meeting in Rivendell[6] and ultimately guide the older brother to Elrond's council. These dreams seem to be further manifestations of divine providence in the world of Tolkien's *Legendarium* – an impression that is strengthened by Elrond's introductory words: "You have come and are here met, in this very nick of time, by chance as it may seem. Yet, it is not so. Believe rather that it is so ordered that we, who sit here, and none others, must now find counsel for the peril of the world" (LotR 236). The same may be said of his encouragement to Frodo after he decided to take the Ring to Mordor: "'If I understand aright all that I have heard,' he said, 'I think the task is appointed to you, Frodo; and if you do not find a way, no one will...'" (264).

The most intriguing dreams in *The Hobbit*, however, are the foreshadowing visions induced by the Elves or Faërie, which we also encounter in the subsequent book, notably in the woodland realm of Lothlórien[7] where Frodo and Sam are granted a look in Galadriel's Mirror and see visions concerning the present and the future. One of the most memorable examples is Sam's vision of the destroyed Shire. The visions in the earlier book are certainly not as bleak and also not as meaningful as the ones we find in *The Lord of the Rings* but they are by no means less prophetic. In Mirkwood Bombur is cast into a long, enchanted sleep after he unintentionally falls into the black river. As familiar motifs like the white stag[8] and the enchanted stream[9] indicate, the dwarves and Bilbo have entered an Otherworld within the borders of Tolkien's fictional mortal lands, which does not only exert an influence over the waking perceptions

---

6   During the council Boromir recounts: "a dream came to my brother in a troubled sleep; and afterwards a like dream came oft to him again, and once to me. 'In that dream I thought the eastern sky grew dark and there was a growing thunder, but in the West a pale light lingered, and out of it I heard a voice, remote but clear, and crying: Seek for the Sword that was broken: In Imladris it dwells; There shall be councils taken, Stronger than Morgul-spells. There shall be shown a token, That doom is near at hand, For Isildur's Bane shall waken, And the Halfling forth shall stand" (LotR 239-240).
7   The short form 'Lórien' is the Quenya word for 'dream land' (cf. Forster 303).
8   The white stag is a familiar animal in Celtic mythology and legend that usually indicates that the Otherworld is near. A similar use of the motif can be found in Pwyll and Arawn, the first branch of the Welsh *Mabinogi*, the romance *Peredur, son of Efrawg*, C.S. Lewis' *The Lion, the Witch and, the Wardrobe*, and also in Tolkien's *The Lay of Aotrou and Itroun*, where Aotroun encounters the witch only shortly after having caught sight of a white doe.
9   The motif of an enchanted stream is also quite familiar in Celtic mythology and appears, for example, in *Life of Brendan of Clonfert*.

of the company but also over the visions that come to them in their dreams. Thus in his enchanted sleep Bombur dreams that

> [he] was walking in a forest rather like this one, only lit with torch-es on the trees and lamps swinging from the branches and fires burning on the ground; and there was a great feast going on, going on forever. A woodland king was there with a crown of leaves and there was a merry singing... (H 137)

Picturing the Elven feast that the company discovers shortly after this scene, it becomes clear that this vision also possesses prophetic value but it notably differs from most of the other dreams discussed so far in that it is perceived as very pleasant. The dwarf's first impulse after he opens his eyes is to get back to his dream as soon as possible and even long after the company had left behind the woodland realm, "he was always trying to recapture the beautiful dreams he had then" (241). Moreover, Bombur's vision has a distinct bearing on the plot because his vivid description of the feast makes the other members of the company ignore all warnings and follow the strange lights they see twinkling in the dark. In so doing Bilbo incautiously stumbles into a fairy ring formed by torches and falls under the same Elven enchantment that the dwarf has experienced and, just like Bombur, he immediately tries to go back to sleep and his gorgeous dream-dinner after waking up.[10]

In the Mirkwood chapter Tolkien thus combines two themes that recur in traditional folk tales and also in medieval romances: enchanted sleep, mostly induced by Elves, and prophetic dreams. The former is often connected to the abduction of mortals to the Otherworld and in *The Hobbit* the Wood-elves use these powers to capture Thorin. However, as we have seen, these enchanted visions have a rather unusual effect. Instead of serving as a warning, a revelation, or some other form of education helping the dreamer to "lead an improved life" (Kruger 124), these enchanted visions induced by the Elves cause an escapist behaviour in the characters. This is by no means the form of escape which Tolkien equated with the 'Escape of a Prisoner'; rather, it is none other than what he described as the 'Flight of the Deserter' (cf. FS 60-61). Bilbo and Bombur wish to lay down and return to a dream rather than trying to improve their situation while they are actually starving. They choose dreams over reality, which, as John Rateliff points out, suggests that these visions are primary

---

10 It is noteworthy that not only the dreams that the Elves can induce are presented as acts of enchantment. Kili suggests that also their torches in the dark forest "must have been lit suddenly and *by magic*" (H 140, emphasis added) and the feast that the company witnesses is described as follows: "The smell of the roast meats was so *enchanting* that, without waiting to consult one another, every one of them got up and scrambled forwards into the ring with the idea of begging for some food" (138, emphasis added).

examples of 'Faërian drama' showing the perilous side of Elven enchantment (cf. HH I 397). In *On Fairy-Stories* Tolkien argues that

> [t]he experience may be very similar to Dreaming... [b]ut in Faërian drama you are in a dream that some other mind is weaving, and the knowledge of that alarming fact may slip from your grasp... You are deluded – whether it is the intention of the elves (always or at any time) is another question. (FS 52)

In the same way the dwarf and the hobbit find themselves under the influence of Elven enchantment and can no longer distinguish between fact and delusion thus giving up and preferring the latter. It is notable that in Tolkien's first manuscript it is not Bilbo who has this dream but Gandalf, which was then still the name of the dwarf king later to be called Thorin (cf. HH I 307).

However, as Rateliff's *The History of The Hobbit* reveals, after Tolkien had added the 'enchanted stream' episode and with that the passage of Bombur's long sleep, which gave him the opportunity to develop the theme of prophetic visions in the Mirkwood chapter, he reassigned the dream to Bilbo. In this way he directly juxtaposed the hobbit's reaction to the dream feast with his subsequent killing of the spider thereby enhancing the significance of Bilbo's development as a hero.

Tolkien made another remarkable modification in the plot, this time concerning the killing of Smaug. We have already discussed his greedy and violent dream which offered some valuable insights into his psyche; yet the dragon has another rather unambiguous vision about his impending fate when "[h]e had passed from an uneasy dream (in which a warrior, altogether insignificant in size but provided with a bitter sword and great courage, figured most unpleasantly) to a doze, and from a doze to wide waking." (H 195).

Tolkien wrote this passage when he still intended to have Bilbo kill the dragon with his sword (cf. HH II 519)[11] and at that point the dream was clearly prophetic. Smaug sees his forthcoming death at the hands of a small hobbit whom he considers as rather unimposing and this vision, which one might be inclined to take as another prophetic dream on first reading, subtly undercuts the pride and self-security that the dragon displays in his ensuing conversation with Bilbo. However, when Tolkien changed the ending so that it

---

11 According to his plot notes, Tolkien planned to have Bilbo put on the ring, creep into Smaug's den and hide until the dragon returns home exhausted from the battle. The hobbit then plunges in his magic knife and floats out in a golden bowl on the dragon's blood. (cf. HH II 496)

significantly differed from the scheme of traditional fairy-stories and he had the newly introduced Bard shoot the vile worm while he is attacking Esgaroth, the dream acquires a different kind of humorous undertone. It evokes readers' expectations of the hobbit performing this most heroic deed and, in so doing, concluding his psychological journey from a timid, unadventurous hobbit to a dragon slayer. But then Tolkien ironically subverts these anticipations by letting Bard, a prototypical hero figure and descendent of the lord of Dale, slay Smaug with a single black arrow – although Bilbo has, of course, considerably contributed to the dragon's defeat with his 'inside information'. The example of this vision, which remained unchanged even after Tolkien had decided not to have the hobbit kill the worm, thus shows how he was also playing on the notion of prophetic dreams in order to create ironic effects.

Unlike the formerly discussed examples, this dream does not turn out to be prophetic – at least not in the final version of the book. In this way Tolkien expresses an awareness that was shared by many scholars before and after him: attempts at dream divination can be unsuccessful and misleading. Moreover, this final dream of Smaug's calls into question the earlier notion that the inhabitants of Middle-earth are entirely at the mercy of providence.

On the one hand, it is possible that the vision is merely deceptive and does not refer to anything meaningful; on the other hand, the dream might also show that Bilbo was in fact destined to free the peoples living in the surroundings of the Lonely Mountain from the threat of the greedy dragon. However, in that case the occurrences following the vision undoubtedly indicate that certain circumstances or deeds can change the foreshadowed course of events. Bilbo unintentionally arouses the dragon and with the self-given name 'Barrel-rider' he puts the worm on track of the men of Lake-town, where Smaug is finally killed. In this way the hobbit's words have countered providence and not he himself but Bard becomes the dragon's bane.

Conclusion

On the whole, it is clear that Tolkien drew from a vast background of medieval dream literature and lore for the visions incorporated in *The Hobbit* and his subsequently written works, notably *The Lord of the Rings*, and this shared motif serves to link the first tale to the latter. Indeed, even the earliest drafts of the book show that in Tolkien's mind the connections between the narrative that was then primarily intended for children and the vast world of his *Legendarium* were already surprisingly strong when he began to write *The Hobbit*. This close relation is reflected, for instance, in a passage in which Bladorthin (only later renamed Gandalf) directly refers to Beren's and Lúthien's victory over the Necromancer,[12] but more subtly also in the recurring motif of prophetic dreams. However, the present discussion has also shown that their significance and application differ remarkably in the different narratives. While the foreshadowing dream visions in *The Lord of the Rings*, for instance, are more ambiguous and usually refer to events that occur across relatively great temporal and spatial distances, the dreams in the earlier book mostly refer to episodes that are far less distant (cf. HH I 147).

Nevertheless, the incorporation of dream visions in *The Hobbit* shows how Tolkien took up a motif he first discovered in his poetry, for example in *You and Me/ and the Cottage of Lost Play* from 1915, and developed it to the elaborated theme we find in his later works.

---

12 In the first chapter of the early text Bladorthin answers to Gandalf's concerns about the Necromancer: "This is a job quite beyond the powers of all the dwarves, if they could be gathered together again from the four corners of the world. And anyway [others >] his castle stands no more and [his >] he is flown [*added*: to another darker place] – Beren and Tinúviel broke his power, but that is quite another story." (HH I 73)

Bibliography

Amendt-Raduege, Amy M. "Dream Visions in J.R.R. Tolkien's The Lord of the Rings". *Tolkien Studies: An Annual Scholarly Review, Vol. 3*, edited by Douglas A. Anderson, Michael C. Drout, and Verlyn Flieger. Morgantown: West Virginia University Press, 2006, 45-55

Aristotle. *De Insomniis De Divinatione Per Somnun*, übersetzt und erläutert von Philip J. Van Der Eijk. Aristoteles Parva Naturalia III. Berlin: Akademie Verlag GmbH, 1994

Carpenter, Humphrey. *The Letters of J.R.R. Tolkien*, edited with the assistance of Christopher Tolkien. London: HarperCollins, 2006

Forster, Robert. *The Complete Guide to Middle-earth: From The Hobbit through The Lord of the Rings and Beyond*. New York: Random House, 2001

Hieatt, Constance B. *The Realism of Dream Visions: The Poetic Exploitation of the Dream-Experience in Chaucer and His Contemporaries*. The Hague and Paris: Mouton & Co, 1967

Hippocrates of Kos. "Regimen IV or Dreams". *Hippoctates Vol. IV*, with an English translation by W.H.S. Jones. London and Cambridge (MA): Harvard University Press, 1931, 421-447

Kruger, Steven F. *Dreaming in the Middle Ages*. Cambridge: Cambridge University Press, 1992

Macrobius, Ambrosius Aurelius Theodosius. *Commentary on the Dream of Scipio*, translated by William Harris Stahl. New York: Columbia University Press, 1990

Mallory, Sir Thomas. *Le Morte d'Arthur: King Arthur and the Legends of the Round Table*. New York: Signet Classics, 2001.

Peden, Alison M. "Macrobius and Mediaeval Dream Literature". *Medium Aevum 54* (1985), 59-73

Rateliff, John D. *The History of The Hobbit, Part One: Mr. Baggins*. London: HarperCollins, 2007

---. *The History of The Hobbit, Part Two: Return to Bag-End*. London: HarperCollins, 2007

Synesius of Cyrene. "De Insomniis". *The Essays and Hymns of Synesius of Cyrene, Vol.2*, translated by August Fitzgerald. London: Oxford University Press, 1930, 326-359

Tolkien, John Ronald Reul. *The Hobbit or There and Back Again*. London: HarperCollins, 1995

---. *The Lord of the Rings*. London: HarperCollins, 1995

---. "On Fairy-Stories". *Tree and Leaf*. John Ronald Reuel Tolkien. London: HarperCollins, 2001, 3-81

---. (translator). *Sir Gawain and the Green Knight, Pearl and Sir Orfeo*, edited by Christopher Tolkien, London: HarperCollins, 2006, 7-13

Ein Quell ergoss sich sprudelnd über die Felsen in ein verborgenes Tal. Dort lag der Ort, den viele das letzte heimelige Haus nennen...

The Hobbit and Desire

Allan Turner (Marburg)

There can be little doubt at the very beginning of *The Hobbit* that we are dealing with a children's book. First of all a little fellow gets into a panic when a wizard turns up and wants to send him on an adventure. Then thirteen dwarves irrupt onto his doormat, eat all his food and sing a nonsense song as they clear the table. In spite of Tolkien's professed dislike of Disney (L 17), up to this point the cartoon-like quality of his tale is evident. However, there is a marked change of tone at the point where the dwarves begin their song about the onetime treasures of Erebor and the coming of the dragon, as arresting for the reader outside the text-world as it is for Bilbo Baggins inside it:[1]

> As they sang the hobbit felt the love of beautiful things made by hands and by cunning and by magic moving through him, a fierce and jealous love, the desire of the hearts of dwarves. Then something Tookish woke up inside him, and he wishes to go and see the great mountains, and hear the pine-trees and the waterfalls, and explore the caves, and wear a sword instead of a walking-stick. (H 25)

The pathos soon ends in bathos as Bilbo is thrown into a further panic by the thought of dragons intruding into his safe life; it is after all his function to ensure that the tale keeps its feet firmly on the ground. Nevertheless the passage has had its effect and the power of the archaic world has been felt. For one thing the text-world now has a historical dimension. But above all, this is where Tolkien most clearly thematises the idea of desire, on two different levels together. Most immediately, and entirely within the Secondary World, there is that of the dwarves for precious and beautiful objects, based on material possession. However, forming a bridge between the Secondary and Primary Worlds, there is a metafictional vignette of how the literary work may evoke desire in the reader; Bilbo, who hears the dwarves' song and is deeply moved by it, also represents the reader, in whom certain literary effects will create a sense of desire for what is not actually present.

---

[1] As an informal check, I have asked three different audiences at what point they first felt *The Hobbit* to be a serious book. On each occasion the majority response was that it was precisely at this point.

It may appear that the term *desire* is being used here with two separate meanings. It would even be possible to paraphrase the one sense with *possessiveness* and the other with *yearning*, or even *daydreaming*. However, there is a significant crossover between the two: the impulse of the dwarves to regain possession of the treasure stolen by the dragon is sublimated in the poetry which encapsulates their aspirations, while the focus on precious objects in their literary art helps to define for the reader their characteristics as a race, and even make them attractive. Perhaps they might best be seen as points on a scale; certainly it will be seen in the following, where each aspect will be explored in turn, that in this narrative and others by Tolkien aesthetic desire can easily become confused with material desire, which in turn can tip over into possessiveness and violence. For the material possessiveness of the dwarves, and in particular Thorin Oakenshield, reference will be made to John Rateliff's detailed study of the writing of *The Hobbit*. In the case of aesthetic desire, some parallels from German literature will be presented to put the remarkable passage cited above into a wider context.

The motif of possessiveness

The phrase "the desire of the hearts of dwarves", in spite of the lofty tone of the passage in which it occurs, nevertheless suggests some kind of practical common knowledge. It could be taken as belonging to the same category of narratorial asides as "That, of course, is the way to talk to dragons", which is pointed out by Shippey (84). The narratorial intrusion is much less overt here than in Shippey's example, but nevertheless the usage strongly suggests that reference is being made to something knowable.

So what did Tolkien "know" about dwarves when he wrote it? Probably not very much. Certainly he was familiar with them from his philological studies (they are mentioned in both *Eddas* and in the *Völsunga saga*), and from folktales (cf. Shippey 69ff), from which he also knew of their association with stone, mining, metallurgy and treasure.

Also he could draw upon what he had already written in *The Nauglafring* in the *Book of Lost Tales*, although significant motifs in this also go back to tradition, in particular the Old Norse *brisingamen*, the necklace of Freyja. This tale generally leaves a negative impression of dwarves, focusing on their greed and treachery. In the 1930 *Quenta* the destruction of Doriath is so abbreviated that only the bare fact of the dwarves' lust for treasure is given as motivation, while this episode is omitted completely from the *Quenta Silmarillion*. Therefore *The Hobbit*, although it was not originally meant to be connected with the mythology,[2] represents the major development in the conception of their character as outlined below; this revised version was subsequently taken up in *The Lord of the Rings* and written into the later 'Silmarillion' texts. Because of this piecemeal elaboration, the depiction of their nature at different stages shows ambiguities that are never fully resolved.

Since all fantasy ultimately has its roots in the Primary World, it can be reasoned that the dwarves are, like the elves, representative in a heightened form of particular facets of human behaviours or concerns (cf. Tolkien's draft of a letter to Michael Straight: "Elves and Men are just different aspects of the Humane", L 236). In the case of the elves, this is "the artistic, aesthetic, and purely scientific aspects of the Humane nature" (*ibid.*). It is difficult to characterise the dwarves in this way without recourse to crude simplifications, not least because of their inherent ambiguities, but one suggestion would be that they embody the technological aspect, the appropriation and crafting of inert materials into products to be owned and used. This aspect of possession is their weakness that can lead to greed and quarrelsomeness, just as the desire of the Noldor for pure knowledge makes them vulnerable to the more materialistic aims of Melkor in Aman in the First Age, or of Sauron in Eregion in the Second Age.

In fact the question of possessiveness and guilt in the development of the 'Silmarillion' is complex and can only be briefly touched upon here. In the early stages Tolkien tended to place the cause in exterior agents rather than individual psychology. The Noldor in Aman begin to lock up their treasures in strongholds and forge weapons to defend them only under the influence of Melkor. In the defence of the dwarves of Nogrod in *The Nauglafring*, their actions come about partly through the baleful influence of the gold of the Rodothlim, a combination of the evil of Morgoth's dragon and Mîm's curse, which acts equally on the supposedly wise elf Tinwelint (the later Thingol) and brings about his fall. In Tolkien's later writings there is a greater balance between individual psychology and any external "magic" force, such as the addictive nature of the Ring as it operates on Gollum or the Ringwraiths. For example, Gollum is already mean and nasty before the Ring concentrates this feature, but there is always the possibility of his redemption through the dormant Sméagol side of his nature.

This external agent still appears in *The Hobbit* in the form of the "dragon sickness". Rateliff provides lots of useful detail about it, comparing its effects here with Tolkien's poem *The Hoard* (originally entitled "Iúmonna gold galdre

---

[2] This is still the widely held view, although Rateliff (84) questions it.

bewunden", and composed several years earlier). However, he emphasizes the aspect of an external, supernatural effect of a curse lying on the treasure, or maybe a property of the treasure itself. In this article I am concerned rather with desire as an urge that is present within the mind of an individual, even if it is intensified or diminished by stimuli from the attendant circumstances. In writing *The Hobbit* Tolkien was still making up his mind about the nature of dwarves. In spite of what he had written in *The Nauglafring*, he was able to start almost from scratch because he was not consciously elaborating on the mythology. Also the development in the character of Thorin is the first occasion on which he was able to trace the transformation of desire into possessiveness over several chapters in a more novel-like manner.

The developments at Erebor

After the striking passage which introduces the desire of the hearts of dwarves, the topic disappears into the background for several chapters while the dangers of the journey form the main source of interest. It reappears only when the company reaches Erebor and the legendary-historical context of the dwarves' song has become a present reality, that is to say the treasure is now near, even if it is not immediately attainable. According to Rateliff's Plot Notes B (364), it was originally intended to be Bilbo who was caught by the "enchantment" of the treasure. "Enchantment" is the concept most frequently used in *The Hobbit* for this attraction, as in "the pale enchanted gold" of the dwarves' song. This is not so purely external as a curse, but is still something that can affect the psyche if the person concerned allows it to happen. As the story develops further, it is the Lake Men and the Wood Elves who are the ones driven by the desire for booty. Paradoxically, even at the late stage of Plot Notes D, just before the final version was worked out, the dwarves appear to be more aware than others of the lure of the treasure, and even have a certain innate immunity to it. According to Rateliff (598), this can be traced back to the *Book of Lost Tales* (LT 2 113f), where Mîm claims to be the only one who can bind the lure of the gold; and indeed the gold fever breaks out after he is killed.

When Tolkien finally re-established the connection between the dwarves and desire, he concentrated its effect by centring it on the character of Thorin Oakenshoeld. Rateliff's research, by providing the contrast with the earlier, blander concept, underlines just how powerful the final version is, particularly for a children's story. A cloud of resentment and suspicion falls upon Thorin (reminiscent of Saul's brooding anger in the *Old Testament*, even to the extent of the dwarves singing songs in an attempt to lighten his mood, like David), Bilbo betrays his companions in an attempt to maintain peace, for which he is grimly rejected by Thorin, and a reconciliation comes only with a moving deathbed scene. Tolkien's changes undoubtedly make for a much more conflicted and serious narrative, in which the "desire of the hearts of dwarves" takes on a new depth of significance, as Christopher Tolkien frequently notes of the plot developments throughout the *History of Middle-earth*.

In view of this, it might be thought that the passage in Chapter 1 was added or revised as Tolkien's conception of motivation in the story developed. However, Rateliff's study of the early workings shows that this is not the case, since the passage is present right from the very first extant draft, the so-called Pryftan[3] Fragment, where almost the final wording is achieved immediately. Admittedly the words "a fierce and jealous love, the desire of the hearts of dwarves" were added, but according to Rateliff this must have happened at a very early stage, before the Fragment was superseded by the Bladorthin typescript, "made very shortly after the manuscript itself, probably as a fair copy" (28).

Because of the reconciliation that is made possible by focusing the motif of possessive greed on the transgression and repentance of an individual character, the "desire of the hearts of dwarves" here is not necessarily a base lust demonstrated by a whole people as in *The Nauglafring*. Rather it is an innate tendency, which can become morbid in individual characters in certain circumstances, but may also be turned to admirable ends, as in the case of Dáin, who rebuilds the Kingdom under the Mountain and uses his accumulated power to resist Sauron in the War of the Ring. It is probable that this new twist in the development of the dwarves was dictated by the way in which the narrative of *The Hobbit* developed. After the fairy-tale-like beginning, Thorin and Company are alternately comic and serious, particularly in their benevolence towards Bilbo as trust and respect increase between them. It was after all written as a children's story, in which one would not expect the hero's companions also to be the villains. In the original outline, after all, it was Bilbo who killed the dragon and then parted amicably from the dwarves with his due reward. Therefore by the time the author had to decide how to bring about the denouement, the generally positive character of the dwarves had been established.

Nevertheless there is some ambiguity in their depiction in the build-up to the turn of events which allows the bumbling comic characters of the early part of

---

3   Rateliff does not comment on the origin of the striking name Pryftan, although it is clearly the Welsh *pryf tân* 'worm of fire'. It is noteworthy as being the only occasion on which Tolkien invents a name based on identifiable Welsh elements, as opposed to the genuine Welsh names borrowed for members of the Brandybuck family, or the hybrid place names such as *Bree Hill*. It is also significant that he rejected this Welshness almost immediately in favour of the Germanic *Smaug*.

the book to achieve both the dogged possessiveness which threatens to lead to a tragic end, but also the larger-than-life heroism with which they leap into battle in the penultimate chapter. The narrator throws in occasional disclaimers to excuse dwarvish gracelessness. For example, he provides the information that it was not Thorin's family who had a quarrel in the past with the Wood-elves (H 179). Later, when the dwarves leave Bilbo to go down the tunnel alone, he explains (again giving the impression that this is common knowledge): "There it is: dwarves are not heroes, but calculating folk with a great idea of the value of money; some are tricky and treacherous and pretty bad lots; some are not, but are decent enough folk like Thorin and Company, if you don't expect too much" (224).

Nevertheless only 26 pages later he warns: "and when the heart of a dwarf, even the most respectable, is wakened by gold and by jewels, he grows suddenly bold, and he may become fierce" (250).

All this is expressed in suitable restrained language which might be thought appropriate for a children's book, and neatly understated with the tongue-in-cheek reference to the "respectability" of dwarves, but the threat of unpredictability and danger can nevertheless not be overlooked.

Tolkien was to resolve this ambiguity only later with the character of Gimli in *The Lord of the Rings*. His friendship with the elf Legolas, in spite of the enmity between the two peoples that had existed for generations, is symbolic of the way in which he combines with the ancestral dwarvish characteristics an elf-like, disinterested (though extremely committed) and non-exploitative love of beauty for its own sake, albeit more of the underground, mineral world than of living, growing things.

Already at an early stage of the tale he is told by Galadriel, when he requests one of her hairs in preference to any other treasure, "[Y]our hands shall flow with gold, and yet over you gold shall have no dominion" (LotR 376). His sensitivity to natural beauty is shown again at the Glittering Caves, where he even attempts to correct the prejudiced view of others towards his people, likening their feeling for stone to that of the elves for trees: "No dwarf could be unmoved by such loveliness... We would tend these glades of flowering stone, not quarry them" (548).

This in turn makes it possible for the last word on the matter, in Appendix F, in the narrative voice of the editor/translator, to stress the essential goodness of the dwarves and puts their reputation for malice down to false reports motivated by envy in the "tales of Men" (1132), which may be a sly metafictional reference either to genuine folklore or to his own earlier writings. That is to say, he was correcting a view which he was aware of partially creating himself, even though *The Nauglafring* was not to appear in print for another twenty nine years.

Desire and the reader

To return to the dwarves' song, there remains the question of how desire operates on the reader/listener. This is in fact an example of how Tolkien's own invention, the hobbits (in this case Bilbo) act as mediators between the archaic world of epic fantasy and the modern-day reader; Bilbo's reaction guides the reader through desire into a state of Secondary Belief. In fact this passage embodies something of what Tolkien was to write a few years later in the essay *On Fairy-Stories*, in which the word *desire* occurs repeatedly. Here the magic of Faëry is said to satisfy "certain primordial human desires" (FS 116), namely

> "to survey the depths of space and time" (116)
> "to hold communion with other living beings" (116)
> to glimpse "Joy beyond the walls of the world" (153)

In particular the last of these is a reminder that Tolkien's philosophy, whether implicit or explicit, is a transcendental one, and however much we may try to practise criticism using purely materialistic arguments, there is no way of escaping from that fact. Any commentary which chooses to ignore it will inevitably miss a hugely important dimension. But that is the "high" desire, straining up out of this world; *The Hobbit*, with its feet kept firmly on the ground by earthy hobbit common-sense, represents the "low" or poetic desire. One possible link between the two is the figure of the dragon. In this tale of adventure and return, "there and back again", we see not the dragon of Hell, into whose gaping jaws the damned are dragged by devils in medieval depictions of the last judgement, but a much more fleshly worm who is nevertheless wonderful. "I desired dragons with a profound desire," claims Tolkien in an autobiographical aside (FS 135), because "the dragon had the trade-mark *Of Faërie* written plain upon him". But still Smaug is a solid part of a world which "holds the seas, the sun, the moon, the sky; and the earth, and all things that are in it" (113). Alarm at the idea of the dragon may at first reduce Bilbo to an unheroic grocer in the eyes of the dwarves, but for him as for the reader it is the possibility of the dragon which also injects wonder into the waterfalls and the pine trees that the dwarves' song evokes for him – or in short, anything which lies outside the everydayness of the hobbit hole. Their encapsulation in the form of a song is all the more powerful because of the additional imagination that the reader has to exercise, since the narrator deliberately draws attention to the fact that what is reproduced in the printed narrative is a fragment and without music.

The passage is remarkable because the young reader, through Bilbo, is given a strong dose of a sense of the potential wonder of the world. This is a metafictional level which is rare in books written for children, so it may well provide a reading experience which is powerful enough to account for its memorability.
But *The Hobbit* is not read only by children. An experienced reader is perhaps more likely to consider what intertextual resonances are set up by the song and Bilbo's reaction to it. For the German reader at any rate, the thematisation of the reader's desire is likely to suggest the German Romantic poets and their concept of *Sehnsucht*, usually translated as 'desire' or 'longing'. Two centuries of familiarity with the standard texts of this period have weakened perceptions, so that *Sehnsucht* is most often regarded by the public as a weak, ineffectual emotion, but at its heart was nevertheless, as with Tolkien, the desire to explore human experience of the transcendental, seen at its most extreme in the fervid desire to embrace death in Novalis' *Hymnen an die Nacht*. Although it is known that Tolkien read German, there is no indication that he read the Romantic poets; nevertheless it may be instructive to trace some of the parallels.

One of the iconic texts of German Romanticism, presenting a review of some of the most typical (or as some would say, clichéd) lyrical motifs of desire, is the poem by Joseph von Eichendorff (1788-1857) entitled simply *Sehnsucht*. In it, the poet is standing by the window late on a starry night and hears the sound of a posthorn, which kindles in him the urge to go and explore the wonders of the world. However, the most significant part for the comparison with Tolkien is the second stanza, where desire is awakened by a song which evokes some of the same images:

> Zwei junge Gesellen gingen
> Vorüber am Bergeshang,
> Ich hörte im Wandern sie singen
> Die stille Gegend entlang:
> Von schwindelnden Felsenschlüften,
> Wo die Wälder rauschen so sacht,
> Von Quellen, die von den Klüften
> Sich stürzen in die Waldesnacht.[4]   (Eichendorff, 20)

The effect on the listening poet figure is not unlike that on Bilbo:

---

4   'Two young journeymen went past on the hillside, I heard them singing as they wandered through the silent surroundings: of vertiginous rocky gorges where the woods rustle so softly, of streams that gush from the gullies into the night under the trees.' (All translations are my own.)

Das Herz mir im Leib entbrennte, / Da hab ich mir heimlich gedacht:
Ach, wer da mitreisen könnte / In der prächtigen Sommernacht!⁵

As in Tolkien, German Romantic desire runs along a spectrum where the urge for discovery of the natural world may merge into material possessiveness, which is also expressed through the motif of mining and jewels. In Novalis' unfinished novel *Heinrich von Ofterdingen* (published 1802) a travelling company at an inn meet a stranger who tells them that he is a miner:

> Von Jugend auf habe er eine heftige Neugierde gehabt zu wissen, was in den Bergen verborgen sein müsse, wo das Wasser in den Quellen herkomme, und wo das Gold und Silber und die köstlichen Steine gefunden würden, die den Menschen so unwiderstehlich an sich zögen.⁶ (Novalis 128)

This curiosity is clearly akin to the "desire of the hearts of dwarves", but it also contains echoes of Gollum's nosing for the secrets at the roots of the mountains. Indeed, the word *unwiderstehlich* ('irresistibly') even suggests the dangerous lure of the Ring or the Silmarils, which can easily tip over into a fatal obsession. That is precisely what E.T.A. Hoffmann depicts in his short story *Die Bergwerke zu Falun* (1819). A young sailor, following the advice of a mysterious stranger, travels inland to where gold, silver and copper are mined from a vast pit in a hillside which exerts a strange fascination on him as soon as he sees it, confirming his resolution to become a miner. Through his hard work and apparent instinct for the job, he becomes highly successful and marries the mine owner's daughter.

However, he becomes increasingly obsessed with the mine, to the point where he believes he sees a supernatural female figure, the spirit of the minerals in the earth, who draws him to her. Finally, abandoning his wife, he rushes off to work all alone at night to dig through to a new seam of ore which he is convinced is not far away, and is buried in a landslide.

It is hard to draw any definite conclusions about the connection between Tolkien and the German Romantics. Certainly he would have received German philosophical ideas from his reading of Coleridge's *Biographia Literaria*, referred to indirectly in *On Fairy-Stories* in the discussion of fancy (or fantasy)

---

5 My heart took fire in my breast, and I thought secretly to myself, "Oh, to go journeying with them in the splendid summer night.
6 'From his youth he had had a powerful curiosity to know what must be hidden in the mountains, where the water in the springs came from, and where the gold and silver and the precious stones were found which drew men so irresistibly to them.'

and imagination (FS 138f). Further German influence could have come through George MacDonald. Philology, itself held by the English to be a German science, had its roots in Romanticism, as seen not only in the famous example of the Grimms, but also in that of Novalis' friend Friedrich Schlegel, who wrote not only works of and about literature, but also a ground-breaking book on the grammar of Sanskrit and its relationship to other languages. However, none of this would explain any similarity of motifs. It is probably safest to say that desire is a universal human emotion, so it is not surprising if literary treatments of it in any of its forms show similarities.

Of course it cannot be argued that *The Hobbit* in any way resembles a psychological novel that depicts in detail a major human weakness. Like the majority of Tolkien's works, it functions on an epic scale, in which the observation of individual characters is subordinate to a broader narrative sweep.

Nevertheless the fall and repentance of Thorin Oakenshield, even though it takes up only a part of the whole story, gives the book a literary value which marks it out as more than just a small-scale prequel to *The Lord of the Rings*, while the thematisation of desire as an element in the aesthetics of art places it within the broader context of European literature.

Bibliography

Carpenter, Humphrey, Ed. *The Letters of J.R.R. Tolkien*. London: George Allen and Unwin, 1981

Eichendorff, Joseph von. *Gedichte: Eine Auswahl*. Stuttgart: Reclam, 1966

Hoffmann, Ernst Theodor Amadeus. *Die Bergwerke zu Falun, Der Artushof*. Stuttgart: Rowohlt, 1966

Novalis (Friedrich von Hardenberg). *Monolog, Die Lehrlinge zu Sais, Die Christenheit oder Europa, Hamnen und die Nacht, Geistliche Lieder, Heinrich von Ofterdingen*. Reinbek: Rowohlt, 1963

Rateliff, John D. *The History of the Hobbit. Part 1: Mr. Baggins, Part 2: Return to Bag-End*. London: HarperCollins, 2007

Shippey, Tom. *The Road to Middle-Earth*, revised edition. London: HarperCollins, 2005

Tolkien, John Ronald Reuel. *The Hobbit* (2nd edition). London: George Allen and Unwin, 1995

---. *The Lord of the Rings*, 50th Anniversary Edition. London: HarperCollins, 2005

---. *The Book of Lost Tales Part II*. London: George Allen and Unwin, 1984

---. "On Fairy-Stories". *The Monsters and the Critics and Other Essays*. London: HarperCollins, 1997, 109-161:

"Some courage and some wisdom, blended in measure": On Moral Imagination in J.R.R. Tolkien's *The Hobbit*

Blanka Grzegorczyk (Wrocław)

Introduction

The last decades have seen a dramatic growth of interest in the idea of fantasy as a discourse within and against which spirituality can be framed. Like much literature, fantasy has been held capable of affecting its readers' moral and ethical awareness much more directly than theoretical speculations and moral philosophy. This, incidentally, is not to suggest that types of literature other than fantasy do not have a potential for moral instruction. Nor is this claim meant to deny the legitimacy of moral philosophy.

Rather, the argument about the ethical value of fantasy implies that moral education is not exclusively the domain of ethics. Questions about good and evil, right and wrong, virtue and vice spring up naturally in the context of narrative fiction. Underlying the moral potential of fantasy is the notion of literature as an appropriate vehicle for the Aristotelian theory of virtue, a conception that much of contemporary moral philosophy and literary criticism continues to espouse.

This paper is concerned with issues central to the contemporary moral debate. Using examples taken from *The Hobbit*, it argues that the Aristotelian theory of virtue can foreground the potential of literature in general and fantasy in particular to assist readers in establishing a value system for a fulfilling human life. The hope is to demonstrate that the Aristotelian process of moral habituation extends well beyond the truism expressed in the phrase that "practice makes perfect." Specifically, the focus is on how and why a structured array of fictional characters who illustrate the Aristotelian pattern of choice and commitment pertains to our concepts of virtue as applied to human relations.

Drawing on Aristotelian ethical perspective and on Noël Carroll's discussion of literary thought experiments, this paper recognizes fantasy as answering, at least in part, our need for an exposition of the ethical code in a narrative form. Most importantly, however, this study argues that *The Hobbit* belongs in a type of literature which is especially nourishing for moral imagination.

"Whose Values? Whose Vision?": The Problems of Definition

It is almost a dogma in ethical criticism that moral imagination needs to be nurtured. Yet criticism so far has not generated a definition of moral imagination which would become a widely recognized foundation within the field of ethical inquiry. Instead, what one encounters is a broad range of definitions with a considerable overlap between them. In its current usage, the term has become a label for an all-inclusive category – the means of embracing realities crucial to the ethical experience of being human and too vast to be adequately depicted. In this paper, moral imagination will be defined as a capacity for building up virtue through the use of imagination, a capacity that allows humans to draw on vicarious imaginative experience with a view to approaching moral dilemmas with confidence.

Potentially present in every human being and rooted in what may generally be called a universal human awareness, moral imagination fulfils an important function: it enables individuals to rehearse responses to moral imperatives in the ordinary world. Though a natural human predisposition, moral imagination can be shaped, nurtured, or stunted in specific social and cultural contexts.

Although various scholars conceive of moral imagination differently, what their approaches share is a simultaneous rediscovery and reappraisal of the Aristotelian model of moral education. The first to shed light on the workings and function of moral imagination, Aristotle still seems especially relevant to the modern debates about it. Perhaps the most important reason for this is that Aristotle's ethics have a palpably "modern" feel to them.

More often than not, Western scholars have focused on the language of Christianity as a natural vehicle for the study of morality and ethics. The link between moral imagination and the Christian tradition, however strong, has nevertheless proven limiting and has had serious practical consequences for the scholarly study of moral imagination. Also modern legal discourse appears to be of little relevance to our understanding of the idea of ethics. Against this background, Aristotelian thought enables the discussion of the workings of moral imagination in a context broader than Christianity or religious worldview as such and more comprehensively than within the perimeters of the legal idiom.

Four key terms that Aristotle adopts for his discussion of ethics – virtue," "habit," "mean," and "happiness" – are especially pertinent to grasping the essence of moral imagination. At the core of Aristotelian moral theory is the concept of virtue as the peak of human excellence. Virtue, Aristotle argues, consists in a steady disposition to choose the golden mean between responses that would be either excessive or deficient. Yet the precise location of the golden mean may not be the same for everyone. Thus, with regard to the golden mean of courage, knowing the type of danger to be faced and recognizing one's own abilities will determine the appropriate behaviour. The habit of choosing the mean between extremes, in turn, gives rise to pleasure, happiness, and fulfilment.

"The Mean Is All?": Virtues, Stories, and Moral Imagination

Since the field of moral imagination has not yet been claimed by one dominant theory, Aristotle's commonsensical approach to ethics may well prove fruitful in isolating a sense of fairness that is independent of the human-made laws of any given community. Accordingly, this perspective seems to resolve the question of whose values we should habituate ourselves to. If moral virtue is taken to be primarily a habit of choosing the mean between extremes, then the readers are offered a pattern for considering possible options and for directing their moral maturation. At issue is *what* moral imagination is and *how* it operates, or, as Aristotle himself asks at the outset of the *Eudemian Ethics*, "how and by what sources does virtue arise" (EE 1216b10-22). The inquiry, as conducted by Aristotle, suggests that a balanced education requires a certain contemplative spirit and that education through stories may prepare a person for "the practice and exercise of virtue."

Building on the Aristotelian concept of the golden mean, Noël Carroll's discussion of literary thought experiments points to the educative power of literature. In his 2002 *The Wheel of Virtue: Art, Literature, and Moral Knowledge*, Carroll addresses the relevance of philosophical thought experiments to the arguments against the educational potential of narratives. For Carroll, reflection on thought experiments makes readers compare and assess the realities that they encounter and fill in the narrative gaps. A literary thought experiment of what Carroll calls "the virtue-wheel variety" can cultivate the readers' capacities for moral perception and stimulate them to an awareness of the criteria they rely on in judging the moral character of others (14). "Virtue wheel," as he defines it, "comprises a studied array of characters who both correspond and contrast with each other along the dimension of a certain virtue" (12).

Fiction, of course, is not the only way to foster a unique pattern of moral habituation. Yet, in the light of the structural criterion, *The Hobbit* may be seen as encapsulating many issues that have been the focus of ethical criticism, most notably the Aristotelian pattern of moral development. What the book images forth are the implications of choosing between right and wrong and the challenges involved in accepting an obligation of righteousness. Those implications and challenges can best be studied through characters' actions and motivations, which cultivate the readers' capacities of recognizing a given vice or virtue. In this respect Tolkien's protagonists may be perceived as "instantiating" certain virtues to greater or lesser degrees. In the remaining part of this paper, I shall use Carroll's term "virtue instantiations" as best capturing the guiding principle of moral exemplification which, I think, Aristotle has in mind.

Courage

Among the virtue instantiations that Tolkien's narrative provides are what we call four cardinal virtues, derived initially from Plato's virtue scheme: courage, temperance, justice, and prudence. The first of these, courage, Aristotle defines as the habit of choosing to act appropriately in dangerous situations, thus avoiding both cowardice and recklessness (NE 1107b1-4). In *The Hobbit* the principle remains the same: what we find is a vast array of comparatively complex characters that permit a large number of differentiations. Reflecting on this array, the readers are able to clarify their concepts of real heroism of the sort found in battle and in everyday life. A good illustration of what may be meant under the notion of recklessness is the behaviour of Bilbo's proud and adventurous companions. As the dwarves draw nearer to their long-lost treasure, they become more obstinate – as when they refuse to parley with the Elvenking – and more careless. They are so when they leave the path in Mirkwood despite the dire warnings of shadows and evil that await them there, or when they indulge in examining the untold riches of Smaug's lair instead of looking for a means of escape. In the course of the quest, they have come to rely solely on Bilbo for common sense in the planning of strategic moves of the company and for salvation from their own tactical blunders. By and large, the dwarves' unthinking boldness and a defiant disregard for the consequences of their actions leave Bilbo with no choice but to further develop his new-found qualities of courage, wisdom, and practical resourcefulness.

Whereas foolhardy daring suggests a defective mode of action, at the opposite end of the spectrum lies excessive fear. It is not irrelevant that most characters in Tolkien's tale are capable of both courage and cowardice. The one in *The Hobbit* who commits perhaps the worst violation of the traditional notion of courage is the Master of Lake-town, who leaves Esgaroth soon after Smaug's terrible approach while others are still willing to defend it. That Bilbo learns the power of fear is clear enough as the story develops; however, his first real test being the dwelling place of the goblins, Bilbo exhibits the kind of courage which is comparable with, or even superior to, that of the dwarves. Now that he has the magic ring, Bilbo wonders, should he not "go back into the horrible, horrible, tunnels and look for his friends" (H 94)? Actually, he "had just made up his mind that it was his duty, that he must turn back" when he hears his companions quarrelling; they are, in fact, quarrelling about whether to turn back and rescue him, and at least one of them answers no: "If we have to go back now into those abominable tunnels to look for him, than drat him, I say" (H 94-95). From this moment onward, the dwarves surely begin to have a very high opinion of Bilbo, and by chapter 12, he "had become the real leader in their adventure" (H 211). Bilbo rescues the dwarves from the giant spiders and from the Elvenking dungeons; still, the real moral test and the trial of his courage comes when he twice faces Smaug and fights "the real battle" before he even sees "the vast danger that [lies] in wait" (H 205). A hobbit "full of courage and resource far exceeding his size" (H 203), Bilbo displays what Zahorski and Boyer in their 1979 *Fantasy Literature* describe as "hidden potential for heroism" (162).

Being courageous is not such an easy thing, however virtuous one's intentions. Paradoxically, the more fallible and prone to fearfulness the characters seem to us, the more formidable their brave deeds become. Indeed, at the outset of the story, Bilbo appears to be an almost inconceivable hero. He is, as Mary R. Bowman in her 2006 *The Story Was Already Written: Narrative Theory in The Lord of the Rings* aptly put it, strongly reminiscent of the Jane Austen heroines, who "have practically to be abducted into narratable zones" (274). Consequently, almost the first thing we hear Bilbo say in *The Hobbit* is that adventures are "[n]asty disturbing uncomfortable things" which "[m]ake you late for dinner" (H 16). While not abducted, he is deceived into sharing the dwarves' adventure by a scheme of Gandalf's, and he repeatedly wishes that he "was at home ... by the fire, with the kettle just beginning to sing" (H 40). Yet Bilbo loves songs and poetry, as well as "wonderful tales ... about dragons and goblins and giants and the rescue of princesses and the unexpected luck of widow's sons" (H 17). He also wishes "to go and see the great mountains, and hear the pine-trees and the waterfalls, and explore the caves, and wear a sword instead of the walking stick" (H 25-26). As Bilbo partakes in the Quest of the Dragon-gold, the unhobbitlike quality inherited from his mother enables him to assume a vital role in the narrative despite his clearly peripheral involvement in fighting goblins, slaying dragons, or winning battles.

Whereas Bilbo's courage is a distinctively modern one – nothing like as striking and noticeable as that found in *Beowulf*, Norse sagas, or the *Eddic* poems – throughout *The Hobbit* it is repeatedly insisted on, as Shippey in his 2000 *J.R.R. Tolkien: Author of the Century* notices, "always in the scenes of solitude [and] always in the dark" (29). Bilbo displays a unique courage when he gives the Arkenstone to the townsfolk to aid them in their bargaining, and does so purely for the sake of others, determined to see justice done. "[T]he best person is not the one who exercises virtue [only] toward himself, but the one who [also] exercises it in relation to another, since this is a difficult task," says Aristotle (NE 1130a7-9). Bilbo's heroic deed is an excellent illustration of this point.

Descriptions of so defined courage abound in Tolkien's narrative, yet chief among those examples is the presentation of seemingly "unheroic" characters as those who are capable of showing what Tolkien calls "the amazing and unexpected heroism of ordinary men 'at a pinch' " (L 158). For in effect, as Tolkien himself says, *The Hobbit* is "a study of simple ordinary man, neither artistic nor ... heroic (but not without the undeveloped seeds of these things) against a high setting" (L 159). The final victory of the noble is achieved not on the battlefield, but through the exercise of what Tolkien calls "the unforeseen and unforeseeable acts of will" and through "deeds of virtue of the apparently small, unseen, [and] forgotten" (L 160). This is the case with hobbits, unambitious folk with "good-natured faces" and "clever brown fingers," who laugh "deep fruity laughs (especially after dinner ...)" (H 14). One would have supposed that courage was the quality least likely to be found in such a creature. And one has, in fact, a sneaking feeling that despite many a decent meal and many an hour of festive cheer, Bilbo will any minute now make a bolt for a snug fireside in his beloved Shire.

Yet there is more to this fellow still. As Richard Purtill brilliantly sums up in his 1974 *Lord of the Elves and Eldils*, "this is the sort of hero [a hobbit] is: not a Beowulf or even a Gawain, but a Jack the Giant Killer, the 'youngest son,' 'the simple one' never expected to succeed but succeeding at last with the aid of courage, resourcefulness, luck, and powerful helpers" (98). It is thus significant that peace, harmony, and order in Middle-earth seem to hang by a thread and that they largely depend on the moral choices of the most untypical, yet by no means accidental, heroes. The balancing of fear and confidence is played out in the narrative against the traditional conception of proper courage and the equally traditional notion of heroism.

Temperance

If this amounts to saying that Aristotle's theory of virtue offers a middle course that embraces the claims of nobility in the harsh necessities of everyday life, *The Hobbit* also reflects Tolkien's idea of proper temperance. The second of the cardinal virtues, as seen by Aristotle, takes the form of a mean between the feelings of inordinate pleasure and excessive pain (NE 1107b5-9). Based on this perspective, it is no coincidence that, by custom, temperance is defined as governing our disposition towards certain tactile pleasures, most notably eating, drinking, and sexual contact. Naturally, in order to consider this particular Aristotelian virtue it is essential to select examples which are, on the whole, representative of a wider trend.

The relevance of the above to Tolkien's work is one of imaginative extension, and makes it possible to see the book as exploring the nature of other human desires. The fact that men, elves, and dwarves are subject to corruption and the craving for wealth seeping into their lives and threatening the social fabric of Middle-earth, obviously makes the protagonists and their actions especially interesting. In this sense *The Hobbit* becomes a framework in which Tolkien addresses the related themes of possessiveness and power.

Inasmuch as the "world-politics" in *The Hobbit* are concerned, one instance of intemperance worthy of serious consideration is the almost proverbial greed on the part of dwarves, elves, and men. All in all, Tolkien's comments leave no doubt that possessiveness is an inherently human tendency by means of which "modern European life" is quickly, if ever so worryingly, becoming "the soon-cloying game of moving at high speed" (FS 64-65).

Taken together, the visions of the present age offered by Tolkien in his *On Fairy-Stories* reflect on the radical change of modern consciousness and look on the "lustful, vengeful, and greedy" nature of human beings as the "essential malady" of the contemporary world (FS 65). Not surprisingly, then, greed becomes an important theme already in *The Hobbit*. It also plays a crucial role in the plot of *The Lord of the Rings*. When the hearts of the dwarves, even the most respectable ones, are fully wakened by "the mere fleeting glimpses" of gold and jewels, the lust for treasure comes heavy upon them and they turn into fierce and hard-hearted companions (H 226).

Also the elves' behaviour presents them as engaged in a power struggle, and anxious to secure their own share of the Dragon-gold: "If the elf-king had a weakness it was for treasure ...; and though his hoard was rich, he was ever eager for more, since he had not yet as great a treasure as other elf-lords of old" (H 163). Nor are the humans free from the lust for wealth. The Master of the Lake-town gives his mind "to trade and tolls, to cargoes and gold" as the only concern worthy of his attention (H 190). By the end of the narrative, he carries off a large part of the gold given by Bard for the help of the Lake-people, and starves to death in the Waste. Deserted by his companions and no longer held in esteem, the Master gets no credit for the new prosperity of the Lake-town.

Those and similar examples suggest that greed is all part and parcel of the human condition. At the same time these episodes may be taken as warnings about how self-defeating – and ultimately fruitless – is an attempt to interfere in the natural order of things. "If more of us valued food and cheer and song above hoarded gold, it would be a merrier world," Thorin says (H 271). The power of gold Tolkien speaks of here – as well as the moral and psychological effects of greed – is increasingly articulated in terms of such metaphors as "bewitchment," "disease," or "dragon-sickness." This inherent acceptance of temperance as what should ideally be part of the natural world is basic to the warp and woof of Tolkien's fictional universe. The unquestioned ideal, here typified by Bilbo, is to have no desire for power or greed of wealth, and this in general is what other characters do. For those who do not, like the Master or the dwarves, the violation is never treated lightly.

Aristotle admits that the habit of yielding excessively to temptation is far more common than that of being insufficiently sensitive to pleasure, and this is the case with *The Hobbit*. Throughout the range of situations that call for moderation Tolkien's protagonists must recognize what is really immoderate and deal with it appropriately.

The moral imperative as Tolkien envisions it thus involves the recognition of the mean between the extremes of intemperance and insensibility but openly acknowledges that the latter is not often found. It follows that if the lure of the Dragon-gold is indeed a test of character for everyone to pass or to fail, then what *The Hobbit* brings forth in relation to temperance are examples of only one of the polar opposites in question and of the mean we all strive to achieve.

Justice

Even more vital for appreciating Tolkien's attempts to uncover the mechanisms on which human societies are based is the conception of justice as represented in *The Hobbit*. The third of the cardinal virtues, justice stands at the very centre of Aristotle's *Nicomachean Ethics* as "complete virtue to the highest degree" (NE 1129b31). Especially on the level of such social relations as those within the city or inside the community, fairness and equality emerge as the ideal mode of human functioning in *The Hobbit*. The masters and the servants change roles, the rulers are good or wicked, prudent or foolish, but the principle remains the same: justice is the Aristotelian mean not as the other virtues are, but because it is "about an intermediate condition, whereas injustice is about the extremes" (NE 1134a1-2).

Among various types of justice that Aristotle distinguishes two deserve special attention in this paper. The first is corrective, or compensatory, justice which involves the restoration of equality between two parties by the compensation of the party that has been wronged or injured. The second is reciprocal justice which governs voluntary exchanges taking place according to strict arithmetical equality or according to some proportion. The former ignores the social status of the individual parties and focuses only on making the amounts in question equal again, the latter takes into consideration the objects exchanged as well as the difficulty of the labour involved, the type of risk taken, and the needs of the parties to be served. Both, however, stem from the habit of choosing to render or receive the right amount at the right time and to avoid the extremes of too much or too little.

Concerning the first type of justice mentioned here, the pattern of compensation for harms imposed and the quest for the restoration of balance are two of the central ethical principles in works of fantasy by virtue of which the moral order of the universe may be implied. Without justice human beings would never have established harmonious and life-enhancing relationships, and thereby would not have developed a conceptual framework geared toward peaceful coexistence.

A significant aspect of fantasy, as Tolkien understands it, compensatory justice represents a close-to-ideal model for giving others their due. Crucial here is the notion of regaining balance and of redressing the wrongs done. That the powers of Good always triumph over the powers of Evil is characteristic of most works of fantasy literature; however, as Tolkien contends in *On Fairy-Stories*, "[t]he verbal ending ... 'and they lived happily ever after' is an artificial device, ... no more to be thought of as the real end of any particular fragment of the seamless Web of Story than the frame is of the visionary scene, or the casement of the Outer World" (FS 80). The idea that closure is never definite and endings never truly final is inscribed into Tolkien's works in a number of more or less explicit ways. Ingrained in this understanding is the additional assumption that a happy ending is not tantamount to "happily ever after"; instead, what such an ending necessarily entails is Tolkien's eucatastrophy.

Justice in *The Hobbit* is not simply the case of what John S. Morris in his 1973 *Fantasy in a Mythless Age* calls "the 'good guys' always winning" (83). Rather, it manifests itself in the healing of wounds suffered and in the sustaining power of order.

In *The Hobbit* the primary instance of this kind of justice is a joyous and miraculous delivery from evil in the form of the goblin's final defeat. Another example is the way Bilbo acts in his dealings with the Elvenking. Concerned with a customary sense of justice, as Aristotle would envision it, the hobbit presents the Elvenking with a precious necklace in an attempt to compensate for his depleted supplies of wine and bread. "Even a burglar has his feelings," says Bilbo filled with remorse, and literally begs the king of the Wood-elves to accept the magnificent gift (H 275). This sense of fairness woven into the narrative fabric of Tolkien's work suggests his strong allegiance to a myth-derived, or natural, justice. Tolkien's, then, is a balanced approach to giving others their due which takes into account the relevant circumstances of a particular course of action. At the same time, it satisfies the readers' deep thirst for justice by compensation rather than by any legal means used in the Western world.

The second major type of justice in *The Hobbit* is the one aimed at establishing harmonious relationships based on reciprocity of voluntary exchanges. "[I]f someone has been gracious to us, we must do a service for him in return, and also ourselves take the lead in being gracious again"; this, Aristotle says, "holds people together" (NE 1133a3-5).

Throughout Tolkien's narrative one important thematic strain which underlies the tale of high adventure in search of a dragon-guarded treasure is a convincing and imaginatively consistent reflection on reciprocal justice as operating within the various societies existing in Middle-earth. On this level *The Hobbit* is a mythopoesis premised upon the Aristotelian belief that one social interaction essential for human well-being is a voluntary exchange motivated by mutual need, and regulated by the ability to satisfy the want of a particular skill or object to be exchanged. Central to this approach, and providing a framework capable of quenching the readers' thirst for justice, is Tolkien's consideration of reciprocal justice as involving a whole set of assumptions concerning fairness, truthfulness, achieving agreement and keeping one's promises.

If Tolkien takes the seemingly Aristotelian perspective as a starting point for an exploration into the workings of justice, he elaborates on this theory in a thoroughly consistent manner. What he insists on is that reciprocal justice is not merely intended to form an economic basis of a particular society; rather, it should also create a precondition for structuring balanced and mutually enriching relationships between different cultures, countries, and races.

The call for being true to one's word and for honouring old alliances is Tolkien's way of emphasizing the ever-present need for a two-way understanding and peaceful cooperation as the means and goal of all life. The identification of reciprocal justice with peaceful coexistence and the social exchanges it entails seems fully justified here as supported by the ample evidence of Middle-earth history. With the hardships and dangers that abound in the Wild, and with dragons that attack human domains, *The Hobbit* tells of how the King under the Mountain and the town of Dale, the people of Thror and the ravens, or the Wood-elves and the Lake-men are brought together in fruitful relationships.

This theme is developed consistently all through the narrative. On the one hand, the parties look to each other for help and support; on the other, neither fails, if need be, to honour the allegiance. When Esgaroth is razed to the ground by an angry dragon, the Wood-elves first come to its people's aid. The Lake-people, in turn, grant the Elvenking "such jewels as he most loved" from their share of the treasure as a reward for his tremendous help (H 273). Indeed, since the people of Middle-earth put much of what hope they have in political allegiances, the obligation not to forsake one's allies becomes an ethical issue at the times of greatest peril.

The fact that the alliance is rooted in the ability to integrate the best each community has to offer makes the connection more fruitful and more powerful than it might otherwise be. Such connections, however, are not unprecedented in Tolkien's narratives. Whatever the nature of the exchange may be, and whatever duties the transaction involves, any oath that is sworn is fully expected to be honoured; it is usually intended to be kept by the speaker, and punishment naturally ensues if it is not. A rejection of this type of justice is unavoidably self-destructive for it leads to a clear violation of the operating principles of reciprocal justice and, therefore, to the loss of the order and of the social structure of being. "We will honour the agreement of the dead," says Dain, and he offers the Lake-people a fourteenth share of the treasure (H 273). It is telling that it contributes to the new prosperity of the Lake-town and Dale, as well as to renewed friendship between elves, dwarves and men.

The point here is not that reciprocity provides a mechanism for healing any particular political division in this or other worlds, but that the fabric of a society hinges on mutual trust. A predominant concern of Tolkien's narrative, this stress on honouring alliances and on reciprocal arrangements is an important component of the emerging ethical field of conflict resolution and coexistence. Truly, to use Aristotle's own words, that is why justice is "the only virtue that seems to be another person's good, because it is related to another; for it does what benefits another, either the ruler or the fellow member of the community" (NE 1130a3-5).

Prudence

If justice can be seen in the light of social and political perspectives, so too can prudence, the fourth of the cardinal virtues. In fact, the interrelation of various virtues as sometimes suggested by Aristotle can best be studied through the blending of the moral and intellectual spheres. Whereas both spheres bring to mind issues that are crucial to moral maturation, virtuous agents necessarily choose and deliberate with a view to achieving virtue of the rational as well as the non rational parts of the soul. And thus, an intellectual component is indispensable for any moral virtue to arise, while a moral component is essential for prudence to occur. To be courageous, temperate, or just, a person has to know the right amount of danger to be faced, the right amount of pleasure to be sought, or the right amount of giving and receiving to arise in social interaction; for all this to happen, prudence must come into play. On the other hand, for the right reasoning in matters of action to occur, one also needs to have a first-hand knowledge of the moral virtues.

Prudence then, as Aristotle defines it, is the habit of "grasping the truth, involving reason, concerned with action about human goods" (NE 1140b21-22). Both an intellectual and a moral virtue, prudence is structured along the lines of the Aristotelian mean between the extremes with regard to its deliberative and judicial constituents. Inasmuch as good deliberation is concerned, the mean is neither deliberating too much nor too little; in good judgment, in turn, the mean is rational calculation "in pursuit of the best good ... achievable in action" (NE 1141b14). Perhaps foremost, Aristotle seems mindful of the interplay between prudence and justice and he sees the human condition as determined both by, as he calls them, "natural" and "legal justice." The former has the same validity "everywhere alike, independent of its seeming so or not," the latter includes "laws passed for particular cases and enactments by decree" (NE 1134b20-24). According to Aristotle natural justice fosters personal responsibility, respect for human dignity, and binding oneself to others by recognizing the law and vision common to all men; legal justice, by contrast, may sometimes encourage faceless bureaucracy, and a depersonalizing of human relations.

Interestingly enough, the concern with how legal justice can be oppressive and depersonalizing, and with how prudence supplies the heart of a judge with a specific conception much closer to natural justice is also inherent in *The Hobbit*. At the same time, the narrative may be seen as revealing Tolkien's strong allegiance to virtue ethics as providing the foundations for moral judgment. A good illustration of this point comes in the happenings of the days following the death of Smaug. Faced with Thorin's refusal to share his newly regained wealth with those against whom his company has aroused the dragon, Bilbo determines to see justice served. The fact that he gives the Arkenstone to the Lake-men, in context, reflects his wisdom and understanding, as much as his unwillingness to bargain in a clear-cut case of inequality and injustice. More satisfying for the readers, Bilbo's judgment provides a sharp contrast to the rule by decree and illustrates how and in what circumstances prudence accords with moral deliberation and complete virtue.

Given all that, underlying the plots and themes of *The Hobbit* is an essentially mythic, Tolkienian notion that natural rather than legal justice, harmony rather than disharmony, and togetherness rather than dissociation are contributive to human happiness and fulfillment.

Conclusion

Tolkien's apparent adherence to the ideas discussed above supports the conclusion that what his narrative endorses and celebrates is the notion of fantasy as a literary form specifically conducive to exploring fundamental moral issues. The peculiar interplay of virtues may take many forms, but invariably involves a slight departure from a linear, objective, Aristotelian model of virtues which can then be expanded on and complemented by Noël Carroll's notion of the virtue wheel. Consequently, while virtue wheels remind us of the Aristotelian concept of the golden mean with their polarized sets of contrasts eliciting conceptual discrimination, the term "wheel" assumes critical importance here inasmuch as it nicely captures the full sweep of Aristotelian virtues in their interpenetrating, symbiotic, and structured relations.

It is suggested in the novel is that a strong overlap between particular virtues makes it difficult, if not altogether impossible, to tell where precisely these patterns of moral life shade into one another. Only together do these virtues work, and only together are they fruitful. It is no coincidence that the ideal of courage, temperance, justice, or prudence must often be tempered with other Aristotelian virtues, such as loyalty, friendship, truthfulness, and courtesy.

What Tolkien does throughout the book can be seen as an extended reflection on what it means to be virtuous, an imaginative response to the ethical experience of being human, or a moving evocation of the intimate relationship between fantasy and moral imagination. In the least, it suggests the validity of fantasy as an appropriate vehicle for the Aristotelian theory of virtue. At its core, the genre is not about inventing hobbit tales or elvish mythologies; instead, it explores an entire range of assumptions aimed at explaining the human condition in the present age.

All in all, Tolkien seems to say that it still lies within our power to be good or wicked according to the same moral laws. One function of fantasy will thus be to draw the readers into imaginative engagement with the story and to stimulate an awareness of what falls under the concept of a given vice or virtue, thereby rendering those concepts newly meaningful. Seen thus, fantasy is a particularly apt form for addressing moral dilemmas and for presenting a practical ideal to be pursued in actual life.

Bibliography

Abbreviations used: EE: see Aristotle 1992 / NE: see Aristotle 1985

Aristotle. *Eudemian Ethics*. Trans. Michael Woods. Oxford: Clarendon Press, 1992

---. *Nicomachean Ethics*. Trans. Terence Irwin. Indianapolis, IN: Hackett Publishing Company, 1985

Bowman, Mary R. "The Story Was Already Written: Narrative Theory in The Lord of the Rings." *Narrative* 14.3 (2006): 272-293

Boyer, Robert H., and Kenneth J. Zahorski (eds.). *Fantasy Literature: A Core Collection and Reference Guide*. New York, London: R. R. Bowker Company, 1979

Carroll, Nöel. "The Wheel of Virtue: Art, Literature, and Moral Knowledge." *The Journal of Aesthetics and Art Criticism* 60.1 (2002): 3-26

Morris, John S. "Fantasy in a Mythless Age." *Children's Literature: The Great Excluded*. Ed. Francelia Butler. Vol. 2. Storrs, CT: Children's Literature Association, 1973. 77-86

Purtill, Richard. *Lord of the Elves and Eldils: Fantasy and Philosophy in C. S. Lewis and J.R.R. Tolkien*. Grand Rapids, MI: Zondervan Publishing House, 1974

Shippey, Tom. *J.R.R. Tolkien: Author of the Century*. Boston, New York: Houghton Mifflin Company, 2000

Tolkien, J.R.R. "On Fairy-Stories." *Tree and Leaf*. London: HarperCollins, 2001, 1-81

---. *The Hobbit*. London: HarperCollins, 1991

---. *The Letters of J.R.R. Tolkien*. Ed. Humphrey Carpenter. Boston, New York: Houghton Mifflin Company, 2000

Der Zwerg lebt nicht vom Gold allein
Vom Umgang mit Reichtum im *Hobbit*

Thomas Fornet-Ponse (Bonn)

Gute Bücher beschäftigen sich mit wesentlichen Fragen. Zum Beispiel mit der aus der Philosophiegeschichte hinreichend bekannten Frage nach einem guten Leben. Was muss gegeben sein, wie muss man leben, welche Werte muss man verfolgen, um ein gutes Leben zu führen? Gerade diesen Fragen nähert man sich aber besser mit einem konkreten Beispiel, das vor Augen führen kann, worin ein gutes Leben besteht und was die Voraussetzungen dafür sind, als mit abstrakten Überlegungen, die letztlich etwas in der Luft zu schweben scheinen. Noch hilfreicher wird dies, wenn dem guten Beispiel ein negatives gegenübergestellt wird.

Genau dies liegt im *Hobbit* vor, wenn wir unseren Blick auf die Frage nach dem Umgang mit Reichtum wenden. Denn schon bei einer flüchtigen Lektüre fällt die Kontrastierung von Bilbo und Thorin hinsichtlich dieser Frage auf. Besonders prägnant zeigen dies die vorletzten Worte Thorins zu Bilbo, indem sie Thorins Sinneswandel illustrieren: »If more of us valued food and cheer and song above hoarded gold, it would be a merrier world« (348). Diese Gegenüberstellung von Thorin und Bilbo kann insofern als bedeutend angesehen werden, als sie erst sukzessive Eingang in den Text gefunden hat. In früheren Entwürfen unterliegt Thorin keineswegs der so genannten »dragon-sickness« (vgl. HH II 595-603).

Im Folgenden soll die im *Hobbit* propagierte Hierarchie von Werten und damit auch die Frage nach dem richtigen und dem verfehlten Umgang mit materiellen und immateriellen Werten zunächst im Blick auf Personen als auch (wesentlich knapper) hinsichtlich der Reichtumskritik als ein den gesamten *Hobbit* durchziehendes Motiv untersucht werden.

Personen: Beispiele guten und weniger guten Lebens

Wenden wir uns nun den Subjekten des guten und weniger guten Lebens zu, sollen anhand der wichtigsten Beispiele die verschiedenen Positionen zum Umgang mit Reichtum dargestellt werden.

Bilbo Baggins – Geld als Mittel zu Frieden und Komfort
Während sich in anderen Aspekten eine deutliche Entwicklung Bilbos zeigt (vgl. u.a. H 269, Bauer 26ff; Ilgner 193-214; O'Neill 57-71), gilt dies nicht für seine grundsätzliche Einstellung zum Reichtum. Das mag auch an seiner finanziellen

Unabhängigkeit liegen. Dessen ungeachtet wird schon auf der ersten Seite sein Hang zu einem komfortablen Leben betont, wenn auf die hohe Zahl seiner Kleiderschränke und Speisekammern hingewiesen wird (vgl. 29ff). Er scheint nachgerade hedonistische Ideale zu verfolgen, die allerdings anderen untergeordnet sind. Dies zeigt sich während der Party, als er sich darum sorgt, »that the cakes might run short, and then he – as the host: he knew his duty and stuck to it however painful – he might have to go without« (38).[1]

Interessanterweise scheinen die im Lied der Zwerge erwähnten Reichtümer keine Rolle bei seinen Phantasien zu spielen, vielmehr steht eine allgemeine Neugier mit der Betonung auf die Natur im Vordergrund: »[H]e wished to go and see the great mountains, and hear the pine-trees and the waterfalls, and explore the caves, and wear a sword instead of a walking-stick« (45). Zugleich fühlt er das Sehnen der Zwerge, das aber als „a fierce and jealous love" charakterisiert und somit schon hier von seinem eigenen abgegrenzt wird.

Auch nach seinem abrupten Aufbruch aus Bag-End hat er vor allem ein komfortables Leben bzw. eine normale Wanderung im Kopf: »I have come without my hat, and I have left my pocket-handkerchief behind, and I haven't got any money« (64). Während der Reise mit den Zwergen wird immer wieder auf seine besondere Sorge um die Mahlzeiten und auf seine sehnsüchtigen Gedanken an Bag-End hingewiesen (vgl. 65f, 88, 107, 115, 142, 161f, 179, 207, 298). Dies ändert sich auch nicht grundsätzlich durch seine immer größer werdende Verantwortung für die Zwerge. Gleichwohl wird seine Veränderung betont, als er zum ersten Mal zu Smaug hinabsteigt: »Already he was a very different hobbit from the one that had run out without a pocket-handkerchief from Bag-End long ago. He had not had a pocket-handkerchief for ages. He loosened his dagger in his sheath, tightened his belt, and went on« (269). Dabei sagt er sich selbst, keine Verwendung für irgendwelche Drachenhorte zu haben und wünscht sich sehnlichst nach Hause.

Völlig unbeeindruckt lässt ihn der Anblick Smaugs und des Drachenhorts jedoch auch nicht; es heißt sogar: »His heart was filled and pierced with enchantment and with the desire of dwarves« (271). Ferner entwickelt er nun auch ein Eigeninteresse und wird zum eigentlichen Anführer des Abenteuers. Wie wenig Gedanken er sich vorher über den weiteren Gang des Abenteuers gemacht hat, zeigt auch, dass er erst durch Smaug auf die Schwierigkeiten der Heimreise

---

1 Vgl. dazu auch: »He suddenly felt he would go without bed and breakfast to be thought fierce« (48). Hier zeigt sich deutlich, was für Bilbo zu Beginn schon größeren Verzicht bedeutet. Eine ähnliche Bedeutung wie den Pflichten des Gastgebers wird dem Dank oder der Bitte zugewiesen, wenn der Erzähler eigens darauf verweist, Bilbo sei sehr verärgert, als die Zwerge ihre Frühstückswünsche ohne ein »Bitte« äußern (vgl. 58), oder daran denkt, die Zwerge seien ohne ein »Danke« verschwunden (vgl. 60). Diese Bedeutung vermag auch Bilbos Ärger über die scheinbare Undankbarkeit der Zwerge nach ihrer Befreiung von den Waldelben zu erklären (vgl. 247). Vgl. seinen Ärger über Thorins Beleidigungen wegen des Arkensteins (vgl. 335).

und eines allfälligen Transports an Reichtümern aufmerksam gemacht wird. Aber auch dabei bleibt er zunächst seinen Freunden gegenüber loyal, indem er Smaug gegenüber das Motiv der Rache als dem Motiv des Goldes vorgängig angibt (vgl. 282) und bedauert, die Worte Smaugs über die Zwerge und ihre angeblichen Absichten, ihn leer ausgehen zu lassen, gehört zu haben (vgl. 286) – die Loyalität seinen Freunden gegenüber wird auch von Purtill herausgestellt (vgl. 68). Hier zeigt sich Bilbo durch die Drachenkrankheit beeinflusst, was sich beim Arkenstein noch dahin steigert, diesen einzustecken und dessen Entdeckung vor den Zwergen zu verheimlichen. Aber er versucht noch, dies rational zu rechtfertigen (vgl. H 293).

Gleichwohl wird sein Verhalten noch deutlich von dem der Zwerge unterschieden, als diese den Hort untersuchen: »All the same Mr. Baggins kept his head more clear of the bewitchment of the hoard than the dwarves did. Long before the dwarves were tired of examining the treasures, he became weary of it and sat down on the floor; and he began to wonder nervously what the end of it all should be« (295f). Seine Gedanken kehren dabei zurück zu Beorns Getränken, für die er viel gäbe. Während die Elben und Menschen vor den Toren lagern, sehnt er sich danach, »to go down and join in the mirth and feasting by the fires« (320f). Die kriegerischen Gesänge der Zwerge vermögen ihn dabei nicht zu befriedigen. Auch die Belagerung ist nicht nach seinem Geschmack. So entscheidet er sich dazu, durch die Übergabe des Arkensteins an Bard seinen (fast) vollständigen eigenen Anteil am Schatz aufzugeben, um Frieden zwischen den verschiedenen Parteien zu stiften – eine eindeutige Prioritätensetzung, für die er auch vom Elbenkönig sehr gelobt wird (vgl. 331).[2]

Erstaunlicherweise – oder vielleicht gerade nicht, wenn man an die Redewendung des »Schlafs des Gerechten« denkt – schläft er nach seiner Rückkehr von seinem heimlichen Ausflug schnell ein, »forgetting all his worries till the morning. As a matter of fact he was dreaming of eggs and bacon« (332). Schon vorher weist er auf ihre geringen Nahrungsvorräte hin und »would have given most of his share of the profits for the peaceful winding up of these affairs« (318). In abgestufter, aber ähnlicher Weise verzichtet er nach der Schlacht abgesehen von zwei kleinen Kisten auf seinen Anteil am Drachenhort, schenkt dem Elbenkönig zum Abschied ein Halsband und will später Gandalf den Trollschatz überlassen (vgl. 351ff). »Bilbo comes from the later arm of the sophrosynic tradition; he is a ›moral‹ hero, who acts when it is right to do so, rather than not acting at all. Nothing he does is for fame or reputation, although this is the way in which he is then measured« (Slack 130f).

---

2   Allerdings weist Rosebury zu Recht darauf hin, dass Thorins Ärger über Bilbo nicht völlig unberechtigt ist, da Bilbo die Zwerge verraten hat – wenn auch mit einer redlichen Motivation (vgl. 112f). Hier zeigt sich sehr deutlich, in welche moralischen Konflikte Bilbo gerät. In seiner Güterabwägung zeigt sich seine Priorität. Zumal er formal aufgrund Thorins Versprechen, er dürfe sich seinen Teil frei aussuchen, ein Argument für seinen ›Diebstahl‹ des Arkensteins anführen kann. Vgl. auch Ilgner 173ff.

So wichtig ihm die Mahlzeiten und seine Erinnerungen an Bag-End sind, so sind sie keineswegs der höchste Wert. Denn schon bei der Begegnung mit den Elben aus Rivendell treten Mahlzeiten für Bilbo in den Hintergrund; er möchte lieber bleiben und den elbischen Gesängen zuhören. Auf Bilbos Vorstellung von einem guten Leben verweist auch sein plötzliches Verständnis Gollums, sein mit Erschrecken verbundenes Mitleid, »a glimpse of endless unmarked days without light or hope of betterment, hard stone, cold fish, sneaking and whispering« (133). So verwundert es auch nicht, wenn sich seine Stimmung hebt, als er im Mirkwood auf den Baum klettert und dort die Sonne sehen sowie den Wind fühlen kann (vgl. 201).

Ferner scheint es für Bilbo keine Frage zu sein, die Zwerge aus den Fängen der Spinnen retten zu müssen – ähnlich wie auch später aus den Gefängnissen der Waldelben, wo er nur kurz vor dem Eingang zögert, aber seine Freunde letztlich nicht aufgeben will (vgl. 223). In beiden Fällen wird im Text nicht (ausführlicher) auf das Handeln bzw. verschiedene Handlungsoptionen reflektiert; vielmehr handelt Bilbo einfach so, wie er handelt. Gleichwohl werden zwei Gründe für sein Verbleiben bei den Waldelben angegeben: »He did not wish to desert the dwarves, and indeed he did not know where in the world to go without them« (226). Aus Freundschaft zu den Zwergen und um sein Wort gegenüber Bombur zu halten, weist er auch das Angebot des Elbenkönigs zurück, bei ihnen zu bleiben (vgl. 331f).

In Einklang mit seinem Umgang mit dem Arkenstein liegen die wichtigsten Prioritäten Bilbos: weniger im Komfort als vielmehr im friedlichen Umgang untereinander und der Treue zu Freunden. Freundschaft kann nicht mit Gold aufgewogen werden, wie er zum Abschied zu Thorin sagt: »This is a bitter adventure, if it must end so; and not a mountain of gold can amend it« (348). Geld dient ihm nur als Mittel, um diese Zwecke zu erreichen. Viel wichtiger aber sind für ein gutes Leben Essen, Freude und Gesang.

Thorin – ein zu spät von der ›dragon-sickness‹ geheilter Zwerg

Während sich bei Bilbo die Grundlinien nicht im Laufe der Geschichte verändern und er nur für eine kurze Zeit und ohne weitere Konsequenzen der Drachenkrankheit verfällt, ist dies bei Thorin deutlich anders. Denn zu Beginn der Geschichte kann von einer derartigen Besessenheit durch den Drachenhort, wie sie sich später in den Diskussionen mit Roäc, Bard etc. zeigt, keine Rede sein. Vielmehr betont er bei der Unexpected Party eine wesentliche Reihenfolge nach dem Essen: »We shan't get through business till late, and we must have some music first« (42). Dementsprechend endet das Lied *Far over the misty mountains cold* mit einer Zeile, in der die Harfen und das Gold als gleichberechtigte Objekte des Wiedererlangens genannt werden: »To win our harps and gold from him« (45).

An dieser Stelle besitzen also auch für Thorin »food and cheer and song« eine hohe Bedeutung – wenn auch nicht notwendig eine höhere als gehortetes Gold.

Obwohl die von den Zwergen gesungenen Lieder eindeutigen Charakter tragen, bleibt ihr Stellenwert als Lied bedeutend, zumal sie dazu geeignet sind, Bilbo die Gegenwart vergessen zu lassen. Bei seinem Bericht über Smaugs Angriff auf Erebor und ihre Pläne spielen die Schätze eine große Rolle, gleichwohl tatsächlich auch der Rachegedanke eine bedeutende Rolle spielt (vgl. 57). Beide Aspekte werden vom Erzähler auch gegenüber dem Erstaunen des Masters von Lake-town angeführt: »... there is no knowing what a dwarf will not dare and do for revenge or the recovery of his own« (253). Aber hier gibt es noch keine Hinweise für eine rationalen Argumenten nicht mehr zugängliche Besessenheit.

Gewisse Anzeichen für eine solche ist sein Schweigen über ihre Pläne gegenüber dem Elbenkönig, auch wenn dieses durch die wenig gute Behandlung noch gefördert wurde, denn seine Familie war bei den Streitigkeiten zwischen Elben und Zwergen nicht beteiligt: »Consequently Thorin was angry at their treatment of him, when they took their spell of him and he came to his senses; and also he was determined that no word of gold or jewels should be dragged out of him« (220).

Aber im Gegensatz zu seinem Verhalten in Erebor führt die lange Haftdauer zur Bereitschaft Thorins, dieses Schweigen doch aufzugeben – bis er von Bilbo gefunden wird (vgl. 227). Zu dieser Zeit scheinen für ihn Lebensmittel und Freiheit letztlich doch noch eine höhere Bedeutung zu besitzen als Gold und Edelsteine. Diese jedoch sind ihm wichtig genug, um auf Bilbos Kreativität zu vertrauen; nun war er entschlossen, »once more not to ransom himself with promises to the king of a share in the treasure, until all hope of escaping in any other way had disappeared« (227).

Indem diese Einstellung aber von allen Zwergen geteilt wird, dürfte sie noch der allgemeinen zwergischen Natur zuzusprechen sein. Dieser entsprechend sind sie nicht sehr erfreut über die in Lake-town entstehenden neuen Lieder, die »spoke confidently of the sudden death of the dragon and of cargoes of rich presents coming down the River to Lake-town« (252).

Auch wenn nur Balin Bilbo bei seiner ersten Erkundung Erebors ein Stück weit begleiten will, wollen sie Bilbo wirklich angemessen für seine Dienste bezahlen und ihrerseits das Ihrige tun, sofern er in Schwierigkeiten geraten sollte. »There it is: dwarves are not heroes, but calculating folk with a great idea of the value of money; some are tricky and treacherous and pretty bad lots; some are not, but are decent enough people like Thorin and Company, if you don't expect too much«[3] (268). Ihr praktischer Sinn zeigt sich besonders deutlich, als sie den Drachenhort sehen – während Fili und Kili die magischen goldenen Harfen spielen, sind die anderen pragmatischer und stecken sich

---

3 Vgl. auch 294: »... when the heart of a dwarf, even the most respectable, is wakened by gold and by jewels, he grows suddenly bold, and he may become fierce.«

soviel wie möglich ein (vgl. 295); auch Thorin ist trotz seiner Suche nach dem Arkenstein keine Ausnahme.

Ferner zeigt sich Thorin Bilbo gegenüber mehrfach sehr dankbar (vgl. 231, 248, 271f). Als Zeichen dafür versichert er ihm, sich seinen Teil selber aussuchen zu können und übergibt ihm später das prächtige Mithril-Kettenhemd (vgl. 286, 295). Während ihres Wartens auf die Rückkehr Smaugs »the enchanted desire of the hoard had fallen from Bilbo« (287), wohingegen die Zwerge ganz darin versunken sind und erst Bilbos Warnung dazu führt, dass Thorin seine Träume abschüttelt und die Tür gerade noch rechtzeitig schließt. Ähnlich besinnt er sich bei der ersten Erkundung des Drachenhortes noch auf Bilbos Einrede hin, den Hort und den Berg zu verlassen (vgl. 296). Aber während Bilbo pragmatisch an das Frühstück denkt und nicht sonderlich guter Stimmung ist, ist Thorin guter Laune. Bis hierhin hat er sich immer wieder von den Gedanken an den Schatz lösen können; dies scheint nach der Benachrichtigung über Smaugs Tod nicht mehr der Fall zu sein, auch wenn er sich grundsätzlich noch dankbar zeigt. Roäc gegenüber sagt er zornig: »You and your people shall not be forgotten. But non of our gold shall thieves take or the violent carry off while we are alive« (318).

Thorin scheint nicht willens zu sein, Gold für Frieden und Freundschaft oder aus Mitleid zu geben. In der ersten Verhandlung mit Bard und dem Elbenkönig ist er nur bereit, für die erhaltene Hilfe zu zahlen, sofern die Elben abziehen.[4] Unklar bleibt allerdings, ob die Verhandlung, zu der er nach dem Abzug der Elben bereit wäre, sich auf mehr als die Bezahlung der erhaltenen Hilfe bezieht. Eindeutig lehnt er ab, Wiedergutmachung für den von Smaug angerichteten Schaden zu leisten; dies bezeichnet er als »your worst cause« und betont, auf den »treasure of my people« habe kein Mensch einen Anspruch (323). Er weiß um ihre recht großen Vorräte an Cram, rechnet auf die Unterstützung Dains und streitet jedem anderen ein Anrecht auf den Schatz ab. In diesem Zustand ist der Schatz für Thorin (und die meisten anderen Zwerge) die absolut höchste Priorität, wofür er sogar die Belagerung in Kauf zu nehmen bereit ist (nach Bilbos Einschätzung sogar den Hungertod; vgl. 329).

Bauer zufolge hat Thorin durch die Verstoßung des ›Heilings‹ Bilbo aufgrund der Lust am alleinigen Besitz nach germanischem Verständnis sein Heil verwirkt, kann aber durch sein Eingreifen in die Schlacht eine kampfentscheidende Verzögerung bewirken, die ihn aber sein Leben kostet. Bei seinem Nachfolger Dain werde ein Umstand betont, »den Thorin so sträflich vernachlässigte« (Bauer 80), nämlich der kluge Umgang mit seinen Schätzen. Der Erzähler betont aber, dass dies nicht nur seiner zwergischen Natur zuzuschreiben ist, sondern er auch durch den Drachenhort affiziert wird, er also der Drachenkrankheit verfällt:

---

4   Nach Bauer verstößt Thorin mit dem Angebot einer pekuniären Abfindung für die erfahrene Bewirtung »gegen die Grundsätze der Tischgemeinschaft und verwirkt so sein Heil, denn die Tischgemeinschaft konnte auf keinen Fall durch materielle Rückerstattung abgegolten werden« (43).

But also he [= Bilbo] did not reckon with the power that gold has upon which a dragon has long brooded, nor with dwarvish hearts. Long hours in the past days Thorin had spent in the treasury, and the lust of it was heavy on him. Though he had hunted chiefly for the Arkenstone, yet he had an eye for many another wonderful thing that was lying there, about which were wound old memories of the labours and the sorrows of his race. (323)

Der letzte Satz deutet auch darauf hin, dass es nicht nur um den materiellen, sondern immer auch um den immateriellen Wert der Gegenstände geht, wofür gerade der Arkenstein paradigmatisch ist. In Verbindung mit der von Martin Sternberg hier vertretenen Deutung, es habe Thorin möglicherweise gar nicht zugestanden, den Arkenstein als »heirloom« zu veräußern, ohne damit Schaden auf seine Familie herabzurufen, stellt sich die moralphilosophische Frage, ob eine Aufgabe seines Anspruches auf den Schatz nicht vielleicht eine für Thorin supererogatorische Handlung gewesen wäre – also eine Handlung, derer er zwar theoretisch fähig gewesen wäre, die aber als seine praktischen Möglichkeiten übersteigend angesehen werden muss. Auch Sternbergs Hinweis auf die kulturelle Diversität Mittelerdes, die sich gerade im Verhältnis zu Reichtum und Schätzen verdichtet, ist zu berücksichtigen – wobei es mir relativ eindeutig scheint, welche Position von Tolkien bevorzugt und primär im *Hobbit* propagiert wird.

Wie sehr Thorin der Drachenkrankheit verfallen ist, dürfte sich am deutlichsten an seinem Verhalten gegenüber Bilbo zeigen, als dieser zugibt, den Arkenstein Bard gegeben zu haben. Nur die Intervention Gandalfs hält ihn davon ab, Bilbo gegen die Felsen zu werfen (vgl. 334). So lässt ihn auch der Arkenstein in den Händen seiner ›Feinde‹ zustimmen, Bilbos Anteil im Austausch gegen diesen auszuliefern. Aber »already, so strong was the bewilderment of the treasure upon him, he was pondering whether by the help of Dain he might not recapture the Arkenstone and withhold the share of the reward«[5] (335). So liefert er nach der Ankunft Dains auch kein Gold aus, woraufhin sich die Heere zur Schlacht rüsten. Erst die tödliche Verwundung Thorins bewirkt bei ihm einen Sinneswandel, so dass er in Freundschaft von Bilbo scheiden will und sich einsichtig über die Bedeutung des Goldes zeigt:

> Since I leave now all gold and silver, and go where it is of little worth, I wish to part in friendship from you, and I would take back my words and deeds at the gate... There is more in you of good than you know, child of the kindly West. Some courage and some wisdom,

---

5 Vgl. Shippey 81: »Thorin's ›bewilderment‹ is physical and mental and moral as well. The ›dragon-sickness‹ which he and the Master of Laketown catch is also simultaneously magical and moral.«

blended in measure. If more of us valued food and cheer and song above hoarded gold, it would be a merrier world. (H 348)

Mithin ist es letztlich bei Thorin der tatsächliche Kontakt mit dem Drachenhort, der ihn recht bald der Drachenkrankheit verfallen lässt. Nach der Information über Smaugs Tod und dem Herannahen der Heere ist er einer rationalen Argumentation kaum mehr zugänglich und will unter allen Umständen den Drachenhort als sein Eigentum verteidigen. Dabei begeht er sogar einen Vertragsbruch, kann aber im Angesicht des Todes die Fehlerhaftigkeit seines Tuns erkennen. Schließlich aber bekennt auch er sich zum Vorrang von »food and cheer and song above hoarded gold«.

Der Master – ein die Legenden vergessender Mensch

Der Master kann wohl als Paradebeispiel eines selbstsüchtigen und ökonomischen Menschen gelten, denn die alten Gesänge spielen keine Rolle für ihn, »giving his mind to trade and tolls, to cargoes and gold, to which habit he owed his position« (250). Rateliff sieht ihn als einen der interessantesten Nebencharakteren Tolkiens an: »... an essentially unsympathetic figure who knows so little about his own town's history that he doubts there ever was a King under the mountain yet who nonetheless helps our heroes a great deal when they need it most« (HH I 453). Angesichts der begeisterten Reaktion vieler Menschen aus Esgaroth auf das Erscheinen der Zwerge bleibt ihm wohl auch nichts anderes übrig.

Durchgängig wird er vor allem über seine Beschäftigung mit Handel, Umsätzen und Gold und seine Ablehnung alter Überlieferungen charakterisiert.[6] So inspiriert er auch jene neuen Gesänge, die zuversichtlich von reichen Geschenken der Zwerge sprechen, und ist doch überrascht und etwas beängstigt, als Thorin sein Vorhaben umsetzen will, denn er »had never thought that the dwarves would actually dare to approach Smaug, but believed they were frauds who would sooner or later be discovered and be turned out« (253). Gleichwohl ist ihr Abschied eine Erleichterung, da sie neben Kosten eine enorme Einschränkung des Handels verursacht haben.

Ganz prägnant wird seine Prioritätensetzung beim Kampf mit Smaug und seinem Umgang mit Bard nach dem Tod Smaugs. Denn während des Kampfes ist es nicht nur Bard, der ihn dazu animieren muss, zum Kampf aufzufordern, sondern vielmehr begibt sich der Master recht bald nach dem ersten Angriff zu seinem »great gilded boat, hoping to row away in the confusion and save himself« (305). So richtet sich die Bevölkerung auch direkt gegen ihn, der die Stadt früher verlassen hat als die letzten Verteidiger, und ruft Bard zum

---

6 Aber auch die Anerkenntnis der alten Überlieferungen durch viele Menschen in Esgaroth ist materialistisch geprägt (vgl. Ilgner 165f).

König aus. Wie man an dessen Reaktion sehen kann und auch der Erzähler hervorhebt, hatte er seine Position aber nicht zu Unrecht inne, da er nicht nur darauf verweist, in Esgaroth seien die Master aus den Alten und Weisen und nicht aus Kriegern gewählt worden und niemand hindere Bard und andere nun daran, nach Dale zurückzukehren. Zudem gelingt es ihm, den Zorn der Bevölkerung von den Geldzählern (und damit sich selbst) weg auf die Zwerge zu lenken (vgl. 309f).

Allerdings kümmert er sich im Gegensatz zu Bard im weiteren Verlauf nicht sonderlich um seine Bevölkerung, sondern nur um sich selbst. Erst nach dem Abzug der Heere zum Berg übernimmt er wieder eine Führungsfunktion beim Aufbau einer neuen Stadt. Fosters Charakterisierung, er sei »ein gieriger und selbstsüchtiger und in der Notlage nicht sehr kompetenter Mann« (Foster 126) gewesen, liegt insofern auf der Linie der Einschätzung der Bevölkerung Esgaroths und zeigt sich deutlich bei seinem Ende.

> The old Master had come to a bad end. Bard had given him much gold for the help of the Lake-people, but being of the kind that easily catches such disease he fell under the dragon-sickness, and took most of the gold and fled with it, and died of starvation in the Waste, deserted by his companions.
>
> (H 362)

Während Thorin also am Ende seines Lebens von der Drachenkrankheit geheilt noch erkennen konnte, dass Gold allein zum Leben nicht ausreicht, lernt der Master das nicht, verfällt ihr und bezahlt mit seinem Leben dafür.

Bard – Gerechtigkeit will ich, nicht Schätze!
Während der Master sich somit als sehr anfällig für die Drachenkrankheit gezeigt hat, kann selbiges nicht von Bard ausgesagt werden. »A dispossessed heir, he lives to achieve unexpected victory over the surpassingly strong hereditary foe who had destroyed his homeland, reestablishes the kingship, and founds a dynasty that renews alliances with nonhuman neighbors and helps bring renewed prosperity to the region« (HH II 557). Auf diese Weise ist er Vorläufer Striders/Aragorns und in Tolkiens *Legendarium* ein Wendepunkt zwischen den unglücklichen menschlichen Helden des Ersten Zeitalters zur triumphalen Rückkehr des Königs im Dritten. Diese Charakterisierung schließt auch ein Verfallen an die Drachenkrankheit aus.

Als Protagonist tritt er erst beim Angriff Smaugs auf. Bei diesem zeigt er sich als der eigentliche Verteidiger Esgaroths und evtl. damit auch als eigentlicher Herrscher; so kümmert er sich auch im Gegensatz zum Master um die Kranken und Verwundeten und hilft bei der Organisation des Nachtlagers. Seine militärische Qualifikation zeigt sich auch, als er die ungünstige Lage der

Zwerge Dains erkennt und zum Angriff ausnutzen will, wovon ihn allerdings der Elbenkönig abhält (vgl. 338).

Die grundsätzlich pessimistische Einstellung (immer wieder wird er als »grim« [vgl. 302ff, 318, 322] charakterisiert) braucht hier nicht weiter entfaltet zu werden. Sie lässt ihn aber angesichts der ›Hetzrede‹ des Masters gegen die Zwerge an deren mutmaßlich schlimmes Ende denken und zeigt sich in seinem anfänglichen Misstrauen Bilbo gegenüber (vgl. 329ff). Ferner verbleibt er zunächst im Dienst an Esgaroth, denkt aber durchaus an einen Wiederaufbau Dales durch den nun verwaisten Schatz (vgl. 310f).

Gleichwohl zeigt er sich von der Drachenkrankheit nicht betroffen. Auch wenn er einen Teil des Schatzes für Esgaroth beansprucht, tut er dies auf der Basis von Rechtsansprüchen – u.a. als legitimer Nachfolge Girions und als Töter des Drachen (vgl. 322). Darüber hinaus erhebt er eine moralische Forderung an Thorin: »Moreover the wealthy may have pity beyond right on the needy that befriended them when they were in want« (323). Ferner weist er auch die harten Worte Thorins dem Elbenkönig gegenüber zurück und diesen als einen Freund aus, der ihnen in ihrer Not geholfen habe, ohne dazu verpflichtet gewesen zu sein.

Welche Werte er für zentral ansieht, wird in den Begegnungen mit Thorin und Bilbo deutlich – er betont die Legitimität seiner Ansprüche. Dementsprechend verlangt er als Drachentöter und Erbe Girions 1/12 des Schatzes, wovon einiges Esgaroth zukommen solle; wolle Thorin aber in Freundschaft mit seinen Nachbarn leben, füge er auch selber etwas hinzu. Die Forderungen Bards an Thorin werden als »fair words and true, if proudly and grimly spoken« (323) bezeichnet. Daher will er auch nach der Absage durch Thorin nicht von den Ansprüchen absehen, zugleich aber auch nicht selber zuerst die Waffen erheben, sondern beginnt die Belagerung und setzt auf die fehlenden Lebensmittel der Zwerge. Auf Bilbos Bemerkung, Thorin sei bereit, auf seinem Gold zu verhungern, antwortet er nur, ein solcher Narr verdiene dies (vgl. 330).

Wie stark sein Gerechtigkeitssinn ausgeprägt ist, zeigt sich in der Verhandlung mit Thorin über den Arkenstein, wo er sagt: »Your own we will give back in return for our own« (334). Er geht auch ohne zu Zögern auf Thorins Angebot ein, für den Arkenstein Bilbos 1/14 des Schatzes auszuliefern, auch wenn dies unter dem von ihm geforderten 1/12 liegt. Hierin zeigt sich, dass es ihm weniger um das Gold als vielmehr um sein Recht geht. Schließlich verteilt er auch den von Dain erhaltenen Teil nach der Schlacht freigebig an den Master, seine Gefolgsleute und Freude und an den Elbenkönig (vgl. 351).

Damit präsentiert sich Bard tatsächlich als ein Vorläufer Aragorns und als ein Herrscher, der gerecht handelt und regiert, sich freigebig zeigt, in der Not seine Führungsqualitäten auch militärischer Art unter Beweis stellt und nicht nur von der Erfüllung alter Legenden profitiert, sondern diese zu einem großen Teil auch selber bewirkt hat.

Der Elbenkönig – »Edelsteine sind schön, aber es gibt dennoch wichtigeres«

Im Gegensatz zum »elf-king« aus alter Zeit, von dessen Streit mit den Zwergen der Erzähler berichtet (vgl. 220), ist zwar auch der Elbenkönig an Schätzen nicht völlig desinteressiert, stellt darüber aber die Hilfe der notleidenden Bevölkerung von Esgaroth, als er von Bards Hilfegesuch erfährt.[7] Gleichwohl ist es schon bezeichnend, dass er sich überhaupt mit einem Heer auf den Weg gemacht hat, noch bevor er dieses erhält, wobei eigens betont wird, auch er habe die alten Legenden über den Reichtum Thrors nicht vergessen (vgl. 311f).

Allerdings tritt er gegenüber Thorin nicht mit einem Anspruch auf, sondern überlässt dies Bard und dient diesem lediglich als Unterstützung. Die Hilfe gewährt er aus Mitleid, »for he was the lord of a good and kindly people« (312), wie auch zuvor die Elben als »Good People« (219) bezeichnet werden. So ist es auch ein hohes Lob, wenn er Bilbo angesichts der Übergabe des Arkensteins als jemanden bezeichnet, der eher wert sei, die Rüstung eines Elbenprinzen als manche, die besser darin ausgesehen hätten, sowie später auch Elbenfreund nennt (vgl. 331, 353). Dementsprechend hält er Bard davon ab, den Kampf gegen Dains Zwerge zu beginnen: »Long will I tarry, ere I begin this war for gold. The dwarves cannot pass us, unless we will, or do anything that we cannot mark. Let us hope still for something that will bring reconciliation« (338).

Diese Ablehnung eines Kriegs um Gold verbunden mit dem Wunsch nach Versöhnung steht allerdings in gewissem Gegensatz zum Bericht über den elbisch-zwergischen Streit, der ungeachtet der Perspektive zweifelsohne über einen Schatz geführt wurde. Tolkien weicht damit zudem von seinen Plot Notes D ab, in denen die Waldelben und andere Berater Bard abraten, Bilbos Angebot anzunehmen (vgl. HH II 570, 572f). Nach dem Tod Thorins zeigt er sich auch freigebig, weil er dessen Schwert Orcrist auf dessen Grab legt (vgl. 350). Vom Schatz erhält er letztlich von Bard »the emeralds of Girion, such jewels as he most loved, which Dain had restored to him« (351).

---

[7] Die von mir vorgenommene Differenzierung zwischen dem »Elvenking« und dem früheren »elf-king« (d.h. Elwe Singollo/ Thingol) basiert auf der unterschiedlichen Schreibweise, da »elf-king« nur zweimal im Text verwendet wird (vgl. 220). Rateliff meint, der *Hobbit* erlaube sowohl die Identifizierung als auch die Differenzierung. »Even after Tolkien eventually, towards the end of work on *The Lord of the Rings*, committed to the decision that the wood-elf king was a separate character, he never fully reworked the original story to completely support that decision« (HH I 410). Weiterhin bezieht er die Charakterisierung des elf-king durch seine einzige Schwäche für Schätze auf den König aus dem *Hobbit*, was von der Narrative her näher liegt. Letztlich entscheidet er sich dafür, zwei unterschiedliche Traditionen für die Verantwortung des elbisch-zwergischen Kriegs anzunehmen: die *Silmarillion*-Tradition sowie die *Hobbit*-Tradition (vgl. 416). Andererseits müsste sich bei einer Identität der Elvenking leichter durch die Drachenkrankheit beeinflussbar zeigen. Für den Skopus dieses Beitrags ist eine Klärung dieser Frage aber letztlich nicht von Belang.

Hinsichtlich seiner Vorstellungen von einem guten Leben können noch die im Wald und in den Hallen regelmäßig gefeierten Feste, seine Vorliebe für guten Wein sowie seine u.a. Gandalf und Bilbo angebotene Gastfreundschaft angeführt werden (vgl. 228, 352f). Es zeigt sich bei ihm also eine deutliche Präferenz für ein friedliches Zusammenleben mit hedonischen Elementen. Bei letzteren spielen auch Schätze eine Rolle, aber sie dürften nicht wie bei den der Drachenkrankheit verfallenden Personen zum primär handlungsleitenden Motiv werden.

Zusammenfassung
In der Zusammenschau dieser fünf Personen ergibt sich ein kohärentes Bild der Vorstellung eines guten Lebens, wie sie im *Hobbit* propagiert wird. In nuce wird dies von Thorin in seinen Abschiedsworten an Bilbo zusammengefasst, in denen er die Bedeutung von »food and cheer and song« für eine fröhlichere Welt betont. Indem bei Thorin bis zu seiner endlichen ›Bekehrung‹ und noch stärker beim Master die Auswirkungen der Drachenkrankheit beobachtet werden können, wird Bilbo als Kontrastfolie noch stärker positiv herausgestellt. Zumal auch die Handlungen Thorins und des Masters primär über die Drachenkrankheit und damit als pathologisch charakterisiert werden – wobei dies bei Thorin wegen der immateriellen Bedeutung des Schatzes und besonders des Arkensteins differenzierter gesehen werden muss.

Bilbos Verhalten und seine Prioritätensetzung dienen mithin als Paradebeispiel des im *Hobbit* propagierten Umgangs mit materiellen und immateriellen Werten; vor allem seine Bereitschaft, seinen Anteil des Schatzes für eine friedliche Lösung des Konflikts aufzugeben. Ferner durch seinen durchgängigen Wunsch nach einem komfortablen Leben. Beide Aspekte finden sich auch beim häufiger als gut charakterisierten Elbenkönig, der sie weit über das Erlangen von Schätzen stellt. Bei Bard hingegen rücken diese Aspekte deutlich in den Hintergrund; er dient vor allem dazu, die Dimension gerechter Ansprüche hervorzuheben (was durch Dain mit seiner klugen Verteilung des Schatzes unterstützt wird).

Dabei wird auch deutlich, dass interpersonale Beziehungen auf mehr als auf einer ökonomischen Grundlage basieren müssen, sollen sie sich als zukunftsträchtig erweisen können. Geld spielt zwar keine völlig zu vernachlässigende, aber grundsätzlich instrumentale Rolle.

Indem letztlich die Prioritätensetzung Bilbos und des Elbenkönigs hinsichtlich eines mit hedonischen Elementen verbundenen friedlichen und freundschaftlichen Zusammenlebens von Elben, Menschen und Zwergen obsiegt, sind »food and cheer and song« von oberster Priorität. Werden die hedonischen Elemente hervorgehoben, darf die Pflege alter Legenden darüber nicht vergessen werden – denn schließlich endet der *Hobbit* mit einem Verweis auf die Erfüllung der Prophezeiungen alter Gesänge und dem eigenen Anteil dabei (vgl. 362f).

Brot oder Gold?

Ist bei der Schilderung der Personen schon die Reichtumskritik als ein durchgängig präsentes Motiv deutlich geworden, insofern die Verabsolutierung des Schatzes durch Smaug, Thorin und den Master letztlich zu ihrem (gewaltsamen) Tod führt, kann selbiges noch etwas weiter untersucht werden. Denn immer wieder leiden die Protagonisten unter Nahrungsmangel und insofern ist die Frage nach dem, was zum Überleben nötig ist, sehr präsent. Vor allem zum Schluss werden dabei Gold und Nahrung als Alternativen gegenübergestellt und die Unzulänglichkeit des Goldes betont.

Während bei der Unexpected Party und auch in der ersten Zeit nach ihrem Aufbruch nicht von Nahrungsmangel gesprochen werden kann, kommen sie recht bald »into the Lone-lands, where there were no people left, no inns, and the roads grew steadily worse« (65). So treibt sie auch vor allem ihr Hunger dazu, nachzusehen, als sie das Licht des Feuers der Trolle erblicken. Auch bei den Trollen spielt die Sorge um ihre Nahrung eine große Rolle, wenn sie sich auch mehr über die Eintönigkeit des Hammelfleisches beschweren sowie der von Gandalf erneut angefachte Streit über die Art der Zubereitung der Zwerge zu ihrer Versteinerung führt (vgl. 71ff). Der Vorrang der Vorräte vor dem Gold zeigt sich schon, indem die Zwerge das Gold der Trolle vergraben, ihre Nahrungsmittelvorräte aber gerne auffüllen. Hier gibt es also noch keine Anzeichen einer Drachenkrankheit.

Nach der Gefangennahme durch die Goblins leiden sie wieder unter Vorratsmangel, den sie erst bei Beorn beheben können. Von diesem werden sie vegetarisch, aber fürstlich bewirtet und gut mit Proviant ausgestattet: »nuts, flour, sealed jars of dried fruits, and red earthenware pots of honey, and twice-baked cakes that would keep good a long time, and on a little of which they could march far« (183). Aber auch diese reichen nicht aus, um den Düsterwald vollständig zu durchqueren, weshalb sie – wiederum aus Hunger – entgegen den Warnungen den Weg verlassen, die Feste der Waldelben stören und schließlich von den Spinnen gefangen genommen werden. Auch nach ihrer Befreiung durch Bilbo sind sie immer noch von Hunger geschwächt, so dass sie nicht ernsthaft an Widerstand gegen die Waldelben denken können. Bei diesen aber erhalten sowohl Thorin als auch die anderen Zwerge Nahrung in ausreichender Menge – und wie schon erwähnt, führt die Dauer der Gefangenschaft bei Thorin allmählich dazu, dem Elbenkönig doch die Wahrheit erzählen zu wollen.

Nach ihrer Befreiung durch Bilbo haben sie wiederum keine Vorräte, erholen sich aber dank der Gastfreundschaft in Esgaroth recht bald. Diese ist wohl die erste, die nicht aus reiner Freundlichkeit gewährt wird, sondern durchaus auch durch die Erinnerungen an die großen Reichtümer des Königs unter dem Bergs und den Wohlstand Dales bedingt sein dürfte.

Bislang aber standen die Zwerge noch nicht vor der ernsthaften Alternative zwischen Überleben und dem Verzicht auf Gold – diese stellt sich nach Thorins Weigerung auf Verhandlung mit Bard bzw. Herausgabe eines Teils des Schatzes. Sie wird auch deutlich vom Herald verkündet: »We will bear no weapons against you, but we leave you to your gold. You may eat that, if you will« (324). Ganz ähnlich auch Bards Reaktion auf Bilbos Meinung, Thorin sei bereit, zu verhungern: »Such a fool deserves to starve« (330). Es wird also unmissverständlich unterstrichen, dass Gold letztlich höchstens zweitrangig sein kann, denn ohne Nahrung habe man auch davon keinen Nutzen – eine Erkenntnis, die Thorin und die Zwerge im Düsterwald abgewandelt noch vertreten, wenn sie lieber den Weg verlassen als zu verhungern (vgl. 204).

Zu diesem sich durchziehenden Grundmotiv des Hungers als Auslöser für weitere Ereignisse und die größten Gefahren für den Ausgang des Unternehmens auf dem Weg passt auch, dass Bilbo auf der Rückreise in keine größere Gefahr gerät – weil auch kein Hunger herrscht.

Die Hierarchie der Werte – oder die Eudaimonie des *Hobbit*

Mithin zeigt sich nicht nur bei der Schilderung wichtiger Personen und ihrer Handlungen bzw. Handlungsreflexionen eine deutlich positive Bewertung der vor allem von Bilbo dargestellten und von Thorin in Worte gefassten Hierarchie mit dem Vorrang von »food and cheer and song above hoarded gold«, sondern dies auch als ein den gesamten *Hobbit* durchziehendes Motiv. Von Gold allein kann man nicht leben und wer das Gold verabsolutiert, endet wie Smaug, Thorin oder der Master: Er stirbt nicht nach einem guten und erfüllten Leben, sondern gewaltsam und von Freunden verlassen – es sei denn, er besinnt sich wie Thorin noch eines Besseren. Wer hingegen bereit ist, für Frieden und Freundschaft auf Gold zu verzichten, oder sich sonst freigebig zeigt, der wird belohnt. Diese Belohnung ist dabei nicht primär als materielle Belohnung zu verstehen, wobei auch diese sich einstellt.

> »Tolkien here creates a near-catastrophe followed by a happy ending appropriate to a fairy-story, in keeping with his ideas of eucatastrophe (cf. OFS): our hero may himself not wind up with a river of gold, but that gold is used instead of hoarded and makes his world a better place, so that in the end ›prophecies do come true, after a fashion‹.« (HH II 600)

Insofern sind diejenigen, die das Gold nicht überbewerten und teilweise auch darauf verzichteten, am Ende finanziell besser gestellt als diejenigen, die es unter allen Umständen zu erlangen suchten. Ferner liegt die Betonung auf dem Einsatz des Goldes und der Kritik am Horten um des Hortens willen.

Werden Mähler, Freude und Gesänge als Hauptelemente eines guten Lebens vorgestellt, geht es dabei nicht einfach um Nahrungsaufnahme, Lachen und Singen, sondern um eine Feierkultur, in der es immer um mehr geht. »Das gemeinsame Mahl, die Teilnahme an der Speise und am Trank, schaffen soziale Bindungen« (Bauer 42). Die Musik dient nicht wie eine Serenade oder ein Divertimento als Begleitmusik oder zur Zerstreuung, sondern besitzt primär kulturtragende Funktion – als Ort der Erinnerung und der Prophezeiungen. Als solche kann sie auch sehr starke Gefühle und Vorstellungen auslösen und so auch Handlungsimpulse bewirken. Ferner wird der Gemeinschaftscharakter der Feiern und Mahlzeiten betont, der ebenso wenig wie Freundschaften durch Gold aufgewogen werden kann.

Insofern zeigt Tolkien sich ein weiteres Mal in seinen Werken nicht als Materialist, sondern als Idealist – sofern man mit solchen plakativen Beschreibungen arbeiten möchte.

Bibliographie:

Anderson, Douglas A. *The Annotated Hobbit*. Revised and expanded edition. London: HarperCollins, 2003

Bauer, Hanspeter. *Die Verfahren der Textbildung in J.R.R. Tolkiens The Hobbit*. Frankfurt a.M. und New York: Peter Lang, 1983

Foster, Robert. *Das große Mittelerde-Lexikon. Ein alphabetischer Führer zur Fantasy-Welt von J.R.R. Tolkien*. Bearbeitet und ergänzt von Helmut W. Pesch. Bergisch Gladbach: Bastei Lübbe, 2002

Ilgner, Oliver. *Biographische, theologische und literaturpsychologische Analysen zur Person und zum Werk J.R.R. Tolkiens*. Aachen: Shaker, 2004

O'Neill, Timothy R. *The individuated hobbit. Jung, Tolkien and the Archetypes of Middle-earth*. Boston: Houghton Mifflin, 1979

Purtill, Richard. J.R.R. Tolkien. *Myth, Morality, and Religion*. San Francisco: Ignatius Press, 2003

Rateliff, John D. *The History of the Hobbit*. 2 Vols. London: HarperCollins, 2007

Rosebury, Brian. Tolkien. *A Cultural Phenomenon*. Basingstoke: Palgrave Macmillan, 2003

Shippey, Tom A. *The Road to Middle-earth*. London: HarperCollins, 1992

Slack, Anna. "Slow-Kindled Courage. A Study of Heroes in the Works of J.R.R. Tolkien". *Tolkien and Modernity 2*. Ed. Thomas Honegger and Frank Weinreich. Zurich and Berne: Walking Tree Publishers, 2006, 115-139

Martin Sternberg

The Treasure of my House: The Arkenstone as Symbol of Kingship and Seat of Royal Luck in *The Hobbit*

Martin G. E. Sternberg (Bonn)

The Arkenstone and its importance for Thorin as "the treasure of my house" drive the action in the last chapters of *The Hobbit* to a considerable degree. In this, the stone is an example of the connection between kingship, the identity of a people and exceptional gemstones that runs through Tolkien's entire work. This connection is not limited to the Silmarils, but can be found among human kingdoms as well. The insignia of royal power in the kingdom Arnor is the Elendilmir, a single white gem upon a fillet of mithril (UT 277). The crown of Gondor bears a gemstone like a flame above a circlet with seven diamonds (RK 297), and the Elessar by its healing powers helps Aragorn not only in being recognized as king, but becomes his royal name as well (RK 164). It is therefore tempting to see the Arkenstone as a link in the tranformation of the Silmarils as sacred jewels containing the light of the Two Trees of Valinor into the more general concept of exceptional gems as insignia of royal rule.

But the development of the Arkenstone through the different versions of *The Hobbit* that can now be traced with the help of John D. Rateliff's *History of The Hobbit* demonstrates that it cannot claim a direct decent from the Silmarils, but has a history of its own. And it must be considered that the Silmarils were unknown to the readers of *The Hobbit* at the time of its publication. From the perspective of its readers, the Arkenstone should be seen in the light of the idea that special gemstones were connected with certain dynasties or countries, an idea with a long history and a strong place in the collective imagination in the 19th and early 20th century.

In the following paper, the development of the Arkenstone shall be analyzed with the help of this idea, and its historical precedents shall be seen less as individual incidents but as sources feeding a stream of ideas that reached the author and his readers at a given point in time. So even if Tolkien had derived the concept of the Arkenstone only from specific Old Norse texts, it met with readers whose ideas about sacred and cursed jewels may have had more and different sources.

Two results of this paper will be that the roots of the Arkenstone reach far beyond medieval texts to sources relevant very much during the time of writing *The Hobbit* and that the currents issuing from these sources carry concepts whith them that create not only a certain moral ambiguity but also raise the question how much effective cultural diversity can be accommodated within Middle-earth.

But before starting off on this enquiry, it is useful to picture its objects in its final form: Its shape is that of a globe with many facets. It glows of its own inner light and splits light falling on it into ten thousand sparks of white shot through with glints of the rainbow. It is unique in the world (H 220, 225), and it is the treasure of Thorin's house, the "Arkenstone of my father" (H 252). It is credited with bringing luck to the people of Erebor, and at the end, it is interred with Thorin on whose tomb the Elvish sword Orcrist is laid too (272f).

The Great Gemstone in History

A stone called Arkenstone is already mentioned in the *Edda* (Grimm *Mythologie* 27, 889). But a more important source for the functions of the Arkenstone of *The Hobbit* is the Norse idea that the luck of a kin was tied to special objects. This meant mainly weapons like swords and axes, though also occasionally arrows that did not miss their target. But a farmer's luck with animals could be embodied in an especially strong and beautiful animal as well. Even in the 19th century, axes and knives could be found on Norwegian farmsteads credited with healing powers (Grönbech II 18-23). When the Arkenstone as the treasure of Thorin's house is deemed to bring luck to Thorin's people, it is the seat of the luck of Thorin's house, even the dwarves of Erebor at large.

It has been noted that the concept of luck is very strong in *The Hobbit* (Shippey 27f, 145). We may therefore assume that Tolkien carried over the idea of luck tied to certain things intentionally, especially as Bard possesses another luck-bearing object with a Norse precedent in his unfailing arrow.

Yet the Arkenstone is no weapon, but a gemstone. And gems have to be seen in connection with the fact that honour, power and an exalted social position are not something residing only in the knowledge of the relevant social group, but are visible phenomena: *in honore fulgore*, to flash in honour, is a description of high social standing, and there is the *splendor imperii*, the splendour of empire. The English word *splendour* has retained this dual meaning of political power and aesthetic radiance to this day (Wolfram 40-43).

In the Germanic world, being adorned with gold is a fact of strong non-material significance that heralds less the economic wealth but the social standing of the adorned person (Leisi 262). And this is more than mere symbolism: The splendid appearance, the *maiestas*, is a force commanding obedience. More than once the idea is expressed that a king lays down his office with laying off the regalia (Wolfram 27), and this idea has survived long after the demise of ideas of kingship that could be called magical: "Magnificence is necessary for a prince as he is the viceroy of God, and God shows forth his magnificence in his visible works", as August the Strong of Saxony once remarked (Wermusch 115).

This concept of *maiestas* has found its strongest expression in Tolkien's work in the description of Aragorn's coronation: "But when Aragorn arose all that beheld him gazed in silence ... Tall as the sea-kings of old, he stood above all that were near; ancient of days he seemed and yet in the flower of manhood; and wisdom sat upon his brow, and strength and healing were in his hands, and a light was about him" (RK 298).

Although of lower intensity, the effects Thorin's appearance has on the guards of Esgaroth belongs to the same kind of aesthetically perceivable royal luck or *Königsheil* (Bauer 78f): "'Thorin son of Thrain son of Thror King under the Mountain!' said the dwarf in a loud voice, and he looked it, in spite of his torn clothes and draggled hood. The gold gleamed on his neck and waist, his eyes were dark and deep" (H 188).

For this reason, it is the king who naturally wants to outshine all others, and the best way to do this is by the possession of an object of singular beauty and radiance. Indeed we find this already in the description of the dragon's hoard in *Beowulf*: Above the treasure hangs a standard which alone, like the Arkenstone, glows of its own inner light and lights up the vault (*Beowulf* 2767-71). It is telling that a standard was chosen for this exceptional role because among the many objects that could serve to mark the position of the king, standards seem to have been of special importance: the first thing Lucifer does to prepare his rebellion is to make his own standard (Raw 172).

But in the Migration Period and the early Middle Ages, the function of demonstrating royal splendour is not yet tied to individual objects. Often enough, insignia are given to churches, remodelled or interred with kings. But the possession of singular gemstones starts to gain a heightened significance.

The Byzantine emperor Romanos IV is said to have possessed such a singular jewel that therefore was aptly called the *orphanos*, the orphan, because there was nothing equal to it and therefore no relations of it in the world. The crown of the Holy Roman Empire once contained a stone called the *Waise* (the German word for orphan) which was credited with glowing in the dark. This stone had a part in the epic *Herzog Ernst* in which it helps the hero by its light to escape from a labyrinth of caves (Schramm, *Herrschaftszeichen* III 806-808). Closer to Tolkien's academic pursuits, the crown of William the Conqueror is described in a poem about the Battle of Hastings as having at its pinnacle a pearl which filled the stones below it with its light. The pearl was situated between two amethysts the colour of which was described as twofold: red like the light of stars in their core, and blue like drifting clouds (Ott 199).

The gleaming pearl thus becomes the image of the moon on the night sky, and it may be more than pure coincidence that the light of the Arkenstone is mainly compared to lights that lights up the night: silver in firelight, water in the sun, snow upon the stars, rain upon the moon (H 220). As an equivalent of the moon, the pearl rules the subordinate gemstones that owe it their light. All this fits in well with calling an Anglo-Saxon King "a splendid gem ... that illuminated our darkness" (Dodwell 27).

Because of their unavailability, big diamonds rose to prominence as leading jewels only in the later Middle Ages. Here Charles the Bold, duke of Burgundy, led the way as supposed first owner of the *Sancy* and the *Florentiner* and the proven owner of the point cut diamond in the *Three Brothers* jewel which later came into English possession (Harlow 133). With him, the possession of great diamonds became a matter of prestige for rulers in Europe.

But it is in India that the connection between kingship and diamonds is the strongest, and from here it infiltrated the collective imagination of its colonial power in the 19th and 20th century. The most important diamond in this context is the *Koh-i-noor* diamond, the *Mountain of Light* and the only historically significant diamond amongst the British crown jewels. To this stone, which is still a household name, many legends and beliefs are tied: That who owns this stone will rule the world and that the diamond had always been in the possession of the rulers of India, a belief so strong that the stone has been reclaimed by the governments of India and Pakistan on various occasions. To his owner, the diamond shall bring good fortune and victory over his enemies, and finally, it is beyond price: if a strong man were to throw a stone into the air and into all four directions, and this space filled with gold and gems, it would nonetheless not equal its worth (Balfour 17-31). Several smaller rulers in Malaysia clung to large diamonds as the last remnants of their kingship (Balfour 99f, 134f).

Another legend tied to many Indian diamonds (even when the way of their acquisition was perfectly well known) is that these diamonds were originally set in the eyes of cult images of Indian deities and than stolen, wherefore they were cursed. Such a stone was the object of Wilkie Collin's highly successful crime story *The Moonstone* which outsold even Charles Dickens' *Great Expectations* (Harlowe 174-176).

When the word Arkenstone is interpreted as a holy stone (HH II 604f), such more contemporary notions should have at least the same weight as precedents in the *Edda* or the results of etymological enquiry.

The fact that the Great Jewels are diamonds means also that the magical powers attributed to diamonds contribute to the function they fulfil. Diamonds were believed to give health and courage to their wearer and victory over his enemies (provided that his cause is just), but only if the diamond had been given to him and not bought (Wermusch 52). This idea had a long life: Napoleon had the *Regent* diamond set in the hilt of his imperial sword (Harlow 106).

To sum it up, the connection between the singular position of the monarch and singular objects appears time and again though the nature of the singular object may change from a shining standard to a large diamond. This singular item is not only an ornament and symbol of rule, but an effective means to it for reasons again varying through the times: the manifestations of family or royal luck, talismanic powers attributed to the gem or memories attached to it. How theses different aspects affect and support the role the Arkenstone plays in *The Hobbit* shall be demonstrated on the following pages.

The Evolving of the Arkenstone

The first thing to note about the evolving of the Arkenstone through the successive versions of *The Hobbit* is that its beginnings lie outside the concept of the Great Jewel so far described. It is introduced for the first time in the plot notes B, then named Girion's Jewel, a "marvellous gem" which Girion gave to the dwarves for the arming of his son. At this stage, the function of the Gem of Girion is only to allow the dwarves to refute Smaug's insinuation against them that they want to cheat Bilbo of his reward because he could not carry home so large a treasure (HH 377). The gem represents just a portable fourteenth share, and although its name already suggests a connection with lordship, it has not reached the status of a Great Jewel because Girion is prepared to exchange it for his son's arms and armour.[1] When the dwarves offer the stone to Bilbo, it is already in his possession because he took it at the first exploration of the case and before the conversation with Smaug. The stone exerts a considerable

---

1 There may be an echo here of the story of the mother of the Gracchi who, upon being shown the jewels of a patrician, called her sons in response. It also may point to the historical fate of some famous diamonds which were sold or pawned for raising troops (Harlow 105-107).

fascination on Bilbo who looks at it often and who decides to kill the dragon to earn the stone as his reward. At the end of the story, Bilbo was meant to choose only a golden dinner service as his reward in addition to the stone. After his return into the Shire, he was meant to become a normal hobbit again with one exception: he looked at the Gem of Girion daily, and would bring it back to Erebor at the end of his life (HH I 364f).

At this early stage, it is Bilbo and not Thorin (then called Gandalf) for whom the gemstone has the greatest motivating power. Bilbo's envisaged character development could be regarded as a kind of "dwarvification": The desire of the hearts of dwarves, the delight in beautiful things and treasure that he felt first during the performance of the dwarves' song in Bag-End (H 25f) has now taken root in his own heart, and in the same way that the dwarves became thieves due to a contention on their reward from the viewpoint of the Elves, Bilbo has become a thief of his own reward. Already here he feels unsure about his claim to it, as returning the stone at the end of his life shows.

In plot notes C this concept is retained. Bilbo "steals a bright gem which fascinates him", but now only after the dwarves told him of the Gem of Girion, but still before Smaug has been killed (HH 496).

In plot notes D, the Gem of Girion turns into the thing that the dwarves appreciate above anything else, and Bilbo takes possession of it only when exploring the treasure after Smaug's death. The latter point is important because his right to choose his own share is now, in contrast to the preceding versions, realized: the treasure is delivered to the dwarves after the death of the dragon, and as the clause "cash on delivery" in Bilbo's contract (H 38) set out, Bilbo's reward is now due to him. More importantly, Bilbo does not take the Gem of Girion with him back to the Shire, but gives it to Bard in an effort to dissuade him from attacking the dwarves when Bard and the Elves besiege the dwarves to get their treasure, something Tolkien regards as unjust at this stage. Bilbo's actions incur at first the anger of the dwarves and Thorin's wrath, but Thorin recognizes the rightness of Bilbo's decision in the end (HH 569f). However precious the Gem of Girion may be for the dwarves, it is not yet a treasure inherited from Thorin's father.

The plot notes D are only carried out in the first typescript in so far as Bilbo takes the stone when inspecting the treasure after Smaugs death: "it was a large gem and heavy – larger than the hobbit's small hand – that was stretched out to it, drawn by its enchantment. Suddenly he stooped, lifted it and put it in his pocket. ‚Now I am a burglar indeed' thought B., – but I suppose I must tell the dwarves what I have done. Yet they said that I could pick and choose my own share – and I think I would choose this, if they took all the rest" (HH II

579f). Bilbo's feeling that he is not entitled to the stone appears here despite the fulfilment of his obligations at this point (though this fact is known only to the author).

The concept of the jewel enters a new phase with the turning of the Gem of Girion into the Arkenstone. The name Arkenstone appears for the first time in alterations to the first typescript and the manuscript in which Tolkien sketched out the concluding chapters of *The Hobbit* (HH 457). The change of name is thus part of the third phase of writing the story in which the transfer of the stone can no longer solve the conflict between Thorin and Bard, without any preceding plot notes pointing to this change of Tolkien's mind. The Arkenstone was now found by the dwarves and has never been in human possession, it becomes the "Arkenstone of my father".

It is very telling that Tolkien in this situation did not just change the name of the first possessor of the stone and rename it into the "Gem of Thrain", but used a name that he already employed in Old- and Middle-English versions of stories of the First Age for the Silmarils: *eorclanstan*, a word that can be translated as precious stone or gemstone, but also as holy stone (HH II 604-606).

But the sacred nature of the Arkenstone may well be connected to sources to which the object points that replaces the Arkenstone as payment for the arming of Girion's son: Girion's necklace of 500 emeralds. Now necklaces have a long history in Europe as marks of a leading position, ranging from the necklace that Wealtheow gives to Beowulf and which Hygelac wears later on (*Beowulf* 1195-1204) to the chains of office of city majors, and the leading position of Thorin himself is marked out by being the only dwarf who wears a golden chain (H 34). But all these real and fictional models would be unable to hold 500 gemstones, least of all emeralds. When migration period necklaces contained gemstones, these were mostly garnets, and the splendid late medieval examples like the Hohenlohe collar contain a few large gemstones, mostly sapphires and spinels.

But exact parallels to the necklace of Girion can be found among the ceremonial multi-strand necklaces of Indian maharajahs which contained up to 2500 stones, and some of which consisted mostly of emeralds. Tolkien's recourse to such models is all the more likely because these Indian rulers had their gemstones reset by European jewellers, often the London branches of Parisian jewellers in London, during the 1920s and 1930s, a fact that the firms involved advertised widely. Their jewels were also sometimes exhibited on the occasion of visits to London, and they adorned their owners in their official portraits (Jaffe 60, 72-84). These Indian necklaces may also be the source for the Nauglamir: In his decision to have his most beautiful gems from Valinor set into a necklace (S 108), Finrod Felagund acts like the Gaekwar of Baroda who had a necklace made up of large diamonds (Balfour 123 ill.). At least since the 17th century, India was the country of the European imagination about gemstones, and Girion's necklace shows that Tolkien was well acquainted with these ideas in the forms current in the time of writing *The Hobbit*.

We may therefore safely assume that the other ideas to Indian diamonds regarding their connection with kingship, magical powers, their sacred nature, cursed laid on them and the recurrent idea of them being objects of sacrilegial thefts were known to him as well as to his audience.

The first thing this means for analysing the Arkenstone in its final form is that it is the Great Jewel of Thorin and his house, the insignia of his kingship and the seat of his royal luck because it brings good fortune to its owner and his people. Thorin's frantic search for the stone is thus due to much more than the desire of the hearts of dwarves. Without the Arkenstone, he lacks an item important for regaining his kingship.

The Arkenstone is therefore *eorclanstan* in the sense of holy stone, and the Indian connotations of the idea of holy stones have to be taken into account with this: Because of its sacred nature, the Arkenstone is also a cursed stone for those not entitled to its possession. When Thorin says of it "I will *be avenged* on anyone who finds it and withholds it" (H 252, emphasis mine), he does not say that he will take vengeance on the finder, but the stone itself that therefore must carry a relevant curse.[2]

This importance of the Arkenstone for Thorin has to be borne in mind when considering Bilbo's appropriation and disposal of the stone. Bilbo seems to be right: Thorin has allowed him to choose is own fourteenth share. According to his original contract he would not have been able to do so, for the fact that he could command a fourteenth share did not mean that he could choose the items that made it up. According to some medieval examples of contract on the distribution of booty, it was either divided by drawing lots, and/or the king had a right to choose the most exceptional items. Such a right Totila claims on the plunder of Rome (Prokop 331, book VII, 20), and a Swedish law states that everyone had an equal share in the spoil, but the king could claim items necessary for the defence of the realm (Wenskus 328f).

So Bilbo originally had no right to choose his own share. But Thorin had ceded his royal prerogative in an attempt of refuting Smaug's insinuations against him, thus adding another case of the long list of oaths and promises in Tolkien's work that turn against those who voiced them.

---

[2] This is underpinned by the fact that in the manuscript of the third phase, Thorin had originally threatened: "I will slay anyone who finds it and withholds it" (HH 658).

But the rightness of Bilbo's actions depends on Thorin being able to dispose of the Arkenstone at all, and this is rather doubtful. The crucial term here is the word *heirloom*. It means something that can only be passed down within the family by inheritance or, in the words of the OED, "chattel that follows the devolution of real estate", a term apt for the heart of the mountain.

Often heirlooms are bound up with certain titles, e.g. horns for land held by conage, or the fate of the family, like the famous "Luck of Edenhall", a Syrian glass beaker of which it is said that the luck of the family would fail if fit broke[3]. But an heirloom is only bound to a family in the course of inheritance. During its lifetime, an owner could confer it on others (Jowitt/Clifford vol. 1, 899). Thus Thorin could dispose of it during his lifetime.

But this is the current legal viewpoint. The problem of disposing of inherited possessions seems to have been well known in the Anglo-Saxon world as well. The *Ramsay Chronicle* mentions an ealdorman who bought land to give it to the church specifically to avoid it being reclaimed by his successors in case it had been inherited (Campbell 230). Again, this limitation extended only to inherited land, but not to things. But apart from the fact that not land but treasure were central to the dwarvish culture and economy, we find several incidents where special objects were formed into a family treasure which the current owner could not transfer to persons outside the family.

In the case of the Habsburg dynasty, a narwal tooth thought to be the horn of a unicorn and an agate bowl believed to be the Holy Grail constituted such an inalienable *Hausschatz* (von Habsburg 96). James I endeavoured to do the same by issuing a decree that the Imperial Crown and a number of royal ornaments including the *Sancy* diamond should be "indivisible and inseparable, forever hereafter annexed to the kingdom of the realm", a decree however soon to be broken by his son Charles I for his chronic lack of money (Balfour 35).

In the 19th century, the legal ambiguities connected to heirlooms are central to Anthony Trollope's *The Eustache Diamonds* in which a widow wants to sell an important diamond necklace which she claims to have received from her deceased husband. This claim is disputed by the family and their lawyer who say that the necklace is an heirloom that cannot be passed outside the family, and even if it could be alienated, this act needed special documentation (e.g. I 145). A legal expert consulted by the family lawyer says that what makes out an heirloom is not its material value, but its capacity to be the embodiment of family pride. Diamonds could not be heirlooms because of their likely recutting and resetting. Only diamonds in medals of honour and gems of the crown

---

3   Grimms *Sagen* provides many examples from the German tradition, e.g. no. 41, 43, 68, 69, 70.

are exempt from this rule. Crown jewels do not represent the possession of the sovereign, but the time-honoured dignity of the crown (I 257f). The Arkenstone is a royal gem and thus qualified to be an heirloom, which in turn means that Thorin either could not alienate it from his family or that such an act needed, in the opinion of many, to refer to the Arkenstone *specifically*.

So when Bilbo answers Bard's question "But how is it yours to give?" with the words "It isn't exactly" (H 256), he may thus not just be expressing moral scruples based on his knowledge that Thorin would not have given away the stone knowingly, but the actual legal situation. In taking the Arkenstone, he is a burglar indeed, as he says himself (H 225). And Bard's words "Your own we will give back in return for our own" (H 259) may have the quite literal meaning that the stone is still Thorin's because Bilbo could not acquire it lawfully.

Apart from legal subtleties, it is quite obvious that the prestige of a ruler is not enhanced when the heirloom of his house falls into the hands of his enemies through treason (at least in his view) and this loss forces him to do what he does not want to, which is to parley with Bard about his share in the treasure before the host of the Elvenking is gone. Having lost the Arkenstone is equal to having lost his luck. In several sagas, losing the family sword spells disaster, and some sagas point to the fact that it was especially grave if a member of a family was wounded or killed with the family heirloom, perhaps because this meant a lessening of the family's luck embodied therein (Grönbech II 26f).

Buying back the Arkenstone bears some resemblance to heirloom weapons turned against the family they belong to. It would mean for Thorin to buy back his kingdom from his enemies, hardly an auspicious condition under which to start a rule[4], especially if we consider the kind of *Königsheil* attached to the stone: As the dwarves are presented not as warriors but as miners, craftsmen and traders, the fact that Thorin had to buy back the stone because of striking a bargain with a foreigner that allowed him to obtain that stone, perhaps even rightfully, is especially grave because this meant bad luck in business. That remains even true if the stone is regarded only as a symbol of royal power, for in this case, the memory of how the King under the Mountain bargained badly and his will was bended would attach itself permanently to the Arkenstone. The stone would become another wonderful thing wound round with memories of labours and sorrows. So there is some reason to regard Thorin's plan to regain the Arkenstone without paying the reward as countering betrayal with

---

[4] It is interesting to note in this context that John of Mandeville's travels reported the notion that a diamond had the power to augment the fortunes of its wearer, but only if it was given to the wearer, not if it was bought. So there might have been ideas that the power of the Arkenstone might lessen if he had to be bought back.

betrayal, and as an attempt to avoid any lessening of the luck that the Arkenstone holds. That does not necessarily replace the effects of dragon-sickness, but adds to them.

So Bilbo's transfer of the Arkenstone cannot resolve the conflict. Redeeming the Arkenstone has such high non-material costs for Thorin that he sees it as a violation of his kingship, and the issue is no longer redeeming the stone, but taking revenge for its loss. It is only the arrival of common enemies, the orcs, which allows the conflicting parties to reunite.

The death of Thorin, Fili and Kili may in a way be even necessary for a fresh start. Thorin's death avoids that the insults he suffered could affect the ordering of the lands around Erebor detrimentally, and the death of Fili and Kili his heirs avoids that they might have to take any kind of revenge for the loss of the Arkenstone. This means the end of Thorin's house, and it is with its end that the interring of the Arkenstone with Thorin gains additional significance from the background of historical precedent which seems to be missing at first. For if insignia are interred with their possessor, they have not yet reached the individuality which is necessary for the idea of the Great Jewel, and when they have reached that status, they are no longer treated as grave goods (Raw 172-173). But with the end of Thorin's house, there no longer is a house to which the heirloom belongs.

It is telling that Bard originally laid the stone into Thorin's tomb with the words "There let it lie with the last of the kings" (HH 680). Because the stone is an heirloom tied to Thorin's house that is even cursed for those not belonging to it, it is unsuited to perform as royal insignia for the new king Dain. So there is no conflict with the reasons given in the final text of *The Hobbit*, which is to honour the agreement between Thorin and Bard, and the idea of the heirloom jewel.

Moreover, the Arkenstone and the Elvish sword Orcrist allow Thorin to be a King under the Mountain after his death: The Arkenstone brings good fortune to his people, and the sword prevents surprise attacks on the Mountain.[5] By virtue of his grave goods, Thorin functions like a Greek heros or a medieval patron saint who protects the city of his church. Finally, it is no coincidence that for the dwarves, who hold dead things in such high regard, dead kings are of such high importance, as the idea of the reborn Durin in Khazad-dûm exemplifies.

---

5 Swords accompanied by crystal spheres have often been found in high status Germanic graves such as the one of king Childerich in Tournai. Today, it is supposed that these spheres stem from a Hunnic tradition and were talismans meant to strengthen the sword they were attached to. One such sphere is in the Ashmolean Museum in Oxford (Schramm, *Sphaira* 22f) and was thus accessible for Tolkien.

Applying the concept of the Great Jewel in its changing historical manifestation calls for a modification of the general consensus that Thorin is just a victim of greed and dragon sickness. Although Thorin remains reprehensible for not honouring the agreement with Bard about the return of the Arkenstone, it has been demonstrated that this stone is much more than just a gemstone, and that the proposed way of redeeming it has a price that consist of much more than gold. The validity of such an interpretation based on historical precedents depends of course on the amount in which the author of the relevant text has drawn on them and how far these precedents were or are familiar to the audience.

But I hope it has been shown that both these conditions were fulfilled, at least at the time of writing, and it is telling that applying the concept of the Great Jewel to *The Hobbit* makes the earlier stages of the story shine through in which men and elves were the principal victims of greed. If the point Tolkien wanted to make in *The Hobbit* were just a critique of possessiveness, this point would have been the stronger by not changing the name of the Gem of Girion, for then it would have been just a precious jewel acquired in trade, and without the significance of heirloom, royal insignia and heart of the mountain.

Finally, the Arkenstone and the many different ways possible of looking at it make it an excellent example of the conditions and effects of real cultural diversity. The Arkenstone may be seen as a variable which can contain a lot of different meanings, from the embodiment of effective royal luck to an item of attached memories and prestige to a precious but expendable gemstone. The more the Arkenstone moves to the former part of this spectrum of meanings, the more do the scales swing in Thorin's favour. The more it moves to the latter part, the scales swing in favour of Bilbo, Bard and the narrator's voice.

The irony of this is that those interpretations that see Thorin only as a victim of greed have to hold a very rationalistic and materialistic worldview in which is no place for royal luck or honour. For this reason, such interpretations can deal neither with effective cultural diversity within Middle-earth nor with value systems different from our own, but treat Tolkien's archaic or at least pre-modern peoples and characters as a masquerade for essentially modern concerns. But even this is not one way only. The opposite view accepts effective cultural diversity, but has to face up to the specific costs of its position: a loss of clear orientation in circumstances of crisis.

At any rate, I hope it has been shown that interpreting *The Hobbit* by applying the criteria of its sources or parallels in real history can unlock a lot of complexity from a tale that all too often is still regarded only as a children's story or a runner up to *The Lord of the Rings*. Michaela Zehetner has demonstrated that remnants of preceding drafts in the finished text led often to the unintentional evolvement of complexity in *The Lord of the Rings*. In the same way, applying the cultural concepts of Tolkien's sources to *The Hobbit* generates complexity and moreover moral ambiguity that may not have been intentional.

Bibliography

Balfour, Ian. *Famous Diamonds of the World*. Colchester: N.A.G. Press, 2nd Ed. 1992

Bauer, Hannspeter. *Die Verfahren der Textbildung in J.R.R. Tolkiens The Hobbit*. Bern/Frankfurt a.M./New York: Verlag Peter Lang, 1983

Beowulf. Seamus Heaney (transl.). Lodon: Faber and Faber, 2000

Grimm, Jacob. *Deutsche Mythologie*. Wiebaden: Marixverlag 2007

Grimm, Jacob and Wilhelm Grimm. *Deutsche Sagen*. Heinz Röllecke (ed.), Frankfurt a.M.: Deutscher Klassiker Verlag, 1994

Grönbech, Wilhelm. *Kultur und Religion der Germanen*. Darmstadt: Wissenschaftliche Buchgesellschaft, 6. Aufl. 1961

Harlow, George E. (ed). *The Nature of Diamonds*. Cambridge: Cambridge University Press, 1998

Hardt, Matthias. *Gold und Herrschaft*. Berlin: Akademie Verlag, 2003

Jaffe, Amin. *Made for Maharajas*. Luxus und Design. München: Christian Verlag, 2007

Jowitt, Earl. *Jowitt's Dictionary of English Law*. London: Sweet & Maxwell, 2nd Ed. 1977

Leisi, Ernst. »Gold und Manneswert im Beowulf«. *Anglia* 71 (1952-53): 259-273

Ott, Joachim. *Krone und Krönung*. Mainz: Philipp von Zabern, 1998

Prokop von Caesarea. *History of the Wars*. Cambridge (MA)/ London, 2000

Rateliffe, John D. *The History of The Hobbit*. London: HarperCollins, 2007

Raw, Barbara. "Royal Power and Royal Symbols in Beowulf". *The Age of Sutton Hoo*. Martin Carver (ed.), Woodbridge: The Boydell Press, 1992

Schramm, Percy Ernst. *Herrschaftszeichen und Staatssymbolik*. Stuttgart: Anton Hiersemann Verlag, 1956

---. *Sphaira. Globus. Reichsapfel. Wanderung und Wandelung eines Herrschaftszeichens von Caesar bis Elisabeth II*. Stuttgart: Anton Hiersemann Verlag, 1958

Shippey, Tom. *J.R.R. Tolkien: Author of the Century*. London: HarperCollins, 2000

Tolkien, John Ronald Reuel. *The Hobbit*. London: Unwin Paperbacks, 1984

---. *The Lord of the Rings*. London: Unwin Hyman 4th Ed. 1988

---. *The Silmarillion*. New York: Houghton Mifflin, 2004

---. *Unfinished Tales of Numenor and Middle-earth*. Christopher Tolkien (ed.), Boston/New York: Houghton Mifflin Company

Trollope, Anthony. *The Eustache Diamonds*. London/New York/Toronto: Geoffrey Cumberlege Oxford University Press, 1950

Wenskus, R. »Beute«. *Reallexilon der Germanischen Altertumskunde*. Johannes Hoopes (ed.), Berlin/New York 1976, Vol.2, 323-330

Wermusch, Günter. *Adamas. Diamanten in Geschichte und Geschichten*. Berlin: Verlag Die Wirtschaft, 3. Aufl. 1987

Wolfram, Harwig. *Splendor Imperii. Die Epiphanie von Tugend und Heil in Herrschaft und Reich*. Mitteilungen des Instituts für Österreichische Geschichtsforschung, Ergänzungsband XX, Heft 3, Graz/Köln: Hermann Böhlau Nachfolger, 1963

Zehetner, Michaela. »Das Erbe der Entwürfe – Ungeplante Qualität(en) im Herrn der Ringe«. *Hither Shore* 3 (2006): 81-93

In der Finsternis an den Wurzeln des Gebirges traf ich auf ein beinahe unheimliches Geschöpf, und ein seltsames Kleinod kam in meinen Besitz...

The Dwarven Philharmonic Orchestra

Heidi Steimel (Scharbeutz)

In a hole in the ground there was a concert. Not a loud, noisy rock concert, with screaming fans, stage diving, and smashed instruments, nor yet a boring, formal, intellectual concert with a dressed-up high-society audience, polite applause, and over-priced champagne: it was a Dwarven concert, and that means... Just what does it mean?

The guests who arrived unexpectedly at Bilbo's home were musicians, and they had their instruments with them. The unexpected party became an unexpected concert, and the music had an unexpected effect on its audience, the hobbit. The emotions that the playing awoke in him directly influenced his involvement in the adventure that followed.

Six different instruments are mentioned in this chapter (H 17); all together, they constituted a string and wind ensemble with percussion. Kili and Fili played small fiddles; Dori, Nori and Ori flutes; Bombur the drum; Bifur and Bofur clarinets; Dwalin and Balin viols; and Thorin a beautiful golden harp. Only Óin and Glóin were left without an instrument. As readers we can only speculate upon the reason for leaving them out of the orchestra. Perhaps they were unmusical; on the other hand, it is also possible that they were the best singers. Since most of the others could not play their instruments and sing simultaneously, they may have been singled out for the vocal part.[1]

In looking more closely at the various instruments as follows, I base my assumptions concerning them on the similarity between the languages and customs of societies in Middle-earth and aspects of our Middle Ages. In this conclusion I am supported by the compositions and performances of numerous musicians, among others by Hargrove, who writes:

> Although in a footnote, Tolkien warns that the adoption of these early medieval languages to represent languages in *The Lord of the Rings* – for example, that of the Riders of Rohan – "does not imply that the Rohirrim closely resembled the ancient English otherwise, in culture or art, in weapons or modes of warfare, except in a general way due to their circumstances," music, or singing, because of its close relationship to the evolution of language in the Middle Ages, is probably an exception to his general warning. (Hargrove 125)

---

[1] It is of course possible that Tolkien simply forgot these two Dwarves; however, in my opinion, his story was revised and corrected often enough to rule out that option. He never, in any of his published papers and letters, mentioned anything about the choices he made.

Historically, the fiddle was the predecessor of the modern violin. Today, when we hear of a "fiddle", we normally think of folk and country dances; the word is used more colloquially, though the instrument may be the same. In addition to being the historically correct expression for the medieval instrument meant here, "fiddle" is the English word for the Italian "violin"; considering Tolkien's emphasis on Englishness, it was logical that he chose this word.[2]

Fiddles are wooden instruments; this material suggests that they were not invented by the mining Dwarves, but adopted from the Elves, perhaps adapted for Dwarven usage.[3] Fiddles are melody instruments with several strings[4] that are usually played with a bow; the strings can also be plucked.

The fiddles are specifically said to be small; perhaps that is the reason for choosing the two youngest Dwarves to play them. They would have a fairly high pitch, possibly sharing the soprano melody line with the flutes. Fili and Kili kept the instruments in their bags, we read; since the fiddles were breakable, they must have had some kind of protective covering as well, to have survived travelling under those circumstances.

It is interesting to note that the Dwarves who were related to one another, either as brothers or cousins (Appendix A, LotR 1418), played the same instruments. That could indicate long family traditions. Today, musical family ensembles often prefer to play different instruments within the group so that they can be combined more interestingly. With no personal experience in instrumental performance, Tolkien may not have been aware of that fact. Of course, it is possible that he was simply attempting to consolidate the large number of Dwarves into small groups that would be easier for his readers to remember.

Three Dwarves played flutes; Dori, Nori and Ori were kinsmen, though we are not told exactly what their relationship was. They produced their instruments from inside their coats, therefore we can assume that they were of a manageable size and stable workmanship. The flutes could have been made of reeds, of hollowed wood, or of metal. If they were played in the same fashion as the flutes we now call "recorders" were in our Middle Ages, they would have been held vertically. It is also possible that they were held horizontally, like transverse flutes.

Because very long flutes would have been unwieldy to carry in a coat pocket, and considering that Dwarves are not very tall, we can assume that the flutes

---

2   Tolkien used the word "fiddle" for the modern violin in one of his letters: "I love music, but have no aptitude for it; and the efforts spent on trying to teach me the fiddle in my youth, have left me only with a feeling of awe in the presence of fiddlers." (L 173)
3   In a letter, Tolkien writes of the Dwarves: "...speaking the languages of the country, but with an accent due to their own private tongue..." (L 229). Since language and music are closely connected, this could apply to their music as well.
4   There are normally four nowadays, though variants with more or less strings, even with a drone, were used (Sachs 276).

were fairly short, producing high notes, perhaps in the same range as the piccolo. We can also safely presume that they had several holes and were able to produce melodies. Were they played in unison or in harmony with the fiddles? Medieval music was most often sung and played in unison[5], but I would like to imagine that the two different instruments could have been played polyphonically with interweaving melodies that generally harmonized with each other. That would not necessarily be as complicated as it sounds – they could have played simple canons, with one instrument beginning and the other starting one or more measures later. I would guess that their melodies were rather slow, in keeping with what we read of the character of the Dwarves.

The Dwarves were long-lived, compared to the race of Men, so that they had time to become proficient on their instruments; because they were few in number, they must have been familiar with each others' style of playing. Whether they played traditional melodies that were passed down orally or in written form, or whether they improvised, they must have been skilful musicians, just as they were artists in the shaping of beautiful objects.

Bifur and Bofur, two cousins, brought their clarinets from among the walking sticks. Clarinets are single reed woodwinds; their playing range would be somewhat lower than that of flutes and fiddles, possibly providing an alto melody to complement them. Musical historians will protest that the clarinet, with its complicated mechanism, is anachronistic, too modern an instrument for Middle-earth. The other instruments in Tolkien's writings all existed in medieval times of our own earth's real history; clarinets not until the Baroque age. Finnamore suggests that "crumhorns" or "chalumeaus", the medieval ancestors of the clarinet, might have been intended here (Finnamore); another possibility would be the oboe, which has a longer history. Though it is a double-reed instrument, this difference may not have been noticeable to laymen. Tolkien was probably quite unaware of any discrepancy and simply used an instrument which could go unnoticed among the walking sticks – a nice comical touch!

Actually, Tolkien did not invent the walking stick instrument – the Romantic age brought forth such curiosities, supposedly to give those who walked in Nature's beauty an opportunity to express their emotions on location (Sachs

---

5   "The musical usage of the Middle Ages was limited to very few elements... Music essentially consisted of unison singing... Purely instrumental music was so rare that it cannot be considered the normal case. In a much greater measure than today, musical instruments had an accompanying function: They served (usually playing in unison) as a support, as guidance for the human voice." [my translation] »Die musikalische Praxis des Mittelalters beschränkte sich auf wenige Elemente... Im wesentlichen war Musik einstimmiger Gesang. Reine Instrumentalmusik war so selten, daß sie nicht als Normalfall gelten kann. Musikinstrumente hatten in weit höherem Grade als heute eine begleitende Funktion: Sie dienten (meist im unisonen Spiel) als Stütze, als Orientierungshilfe für die menschliche Stimme.« (Schulz 12-13)

390).[6] It is possible that Tolkien saw such an instrument and was amused by it, adopting it for his story. In the *History of the Hobbit*, Rateliff says that Tolkien's original intention was to have the instruments produced magically; walking sticks would be turned into clarinets (HH 36, 54). He later changed that idea, though he did not give any reasons for doing so.

Bombur, Bofur's brother, is singled out as the drum player. Since he is the Dwarf who is frequently called fat by the narrator of the story, he might have been chosen for that instrument because of his girth. The big drum would seem to suit him better than a small instrument would. However, Tolkien probably had a linguistic reason for his choice; according to Rateliff, "'bombur' means *drum* in Old Norse" (HH 784).

This was the only non-melodic instrument in the group; it must have been there for the purpose of keeping the beat so that all of the players stayed together. The drum could have been held horizontally, which would correspond with the typical medieval usage, or vertically. We do not read whether it was beaten by the hands directly or by using one or more sticks.

Balin and Dwalin, again brothers, played viols as big as themselves, which they had left in the porch.[7] Historically, a viol would mean the *viola da gamba*, a large string instrument played like a cello (Sachs 347). However, if the viols were as large as their players, the Dwarves would have had to stand rather than sit to play them, just as string bass players usually do. The low tones of the instruments would provide the bass line for the ensemble. Not knowing the size of the harp, we can conjecture that these were probably the largest of the Dwarves' instruments – and the most unwieldy to transport.

Thorin Oakenshield, the leader of the group and the Dwarves' king by hereditary right, played the harp. This instrument has a very old history and was often associated with kings and their courts. It originated as a musical bow, though it was not necessarily derived from the similar weapon (Sachs 56). Here it is said to be made of gold, an expensive and therefore valuable material. It is beautiful, so it must have been fashioned by expert craftsmen who shaped it to be aesthetically pleasing both visually and audibly.

How many strings Thorin's harp had, and whether those were plucked melodically or strummed harmonically is not mentioned. With so many melody instruments already included in the group, I would like to think that the harp was played in chords to accompany them, although that would not necessarily

---

6 "Even on a solitary walk one had to be prepared to react to sunsets or ruins, for which occasions there were canes that in a twinkling could be transformed into flutes, clarinets, violins." (Sachs 390)
7 This in itself is curious, because as far as I know, it is the only time a "porch" is mentioned as a feature of a Hobbit hole.

correspond with medieval usage. It could have been played differently for various occasions and styles. The harp is the one instrument which allows its player to sing while playing, aside from the drum and perhaps the viols. The reader of this scene can easily imagine Thorin's voice leading the others in song.

Now the instruments are all assembled; their players are ready to commence. What follows is an unusual account in Tolkien's works – music that is at first, for a length of time, only instrumental before being joined by voices in song. We can compare the performance to the overture of an opera – hinting at the themes to come and preparing the way for the vocal drama, yet a work of art in its own right.

The effect of the playing on its audience – in this case, Bilbo – is described as "sudden and sweet" (H 17), sweeping him away to strange lands. The Dwarves must have played for quite a while, since we are told that it became dark before they began to sing. Twice the narrative says that the Dwarves "still played on"(H 17), though daylight faded into darkness. Then we read that they began to sing while the playing continued, first one, then another. Perhaps several put their instruments aside, as they could not sing while playing, and the others accompanied the singing with subdued volume, to allow the words to be heard.[8]
Here, with the advent of words, the effect of the music became stronger – Bilbo felt within himself the spirit of the Dwarves and awakened to an understanding of their nature. This identification with his guests made it easier for him to subsequently join in their adventure. The music had an important part in preparing him for what was to come. Though he did not consciously understand the words of the song, he was affected emotionally by them. Only later did he realize that the lyrics told the story behind the planned quest.

Then the instruments were put away to discuss plans, and that is the last that we hear of them. "What happened to the musical instruments used by the Dwarves at Bag-end?" is a question that even Tolkien asked himself, in a note he wrote years later when pondering the possibility of revising Bilbo's tale to fit in with *The Lord of the Rings* (HH 809-810).[9]

They can't have stayed in Bag-End, because the Dwarves took all of their belongings with them, so we must assume that they were packed onto the ponies with the luggage. In that case, we actually do know what happened,

---

8   The text specifically says that they "began to sing as they played" (H 17), therefore indicating that strict medieval standards could not be applied to this performance. Of course, strict adherence to historical standards of our own world's history is not applicable to a work of fantasy fiction.

9   He also asked: "Why did they bring them to B-End?", a question that remains unanswered. (HH 809) Rateliff comments, "Given his attempt throughout the 1960 *Hobbit* to reduce the whimsy and comic touches of the original, however, it seems likely that in the end this bit of dwarven exuberance would have been sacrificed to probability and all but the most portable instruments deleted." (HH 810)

though the instruments are not specifically mentioned. When the goblins took the ponies and luggage, it is said that the Dwarves never saw their belongings "and paraphernalia" (H 70) again. Would the goblins have known and used the instruments? I doubt it; they were probably taken apart for the value of their materials. When the Dwarves and Bilbo are taken into the goblins' cavern, we read: "There were all the baggages and packages lying broken open, and being rummaged by goblins, and smelt by goblins, and fingered by goblins, and quarrelled over by goblins." (H 73)

We read that the Dwarves found harps and other instruments in Smaug's hoard near the end of the story and were thus able to play again. Those are described in the narrative:

> Fili and Kili were almost in a merry mood, and finding still hanging there many golden harps strung with silver they took them and struck them; and being magical (and also untouched by the dragon, who had small interest in music) they were still in tune. The dark hall was filled with a melody that had long been silent. (H 277)

Aside from this reference, musical instruments are mentioned only in their songs. In *Far over the Misty Mountains* the Dwarves sing of hammers which fell like ringing bells (H 18). That evokes the musical accompaniment of the Anvil Chorus in Verdi's opera *Il Trovatore* and seems very appropriate for a race that concentrates on the mining and working of metal. Perhaps we can see there a reference to a secret form of music known only to them, like their secret language.

Bilbo titled the account of his adventures "There and Back Again". Though he did come home to Bag-End, he himself was no longer the same Hobbit who began the quest with the Dwarves. Music had an important role in sending him on his way; what part did it play in his changed life thereafter?
 Though we do not know if Bilbo was an active musician before he left the Shire, we read that he wrote poetry and composed song melodies afterwards. The lyrics reflect various aspects of his life; many of them, some comical, some serious, are recorded in *The Lord of the Rings*, in addition to several that are printed in *The Adventures of Tom Bombadil*. He passed them on to his relatives and friends; his nephew Frodo sang them, as did the other hobbits who joined the Fellowship.
 Apparently Bilbo never learned to play an instrument, though he must have enjoyed instrumental music. At the long-expected birthday party, musical crackers were given away: trumpets, horns, pipes, flutes and others – "instruments, small, but of perfect make and enchanting tones" (LotR 38). They came from

Dale, so we can assume that they were of Dwarven make. At least some of the Hobbits must have been skilled and experienced players, since they made up an impromptu orchestra and played dance tunes.

That is the only occasion upon which we read of Bilbo himself playing an instrument. Before making his speech, he took one of the horns and blew three loud hoots to get everyone's attention – a performance that sounds quite unmusical.

Middle-earth is filled with music; it was the means by which Arda was created, and it continued to be a vital part of daily life and of special occasions. No wonder that Tolkien's writing has inspired many of his readers to embark upon musical adventures of their own, following Bilbo's steps: there, to Middle-earth, and back again, to our own world.

Bibliography

Carpenter, Humphrey, Ed. *The Letters of J.R.R. Tolkien*. London: HarperCollins, 1995

Finnamore, David J. *Essay on the Development of Music for Middle-earth*. http://www.elvenminstrel.com/tolkien/memusic.htm (14.09.2008)

Hargrove, Eugene C. *The Music of Middle-Earth*. Denton, Texas: Old Forest Sounds, 2001

Rateliff, John D. *The History of the Hobbit*. 2 Vols. London: HarperCollins, 2007

Sachs, Curt. *The History of Musical Instruments*. Mineola, New York: Dover Publications, 2006

Schulz, Georg Friedrich. *Alte Musikinstrumente*. München: Schuler Verlagsgesellschaft, 1973

Tolkien, John Ronald Reuel. *The Hobbit*. London: HarperCollins, 2006

---. *The Lord of the Rings*. London: HarperCollins, 2007

Singen oder nicht singen: Lieder und Gedichte in J.R.R. Tolkiens *Der Hobbit*

Julian Tim Morton Eilmann (Aachen)

Goblins, die mehrfach metrisch anspruchsvolle Lieder zum Besten geben, Elben, die sich als Meister des Spottgedichts präsentieren, ein Held wider Willen, der angesichts existentieller Bedrohung humoristische Verse erdichtet, Zwerge und Stadtbürger, die ihre politischen und ökonomischen Interessen mithilfe von Liedern zu erkennen geben, und ein Hobbit, der am Ende einer Abenteuer- und Bildungsgeschichte zum Dichter wird.

Womit haben wir es hier zu tun? Wir sind konfrontiert mit den Protagonisten eines Kinderbuches, die sich offensichtlich zum Singen berufen fühlen. Warum aber singen bzw. dichten die Figuren in Tolkiens *Hobbit*? Wer singt zu welchem Anlass und warum? Welche Inhalte werden mithilfe von Lyrik vermittelt und welche Funktion erfüllen die Lieder innerhalb des Romantextes? Aufgrund der immensen Bedeutung, die dem Gesang in Tolkiens Roman zukommt, stellt sich offensichtlich – um mit William Shakespeare zu sprechen – die Frage: Singen oder nicht singen?

Am Ausgangspunkt meiner Untersuchung steht die Beobachtung, dass erstaunlich viele von Tolkiens Romanfiguren die Frage „Singen oder nicht singen?" implizit mit Ja beantworten, denn sie singen und dichten zu erstaunlich vielen Anlässen und Gelegenheiten innerhalb des Werkes. Insgesamt finden wir 16 Gedichte bzw. Lieder sowie acht Rätsel im *Hobbit*. Dies stellt ein ähnliches Verhältnis von Lyrik und Prosatext dar wie im *Herrn der Ringe*.

Die leitenden Fragestellungen, um die es im Folgenden gehen soll, lauten: Warum hat Tolkien Lieder und Gedichte in seinen Prosaroman integriert? Lassen sich die Verse von Tolkiens erstem Hobbit-Roman mithilfe bewährter literaturwissenschaftlicher Termini strukturieren? Und kann auf diese Weise die Funktion der Lyrik im Romantext erhellt werden? Bestehen Unterschiede oder Gemeinsamkeiten hinsichtlich des Liedgebrauchs im *Hobbit* und im *Herrn der Ringe*?

Einleitung: *Der Hobbit* – Roman der Irritationen

Wenn man sich eingehender mit dem Thema Tolkien-Lyrik auseinandersetzt, wird man zu der ernüchternden Erkenntnis gelangen, dass auf diesem Forschungsgebiet noch eine große Lücke klafft: Seit meiner Bestandsaufnahme des Forschungsstandes im Jahre 2005 hat sich bei der Literaturlage nichts Wesentliches geändert (vgl. Lied 106-108): Eine Erforschung dieses Themenbereiches hat bisher so gut wie nicht stattgefunden, was u.a. deshalb erstaunt, weil die literarische Qualität von Tolkiens Lyrik zwar mitunter vehement in Zweifel gezogen wurde (vgl. Moseley 49, u. Rosebury 84), es jedoch außer Frage steht, dass die Lieder in Tolkiens Mittelerde-Romanen in hohem Maße dazu beitragen, Tolkiens Anspruch zu erfüllen, eine lebendige literarische Sekundärwelt zu erschaffen (vgl. *Lieder* 246ff).

In Bezug auf die Lieder des *Hobbit* sieht die Forschungslage ähnlich enttäuschend aus wie hinsichtlich der Tolkien-Lyrik im Allgemeinen. Auch hier fehlen einschlägige Monographien, Aufsätze und eine umfassende literaturwissenschaftliche Analyse der *Hobbit*-Gedichte, sodass sich nur vereinzelte Kommentare und bescheidene Forschungsansätze in Studien mit anderen Fragestellungen finden lassen. Das Tolkien Seminar 2008 in Jena, der höchst aufschlussreiche Vortrag von Heidi Steimel zur Rolle der Musik im *Hobbit* sowie die anregende Diskussion im Anschluss an die dort von mir vorgestellten Thesen (s.u.) haben jedoch mehr als deutlich gemacht, dass auf dem Gebiet Tolkien-Poesie noch zahlreiche Erkenntnisse zu gewinnen sind. Darüber hinaus verspricht ein für 2009 angekündigtes Forschungsprojekt zum Thema Musik in Mittelerde, dass von der deutschsprachigen Tolkien-Forschung wichtige Impulse für das bisher stark vernachlässigte Thema Tolkien-Poesie und -Musik zu erwarten sind.

Aber nicht nur aufgrund der beklagenswerten Forschungslage steht der *Hobbit* unter dem Verdikt eines Forschungsproblems, handelt es sich hier doch um einen Roman, der sowohl den interessierten Leser als auch die Tolkien-Forschung irritiert. So konstatieren wir offensichtliche Disparitäten zwischen dem hohen epischen Stil des *Herrn der Ringe* und dem märchenhaften Kinderbuch-Charakter des *Hobbit*, eine Problematik, die bereits Tolkien beschäftigt hat:

> ... the [novel's] tone and style change with the *Hobbit*'s development, passing from fairy-tale to noble and high and relapsing with the return. (L 159)

In späteren Jahren hat Tolkien bekanntlich den Versuch unternommen, den Roman zu überarbeiten, um ihn inhaltlich und sprachlich dem hohen mythischen Stil des *Herrn der Ringe* anzupassen, ein Versuch, der ihm, wie er selbst ernüchternd feststellen musste, nur teilweise glücken sollte. Betrachtet man beide Hobbit-Romane, wie insbesondere vonseiten der Tolkien-Verlage vehement betrieben, lediglich im Verhältnis von Vorgeschichte und Fortsetzung, so muss eine gänzlich homogene Leseerfahrung angesichts der vorhandenen Irritationen ausbleiben.

Dementsprechend gelangt John Rateliff bei seiner Analyse der *Hobbit*-Rezeption zu der zutreffenden Beobachtung, dass der Einfluss des *Herrn der Ringe* der unbefangenen Auseinandersetzung mit Tolkiens erstem großem Romanerfolg geschadet hat:

> 'Recovery' is particularly apt in case of *The Hobbit*, which in recent years has come to be seen more and more as a mere 'prelude' to *The Lord of the Rings*, a lesser first act that sets up the story and prepares the reader to encounter the masterpiece that follows.
>
> (HH I xi)

Ein ähnlich profunder Kenner der Quellenlage des *Hobbit*, Douglas A. Anderson, kommt zu einer vergleichbaren Einschätzung, wenn er im Vorwort zu seiner kommentierten Werkausgabe des Romans betont:

> I have prefered to let *The Hobbit* stand on its own as a work of art and have not relegated it to the mere status of 'prequel' to *The Lord of the Rings*. *The Hobbit* remains a great work, though *The Lord of the Rings* is greater.
>
> (Anderson ix)

Anderson ist sicherlich zuzustimmen, dass die Klassifikation des *Hobbit* als Vorgeschichte einem Roman, der ganze 17 Jahre erfolgreich als eigenständiges literarisches Werk bestanden hat, nicht gerecht wird. Für meine Fragestellung ist entscheidend, dass die intertextuellen Irritationen, die der Romantext des *Hobbit* beim Tolkien-Leser auslöst, auch die Lyrik betreffen, da der Ton der Gedichte auch bei einer wiederholten Lektüre nicht mit den Eindrücken des *Herrn der Ringe* übereinstimmt. So spiegeln auch die Lieder und Gedichte im *Hobbit* den für die Rezeption des Romans problematischen Status zwischen Kinderbuch und epischem Roman im Sinne Tolkiens.

Wie sieht dies im Detail aus? Erstaunlich ist bereits das große Spektrum an unterschiedlichen Romanfiguren, die im *Hobbit* als Dichter, Sänger oder Rezitatoren in Erscheinung treten: Denn im Gegensatz zum *Herrn der Ringe* sind nicht nur die Vertreter der freien Völker, sondern auch Goblins mit ganzen drei Liedern im Roman vertreten. Weiterhin singen und dichten einige Protagonisten in ungewohnter Weise, präsentieren sich doch ausgerechnet Tolkiens Elben als Meister des Spottgedichts und verfassen an Kinderreime erinnernde Nonsense-Gedichte (»Tra-la-la-lally/ Fa-la-la-lally/ Fa-la!«, H 266), die im *Herrn der Ringe* den Hobbits oder Tom Bombadil vorbehalten bleiben. Dichtende Goblins und Spottlieder singende Elben wird man im *Herrn der Ringe* vergebens suchen. Rateliffs pointierte Einschätzung in Bezug auf die sangesfreudigen Goblins trifft die irritierende Textsituation demnach sicherlich gut:

> Not only are Tolkien's goblins ... unafraid of a little verse, they seem as fond of breaking into a song as the villains of a Gilbert and Sullivan operetta.
>
> (HH I 141)

Da die erste Lektürebeobachtung sich demnach auf die Unterschiede der beiden Hobbit-Romane richtet, stand am Beginn meiner Untersuchung die ursprüngliche Arbeitshypothese, dass sich der Liedgebrauch im *Hobbit* grundlegend vom *Herrn der Ringe* unterscheidet, in ähnlicher Weise in der beispielsweise die Rolle des Erzählers oder der Sprachgebrauch in beiden Romanen divergiert.

Wie im Folgenden deutlich wird, kann anhand einer eingehenden Analyse der Lyrik jedoch gezeigt werden, dass sich die Merkmale, die den Liedgebrauch im *Herrn der Ringe* kennzeichnen, auch im *Hobbit* feststellen lassen. So besteht auch im *Hobbit* jene charakteristische Spannung zwischen kollektiver Liedtradition und individueller Kunstschöpfung. Darüber hinaus lassen sich die literaturwissenschaftlichen Kategorien Volkslied und Gelegenheitslyrik erfolgreich auch auf den *Hobbit* anwenden.

Volkslieder und kollektive Liedtradition

Im *Herrn der Ringe* treten nahezu alle gesellschaftlichen Schichten der freien Völker Mittelerdes als Liedschöpfer oder Sänger in Erscheinung. Tolkien kreiert hier den interkulturellen Austausch von verschiedenen Gesellschaften, deren Repräsentanten auf lyrisches Sprechen angewiesen sind, um in sozialen, politischen und alltäglichen Kommunikationssituationen bestehen zu können. Darüber hinaus ist das Verhältnis von Vortragendem und eigentlichem Schöpfer der Lieder in Tolkiens großem Roman äußerst vielschichtig (vgl. *Lieder* 246-253).

So konnte ich bei meinen Forschungen zur gesellschaftlichen Funktion der Poesie im *Herrn der Ringe* feststellen, dass ein wechselseitiger Zusammenhang zwischen kollektiver Liedtradition und individuellem Liedgebrauch besteht: Charaktere schöpfen aus einem tradierten Liedfundus und adaptieren bewährte poetische Formen und Melodien für ihren eigenen Gebrauch (vgl. 253ff). Lässt sich diese für Volkspoesie charakteristische Wechselwirkung zwischen einer anonymen, zunächst nicht schriftlich überlieferten Kunstschöpfung und der Inanspruchnahme des tradierten Liedfundus durch unterschiedliche Individuen (vgl. Trost 171f, Schulz 794 u. Weidhase, *Volkslied* 492) auch für den *Hobbit* nachweisen?

Von den 16 Liedern, die im Roman wiedergegeben sind, lässt sich anhand der Zwergenlieder deutlich machen, dass diese auf Mechanismen der Volksliedproduktion und -überlieferung beruhen. Die Zwerge im *Hobbit* verfügen offenbar, ähnlich den Hobbits und Rohirrim im *Herrn der Ringe* (vgl. *Lieder* 254-256) über einen Fundus an charakteristischen Liedstrukturen und Melodien, auf den sie immer wieder zurückgreifen können, um aktuelles Geschehen poetisch zu fassen und zu deuten. So stimmen Thorin & Co. (H 28) im Roman insgesamt vier Lieder an, von denen drei größere Aufmerksamkeit verdienen:

Far over the misty mountains cold (14f), *The wind was on the withered hearth* (116f) und *Under the Mountain dark and tall* (235f). Das letztgenannte Lied wird uns später in Bezug auf die Verwendung panegyrischer Topoi innerhalb der *Hobbit*-Lyrik noch beschäftigen (s.u.). Vergleichen wir nun beispielhaft die jeweils zweite Strophe aus den Gedichten *Far over the misty mountains cold* und *The wind was on the withered hearth*:

> The dwarves of yore made mighty spells,
> While hammers fell like ringing bells
> In places deep, where dark things sleep,
> In hollow halls beneath the fells. (14)

> The wind came down from mountains cold,
> and like a tide it roared and rolled;
> the branches groaned, the forest moaned,
> and leaves were laid upon the mould. (116)

Liest man beide Strophen wie hier hintereinander und wüsste nicht, dass es sich um zwei Strophen aus unterschiedlichen Gedichten handelt, dann wäre man geneigt, die Verse für Auszüge aus einem einzigen zusammenhängenden Gedicht zu halten, so ähnlich sind sich die Strophen in ihrer metrischen Struktur und ihrem lyrischem Klang. Dieses Schema von identischen Versfüßen und Silbenabfolgen wird bei allen drei Zwergengedichten, um die es hier geht, nur minimal abgewandelt.

Welche Merkmale zeichnen die hier wiedergegebenen Strophen aus? Jedes der Zwergengedichte bzw. -lieder besteht aus jeweils vierzeiligen Strophen mit einem durchgehend steigenden, alternierenden, vierhebigen Jambus, der dem Reimschema AABA folgt. Weiterhin weisen die Strophen einen charakteristischen Binnenreim im dritten Vers auf. Binnenreime verstärken die Klangwirkung eines Gedichtes, bringen sie doch einen Gleichklang innerhalb eines kürzeren Abstandes. Betrachtet man all diese Merkmale zusammen, dann wird deutlich, dass es sich hier um eine typische Volksliedstrophe handelt.

Die Volksliedstrophe ist in ihrer häufigsten Form vierzeilig, mit drei oder vier Hebungen alternierend, d.h. im regelmäßigen Wechsel von Hebung und Senkung (Jambus). Insbesondere deutsche und englische Volkslieder basieren oft auf vierfüßigen Jamben und erzeugen so ein eingängiges rhythmisches Muster, das ein leichtes Memorieren, gemeinsames Sprechen und Singen begünstigt (vgl. Neureuter 797f). Der Erzähler des *Hobbit* betont darüber hinaus explizit, dass die Zwerge die Lieder singen (vgl. H 12, 14, 116, 235), zweimal sogar mit musikalischer Begleitung (14 u. 235), wodurch wir uns darin bestätigt sehen, dass es sich bei den Zwergenliedern tatsächlich um Lieder handelt.

Darüber hinaus wenden Thorin und seine Begleiter bei ihren Gesangsdarbietungen ein Verfahren der Volksliedproduktion an, das in der Musik- und Literaturwissenschaft als Prinzip der Kontrafaktur bezeichnet wird. Was hat es damit auf sich? In der Forschung versteht man unter Kontrafaktur die Übernahme populärer Melodien und Liedformen für neue Liedtexte. Melodie, Rhythmus, die Struktur der Strophen und Verse, womöglich auch ganze Teile des Wortmaterials, insbesondere seine Klangqualitäten bleiben dabei erhalten. Auf diese Weise kann der neue Text bzw. das neue Lied vom Bekanntheitsgrad und der sprachlich-musikalischen Eingängigkeit der Vorlage profitieren (vgl. Delbrück 250). Für Repräsentanten einer auf mündlicher Kommunikation und Überlieferung basierenden Gesellschaft bietet sich ein solches Tradierungsverfahren in hohem Maß an, da die Übernahme gebräuchlicher Melodien die Aneignung neuer Liedtexte erleichtert.

Die Zwergenlieder des *Hobbit* weisen dementsprechend nicht nur eine nahezu identische metrische Liedstruktur auf (s.o.), sondern übernehmen teilweise auch ganze Strophen voneinander: So taucht die genannte Strophe »The dwarves of yore made mighty spells« identisch in den Liedern *Far over the misty mountains cold* (H 14f) und *Under the Mountain dark and tall* (235f) auf. Die Zwerge greifen hier offensichtlich auf einen spezifischen Volksliedtypus zurück, der zum Zwecke poetischer und gesellschaftlicher Kommunikation adaptiert und damit aktualisiert werden kann.

Da das Volkslied geradezu auf Aktualisierungen in Form von Kontrafakturkompositionen angewiesen ist, um seine identitätsstiftende Kraft zu entfalten, besteht die schöpferische Tätigkeit der Vortragenden darin, den Text und die Struktur des Liedes dem gegebenen Anlass anzupassen. Dass die Zwergenlieder des *Hobbit* auf eine kollektive Liedtradition zurückgehen, die von den Sängern mithilfe des Prinzips der Kontrafaktur aktualisiert wird, macht u.a. ein Bezug zum *Herrn der Ringe* deutlich: Pippin und Merry bearbeiten das aus dem *Hobbit* bekannte Lied *Far over the misty mountains cold* (14f), ändern jedoch nur den Text. Die erste Strophe lautet wie folgt:

> Farewell we call to hearth and hall!
> Though wind may blow and rain may fall,
> We must away ere break of day
> Far over wood and mountain tall. (LotR 104)

Man vergleiche hierzu ebenfalls die erste Strophe aus dem entsprechenden Zwergenlied des *Hobbit*, um sich ein Bild der Übereinstimmungen in Metrik (u – u – u – u -) und Melodie (vierhebiger alternierender Jambus) zu machen:

> Far over the misty mountains cold
> To dungeons deep and caverns old

> We must away ere break of day
> To seek the pale enchanted gold. (H 14)

Im Erzählkommentar des *Herrn der Ringe* heißt es denn auch zutreffend über Pippins und Merrys Lied: »It was made on the model of the dwarf-song that started Bilbo on his adventure long ago, and went to the same tune« (LotR 104). Das Prinzip der schöpferischen Aneignung findet hier explizit Erwähnung. Tolkien stellt auf diese Weise intertextuelle Bezüge zwischen seinen beiden Hobbit-Romanen her und verbindet die Volksliedtradition seiner Mittelerde-Mythologie.

Darüber hinaus legt die Verwendung des Zwergenliedes durch die Hobbits nahe, dass die Aneignung und Übernahme von Volkspoesie auch zwischen verschiedenen Kulturen stattfinden kann, sofern lyrisch begabte Dichter wie Bilbo den Poesie-Transfer gewährleisten.

Wir können also festhalten, dass die Integration von Volksliedern, wie sie für den *Herrn der Ringe* charakteristisch ist, auch auf den *Hobbit* zutrifft. Welche expositorische Funktion das Zwergenlied *Far over the misty mountains cold* (H 14f) darüber hinaus im Roman hat, wird uns später noch beschäftigen. Im Folgenden geht es um die gesellschaftliche und politische Funktion von (Volks)Liedern im *Hobbit*.

Die politische Funktion von Liedern und poetischer Überlieferung

Meine Analyse der Lieder und Gedichte im *Herrn der Ringe* als Teil der kulturellen Kommunikation kam zu dem Ergebnis, dass poetische Überlieferung einen Zusammenhang zwischen historisch-mythologischer Vergangenheit und gegenwärtigem Geschehen herstellen kann (vgl. *Lieder* 246-249). Durch Rezitation alter Verse können Handlungsanweisungen für den situativen Kontext gewonnen werden. Dieses Verfahren des Liedgebrauchs findet an einer signifikanten Stelle auch im *Hobbit* statt.

Nachdem sich Thorin in Seestadt mit der Nennung seines Königstitel vorgestellt hat und seine Proklamation mit den bedeutungsvollen Worten »I return!« (H 177) beendet, wird alte Lyrik in einer bemerkenswerten Weise aktualisiert. So besinnen sich die Seestädter zur Deutung des Geschehens ihrer poetischen Überlieferung: »Some began to sing snatches of old songs concerning the return of the King under the Mountain« (H 177f). In diesem Falle sind es »snatches of old songs« (ebd.), die eine politische und legitimatorische Funktion innehaben, im *Herrn der Ringe* erfüllen »rhymes of old days« (LotR 847) dieselbe Funktion. Schauen wir uns die Verse der Seestädter etwas genauer an:

The King beneath the mountains,
The King of carven stone,
The lord of silver fountains
Shall come into his own!

His crown shall be upholden,
His harp shall be restrung,
His halls shall echo golden
To songs of yore re-sung.

The woods shall wave on mountains
And grass beneath the sun;
His wealth shall flow in fountains
And the rivers golden run.

The streams shall run in gladness,
The lakes shall shine and burn,
All sorrow fail and sadness
At the Mountain-king's return! (H 178)

Das Erste, was bei einer Lektüre unter Berücksichtigung der obigen Ausführungen ins Auge fällt, ist die Tatsache, dass die metrische Struktur dieses Liedes ähnlich den bereits oben analysierten Zwergengedichten einer gebräuchlichen Volksliedform entspricht (s.o.): Wir haben es hier mit einem dreihebigen Jambus (u - u - u - u) und Kreuzreim (ABAB) zu tun.

An dieser Stelle soll jedoch das Augenmerk auf die gesellschaftlich-politische Funktion des Seestadtliedes gerichtet werden: So artikulieren die Seestädter unter Bezugnahme auf eine historisch-mythologische Vergangenheit ihre Hoffnung auf die Wiederherstellung eines ehemaligen Herrschaftszustandes: Bereits die erste Strophe konzentriert den Gehalt des Liedes, wird hier doch in drei Versen das Bild eines ins Heroische gesteigerten Herrschers gezeichnet, der mit drei unterschiedlichen Titelvarianten porträtiert wird (König unter dem Berg, König des geschliffenen Steins, Herr der silbernen Quellen), und dessen Rückkehr man sehnlichst erwartet. Durch die Beschwörung einer historischen Herrscherpersönlichkeit wird eine Verbindung zwischen der (Kunst-)Welt der Lieder und der Gegenwart der Sänger/Zuhörer hergestellt.

Die Tatsache, dass das Volk zwar die Heimkehr des so vehement gepriesenen Königs fordert, es bei der Generationenfolge der Herrscher jedoch nicht allzu genau nimmt, wird vom Erzähler scharfzüngig kommentiert und das Pathos der Verse damit ironisch gebrochen: »that it was Thror's grandson not Thror himself that had come back did not bother them at all« (ebd.). Das zentrale politische Begehren, das mit diesem Lied artikuliert wird, nämlich die prophetische Antizipation einer erwünschten Zukunft, manifestiert sich u. a. durch die Dominanz des Verbs ›shall‹. So findet das in die Zukunft gerichtete Verb in 16 Versen ganze achtmal Verwendung, und ermöglicht auf diese Weise die sprachliche Vorwegnahme des ersehnten Herrschaftszustandes.

Wichtig ist für unser Verständnis der politisch-gesellschaftlichen Konnotationen des Liedes, dass die Seestädter mit ihrem lyrischen Herrscherlob auch handfeste Ansprüche am erwarteten zukünftigen Wohlstand artikulieren: So erhoffen sie sich, dass der Reichtum des neuen/alten Königs wortwörtlich in Strömen fließen möge, wobei das Lied mehr als deutlich macht, dass zumindest ein Teil dieses Wohlstands auch seinen Weg nach Seestadt finden. Auch der Erzählkommentar betont die ökonomischen Interessen der Seestädter, die mithilfe von Liedern ihren Ausdruck finden:

> Some of the songs were old ones; but some of them where quite new and spoke confidently of the sudden death of the dragon and of cargoes of rich presents coming down the river to Lake-town.
>
> (179)

Darüber hinaus bestätigt diese Textpassage das Vorhandensein einer gemeinsamen Liedtradition, auf die zur Bewältigung aktueller Probleme zurückgegriffen werden kann. Gleichermaßen erfahren wir, dass die Seestädter auch neue Lieder anstimmen, um ihre Wünsche öffentlich kundzutun. Lyrik wird hier in Form von Herrscherpanegyrik funktionalisiert, ein Aspekt, der auch in Bezug auf die Zwergenlieder von Bedeutung ist (s.u.).

Der Umgang der Seestädter mit ihrer poetischen Überlieferung ist für unser Verständnis des Liedgebrauchs im *Hobbit* höchst aufschlussreich. Dies wird anschaulich, wenn wir uns näher mit Bilbo und der ›Lücke‹ innerhalb der Liedtradition auseinandersetzen, die durch seine Anwesenheit zutage tritt. So erfahren wir, dass die Seestädter es als ein ungeahntes Kuriosum ansehen, dass ein Hobbit den zurückkehrenden König begleitet, findet sich in der poetischen Volksüberlieferung doch nicht ein einziger Hinweis auf diesen unerwarteten Gast (»no songs had alluded to him even in the obscurest way« ebd.). Hierdurch wird ersichtlich, dass Lieder auch im *Hobbit* zwischen Vergangenheit und Gegenwart prophetisch vermitteln (»songs of yore re-sung«; 178), Sinnstiftung leisten und somit eine gesellschaftliche Deutungsfunktion ausüben.

Dabei ist aufgrund der Dominanz der poetischen Überlieferung grundsätzlich alles, was nicht in ihr erscheint, verdächtig. Die orale Liedtradition ist immer schon vorher da. Individuen werden an ihr gemessen und müssen sich in sie einfügen. Da dies bei Bilbo nicht der Fall ist, ist seine Legitimation vehement in Frage gestellt. Eine solche Problematik ist auch für die Protagonisten des

Julian Eilmann

Herrn der Ringe von Bedeutung. Dort steht der designierte König Aragorn vor der Herausforderung, seine Taten mit der prophetischen Liedtradition in Übereinstimmung zu bringen (vgl. Lieder 247f).

Das Seestadtlied ist jedoch nicht der einzige lyrische Text im *Hobbit*, der eine panegyrische Funktion erfüllt. Auch im Zwergenlied *Under the Mountain dark and tall* (H 235f) kommen panegyrische Topoi zur Anwendung.

Als eine Gattung der Rhetorik, die seit der römischen Kaiserzeit besondere Bedeutung erhielt, bezeichnet Panegyrik die prahlende öffentliche Dichtung, das festliche Herrscherlob und die poetische Huldigung (vgl. Weidhase, *Panegyrikus* 339). Das Zwergenlied *Under the Mountain dark and tall* (H 235f) weist dieselbe Struktur auf wie die oben analysierte Zwergenlyrik (vierzeilige Strophen, alternierender Jambus mit vier Hebungen, Reimschema AABA, Binnenreim im dritten Vers), was deutlich macht, dass es sich auch in diesem Falle um eine typische Volksliedstrophe aus dem Liedfundus der Zwerge handelt.

An diese Stelle sind jedoch die panegyrischen Topoi entscheidend, die hier zur Anwendung kommen. So wird ähnlich dem Seestadtlied die Rückkehr des rechtmäßigen Königs proklamiert (»The king has come unto his hall!«; 235, »The mountain throne once more is freed!«; 236), die immense kriegerische Macht Thorins gepriesen und gleich zweimal der Sieg über seinen Erzfeind besonders herausgestellt (»His foe is dead, the Worm of Dread«; 235, »The Worm of Dread is slain and dead,/ And ever so our foes shall fall!«; 236). Hinzu kommt die additive Aufzählung der königlichen Macht als Ausdruck eines einschüchternden Machtpotentials (»The sword is sharp, the spear is long,/ The arrow swift, the Gate is strong;/ The heart is bold that looks on gold«; 235).

Die poetische Huldigung Thorins beschränkt sich jedoch nicht allein auf die Hervorhebung seiner militärischen Wehrhaftigkeit. Auch die Beschenkung derjenigen, die dem König zu Diensten sind, wird als ausgewiesene königliche Qualität hervorgehoben (»Here at the gates the king awaits,/ His hands are rich with gems and gold.«; 236).

Resümieren wir die Aspekte, die im Zwergenlied zur Huldigung königlicher Autorität herangezogen werden, dann lässt sich feststellen, dass hier ein Großteil der klassischen panegyrischen Topoi Verwendung finden: Verkündigung der Rechtmäßigkeit des königlichen Machtanspruchs, Betonung der kriegerischen Machtfülle und Lob der fürstlichen Freigiebigkeit (vgl. Mause 496).

Im Handlungszusammenhang wird somit deutlich, dass die Funktion des Liedes darin besteht, die Zwergengemeinschaft in einer Situation, in der der eigene politische Machtanspruch von anderen Völkern in Frage gestellt ist, zu stärken.

Gelegenheitslyrik im *Hobbit*

Wie bereits oben festgestellt wurde, singen und dichten die Figuren im *Hobbit* zu vielfältigen Anlässen und Gelegenheiten. Dabei hat die Lyrik nahezu ausnahmslos einen unmittelbaren Situationsbezug.[1] Was ist das Charakteristische an dieser lyrischen Gattung, die von der Literaturwissenschaft als Gelegenheits- bzw. Gebrauchslyrik bezeichnet wird?

Nach Einschätzung der Forschung handelt es sich bei Gelegenheitsdichtung um eine stark kontext- und anlassgebundene Dichtung, bei der intra- und extratextuelle Wirklichkeit in hohem Maße übereinstimmen (vgl. Segebrecht 688). In gleichem Maße besteht eine weitgehende Identität zwischen dem lyrischem Ich/Inhalt und dem Sprecher/Sänger, was eine Einschränkung des fiktionalen Gehalts der Dichtung, aber auch eine höhere alltagspraktische Anwendbarkeit zur Folge hat. Künstlerisch oft von nachrangiger Bedeutung ist für die Gattung weiterhin charakteristisch, dass oftmals Aktualisierungen tradierter Liedformen vorgenommen werden (vgl. Trost 171f). Insgesamt handelt es sich bei einem Lied dieses Typus um eine Dichtung für einen speziellen, zeitlich datierbaren Anlass.

Meine Analyse des Liedgebrauchs im *Herrn der Ringe* hat gezeigt, in welch großem Maße die Romanfiguren auf Mechanismen zurückgreifen, die bei der Produktion von Gelegenheitslyrik zur Anwendung kommen (vgl. *Lieder* 253-256). »I feel I could sing, if I knew the right song for the occasion« (LotR 220), wünscht sich Pippin im *Herrn der Ringe*, um einer besonderen Situation poetischen Ausdruck zu verleihen.

Tolkien hat selbst darauf hingewiesen, dass die Verse im *Herrn der Ringe* alle ›dramatisch‹ seien, d.h. im situativen Kontext und in Bezug auf die jeweilige Figur interpretiert werden müssen:

> My 'poetry' has received little praise – comment even by some admirers being as often as not contemptuous ... Perhaps largely because in the contemporary atmosphere – in which 'poetry' must only reflect one's personal agonies of mind or soul, and exterior things are only valued by one's own 'reactions' – it seems hardly ever recognised that the verses in The L.R. are all dramatic: they do not express the poor old professor's soul-searchings, but are fitted in style and contents to the characters in the story that sing or recite them, and to the situations in it. (L 396)

---

[1] Als Beispiele seien die Lieder *Chip the glasses and crack the plates!* (H 12f), *Clap! Snap! the black crack!* (56ff), *Fifteen birds in five firtrees* (97), *Lazy Lob and crazy Cob* (145), *Roll – roll – roll – roll* (165) und *Down the swift dark stream you go* (166) genannt, in denen Zwerge, Goblins, Hobbits und Elben aktuelle Ereignisse lyrisch kommentieren.

Tolkiens Einschätzung seiner Lyrik trifft auch auf den *Hobbit* zu, denn auch dort sind die Gedichte in das dramatische Geschehen eingebunden und geben Auskunft über die Stimmung der Protagonisten. Der personale und situative Bezugsrahmen, die »Okkasionalität« (Drux 655) der Gedichte ist dabei, wie oben ausgeführt, charakteristisch für Gelegenheitslyrik und wird bereits am ersten Lied des Romans deutlich.

So stimmen die Zwerge nach Beenden ihres Mahls ein Lied an, das regelrecht als lyrische Antwort auf Bilbos vorangegangene Warnungen und Bitten (»please be carefull! and please, don't trouble! I can manage.« H 12) verstanden werden kann. Ihre spöttische Verhöhnung des Gastgebers verweist auf die eindeutige Übereinstimmung von intra- und extratextueller Wirklichkeit. Dass die Zwerge tatsächlich von sich und niemand anderem singen, wird nicht zuletzt daran deutlich, dass Bilbo als Adressat des Liedes gleich zweimal im Text erwähnt wird (»That's what Bilbo Baggins hates!«; 13). Auch der Erzählkommentar weist auf den situativen Kontext des Liedes hin: »And of course they did none of these dreadful things« (ebd.).

Ein weiteres Beispiel für diesen poetischen »Gestus der Ereignisnähe« (Kellermann 50f) im *Hobbit* sind Bilbos Spinnenlieder. Die Funktionalisierung der Lieder für einen aktuellen Anlass wird vom Erzähler explizit erwähnt: »then dancing among the trees he began to sing a song to infuriate them and bring them all after him« (H 144). Auch der Inhalt der zwei im Text wiedergegeben Lieder lässt keinen Zweifel daran, dass Bilbo gegenwärtiges Geschehen in seinen improvisierten Liedern reflektiert und einen ausdrücklichen Zweck verfolgt, nämlich die Spinnen in Rage zu versetzen. In einer weiteren Textbemerkung kommt nicht nur der Stegreifcharakter der Verse zum Ausdruck, es wird auch die viel grundlegendere Frage aufgeworfen, wie es den Protagonisten möglich ist, in einem existenziell bedrohlichen Moment lyrisch zu improvisieren: »Not very good perhaps, but then you must remember that he had to make it up himself, on the spur of a very awkward moment« (145). Die Fähigkeit, im Angesicht des Todes zu dichten, stellt ein bemerkenswertes Charakteristikum vieler Tolkien-Figuren dar (vgl. *Lieder* 252).

Auch die Gesänge der Bruchtal-Elben sind in diesem Zusammenhang aufschlussreich, insbesondere für unser Verständnis der oben angesprochenen Irritation, die für die Rezeption des Romans konstitutiv ist und die in hohem Maße durch die elbischen Lieder bedingt wird. Nichts charakterisiert die albernen, feenhaften Elben des *Hobbit* so deutlich wie ihre Lyrik: »Just then there came a burst of song like laughter in the trees ... pretty fair nonsense I daresey you think it« (H 45f).

Hier berührt sich die klassische britische Elbentradition, wie wir sie bei Drayton und Shakespeare vorgeprägt finden, mit den erhabenen Eldar von Tolkiens Mythologie (vgl. HH I 120). In einem Kinderbuch können Elben problemlos drollige Spottlieder (H 45f) und weinselige Trinklieder (165) zu Besten geben, genauso wie es möglich ist, dass Goblins metrisch anspruchsvolle Lieder anstimmen. Die Figuren der beiden Hobbit-Romane sind eben nur bedingt identisch (vgl. Brückner 106). Angesichts des Ungleichgewichts von Tolkiens Darstellung der Elben ist John Rateliff sicherlich zuzustimmen, wenn er in Bezug auf die Bruchtal-Elben des *Hobbit* zu der Einschätzung gelangt: »the elves of the valley echo the worst excesses of Edwardian and Georgian fairy sentimentally« (HH I 120).

Die Klassifikation der Elbenpoesie als »pretty fair nonsense« (H 45) wird durch die Analyse ihrer metrischen Struktur erhärtet. So hat sich Tolkien in diesem Falle für einen Amphibrachys (u – u u – u) entschieden, einen dreisilbigen Versfuß klassischer Herkunft, der häufig in Marsch- und Schlachtliedern sowie in Spottliedern Verwendung findet. Hierdurch entsteht ein Versmaß, das Bewegung erzeugt und fließendes Sprechen bzw. Gesang begünstigt. Tolkien verwendet folglich ein Versmaß, das dem spöttischen Tonfall der Szene eine passende metrische Struktur gibt.[2]

Darüber hinaus wird deutlich, dass die Elbenlieder für unser Verständnis von Gelegenheitslyrik und kollektiver Liedtradition im *Hobbit* bedeutsam sind. So poetisieren die Elben in ihren Gesängen aktuelles Geschehen und richten ihr Lied direkt an die Reisegemeinschaft, die sowohl Gegenstand als auch Publikum des Liedes darstellt:

> What brings Mister Baggins
> And Balin and Dwalin
> down into the valley
> In June
> ha! ha! (46)

Auch bei Bilbos Rückkehr nach Bruchtal stellen die elbischen Sänger einen eindeutigen Situationsbezug her, besingen den Tod des Drachen Smaug und greifen auf dieselbe metrische Liedstruktur zurück, sodass beide Lieder große formale Übereinstimmungen aufweisen[3]:

> The dragon is withered,
> His bones are now crumbled;
> His armour is shivered,
> His splendour is humbled! (265)

---

2   Bei der Analyse der metrischen Struktur der Elbenlieder bin ich Jens Burkert zu Dank verpflichtet, der mir wichtige Hinweise zur Klassifikation der Verse geliefert hat.
3   Auch der Erzähler verweist auf die Ähnlichkeiten der beiden Lieder: »Bilbo heard the elves ... burst into a song of much the same kind as before« (H 265).

Ähnlich den Zwergen scheinen die Bruchtal-Elben demnach über tradierte, populäre Liedformen zu verfügen, derer man sich zu gegebenem Anlass bedienen kann. Es handelt sich um einen spezifischen Liedtypus, der zum Zwecke poetischer und gesellschaftlicher Kommunikation aktualisiert werden kann.

In der narrativen Struktur des Romans üben die Elbenlieder darüber hinaus eine Klammerfunktion aus: Sie markieren und akzentuieren Beginn und Ende der gefahrvollen Reise. Der Untertitel des Romans *There and Back Again* spiegelt sich somit auch in der Anordnung der Lyrik. Die Verwendung einer bereits bekannten Liedstruktur erhöht den Wiedererkennungsfaktor für den Leser. Auch für ihn schließt sich der begonnene Kreis der Reise und des Romans.

Die lyrische Exposition des Romans

Far over the misty mountains cold (H 14f), das zweite Lied, das im Roman angestimmt wird, ist auch eines der wichtigsten, denn es erfüllt eine wichtige erzähltechnische Funktion innerhalb des Romans. Die Enthüllung der Zwergenmission findet nicht innerhalb des Prosatextes, sondern mithilfe dieses Liedes statt. Vorher wird nur ein obskures »business« (12) erwähnt, so dass der Leser ähnlich der Hauptfigur bis zur Anstimmung des Liedes im Unklaren über das wahre Anliegen der unerwarteten Gäste bleibt, eine Erzählstrategie, die zum Spannungsaufbau beiträgt.

Mit ihrem Lied, das die drei Zeitebenen Vergangenheit (Was hat uns hergebracht?), Gegenwart (Wer sind wir?) und Zukunft (Was sind unsere Ziele?) berührt, stellen die Protagonisten sich, ihre Geschichte und ihre selbstgewählte Aufgabe vor. Gleichzeitig geht das Anstimmen der Verse mit einer auffallenden Verlagerung des Tonfalls einher. Von der fröhlichen Ausgelassenheit der bisherigen Szene mit ihren stark komödiantischen Elementen (Einführung der Zwerge) geht die Stimmung über zu einer dunklen und gefährlichen Atmosphäre.

Das Zwergenlied vermittelt zwischen Innen und Außen, vertrauter Heimat und abenteuerlicher Fremde und initiiert maßgeblich den Bildungsweg des Titelhelden, was u.a. daran deutlich wird, dass bezeichnenderweise die Musik und der Gesang die nächtliche Dunkelheit in das Zimmer hereinholen (vgl. 14). Tolkien legt sehr viel Wert darauf, den appellativen Charakter des Liedes für Bilbo hervorzuheben, und schildert in einer bemerkenswerten Passage Bilbos visionäre Schau unter dem Einfluss der zwergischen Poesie und Musik (vgl. 15f). An dieser Angelstelle des Romans ist der Beginn des persönlichen Reifeprozesses der Titelfigur zu verorten.

Für die expositorische Funktion des Liedes innerhalb des Romans ist im hohen Maße sein Aufbau ausschlaggebend. Wie bereits oben erwähnt, handelt es sich bei *Far over the misty mountains cold* (14f) um ein Lied mit einer typischen Volksliedstrophe aus dem Liedfundus der Zwerge. Strukturiert werden die zehn Strophen des Liedes durch die dreimalige Wiederholung des einstrophigen Titel gebenden Refrains.⁴ Diese Refrains umschließen jeweils zwei Erzählblöcke, wodurch eine pointierte, auf Spannungssteigerung ausgerichtete Erzählung entsteht.

Wie sieht der Strophenaufbau im Detail aus? Das Lied beginnt mit einem Refrain, der das für Lied und Roman leitmotivische »Far over the misty mountains cold« einführt. Hieran schließen sich drei Strophen zum historisch-mythologischen Hintergrund der Handlung an. Die Sänger zeichnen das glanzvolles Bild eines vergangenen goldenen Zeitalters und beschwören die Glorie der »dwarves of yore« (14). Durch einen Bezug zur Geschichte von Thingol und dem Nauglamír (ebd.) stellt Tolkien eine intertextuelle Verbindung zum Hintergrund seiner Mythologie her.

Auf diesen Erzählblock folgen ein weiterer Refrain und anschließend vier Strophen zur direkten Vorgeschichte der Romanhandlung. Hier wird der Untergang des Zwergenreiches unter dem Berg in schillernden Farben ausgemalt (vgl. auch Brückner 105). Formal und inhaltlich abgerundet wird das Lied durch einen finalen Refrain.

Die Refrainstrophe »Far over the misty mountains cold« (H 14) ist jedoch nicht nur für die strukturelle Rahmung des Liedes entscheidend. Darüber hinaus findet innerhalb der Refrains auch eine dreifache inhaltliche Steigerung statt. So folgt auf die jeweils identischen ersten drei Verse in jeder Refrainstrophe ein unterschiedlicher letzter Vers. Dass hier eine Zunahme an emotionaler Eindringlichkeit und eine Präzisierung der Mission stattfinden, wird ersichtlich, wenn man diese drei Verse miteinander vergleicht:

> To seek the pale enchanted gold. (ebd.)
> To claim our long-forgotten gold. (15)
> To win our harps and gold from him! (ebd.)

Aus dem vagen Suchen (seek) des ersten Refrains wird ein Einklagen bzw. Fordern im zweiten Refrain (claim), gefolgt schließlich von einem emphatischen Zurückgewinnen (win) im letzten Vers des Liedes. Die Frage, was zu tun ist, nämlich die Harfen und das Gold der Zwerge vom Drachen Smaug zurückzugewinnen, wird innerhalb des Liedes immer weiter entfaltet und die persönliche Anteilnahme und Motivation der Sänger (»our harps and gold«; ebd.) stärker in den Vordergrund gerückt. Erstaunlich ist, dass die Harfen für die Sänger offensichtlich einen bedeutenden Wert darstellen und im letzten Vers an exponierter Stelle Erwähnung finden und somit noch vor dem Gold genannt werden.

---

4   Far over the misty mountains cold/ To dungeons deep and caverns old/ We must away ere break of day/ To seek the pale enchanted gold. (H 14)

Weiterhin ist es bezeichnend, dass der Antagonist der Zwerge das ganze Lied über namenlos bleibt. Zwar wird bereits in der achten Strophe ein Drache als Verheerer des Zwergenreiches erwähnt, aber auch im letzten Vers, der sich explizit auf einen Widersacher bezieht (»To win ... from him!«; H 15), wird dieser nicht namentlich genannt. Die verhasste Nemesis wird zwar lyrisch beschworen, ihr Name allerdings bewusst nicht ausgesprochen, was dem sinnbildhaften Charakter Smaugs als Geißel und Fluch der Zwerge durchaus angemessen erscheint.

Dass das Lied offensichtlich aus einem kollektiven Liedfundus stammt, wird sowohl aus dem oben analysierten volksliedhaften Metrum deutlich, als auch daran, dass sein Text veränderlich ist. So murmelt Thorin am Ende des ersten Kapitels vor dem Einschlafen den Refrain des Zwergenliedes und verändert dabei marginal den Text: Während die Zwerge im zweiten Refrain des Liedes singen »To claim our long-forgotten gold.« (ebd.), variiert Thorin diese Verse zu den Worten »To find our long-forgotten gold.« (26). Zwar handelt es sich hierbei nur um eine kleine Veränderung, die im Erzählzusammenhang auch Thorins fortgeschrittener Müdigkeit geschuldet sein kann.

Nichtsdestotrotz ist dies ein Beispiel für die Veränderlichkeit der oralen Liedtraditionen Mittelerdes. Indem Thorin den Refrain des für den Roman so bedeutsamen Zwergenliedes noch einmal anstimmt, wird die Exposition abgeschlossen, sodass die Handlung sich im Folgenden entfalten kann.

Zusammenfassung

Beim Thema Lyrik handelt es sich um einen Forschungsgegenstand mit hohem Erkenntniswert für die Tolkien-Forschung, so dass bei einer systematischen Bearbeitung dieses Bereiches noch viele Ergebnisse zu Tolkiens Werk zu erwarten sind. Meine ursprüngliche Arbeitshypothese, dass der Liedgebrauch im *Hobbit* sich grundlegend vom *Herrn der Ringe* unterscheidet, musste revidiert werden, da auch die Lyrik im *Hobbit* von jener für die Mittelerde-Mythologie bezeichnenden Spannung zwischen kollektiver Liedtradition und individueller Kunstschöpfung geprägt ist. Die Irritation hinsichtlich des Liedgebrauchs wird begründet durch den Gegensatz von mythologischem Werkkontext und märchenhaftem Kinderbuch-Charakter des *Hobbit*.

Die Zwergenlieder des Romans weisen eine übereinstimmende typische Volksliedstruktur auf und verweisen so auf die Verwurzelung in einem kollektiven Liedfundus. Lieder werden darüber hinaus in Form von Gelegenheitslyrik verwendet und können mithilfe des Prinzips der Kontrafaktur aktualisiert und dem situativen Kontext angepasst werden. Indem im *Herrn der Ringe* Bezug auf Gedichte des *Hobbit* genommen wird, stellt Tolkien intertextuelle Bezüge zwischen seinen beiden Romanen her.

Wie am Beispiel des Seestadtliedes deutlich gemacht werden konnte, werden Verse im *Hobbit* für politische bzw. wirtschaftliche Zwecke funktionalisiert und leisten damit Sinnstiftung. Weiterhin kommen Topoi der Herrscherpanegyrik zur Anwendung. Darüber hinaus erfüllt Poesie erzähltechnische Funktionen im Roman, sie dient, wie die Elbenlieder als narrative Erzählklammer bzw. hat sogar expositorische Qualitäten.

Bibliographie

Anderson, Douglas A. *The Annotated Hobbit*. London: Unwin Hyman, 1988

Brückner, Patrick. »Das Drachenmotiv bei Tolkien als poetologisches Konzept zur Genese des Episch-Historischen«. *Hither Shore 4* (2007): 99-118

Delbrück, Hansgerd. »Kontrafaktur«. *Metzler Literatur Lexikon. Begriffe und Definitionen*. Hg. Günther u. Irmgard Schweikle. Stuttgart: Metzler, ²1990: 250

Drux, Rudolf. »Gelegenheitsgedicht«. *Historisches Wörterbuch der Rhetorik*. Hg. Gert Ueding. Bd. 3. Tübingen: Max Niemeyer, 1996: 653-667

Eilmann, Julian. »Das Lied bin ich. Lieder, Poesie und Musik in J.R.R. Tolkiens Mittelerde-Mythologie«. *Hither Shore 2* (2005): 105-135

---. »Lieder und Poesie als Teil der kulturellen Kommunikation Mittelerdes«. *Hither Shore 3* (2006): 246-259

Kellermann, Karina: *Abschied vom ›historischen Volkslied‹. Studien zu Funktion, Ästhetik und Publizität der Gattung historisch-politische Ereignisdichtung*. Tübingen: Max Niemeyer, 2000

Mause, Michael. »Panegyrik«. *Historisches Wörterbuch der Rhetorik*. Hg. Gert Ueding. Bd. 6. Tübingen: Max Niemeyer 2003: 495-501

Moseley, Charles: *J.R.R. Tolkien*. Plymouth: Northcote House, 1997

Müller, Jan-Dirk. »Gebrauchsliteratur«. *Historisches Wörterbuch der Rhetorik*. Hg. Gert Ueding. Bd. 3. Tübingen: Max Niemeyer 1996: 587-605

Neureuter, Hans Peter. »Volksliedstrophe«. *Reallexikon der deutschen Literaturwissenschaft*. Bd. 3. Hg. Jan-Dirk Müller u.a. Berlin: Walter de Gruyter, 2003: 797-799

Rateliff, John D. *The History of The Hobbit*. 2 Bde. London: HarperCollins, 2007

Rosebury, Brian: *Tolkien. A critical Assessment*. New York: St. Martin's Press, 1992

Schulz, Armin. »Volkslied«. *Reallexikon der deutschen Literaturwissenschaft*. Bd. 3. Hg. Jan-Dirk Müller u. a. Berlin: Walter de Gruyter, 2003: 794-797

Segebrecht, Wulf. »Gelegenheitsgedicht«. *Reallexikon der deutschen Literaturwissenschaft*. Bd. 1. Hg. Klaus Weimar u. a. Berlin: Walter de Gruyter, 1997: 688-691

Tolkien, J.R.R. *The Hobbit or there and back again*. Boston, New York: Houghton Mifflin 1996

---. *The Lord of the Rings*. London: HarperCollins, 1995

---. *The Letters of J.R.R. Tolkien*. Hg. Humphrey Carpenter. London: HarperCollins, 1981

Trost, Karl. »Gelegenheitsdichtung«. *Metztler Literatur Lexikon. Begriffe und Definitionen.* Hg. Günther u. Irmgard Schweikle. Stuttgart: Metzler, ²1990: 171f

Weidhase, Helmut. »Volkslied«. *Metztler Literatur Lexikon. Begriffe und Definitionen.* Hg. Günther u. Irmgard Schweikle. Stuttgart: Metzler, ²1990: 492f

---. »Panegyrikus«. *Metztler Literatur Lexikon. Begriffe und Definitionen.* Hg. Günther u. Irmgard Schweikle. Stuttgart: Metzler, ²1990: 339

Sein Anwesen lag zwischen dem Carrock und dem Düsterwald – bevölkert von zahlreichen Tieren der verschiedensten Arten, manche so eigenartig wie er selbst ...

Sehen und (nicht) gesehen werden
Augen als Schutz und Bedrohung im *Hobbit*

Christian Weichmann (Braunschweig)

Dieser Artikel untersucht die Bedeutung von Augen und Gesichtssinn in *The Hobbit*, denn dies ist ein Motiv und Gestaltungsmittel, das Tolkien gerade in dieser Geschichte immer wieder verwendet. Das Nicht-gesehen-werden aufgrund des Ringes und die daraus erwachsenden Folgen sind ein recht offensichtliches Thema des Buches. Aber dies ist nicht der einzige Punkt, an dem das Sehen und das Gesehen-werden beziehungsweise die Augen eine wichtige Rolle spielen. Andere Aspekte sind nicht unwichtiger, aber oft leichter zu übersehen.

Dunkle Geschäfte

Zunächst will ich auf eine Stelle hinweisen, die man zwar leicht überliest, die aber, wenn man darüber nachdenkt, zunächst sehr seltsam erscheint. Im ersten Kapitel antworten die Zwerge, als Bilbo vorschlägt, etwas Licht zu machen, unisono[1]: »We like the dark... Dark for dark business!« (H 46).

Es ist doch verwunderlich, dass die Zwerge ihre Unternehmung als »dunkles Geschäft« bezeichnen. Denn eigentlich ist es ja kein im üblichen Sinne dieses Ausdrucks geheimes, zweifelhaftes oder sogar illegales Geschäft, zumindest aus der Sicht der Zwerge.

Natürlich ist es sinnvoll, den Plan vor Smaug geheim zu halten, aber die Wahrscheinlichkeit, dass dieser Spione im Auenland hätte, die sie hier beobachten könnten, ist eher gering. Eventuell sollte die Reise auch vor anderen Zwergen geheim gehalten werden, um im Falle eines Misserfolgs den Spott zu vermeiden.

Und was die Rechtmäßigkeit angeht, so waren sie ja völlig davon überzeugt, dass der Schatz und der Berg ihnen gehören und dass Smaug ein Räuber sei, der auch zu Recht getötet werden könnte.

Was also könnte »dark business« hier bedeuten? Wenn man die gesamte Geschichte durchliest, ergibt sich im Rückblick eine interessante und viel wörtlichere Deutung dieses Ausdrucks. Nämlich dass es sich um ein Unternehmen

---

[1] Und dieser Ausdruck scheint schon von der frühesten Entwicklung des *Hobbit* an da gewesen zu sein, denn er findet sich schon im „Pryftan Fragment" (HH I 7), wie Rateliff die ältesten überlebenden Manuskriptseiten des *Hobbit* nennt.

handelt, das wesentlich im Dunklen stattfindet. Ein Großteil der wichtigen Szenen spielt sich unterirdisch oder in der Nacht ab, teilweise dann doch künstlich erleuchtet, teilweise aber auch in weitgehender oder völliger Dunkelheit.[2]

Das beginnt mit der Unexpected Party (H 36-59), die sich weit in die Nacht hineinzieht und nach der oben zitierten Stelle noch eine Weile ohne Licht auskommt.

Das Zusammentreffen mit den Trollen findet dann in einer regnerischen Nacht statt, in der es den Zwergen nicht gelingt, Feuer zu machen (H 68). Und es ist gerade das Licht des Feuers der Trolle, das Bilbo und die Zwerge anlockt. Die Zwerge zumindest haben nicht viel davon, denn sie landen in dunklen Säcken, in denen sie die Nacht verbringen, bis sie von Gandalf und dem zurückkehrenden Licht des Tages gerettet werden.

Als nächstes ist natürlich die gesamte Goblin-Gollum-Geschichte unterirdisch und zumindest in dem Teil, in dem Bilbo allein ist (nach seiner Ohnmacht), herrscht Dunkelheit: »When Bilbo opened his eyes, he wondered if he had; for it was just as dark as with them shut« (H 115). Zwar bekommt er etwas Licht, nachdem er Stich hervorgeholt hat, das aufgrund der Nähe der Orks leuchtet, aber als er an Gollums See ankommt, reicht das Licht nicht mehr, um festzustellen, in was er da hinein getreten ist, denn »[t]he sword was hardly shining at all« (H 117). Dies ist umso erstaunlicher, als dass gerade diese Szene für viele Leser sehr optisch wirkt und viel illustriert wird.

Dabei ist Tolkiens Wiedergabe dieser Tatsache gemischt gelungen. Bilbos[3] Beschreibung Gollums beschränkt sich weitgehend auf die Dinge, die er in der Dunkelheit wahrnehmen konnte:

> ... old Gollum, a small slimy creature... as dark as darkness, except for two big round pale eyes in his thin face... He paddled it with large feet dangling ... (H 118-119)

Nur bei den »long fingers« (H 119) und dem »long webby foot« (H 124) ist man sich nicht sicher, ob Bilbo diese wirklich so gut gesehen oder sich nur eingebildet oder nach späteren Beschreibungen ergänzt hat. Denn Gollum kommt ihm zwar recht nah, aber ob die Beleuchtung für solche Details ausreicht, kann bezweifelt werden. Und außerdem wird gerade in Zusammenhang mit Gollum vieles berichtet, was Bilbo nicht so genau wissen konnte, wie Gollums Ess- und Jagdgewohnheiten oder seine Insel, von der es später explizit heißt »his island, of which Bilbo knew nothing« (H 127).

---

2 Es muss aber auch dazu gesagt werden, dass dies nicht immer sehr deutlich gemacht wird, so dass es dem Leser leicht entgehen kann. Häufig lässt sich die Tatsache absoluter Dunkelheit nur von den Beschreibungen im Umfeld der entsprechenden Stelle ableiten.

3 Bilbo hier als Autor des dem *Hobbit* zugrunde liegenden Tagebuchs und einzige Person, die Gollum vor dem Ringkrieg kannte.

Zusätzlich betont Tolkien immer wieder, dass es dort dunkel ist[4]: So als er von Fischen berichtet, deren »eyes grew bigger and bigger and bigger from trying to *see in the blackness*« (H 118), und anderen Bewohnern, die von draußen kamen, um sich »in the dark« (H118) zurückzuziehen. Auch konnte Bilbo Gollum auf seiner Insel nicht sehen, dieser aber mit seinen speziell angepassten Augen ihn schon. Erst als Gollum deutlich näher kommt, sieht Bilbo ihn.

Später, als es um Gollums Rätselvorliebe geht, wird erklärt, dass Rätsel das einzige Spiel war, das er gespielt habe, bevor er vertrieben wurde und »crept ... down, into *the dark* under the mountains« (H 121). Und bei Gollums dritten Rätsel, dessen Lösung ja »Dark!« (H 123) ist, wird betont, dass es für Bilbo auch deshalb einfach war, weil »the answer was all round him« (H 123). Vor Bilbos letzter Frage kehrt Gollum nicht in sein Boot zurück, das er in der Hoffnung, Bilbo könne seine Frage nicht beantworten, zuvor verlassen hatte, sondern »sat down in the *dark* by Bilbo« (H 125).

Als Gollum seinen Ring holen will, spricht er mit sich selbst, wie er es »in the endless *dark* days« schon oft getan hatte. Dann wird sein Umgang mit dem Ring beschrieben, mit dem er wieder »dark passages« (H 128) entlang kroch und sich selbst in Gebiete wagte, die mit Fackeln erleuchtet waren und die »made his eyes blink and smart« (H 128). (Das heißt, seine Augen vertragen keine Helligkeit mehr. Da seine Augen im Moment aber keine Probleme haben, muss es dunkel sein. Aber das ist natürlich nur ein indirekter Hinweis.) Jedenfalls verlässt er Bilbo und verschwindet »off into the dark« (H 128).

Als Gollum dann an dem auf dem Boden liegenden Bilbo vorbei rennt, wundert sich dieser, denn »Gollum could see in the *dark*« (H 132). Zum Abschluss folgt dann noch Bilbos Sprung über Gollum, »a leap in the dark« (H 133).

Andererseits werden Gollums Bewegungen immer relativ genau beschrieben, so dass der Leser leicht vergisst, dass sie von Bilbo immer nur schemenhaft gesehen werden. Obwohl natürlich meist damit auch Geräusche verbunden sind, die eine bessere Wahrnehmung erlauben.

Die nächste Gefahr, nachdem Bilbo die Höhlen der Goblins hinter sich gebracht hat, droht auch schon wieder, als es Nacht wird. Noch bevor sie Ihr Nachtlager machen wollen, ist es so »dark that he [Bilbo] could only just see Thorin's beard wagging beside him« (H 144). Allerdings wird es wieder heller, bevor die Gesellschaft von den Wargen überrascht und eingekreist wird, denn der »moon was up and was shining into the clearing« (H 144). Und später wird es noch viel heller, nachdem zuerst Gandalf mit Feuer wirft und dann die Goblins das Feuer unter den Bäumen, in die sich Thorin & Co. geflüchtet haben, schüren. Wahrscheinlich hätte der Fürst der Adler sie sonst auch nicht sehen können.

---

4 Die Hervorhebungen in den folgenden Zitaten sind meine.

Wieder richtig dunkel wird es im nicht umsonst so genannten Mirkwood (Düsterwald). Gleich zu Anfang wird gesagt, dass sich ihre Augen erst an die »Dimness« (H 191) gewöhnen mussten, bevor sie etwas in den Wald hineinsehen konnten. Und direkt darauf folgt die poetische Beschreibung des Schicksals eines Lichtstrahls im Düsterwald:

> Occasionally a slender beam of sun that had the luck to slip in through some opening in the leaves far above, and still more luck in not being caught in the tangled boughs and matted twigs beneath, stabbed down thin and bright before them. But this was seldom, and it soon ceased altogether. (H 191)

Dieser Lichtmangel wirkt sich auf die Reisenden aus: »they were sick for a sight of the sun« (H 192), sogar »the dwarves felt it, who ... lived at times for long whiles without the light of the sun« (H 193). Wie wenig Licht vorhanden ist, erkennt man auch aus Bilbos Aussage, als er versucht zu erkennen, ob das 12 yard (knapp 11m) entfernte Boot am anderen Ufer des Nachtwaldflusses angebunden ist: »I can't be sure in this light« (H 195). Und das war tagsüber, als wenigstens noch etwas Licht da war.

> The nights were the worst. It then became pitch-dark – not what you call pitch-dark, but really pitch: so black that you really could see nothing. Bilbo tried flapping his hand in front of his nose, but he could not see it at all. (H 193)

Und auch den Versuch, durch Feuer die Nacht erträglicher zu machen, geben sie bald auf, weil das Feuer zu viele Augen und Schmetterlinge anlockt, so dass sie »sat at night and dozed in the enormous uncanny darkness« (H 194).

Erst vier Tage nach Passieren des Nachtwaldflusses wird es wieder etwas heller, als sie in einen Buchenwald kommen: »the shadow was not so deep. There was a greenish light about them, and in places they could see some distance to either side of the path« (H 199). Es wird allerdings nicht gesagt, ob sich nachts dann auch etwas bessert, und auch tagsüber ist die gefühlte Verbesserung für die Reisenden sehr gering. Als Bilbo noch einmal zwei Tage später von der Eiche herunter klettert, auf der er Ausschau gehalten hatte, »he could not see anything in the gloom below when he got there« (H 201), da es so viel dunkler ist als oben im Sonnenschein.

Und als sie dann den Pfad verlassen, um die nächtlichen Elbenfeste zu erreichen, ist es wieder so dunkel, dass die Zwerge Bilbo, der eingeschlafen ist, nur zufällig finden, als Dori über ihn stolpert. Und als Bilbo die Zwerge dann wirklich verloren hat, gibt er die Suche irgendwann auf, um den nächsten Morgen »with some little light« (H 207) abzuwarten, was wieder völlige Dunkelheit impliziert. Tatsächlich bringt der Morgen nach dem Kampf im Dunklen gegen die Spinne (von der er nur die Augen sieht) wieder »dim grey light of the forest-day« (H 208), aber schon bald entdeckt Bilbo »a place of dense black shadow ahead of him, black even for this shadow, like a patch of midnight that had never been cleared away« (H 209) und dieser Platz der Dunkelheit (hervorgerufen durch Spinnweben) ist genau der Platz, wo die Zwerge gefangen gehalten werden und wo Bilbo seine Befreiungsaktion durchführen muss. Es stellt sich aber heraus, dass dieser Eindruck von Dunkelheit nur von der Ferne her herrscht. Dort angekommen ist es hell genug, dass Bilbo keine Probleme hat, die eingesponnenen Zwerge aus einiger Entfernung zu sehen und sogar einen gezielten Steinwurf durchzuführen.

Auch beim nächsten Abenteuer, der Gefangennahme durch die Elben, sind die Reisenden wieder unterirdisch. Allerdings ist es nicht klar, ob und wie lange sie sich dabei im Dunklen aufhalten, denn die Höhlen des Elbenkönigs sind mit Fackeln erleuchtet, aber Bilbo zieht sich zum Schlafen in die »darkest and remotest corners« (H 225) zurück, und Thorin ist »in a specially deep dark place« (H 226) eingesperrt. Die Beleuchtung ist also sehr unterschiedlich. Und bei ihrer Flucht wird wieder erwähnt, dass die Zwerge sich nicht nur wegen ihrer langen Gefangenschaft, sondern auch wegen der Dunkelheit so ungeschickt anstellen, dass Bilbo sich Sorgen wegen des Lärms macht (H 230).

Die Flucht selbst ist für die Zwerge sehr dunkel, da sie in Fässer eingesperrt sind. Und auch Bilbo stürzt sich mit dem letzten Fass durch die »dark trapdoor« (H 234) in den »dark tunnel« (H 236) darunter.

Der nächste und letzte Ort, an dem Thorin & Co. »dunkle« Abenteuer erleben, ist dann der Einsame Berg. Dieser ist anfangs innen nur von Smaugs Feuer erleuchtet, und die Reisenden wollen natürlich kein Licht machen, um nicht auf sich aufmerksam zu machen. Entsprechend ist auch ihr Eindruck, als sich die Seitentür in den Berg das erste Mal öffnet:

> It seemed as if darkness flowed out like a vapour from the hole in the mountain-side, and deep darkness in which nothing could be seen lay before their eyes. (H 266)

Bilbo ist der einzige, der sich in die vollständige Dunkelheit hinein traut, denn Balin begleitet ihn nur so lange, wie er gerade noch den »faint outline of the door« (H 269) erkennen kann, während Bilbo weitergeht, »till all sign of the door behind had faded away« (H 269). Allerdings bleibt es nicht lange völlig dunkel, denn schon bald zeigt sich »a kind of glow« (H 269), was sich bald als »[t]he glow of Smaug« (H 270) herausstellt. Entsprechend ist die Szene beim Drachen auch beleuchtet.

Der Rest der Nacht wird aber wieder von Dunkelheit beherrscht, nachdem sie vor Smaugs Zorn in den Tunnel flüchten mussten, und am nächsten Mittag begibt sich Bilbo wieder in den Tunnel, der nun noch schneller dunkel ist, da die Tür fast geschlossen ist.

Schließlich werden sie in der nächsten Nacht völlig in der Dunkelheit eingeschlossen. Denn als sie wieder im Tunnel warten und »Darkness grew deeper« (H 287), wird Bilbo nervös und fordert sie auf, die Tür zu schließen, woraufhin sie »in darkness« (H 289) sitzen und »still to darkness« (H 289) erwachen.

Als sie endlich tiefer in die Höhle eindringen, »the darkness was complete, and they were all invisible... There was not a gleam of light« (H 290). Doch nun können sie wieder Licht entzünden, da Smaug nicht zu Hause ist. Entsprechend hilflos ist Bilbo dann, als ihn am anderen Ende der Halle eine Fledermaus überrascht und seine Fackel erlischt, so dass ihn nur noch »wide blackness« (H 294) umgibt. Auch die Tötung Smaugs ereignet sich in der Nacht, und die Drossel, die Bard den entscheidenden Hinweis gibt, kommt »out of the dark« (H 307).

Das vielleicht im üblichen Sinne »dunkelste« Geschäft, weil es ja gegenüber seinen Begleitern geheim gehalten werden muss, ist Bilbos Ausflug zu den Belagerern des Einsamen Berges. Auch dieser findet deshalb nachts statt und »[i]t was very dark« (H 328), weshalb Bilbo dann auch in den Fluss fällt.

Und noch einmal wird es dunkel, bevor das Buch sein Ende erreicht, plötzlich und unerwartet vor der Schlacht der fünf Heere:

> Still more suddenly a darkness came on with dreadful swiftness! ...
> And beneath the thunder another blackness could be seen whirling forward. (H 338)

Die Fledermäuse der Orks verdunkeln den Himmel, um den lichtempfindlichen Orks zu helfen.

Es zeigt sich also wirklich, dass ein nicht unerheblicher Teil der Abenteuer, die im *Hobbit* geschildert werden, in der Dunkelheit stattfindet, was für Bilbo und die Zwerge eine Behinderung ist, auch wenn es nicht immer so dargestellt wird. Oft aber gelingt es Tolkien, dem Leser zu zeigen, welche Auswirkungen diese Einschränkung der Sehfähigkeit hat.

Ein Wendepunkt in seiner Karriere

Diese Behinderung wirft dann noch ein neues Licht auf Bilbos Ringfund und die Einschätzung des Erzählers, dass dieser »a turning point in his career« (H 328) gewesen sei. Denn nun erhält Bilbo jene Eigenschaft, die seine Umgebung so häufig hat, die Unsichtbarkeit. Damit wird er in diesem Sinne mit seiner Umgebung gleichgestellt, der er zuvor als Opfer ausgeliefert war. Auch in diesem Sinne ist der Ring also ein »Equalizer« (Shippey 70f), auch wenn Shippey mehr eine Angleichung an seine Gefährten, also die Zwerge meint.

Zwar bietet Tolkien wenige Vergleichspunkte, um diese Veränderung wirklich zu zeigen, da Bilbo in den vier Kapiteln vor dem Ringfund natürlich deutlich weniger aktiv ist als in den 15 ab dann. Aber einige Punkte zeigen sich schon, die diese Gleichstellung deutlich machen.

So ist Bilbo beim Überfall der Goblins in der Höhle in den Nebelbergen nicht nur einer der Gefangenen, sondern auch noch der schwächste, denn während die Zwerge jeder von mindestens sechs Gegnern angegriffen wurden, genügten zwei für Bilbo. Ganz anders ist es dann bei den Spinnen (wobei es allerdings nichts mit dem Ring zu tun hat und nur Glück ist, dass er rechtzeitig aufwacht, bevor er eingesponnen wurde) und den Waldelben, bei denen er der Gefangennahme dadurch entkommt, dass er den Ring aufsetzt. In diesen Fällen ist er nun derjenige, dessen Aufgabe es ist, die Zwerge zu retten, da er der einzige ist, der noch frei handeln kann.[5]

Natürlich gibt der Ring Bilbo ganz neue Handlungsoptionen, aber diese sind vielleicht nicht das wichtigste für ihn. Stellen wir uns zum Beispiel vor, er hätte den Ring schon gehabt, als die Sache mit den Trollen geschah. Hätte es ihm genutzt? Man weiß es nicht. Natürlich hätten die Trolle ihn nicht gesehen, und vielleicht hätte das gereicht, um ihm die Flucht zu ermöglichen. Aber entdeckt wurde er ja dadurch, dass die magische Trollbörse gesprochen hat. Dies wäre auf jeden Fall geschehen und hätte möglicherweise den Trollen genügt, ihn zu finden.

Ebenso wenig hilft der Ring gegen die Warge oder gegen Smaugs Feuer nach der zweiten Unterhaltung (H 283). Und auch in der Schlacht der Fünf Heere bietet er nur eingeschränkten Schutz:

> A magic ring of that sort is not a complete protection in a goblin charge, nor does it stop flying arrows and wild spears; but it does help in getting out of the way, and it prevents your head from being specially chosen for a sweeping stroke by a goblin swordsman.   (H 341)

Ja, wie Bilbo nach der Schlacht sogar feststellen muss: »This invisibility has its drawbacks after all« (H 347). Denn sonst wäre er viel früher gefunden und versorgt worden. Die wahrscheinlich wichtigere Wirkung des Rings ist die doppelte psychologische, zum einen auf Bilbo selbst, zum anderen auf die Zwerge. Bilbo selbst fühlt sich nun deutlich mehr den Aufgaben gewachsen, die seine Position

---

5   Interessanterweise ist es, trotz allem, was die Zwerge sagen, und auch was der Erzähler einstreut, doch weitgehend so, dass die Zwerge durchgehend gerettet werden müssen. Die einzige Rettungsaktion, die sie selbst vornehmen, als Bilbo sich von den Trollen fangen lässt, geht so völlig schief, dass Gandalf als Retter eingreifen muss. Und Bilbo übernimmt die Rolle des Retters am Eingang des Düsterwaldes, als Gandalf sie verlässt und ihm diese Rolle mit den Worten »I am sending Mr. Baggins with you« (H 187) implizit übergibt. Wirklich hilfreich sind die Zwerge nur im Kleinen, dadurch dass sie Fackeln anzünden (H 292), Bilbo eine neue Fackel bringen (H 294) oder einen Unterschlupf kennen (H 299).

als »burglar« der Expedition mit sich bringt. Die Zwerge auf der anderen Seite erkennen an, dass er doch nicht »more like a grocer than a burglar« (H 48) ist, wie Gloins erster Eindruck ist, sondern entwickeln »a great respect for him« (H 217), da er »some wits, as well as luck and a magic ring« (H 217) hat.

Diese Wandlung beginnt mit Bilbos unerwartetem Wiedererscheinen, nachdem er in den Goblin-Höhlen verloren gegangen war und den Ring gefunden hatte, mit dem er sich an das Lager anschleichen konnte. Und sie erreicht mit der Rettung vor den Spinnen wohl ihren Abschluss in dem Sinne, dass Bilbo ab da nicht nur ein vollständig anerkanntes Mitglied der Reisegesellschaft ist, sondern auch ihr Führer in Krisensituationen. Selbst Thorin, der immer noch die Richtlinien bestimmt, folgt ihm beispielsweise, als Bilbo sie auffordert, die Tür zum geheimen Eingang zu schließen (H 287).

Vergleicht man die Stellen, an denen die Zwerge ihn vorschicken, so gibt es da eine klare Entwicklung:

Bei den Trollen wird er ohne viel zu fragen losgeschickt, obwohl er die gewünschten Signale nicht geben könnte. Und als er (durch sein natürliches Talent sich leise zu bewegen) bis in die Nähe des Feuers vorgedrungen war, weiß er nicht, was er nun tun soll. Eigentlich will er gar nicht dort sein, fühlt sich aber trotzdem nicht wohl bei dem Gedanken, zu den Zwergen zurückzukehren, ohne etwas gestohlen zu haben.[6] Entsprechend verhält er sich auch völlig falsch und gefährdet die ganze Expedition.

Beim zweiten Fest der Waldelben verläuft es noch sehr ähnlich. Bilbo wird losgestoßen, ohne ihm Zeit zur Vorbereitung zu geben, und die ganze Sache geht schief (H 205). Aufgrund der anderen Umstände ist die Form des Schiefgehens zwar weniger schlimm, aber trotzdem gibt es keine wesentliche Veränderung. Allerdings wissen die Zwerge zu dieser Zeit auch noch nicht, dass Bilbo den Ring hat. Und dieser versucht noch ihn anzuwenden, kommt aber wegen der Ungeduld der Zwerge nicht dazu.

Aber beim dritten Mal, als es darum geht, das Innere des Einsamen Berges zu erkunden[7], ist es Bilbo, der ungeduldig wird, als Thorin ihn mit einer ge-

---

6 Hier wird ausnahmsweise mal nicht der Unterschied zwischen der Baggins- und der Took-Seite von Bilbo erwähnt. Erstere ist es wohl, die ihn wegwünscht, letztere die ihn zur Tat treibt. Vielleicht kommt es daher, dass hier ausnahmsweise die Took-Seite über das Ziel hinausschießt und unnötigen Ärger bereitet. Natürlich ist aus Sicht der Baggins-Seite jeglicher Ärger und die ganze Angelegenheit unnötig, aber der Erzähler und mit ihm der Leser sympathisiert sonst mit der Took-Seite, ohne die nichts Interessantes passieren würde. Hier aber ergibt sich eine Art implizite Kritik an dem unnötigen Heldentum, das fordert, nicht ohne Trophäe zurückzukehren. Und das könnte die Sympathie für die Took-Seite dämpfen, wenn es ihr explizit zugeordnet würde.

7 Auch hier stiehlt Bilbo, wie bei den Trollen, wieder einen Gegenstand, einen großen Pokal, was verheerende Folgen hat, indem es Smaug auf sie aufmerksam und wütend macht und schließlich zur Zerstörung Seestadts führt. Aber dies wirkt auf den Leser wesentlich weniger »dumm«, denn wie Bilbo selbst gegenüber den Zwergen sagt, war es ja genau das, wofür die Zwerge ihn mitgenommen hatten: Schätze zu stehlen.

wundenen Rede auffordern will, dies zu tun. Und er unterbricht den Zwergenanführer, indem er erklärt, dass er sich weigern könnte, dies aber nicht tun wird. Dies begründet er damit, dass er begonnen habe »to trust [his] luck more than [he] used to in the old days« (H 267).

Aber dies ist sicher nur ein Aspekt, der selbstverständlich auch durch den Ringfund gefördert worden ist. Denn bei seinem zweiten Besuch bei Smaug, den er nun ganz aus eigenem Antrieb macht, ohne von den Zwergen geschickt worden zu sein, äußert er zweimal deutlich, was ihm hier Mut macht: Zuerst bei seinem Angebot, diese Expedition zu unternehmen: »I have got my ring and will creep down this very noon« (H 277) und dann als er sich Smaug nähert, »He can't see me and he won't hear me. Cheer up Bilbo!« (H 278). Die Tatsache, dass er sich als unwahrnehmbar fühlt, gibt ihm die Ermutigung, die er braucht. Und es ist nur der Erzähler, der den Leser, aber nicht Bilbo an dieser Stelle daran erinnert, dass Drachen auch einen guten Geruchssinn haben.

Tatsächlich hilft der Ring bei seinem ersten Besuch bei Smaug gar nicht. Der Drache schläft sowieso und hätte ihn mit oder ohne Ring nicht wahrgenommen. Nur seine geräuschlose Bewegung hilft ihm, den Drachen nicht zu wecken. Der Ring wirkt nur als Rückversicherung und eben als psychologische Unterstützung.

Erst beim zweiten Besuch wird er wichtig, indem er Bilbo erlaubt, soweit in Smaugs Blickfeld einzutreten, dass er die ungeschützte Stelle am Bauch erkennen kann. Natürlich kann Smaug ihn auch so relativ gut orten, was Bilbo nach seiner unglücklichen Verabschiedung schmerzhaft feststellen muss. Bilbo ist das auch klar und er zieht sich weitgehend in den Eingang des Ganges zurück (H 278)[8]. Aber die Unsichtbarkeit trägt sicher zu Smaugs Neugier in Bezug auf diesen Dieb bei, die dann dazu führt, dass er sich lieber erst ein bisschen mit ihm unterhält, was Bilbo auch relativ geschickt nutzt (bis auf ein paar sehr böse Fehler, wie die Verabschiedung und »Barrel-rider«, H 280).

Das Schlimmste aber waren die Augen

Angesichts der großen Bedeutung, die die Unsichtbarkeit hat, ist es nicht verwunderlich, dass Augen im *Hobbit* als bedrohlich dargestellt werden. Dabei sind es im Wesentlichen drei Szenen, in denen das eindrücklich geschieht.

Zunächst nachdem Gollum festgestellt hatte, dass sein »precious« (H 128f, interessanterweise durchgehend nur mit einem s) verschwunden ist, und auf den richtigen Verdacht in Bezug auf die Antwort auf Bilbos letzte Frage gekommen war:

---

8   Hier ist Tolkiens eigene Illustration *Conversation with Smaug* (H 277) irreführend, da sie Bilbo mitten im Saal zeigt.

> ... to his alarm Bilbo now saw two small points of light peering at him... the light in his [Gollum's] eyes burned with a pale flame... But now the light in Gollum's eyes had become a green fire, and it was coming swiftly nearer... He turned now and saw Gollum's eyes like small green lamps coming up the slope. (H 129f)

Hier sind es zunächst Gollums Augen, die Bilbo dessen Gemütszustand und die von ihm ausgehende Gefahr mitteilen. Damit auch im gewissen Maße die Bedrohung darstellen und ihm Angst machen. Ein Punkt der noch einmal aufgenommen wird, als Bilbo durch den glücklichen Zufall des »in den Ring Rutschens« gerettet wird, als er auf der Flucht vor Gollum hinfällt: »What could it mean? Gollum could see in the dark« (H 130). Gollum hätte ihn also eigentlich sehen und angreifen müssen. Eine Gefahr, vor der Bilbo nur durch den Ring gerettet wurde.

Dann im Düsterwald, wo im Anschluss an die oben schon zitierte Stelle über die nächtliche Dunkelheit erwähnt wird, dass sie doch nicht nichts sehen:

> ... they could see eyes... he would see gleams in the darkness round them, and sometimes pairs of yellow or red or green eyes would stare at him from a little distance, and then slowly fade and disappear and slowly shine out again in another place. And sometimes they would gleam down from branches just above him; and that was most terrifying. But the eyes that he liked the least were horrible pale bulbous sort of eyes. "Insect eyes," he thought, "not animal eyes, only they are much too big." (H 193f)

Es wird also der Eindruck erweckt, dass sie von Tieren beobachtet werden (dass es Tiere und keine Menschen, Elben oder ähnliches sind, wird durch die genannten Farben und natürlich Bilbos Gedanken nahe gelegt). Welcher Art diese Tiere sind, warum sie sie beobachten und warum sie sich nie deutlicher zeigen, als nur durch ihre Augen, wird nicht klar gemacht. Aber das ist ein Teil der bedrohlichen Stimmung, die mit dieser Schilderung erreicht wird.

Einzig die zuletzt genannten Augen sollen wohl die Augen der Spinnen darstellen. Auch wenn es keine biologisch korrekte Darstellung von Spinnenaugen ist, sondern tatsächlich eher Insektenaugen zeigt, so entspricht es doch Tolkiens Darstellung von Kankras Augen in *The Lord of the Rings* (LotR 704). Zusammen mit den Spinnweben bereiten sie also auf die weiteren Erlebnisse mit den Spinnen vor.

Dass die Reisegesellschaft diese Augen als sehr bedrohlich empfindet, zeigt sich auch darin, dass einer der Gründe dafür, bald kein Feuer mehr zu entzünden, war, dass dieses die Augen noch vermehrt anlockte. Und zwar weiterhin nur Augen, denn die dazugehörigen Wesen waren sehr vorsichtig »never to let their bodies show in the little flicker of the flames« (H 194).

Das dritte Mal, wenn eine Bedrohung speziell durch Augen dargestellt wird, ist Bilbos zweiter Besuch bei Smaug:

> Bilbo... was just about to step out on to the floor when he caught a sudden thin and piercing ray of red from under the drooping lid of Smaug's left eye... He was watching the tunnel entrance. (H 278)

Wieder geht die offensichtliche Bedrohung von den Augen des Drachen aus, die Bilbo ausspähen wollen und die ihn warnen, dass der Drache doch nicht schläft. Da Bilbo aber den Ring trägt, wirken die Augen gar nicht, und es sind eigentlich andere Sinne, die es Smaug erlauben, den Eindringling zu erkennen, wie jener selbst sagt: »I smell you and I feel your air. I hear your breath« (H 278).

Leuchtende Augen

Eine auffällige Gemeinsamkeit der geschilderten Szenen ist, dass die Augen mit einem eigenen Licht leuchten. Gollums Augen so stark, dass Bilbo, nachdem jener an ihm vorbeigelaufen war, »could see the light of his eyes palely shining even from behind« (H 130). Er sieht also die Reflektion des Lichts aus Gollums Augen.

Die Augen im Düsterwald können die Reisenden sehen, obwohl sie sonst nichts sehen können, wie oben zitiert, weil eben diese Augen leuchten. Und auch Smaugs Auge wird durch einen roten Strahl verraten.

Auch beim vergeblichen Versuch der Warge, die auf die Bäume geflüchteten Zwerge zu erreichen, werden sie »with eyes blazing« (H 146) beschrieben. Diese Stelle ist zwar nicht so deutlich wie die anderen, da es sich hier auch um reflektiertes Mondlichts handeln kann, aber das Licht aus den Augen wird auch hier genutzt, um die Wut der Warge deutlich zu machen.

Doch nicht nur die Gegner haben gelegentlich leuchtende Augen im nicht übertragenen Sinne. In der am Anfang dieses Artikels zitierten Stelle, als Bilbo sich von der Unexpected Party davonschleichen will, stellt er fest, dass »they were all looking at him with eyes shining in the dark« (H 46). Zwar kann man auch hier noch andere Erklärungen anführen, die kein eigenständiges Leuchten erfordern, aber die Kombination von »shining« mit »in the dark« deutet schon stark darauf hin, dass tatsächlich so etwas gemeint ist. Zuvor wird ja festgestellt, dass die Dunkelheit hereinbricht und das Feuer herunterbrennt (H 44), Lichtquellen, die sich in den Augen der Zwerge und Gandalfs spiegeln könnten, scheint es also nicht mehr zu geben.

Dieses Phänomen erinnert an eine antike Sehtheorie, wie sie beispielsweise in Platons Dialog *Timaios* dargestellt wird: »Sie [die Götter] machten nämlich, daß das in uns befindliche, diesem verwandte unvermischte Feuer durch die Augen hervorströmte« (45b). Es wird also davon ausgegangen, dass man aktiv sieht, also ein Sehkegel aus dem Auge hervortritt, sich mit dem Licht der Umgebung verbindet und auf den Menschen zurückwirkt.

Von der Ausbildung Tolkiens her, mit Griechischunterricht an der Schule und einem begonnenen Studium der Classics, ist davon auszugehen, dass er diese Theorien kannte. Auf den ersten Blick passen sie auch gut zu Tolkiens Beschreibung des Lichts, das aus den Augen hervordringt. Aber zumindest Platons (oder Timaios, der hier spricht) Darstellung widerspricht dem im Folgenden deutlich:

> Schwand aber das ihm verwandte Feuer zur Nacht, dann ist es von ihm abgeschnitten; denn zu etwas ihm Unähnlichen herausdringend, erfährt es selbst eine Veränderung und erlischt, indem es nicht mehr mit der kein Feuer mehr enthaltenden benachbarten Luft in eins verschmilzt. (45d)

Gerade in den Situationen, in denen Tolkien also das Leuchten der Augen verwendet, würde es bei Platon erlöschen. Nichtsdestotrotz ist es denkbar, dass Tolkien hier seine eigene Fortschreibung solcher Theorien einsetzt.

Ein weiterer Punkt, der mehrfach in die Diskussion eingebracht wurde, ist die bei Tolkien an verschiedenen Stellen seines Werkes auftretende Eigenschaft von Gegenständen, Licht dauerhaft speichern zu können.

Das bekannteste Beispiel sind die Silmarilli, deren inneres Feuer aus dem »blended light of the Trees of Valinor, which lives in them yet«(S 78) bestand. Und natürlich darf in diesem Zusammenhang beim Thema des Seminars auch der Arkenstein nicht vergessen werden, der auch »of its own inner light« (H 293) leuchtet. Wenn also diese unbelebten Edelsteine von sich aus leuchten, so wäre es nicht verwunderlich, wenn auch die Augen einiger oder aller Lebewesen in unterschiedlichem Maße die Eigenschaft hätten, Licht aufnehmen, speichern und dann wieder abgeben zu können.

Allerdings gibt es dazu keine veröffentlichte Äußerung Tolkiens, so dass diese Annahme nicht mehr Autorität besitzt als die Zurückführung auf eine antike Sehtheorie. Die beiden müssen sich noch nicht einmal ausschließen, da die Sehtheorie oder die ihr zugrunde liegende Theorie der Elemente auch Tolkiens Vorstellungen vom Licht, speziell vom Licht der zwei Bäume (das auch als flüssig und schwer dargestellt wird, S 44) beeinflusst haben könnte.

Fazit

Im *Hobbit* setzt sich Tolkien gekonnt mit mehreren Aspekten des Gesichtssinns auseinander. Zum einen den Vor- und Nachteilen einer Einschränkung der Sehfähigkeit: Nachteile, wenn man selbst nicht sehen kann. Vorteil, wenn andere einen nicht sehen können.[9] Diese werden in eindrücklichen Szenen dargestellt.

Diese Auseinandersetzung bildet in gewissem Maße den Hintergrund für Bilbos Ringfund und die damit erworbene Fähigkeit der Unsichtbarkeit, die ihn in einem Abenteuer, in dem er sich viel in Dunkelheit bewegt und Gegnern begegnet, die im Dunklen sehen können, einen Chancenausgleich bringt.

Zum anderen stellt Tolkien die Augen häufig als Lichtquellen dar. Dies könnte auf eine geschickte Nutzung antiker Sehtheorien hindeuten oder aber auch einer mehr in seinem eigenen *Legendarium* verwurzelten Lichtmythologie entsprechen, die auf jeden Fall Edelsteinen, aber vielleicht eben auch Augen, die Fähigkeit zuschreibt, Licht zu speichern und später abzugeben. Was hier überwiegend ist, lässt sich aus dem vorhandenen Material nicht ableiten, und auch Tolkien hat sich in keiner veröffentlichten Stelle dazu geäußert.

Bibliographie

Anderson, Douglas A. *The Annotated Hobbit*. Revised and expanded edition. New York: Houghton Mifflin, 2003

Carpenter, Humphrey, (ed.). *The Letters of J.R.R. Tolkien*. London: HarperCollins, 1995

Platon, *Timaios*. (Übersetzung Friedrich Schleiermacher) aus Platon: Sämtliche Werke. Band 4, Reinbek: Rowohlt, 2006

Rateliff, John D. *The History of the Hobbit*. 2 Vols. London: HarperCollins, 2007

Shippey, Tom A. *The Road to Middle-Earth*. London: Grafton, 1992

Tolkien, John Ronald Reuel. *The Lord of the Rings*. London: HarperCollins, 2001

---. *The Silmarillion*. London: Unwin Paperbacks, 1988

---

9 Was häufig ein Vorteil ist, jedenfalls in den Situationen, die Bilbo erlebt. Aber nicht immer, wie die zitierte Szene nach der Schlacht der Fünf Heere zeigt.

Seeing Fire and Sword, or Refining Hobbits
Anna E. Slack (Palermo)

> I need a hero. I'm holding out for a hero until the end of the night. He's gotta be strong, he's gotta be fast... he's gotta be larger than life.[1]

So sings Bonnie Tyler as she holds out for her hero. But is her definition of a hero a kind of 'one-size-fits' all? There are many different types of stories and, unsurprisingly, there are as many different kinds of heroes in them. Like the specimens in a peculiarly literary nature documentary, each hero tends to be well adapted to, or perhaps, the curious product of, the world that he (or she) inhabits.

Most heroes are also in some way beyond the scope of our ordinary world. They are men and women who are accustomed to and refined by experiences of fire and sword. Here are some well-known, predominantly literary, heroes: Achilles; Odysseus; Aeneas; Saint George; Beowulf; Charlemagne; Roland; Lancelot; Hamlet and Bilbo.

Many would agree in classing these men as heroes and also in observing that they are not all heroic in quite the same way. Achilles is the epitome of a classical hero – to use Bonnie Tyler's terms, he is fast, strong and larger than life. Odysseus' epithet, 'wily', runs before him like fire fanned through dry grass. We have 'pius Aeneas' as the keystone of the new Roman heroism; on the more saintly side we find Saint George and his dragon and, as we can read in dozens of hagiographies, scores of saints who followed similar patterns. Beowulf did better against his monsters than his critics while other heroes, sometimes with the help of those same critics, became literary tropes in their own right. Lancelot, father of the only man who could sit in the *siege perilous* is, for example, more than partially responsible for both Victorian and modern notions of chivalry. Hamlet, existential thinker caged in a stalling revenge tragedy, has become one of the most famous 'heroes' in literature, aped and marvelled at across the globe.

And Bilbo? It doesn't take critics and academics to note that he is in a completely different league to the other heroes mentioned here. Try imagining him, for example, at the siege of Troy, or facing Grendel's mother in Denmark's swamps, or winding the horn of Roland... It doesn't quite work.

---

[1] From 'Holding Out for a Hero'; lyrics by Jim Steinman and Dean Pritchford, sung by Bonnie Tyler on her album *Secret Dreams and Forbidden Fire*, first released in 1986 by Columbia Records

So what kind of hero is Bilbo? Many will answer that he is an everyman, a kind of hero who, perhaps more than any other, is tested by seeing fire and sword. The examination of Bilbo's everyman heroism is the scope of this paper.

Everyman and the Hero's Journey

Our first question has to be: what is an 'everyman'? Enter the *Oxford English Dictionary*, defining an everyman as "an ordinary or typical human being". In fact, the term 'everyman' has been with us a long time, dating back at least as far as mediaeval morality plays. Study of these plays and the OED's definition swiftly leads us to the conclusion that an everyman hero is ordinary or typical, with the purpose of communing with his readers and spectators in a particularly intimate way by means of appealing to common human traits.

We identify keenly with a protagonist who reminds us of ourselves and as we interpret his (or her) experiences through our own eyes, we may even see a trace of ourselves in the unfolding drama. The everyman hero makes the story applicable to us; he both represents us in the story and mediates it to us.

This is, of course, precisely why the everymen are cherished. They differ from the other breeds of heroes – the warriors, thinkers and saints – by being like us: ordinary and typical. Everyman has no supernatural connections, no lost kingdoms, and no murdered fathers. He is the black sheep at the high table of heroes.

Every hero, of course, has a hero's journey, but the everyman's journey is different; he must be pitted against circumstances that are beyond the scope of his experience – and occasionally his understanding – and somehow he must use his wit and noble ordinariness to resolve them. Everyman isn't capable of this at first, and we're used to seeing so-called 'montage' sequences in films where he must be trained, stumbling and failing (usually with a musical accompaniment), before his determination shines through and he succeeds in his task. Once his skills have been finely honed in practice, everyman's journey usually entails demonstrating to the world how the very ordinary can be a mark of greatness in halls peopled by the superhuman.

His task done, everyman returns home happily, enriched in all spheres – but principally in terms of character – by his adventure. Sometimes he even helps to remedy a terrible problem in his society or culture. His story is that of someone unexpectedly called from their normal life to a 'there and back again' adventure. They are, as Shakespeare put it, those who have had "greatness thrust upon them" (*Twelfth Night*, Act II Scene V); they are the unexpecting – and sometimes unwilling – subjects for a work of ennoblement in a world beyond their own.

For an example, cast your mind back to the scene at the beginning of Ridley Scott's film *Gladiator*[2], where the old emperor tells the hero, Maximus, that he wants him to be nominated as emperor after him. Maximus, contrasted against the emperor's own immoral son, has no desire to do so. This is the mirror image to a sentiment expressed in Douglas Adams' *The Hitchhiker's Guide to the Galaxy*, where it is stated that: "Anyone who is capable of getting themselves made President should on no account be allowed anywhere to do the job" (*The Original Radio Scripts* 242).

In Tolkien's own view, the matter of becoming a hero is very similar to that of becoming an emperor. "*Nolo heroizari*" he wrote, "is as good a start for a hero as *nolo episcopari* for a bishop" (L 215). Saying 'I do not want to be a hero' shows a measure of humility found far too often only in ordinary men. It is that same humility which, at least to the modern eye, forms a fine basis for heroism.

Bilbo: 'Nolo Heroizari!'

At a first glance Bilbo looks to be the perfect candidate for an everyman hero precisely because he has no desire to be one, and certainly not if it means being the protagonist in an adventure. "'Sorry,' he says to Gandalf, 'I don't want any adventures, thank you. Not today. Good morning!'" (H 7) Bilbo hides from adventures behind the cloak of his ordinariness. He 'good mornings' Gandalf until he thinks he has 'escaped adventures very well' (H 8). How many of us have escaped potentially unpleasant – or decidedly unwelcome – situations, in exactly the same fashion?

Tolkien himself sets the frame for us to view Bilbo as the everyman. In a letter to Milton Walden he wrote that *The Hobbit* was "in effect... a study of simple, ordinary man, neither artistic nor noble and heroic" (L 159). Bilbo's ordinariness is intrinsically borne out in the details and initial representation of his character and in the way his society and culture are figured in the narrator's opening strokes: Bilbo is hedged round by letters, smoke-rings, the Hill and the Water, tea and cakes, spare beds and pocket handkerchiefs.

From the picture of the pressed and frustrated host trying to be polite to the idly pronounced 'good morning', Bilbo is a well-crafted image of a not quite well-off enough, and comfortingly ordinary, English country gentleman.

But there is a spark in Bilbo that loves tales of the world beyond:

> As [the dwarves] sang the hobbit felt... something Tookish [wake] up inside of him, and he wished to go and see the great mountains, and hear the pine-trees and the waterfalls, and explore the caves,

---

2   *Gladiator*, dir. Ridley Scott, released in May 2000

and wear a sword instead of a walking-stick. He looked out of the window. The stars were out in a dark sky above the trees. He thought of the jewels of the dwarves shining in dark caverns. Suddenly in the wood beyond the water a flame leapt up – probably someone lighting a wood fire – and he thought of plundering dragons settling on his quiet Hill and kindling it all to flames. He shuddered; and very quickly he was plain Mr Baggins of Bag-End...again. (H 16)

This passage is instrumental in illustrating Bilbo as our everyman; the dwarves' song stirs something in him near to a desire for adventure – but the real-world implications of dragons quickly ground him again.

It is about here that our definition of Bilbo as an everyman runs into trouble, for though he may be ordinary Bilbo is not typical in our modern sense. Emphasis is consistently given to the Tookish part of Bilbo and the fact that the dwarves' song moves him at all is further proof of his a-typicality – other hobbits, like Ted Sandyman in *The Lord of the Rings*, would dismiss the kind of song that so affects Bilbo as nonsense.

It seems, therefore, that everyman heroes must be distinguished into at least two groups: the typical everyman, and his ordinary counterpart. Tealess and bumbling around the galaxy in his dressing gown, Arthur Dent from *The Hitchhiker's Guide to the Galaxy* is a fine example of a typical everyman but Bilbo seems to be an ordinary everyman. That is to say, there is something about him that sets him apart from the typical hobbits that surround him, something that is not quite enough to make him extraordinary.

Tolkien commented that "Bilbo was specially selected by the authority and insight of Gandalf as abnormal" (L 365). Returning to his letter to Walden we find that Tolkien's study of the simple, inartistic man (in this case Bilbo), is actually a study of one who is '*not without the undeveloped seeds of these things*' (L 159, emphasis mine).

In contrast to the typical everyman the ordinary everyman has the undeveloped seeds of greater things within him; more than this, perhaps the ordinary everyman is disposed towards making some use of such virtues while a typical everyman is not.

So what ordinary, hidden virtues does Bilbo possess? Tolkien enumerates them in his letters as: "shrewd sense, generosity, patience and fortitude, and also a strong 'spark' yet unkindled" (L 365). Bilbo has many of these virtues 'blended in good measure' but it is clear that the spark in him is simply waiting to be kindled. The narrator tells us that "Bilbo... got something a bit queer in his make-up from the Took side, something that only waited for a chance to come out" (H 5).

It is in this part of Bilbo that Gandalf recognises the untapped potential indigenous in his chosen burglar. The hobbit is a perfect subject for the ennoblement that goes with the fire and sword experiences of a hero's journey and we do indeed see ordinary Bilbo from the Shire go from fainting dinner host to dragon-riddler. Many would comfortably call it the standard fire and sword journey of an everyman. Except for another small problem.

We have seen how, possessing a spark yet unkindled, Bilbo cannot be seen as a typical hobbit – he is an ordinary one. But Bilbo is not simply an ordinary hobbit; he is unexpectedly unconventional, perhaps to the point of disqualifying him from traditional everyman status.

From the outset of the story we are constantly being reminded by the narrator that Bilbo may descend from a line of hobbits who have done exceptional things, like being big enough to ride a horse. And: "it was often said (in other families) that long ago one of the Took ancestors must have taken a fairy wife" (H 4).

Whether or not Bilbo is disqualified from his everyman status depends very much on our reading of this line. Either it is true that a Took took a fairy wife – meaning that, like more classical heroes, Bilbo has some 'supra-human' ancestry a great distance back – or we must read Tolkien as making an astonishing statement about the nature of being ordinary. In this latter case, it appears that it is perfectly in line for an 'ordinary' hobbit to have a spark that connects him to the fairy world and perhaps this is where the seeds of his undiscovered greatness come from. This unconventional, but apparently ordinary, root further demarks Bilbo from the typical hobbit.

This root engenders a conflict in Bilbo's blood that lends him a veritable verisimilitude: Bilbo both desires and is terrified of adventures, he is entranced and repelled by them. Without this atypical conflict no amount of nudging would have got him to leave his hobbit hole.

This conflict also prepares Bilbo for a much more serious everyman role, that of straddling several worlds. Bilbo has a spark and lives in a commonplace 'familiar' world (being Hobbiton and the Hill). As he is sent running from his hobbit hole by Gandalf he steps into the 'legendary' world of Middle-earth. Just as a good everyman should be, Bilbo is a piece of the ordinary world being driven into the legendary one. And, as he is an ordinary everyman, Bilbo is by no means at ease with the world of wizards, dwarves, goblins and dragons that he goes into.

Bilbo's unease means that he is quick to note discrepancies between the actuality of the legendary world and the depiction of it in the ordinary world from which he came. As they set out the narrator notes that: "Mostly [the weather] had been as good as May can be, even in merry tales, but now it was cold and wet". Bilbo is even less enthused: "'To think it will soon be June,' grumbled Bilbo" (H 31).

In contrast to Bilbo, the ordinary everyman adjusting to the legendary world, we have a whole company of dwarves and Thorin Oakenshield. The ordinary world of Bilbo's hobbit hole seems, both literally and metaphorically, scarcely enough to hold them. Thorin, dispossessed heir to the King under the Mountain, holds a role comparable in type to that of Aragorn in *The Return of the King*. Yet Thorin is a diminished shadow of the world that he represents.

This seems to be caused not by being represented in a tale about a hobbit but by his own nature. Gandalf's description of Thror's exploits in the Necromancer's dungeon sounds as grand and tragic as a heroic exploit should. As the narrator delights in telling us, Thorin's own speech is unnecessarily protracted: "This was Thorin's style... he would probably have gone on like this until he was out of breath, without telling anyone there anything that was not known already" (H 17). While Gandalf observes repeatedly that there is more to Bilbo than meets the eye, of Thorin, but pages after we have met him, we see Gandalf say that he has been set tasks 'big enough' for him (H 25).

Set side by side in this fashion we might see Bilbo and Thorin as parallel figures of two descending lines. Bilbo, the ordinary everyman, can either diminish into a quotidian and typical figure by rejecting the call to adventure, or may live to prove the spark in him that does not meet the eye. Thorin, descendant of the legendary world of heroic history, may either become a protracted Lilliputian or a reinstated king.

The stage is set for a tale that explores what it means to be ordinary in the legendary world; it is the very stuff that forges the mettle of the everymen. But the tale isn't just about wringing out the destinies of Bilbo and Thorin by seeing fire and sword, or seeking to reconcile the ordinary and heroic worlds: through Bilbo, Tolkien is also refining the heroism of hobbits and their place in the legendary history of Middle-earth.

Legendary and Commonplace

Alfred Lord Tennyson once observed that the writing of a good hymn was the most difficult thing in the world for: "In a good hymn you have to be both commonplace and poetical" (*Memoir* 754).

Bilbo's story is in many ways like the elusive 'good hymn'; he is caught between the commonplace world and the poetical or legendary one that he knows of primarily through his reading. As soon as he becomes the dwarves' burglar he finds himself pinned between the two. He is no longer seeing fire and sword on the pages of a book – he is living it. Thrust into an adventure beyond his control, Bilbo's occupation of both territories forces him to interpret the dialogue between his own ordinary life and what he meets in the world beyond it.

It is in his interpretation that he becomes an unwitting mediator, both of daily business and sometimes unpleasant legend, to the reader: this mediation and interpretation is the basis of his hero's journey and of his status as an everyman. But it is more than this: the process of interpretation is also the process of his *integration* into the legendary world.

Initially, Bilbo can only really negotiate the legendary world by relying on Gandalf. It is the wizard who 'interprets' the dwarves' letter, telling Bilbo that he will have to run to be punctual, and frequently it is Gandalf who acts on behalf of Bilbo and the entire company in the various stages of their adventures (such as with the eagles, or in meeting Beorn). A fully integrated part of the world through which they move, the wizard is Bilbo's comfort and encouragement. But as he journeys on Bilbo begins to integrate into the legendary world and as he does so his interpretations of it also become shrewder.

We can exemplify Bilbo's growing (and yet still awkward) integration by looking at his dream in the Misty Mountains: "He dreamed that a crack in the back of the cave got bigger and bigger, and opened wider and wider, and he was very afraid but could not call out or do anything but lie and look. Then he dreamed that the floor of the cave was giving way and he was slipping – beginning to fall down, down, goodness knows where to..." (H 57)

Dreams are very much in the mechanics of fairy and heroic story, and this one is rather prophetic. Bilbo's inability to cry out in the dream is indicative of the fact that he is still only an interpreter or onlooker on the heroic world. In his fear he wakes Gandalf, who will be the key to the dwarves' and hobbit's escape from the goblins. Bilbo's cry, elicited by his dream, affects the waking world – and Gandalf, a key actor in that world – even if it does not grant Bilbo the active ability to do so. It is the first step of an everyman towards not just seeing, but affecting his new surroundings.

The importance of interpretation and its relationship to integrating into and affecting the legendary world is shown keenly in the riddle contest with Gollum. The narrator observes that the finding of the ring, and what follows it, "was a turning point in [Bilbo's] career, but he did not know it" (H 66). Ironically, it is alone and in the dark that Bilbo begins to recognise the legendary world – he sees that his own blade, glinting dimly in the dark, "is an elvish blade, too" (H 67). The riddle contest itself has heroic roots; Bilbo knows that "[it] was sacred and of immense antiquity" (H 76). Like Bilbo, it is a tradition that inhabits both the legendary and commonplace world – many of the riddles exchanged are ones that Bilbo and Gollum know from their time spent living in the latter. Bilbo trades in riddles as simply and deftly as a great hero but does so as an ordinary man. The turning point is in the fact that, alone in the dark, Bilbo has the wit to escape both Gollum and the goblins at the gate. As a prize he retains the ring, itself a tool from the heroic world, and it grants him a legendary aspect when he reappears before the dwarves.

The intertwined nature of the riddling contest is not too far from Bilbo's ordinary experience and yet it is also a heroic and legendary act. Without realising it, Bilbo has come through his first proper deed of fire and sword and gone towards the legendary by interpreting it with the eyes and sense of an ordinary man.

Ordinary towards Legendary

This is the first of various legendary successes for Bilbo, and his growing integration into the legendary world begins to find expression in heroic tropes: in Mirkwood Bilbo kills the first spider alone and unaided, then names his sword. It makes "a great difference" to him (H 146). Both killing and naming are steps towards legendary status and yet, just as when Samwise Gamgee battles Shelob, heroism and legends could not be further from Bilbo's mind; his naming of the sword, Sting, seems to come to Bilbo naturally and without any pretensions to heroism. In this Tolkien gives us both the stereotype and pure type of heroism. We are allowed to appreciate Bilbo's heroism without the blinkers of the heroic canon, even though we are aware of it, and this refreshed appreciation of heroism comes from Bilbo being our everyman.

It can be argued that from this point the narrator's tone keeps us from seeing the full-fledged scale of Bilbo's deeds in Mirkwood. The narrator maintains Bilbo firmly in the guise of an everyman rather than a legendary hero; the details of the time he spends hidden in Thranduil's palace, for example, are kept very much behind the scenes. By means of the ring Bilbo becomes the un-looked-for help in Thorin's despair, using all his cunning to orchestrate the dwarves' escape. It is a testing time of fire and sword in which Bilbo has no help and is, in a sense, more in peril than in his solitary combat with the spiders.

After the great escape the narrator, still showing us the common nature of the protagonist, gives account of Bilbo's cold in reasonable detail. This detail, as well as being one which we would expect from someone who had smuggled himself out of a dungeon in a barrel, seems comic in conjunction with the legendary nature of the escape which Bilbo has effected. With Bilbo's cold it is suddenly the intrusion of the ordinary into the legendary, rather than legendary into the life of the ordinary everyman, that has become the root of the comedy.

This is a key shift in the narrator's tone and demonstrates how far Bilbo's integration has gone. It is relieving to see that our everyman is still 'ordinary', and it is just as well, for it is Bilbo's ordinary everyman nature that saves him from some of the more annoying flaws of traditional and classical heroism: namely, doom and hubris.

Conversing with dragons is, by all accounts, a dangerous business. The narrator tells us as much and we see for ourselves the disturbing and disquieting effect that it has on Bilbo, encouraging him to distrust his friends and allies. Standing before Smaug, however, Bilbo begins to riddle on his names and adventures:

> I am he that walks unseen… I am the clue finder, the web-cutter, the stinging fly. I was chosen for the lucky number… I am he that

buries his friends alive and drowns them and draws them alive again from the water. I came from the end of a bag, but no bag went over me.... I am the Ring-winner and Barrel-rider... (H 207)

Bilbo is 'very pleased with his riddling', but if our hero were any kind of hero other than an everyman this would be a moment of terrible hubris. We could compare it, for example, to the consequences of Odysseus giving his name as *nemo* to the Cyclops, or of Turin speaking with Glaurung. If Bilbo was an epic hero, turning the page would likely reveal Laketown destroyed by Smaug, the dwarves killed as a consequence of Bilbo's words and Bilbo realising that it had all been his doing before dying in heroic combat against his foe.

But Bilbo is an everyman – he is commonplace, and to Smaug he is out of place: hobbit smell is "quite outside [Smaug's] experience and [puzzles] him mightily" (H 209). Smaug is confident in his unassailability observing, like Gandalf in the very first chapter, that the like of the heroes of old is "not in the world today" (H 21, 210). What he fails to recognise is the new kind of hero before him, just as he fails to recognise Bilbo's similarity to his uneasy dream "in which a warrior, altogether insignificant in size but provided with a bitter sword, figured most unpleasantly" (H 202). Smaug misinterprets his dream because he cannot interpret the ordinary and, in the contest of hobbit and dragon, it is Bilbo's ordinariness that saves him. He extricates himself from his meeting with Smaug with the same platitudes and manner which one might adopt to avoid an awkward dinner with ungainly relatives. It is an everyday skill with which it is likely Bilbo has some experience.

It is Bilbo's unconventional and goading ordinariness that prompts Smaug to go to Laketown where he is slain by Bard. Bilbo's engagement in the heroic trope of speaking with dragons has a good end – except for the dragon – which is as it should be.

Following Smaug's death Thorin is elevated to a legendary status, being at his most eloquent and epic in treating with Bard. But with this elevation he also becomes arrogant. Thorin is not defended from the effect of a dragon hoard and so his reunion with his ancestors' treasure brings him clearly, and negatively, into the legendary heroic canon. On the other hand Bilbo, after various encounters with both dragon and horde, seems to return firmly to his commonplace status.

In the matter of the Arkenstone Bilbo's piercing common sense takes him through the gestures of heroic betrayal in the business-like guise of an ordinary man doing the best thing that he can think of doing. It is a motive that is not understood by Bard, another representative of the legendary world:

> "...Are you betraying your friends, or are you threatening us?" asked Bard grimly. "My dear Bard!" squeaked Bilbo. "... I am merely trying to avoid trouble for all concerned!" (H 251)

Bilbo's one true act of burglary – the delivering of the Arkenstone to Bard – is by no means epic. All the same the outcome of the wider adventure rests on it. Even though the theft is little more to Bilbo than an act of common sense, the elves interpret it as a grand gesture:

> The Elvenking looked at Bilbo with a new wonder. "Bilbo Baggins!" he said. "You are more worthy to wear the armour of elf-princes than many who have looked more comely in it."   (H 251)

Bilbo's ordinariness has metamorphosed before our eyes into a keystone of greatness. It is just this that Thorin notes when he speaks with Bilbo for the last time: "There is more of good in you than you know, child of the kindly west. Some courage and some wisdom, blended in measure. If more of us valued food and cheer and song above hoarded gold, it would be a merrier world" (H 266).

By Thorin's death two remarkable things have happened: Bilbo has been reconciled enough to the legendary world to feel honoured to have shared Thorin's perils, and Thorin sees that there is more to the ordinary world than meets the legendary eye. Through the adventures and interactions of dwarf and hobbit, the ordinary and legendary worlds have been powerfully integrated with each other, to the enrichment of both.

Ordained Goodness, Unexpected Greatness

In his book *The Hero with a Thousand Faces*, Joseph Campbell writes that the hero's journey can begin by means of "a blunder ... the merest chance" which "reveals an unexpected world, and the individual is drawn into a relationship with forces that are not rightly understood. The blunder may amount to the opening of a destiny" (Campbell 51).

Campbell's definition of a blunder amounting to a destiny might not seem to have a place in the life of an everyman, but it is a key aspect of Bilbo's journey and, through him, a defining and crucial facet of Tolkien's hobbits.

Tolkien wrote that *The Hobbit* was "about the achievements of ... ordained individuals, inspired and guided by an Emissary to ends beyond their individual education and enlargement" (L 365).

So Bilbo Baggins, though sharing every nuance of an ordinary everyman, is actually from start to finish to be considered as an ordained everyman, a "chosen burglar" (H 19). Yet this ordination is beyond the ken of the world in which Bilbo has been ordained to move: the narrator of *The Hobbit* advises us that "no songs alluded ... to [Bilbo] even in the obscurest way" (H 185). Bilbo is both chosen and unforeseen by the conventional wisdoms of either the ordinary or legendary world. As Elrond will later put it in *The Lord of the Rings*:

"This is the hour of the Shire-folk, when they arise from their quiet fields, to shake the towers and counsels of the Great. Who of all the Wise could have foreseen it?" (LotR I, 355)

Bilbo's ordinariness has been a platform for the working out of an ordained role. It is the ordinariness that makes our everyman an unlikely candidate; it is beyond the wisdom of the wise (cf. *1 Corinthians* 1:20). It is this straddling between being elect and being unforeseen, first shown in Bilbo, that refines the hobbits into a race adapted to perform the tasks too great for the heroic races all around them. Bilbo's trial by fire and sword has been a testing ground for the unexpected yet ordained slow-kindled courage that other notable hobbits will exhibit by merit of being ordinary. Hobbits are the distinctly anti-heroic element of Middle-earth and, in this sense, are the ultimate and completely unforeseen channel for the unconventional heroism of the everyman. As heroes, this makes them, in Tolkien's words, "more praiseworthy than the professionals" (L 215).

It is this praiseworthy channelling of unforeseen heroism which gives hobbits a very literally other-worldly capacity to deliver and reconcile the legendary world into which they travel. The hobbits become agents of eucatastrophe, a means by which a glimpse of *evangelium*, the unlooked for turn, strikes through into Middle-earth. In this, the way in which Tolkien figures the hobbits is partly informed by Tolkien's Christian belief, where an unconventional hero, Christ, by taking an ordinary and human guise eucatastrophically reconciles the historical and eternal worlds.

Hobbits in general – and Bilbo in particular – cannot quite be said to foreshadow Christ, but Bilbo does serve a purpose beyond interpreting and mediating the story to us. In his eucatastrophic journey towards interpretation, integration and reconciliation, Bilbo reminds us to look for the spark in ourselves. We are also everymen – and our ordinary lives are just as capable of being the springboards for unexpected heroism, or even ordained eucatastrophe, as a hobbit's. In this sense Bilbo's tale is a call to arms, one that urges us to rise above the typical and ordinary everymen and hear the music of the Lonely Mountain in our hearthside kettle.

Bibliography

Campbell, Joseph. *The Hero with a Thousand Faces*. New York: Princeton University, 1949

Carpenter, Humphrey, Ed. with assistance of C. Tolkien. *The Letters of J.R.R. Tolkien*. London: HarperCollins, 1995

Gill, Roma (ed.) and Shakespeare, William. *Twelfth Night*. Oxford: Oxford School Shakespeare, 2001

Tennyson, Hallam. *Tennyson: A Memoir*. London, 1899

Tolkien, J.R.R. *The Hobbit*. London: HarperCollins, 1999

---. *The Lord of the Rings*. London: HarperCollins, 1995

Other Sources:

Adams, Douglas. *The Hitchhiker's Guide to the Galaxy: The Original Radio Scripts*. London: Pan Books Ltd, 1985

The Holy Bible: New International Version. London: Hodder and Stoughton, 2000

The Oxford English Dictionary. Oxford: Oxford University Press, 2006

The Not-Quite-Moving Pictures: The Comic Book Adaptation of Tolkien's *The Hobbit*
Dirk Vanderbeke

"In a hole in the ground there lived a hobbit". The first sentence of Tolkien's *The Hobbit* has by now joined many other famed first lines like "It was the best of times, it was the worst of times", "Stately, plump Buck Mulligan came from the stairhead ...", "Call me Ishmael", "For a long time I would go to bed early", or "It was a wrong number that started it", all of which are easily recognized by readers who have not yet managed to reach page one of the respective book or even some of those who would never think of touching it. Each first sentence presents the reader with a different kind of world and thus also with some problems, and so does the first sentence of *The Hobbit*.

The question of the reader, who first encounters the text, can probably be summed up as: In what kind of hole in the ground does what exactly live? Of course, we all know what a hobbit is, but then I think we also remember how we first came across this word without any preconception and asked ourselves whether it was a kind of mouse or rodent, a fox-like creature or a strange kind of humanoid like a dwarf, a fairy or a pixie. We found out soon enough, but we will never again be able to feel the wonder and magic of this first encounter with the unfamiliar.

In his book on *The Language of Comics*, Mario Saraceni points out that in the illustrations of children's books, in particular of small children's books, we usually find a strict correlation between the pictures and the words in the style of "See Spot jump", as they serve to support each other. He then adds:

> In comics things are very different: words and pictures are far from being redundant. In comics, that is, words and pictures don't just mirror one another, but interact in many different ways, and each of the two contributes its own share for the interpretation of the text. (Saraceni, 29)

However, this rather prescriptive view on the difference between children's books and comics or graphic novels cannot easily be maintained when we deal with the adaptation of a literary work, and the way the opening words are rendered offers a good example of one of the major problems in the adaptation of literature to sequential and visual arts.

We can assume that every comic book adaptation of *Moby Dick*, *Ulysses*, *Remembrance of Things Past*, *The Tale of Two Cities* or *City of Glass* will attempt to fulfil the audience's expectation by preserving the iconic first lines, and so

Dirk Vanderbeke

will an adaptation of *The Hobbit*. For an adaptation to a different medium like a movie or a comic book or graphic novel, the famed first line may then present the artist with a challenge if he wants to present the audience with a similar first impression of the world we are about to experience. In consequence, it also requires some decisions by the artist. Here is the first panel of David Wenzel's and Charles Dixon's *The Hobbit*.

Formally, the questions are preserved in the quotation of the first paragraph: not only do we still not know what kind of hole the text refers to, there is also no indication of a Hobbit, whatever that may be. However, a comic or graphic novel differs very much from a written text which we normally read linearly, and the panels on a page are at first not viewed consecutively but simultaneously. In consequence, we already know more than we are supposed to before we even read the first lines, for in the larger frame we immediately see not only the image of a hobbit-hole but also a view of the Hill with the neighbouring habitations.

This fundamental aesthetic difference alters the reading of the first lines completely, and thus the questions posed by the first sentence will no longer be asked but also immediately answered by a specific image, and in consequence the opening of the new version will include a redundancy, i.e. we get the text and an image repeating what the text has just said. And this now includes also that unfamiliar being, the Hobbit, who actually dominates the first page:

This redundancy of text and image becomes even more prominent as the new version also tries to preserve the straightforward repetition of the implied question that haunts the first paragraphs and the various references to the unknown, and as of yet undefined, being: "What is a Hobbit?" (p.30).

In this situation, the artist has to face the new decision of how much and which parts of the text he or she will actually try to preserve and in how far the new imagery will be trusted to carry the tale and the style independently.

In this case the decision is awkward.

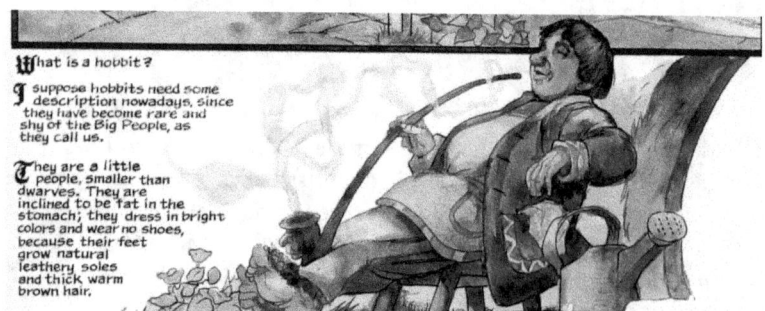

The text that accompanies the image describes what we actually see, while those features of the *Hobbit* that resist pictorial representation are not quoted at all (below you see the original text, the passages underlined being the ones quoted in the comic and the ones in italics those that present the reader with 'invisible' features).

> <u>I suppose hobbits need some description nowadays, since they have become rare and shy of the Big People, as they call us.</u> <u>They are</u> (or were) <u>a little people</u>, about half our height, and <u>smaller than the</u> bearded <u>Dwarves</u>. Hobbits have no beards. *There is little or no magic about them, except the ordinary everyday sort which helps them to disappear quietly and quickly when large stupid folk like you and me come blundering along, making a noise like elephants which they can hear a mile off.* <u>They are inclined to be fat in the stomach; they dress in bright colours</u> (chiefly green and yellow); <u>wear no shoes, because their feet grow natural leathery soles and thick warm brown hair</u> like the stuff on their heads (which is curly); have long clever brown fingers, good-natured faces, and *laugh deep fruity laughs (especially after dinner, which they have twice a day when they can get it).* Now you know enough to go on with. (p. 30)

All in all, Wenzel's and Dixon's *Hobbit* is rather wordy for a comic, and it tries to maintain as much of the actual text in the specific words of Tolkien as can be reasonable or even unreasonably managed.

Compared to other comic book adaptations of novels this is quite striking. The first panel of Stéphane Heuet's comic book version of Marcel Proust's *Á la recherche du temps perdu* of course presents us with the famed first line, but then there is a jump of about four pages to the memories of Marcel when he wakes up in the middle of the night. Moreover, every panel shows something new, while Wenzel and Dixon's first page contains three pictures of Bilbo which are almost interchangeable and thus add a new redundancy to the comic book. In fact, the first panel of the Proust adaptation departs from the actual text it repeats from the novel. It does not show us the narrator or the room he goes to bed in, but the shutters from the outside, and indeed, it is not dark yet. It thus establishes a double perspective, the internal view of the young boy and the external view of the narrator who remembers.

Just like the Proust adaptation, Bill Sienkievicz's *Moby Dick* only quotes the famed first sentence and then moves on to sum up the first three chapters all on the first page. What we actually see is a man with white hair looking distractedly on a street, probably Nantucket, where a younger man seems to have just arrived. The first line is not presented in a speech balloon, but in a banner. In consequence, the times of experience and narration are clearly divorced, and it even remains questionable whether the elderly man is, indeed, Ishmael or someone listening to the tale.

In the adaptation of Paul Auster's *City of Glass*, the ratio of text that has been preserved from the first pages looks like this:

> <u>It was a wrong number that started it, the telephone ringing three times in the dead of night, and the voice on the other end asking for someone he was not.</u> Much later, when he was able to think about the things that happened to him, <u>he would conclude that nothing was real</u> except chance. But that was much later. In the beginning, there was simply the event and its consequences. <u>Whether it might have turned out differently, or</u> whether it <u>was all predetermined</u> with the first word that came from the stranger's mouth, <u>is not the question. The question is the story itself, and whether or not it means something is not for the story to tell.</u>
>
> <u>As for Quinn</u>, there is little that need detain us. Who he was, where he came from, and what he did are of no great importance. We know, for example, that <u>he was thirty-five years old.</u> We know that he had once been married, had once been a father, and that <u>his wife and son were now dead.</u> We also know that he wrote books. To be precise, we know that <u>he wrote mystery novels.</u> These works were written <u>under the name of William Wilson</u>, and he produced them at a rate about one a year, which brought in enough money for him to live modestly in a small New York apartment.
>
> (Auster, *Trilogy*, p. 3)

As in Wenzel and Dixon, this is quite a lot, and it is actually mixed with passages of the text from a page or two later. However, if we then look at the imagery, things change, for the text/image ratio is quite different; the pictures are not loaded with words and they present us with a variety of motifs, even though there is a fair share of redundancy.

The very fist page seems to be straightforward but slightly uninteresting, being completely black with only the words "It was a wrong number that started it". But while the reader probably expects the blackness to represent a dark room, the following panels make clear that it was an extreme close up on a black telephone which then turns out to be only a small icon on a telephone directory. Things are from the very beginning not quite what they seem to be. And after three pages, all we have seen of the protagonist is his right foot.

The attempt to maintain as much as possible of the original text can be felt throughout the adaptation of *The Hobbit*, and, as already mentioned, it leads not only to a persistent redundancy of text and image, but also to a redundancy of the images themselves. And sometimes they both add up, and a repetitive imagery repeats the content of the text that it is supposed to adapt to a new medium. Thus an important aspect of the comic is lost, the pictorial equivalent of a poetic of absence.

As comics necessarily use hard cuts from one image to the next, a lot of the action takes place in the so-called gutter, the space between the images. This allows for various artistic possibilities – unexpected contrasts, scenic variation, radical shifts in the point of view, gaps which demand to be filled in by the reader. *The Hobbit*, however rather resembles the books of the Films Classics Library of the pre-video era, in which each shot and the complete dialogue are preserved.

Repetition in a comic can, of course, evoke the passing of time (cf. McCloud, 100-101), and thus it could make sense, for example, to present the seemingly endless journey in a series of similar images, However, the immense amount of text that accompanies each image rather indicates that the artist primarily tried to preserve Tolkien's words and thus needed more pictures as background. This unwillingness to depart from the text and to trust in the ability of the new medium to carry the message quite clearly results from an inordinate deference towards the words of the master; the text is treated as taboo and sacrosanct, even more so than the novels of Proust or Auster in the respective graphic novels.

And this can even lead to a kind of absurdity, when the text cannot be meaningfully adapted to the new medium. When the text tells us that the night in the forest was "pitch-dark – not what you call pitch-dark but really pitch: so black that you could see nothing" (p. 193), this does not offer too many opportunities for visualization. Of course, it would not make any sense to present a panel so dark that you cannot see anything, but instead of simply dropping the sentence, it is inserted into a kind of late afternoon panel akin to day-for-night shots in the movies (cf. Dixon and Wenzel, p. 76), simply because the authors could not let go of the original text.

Enough of that. An important aspect of comic book adaptations of literary text is, of course, the specific way in which elements of intertextuality are transported to the new medium. One should expect then that instead of literary allusions one would find references to artistic images or styles.

On the third page of *City of Glass*, for example, the image of the detective closely resembles the stereotyped P.I. of earlier comic books like Dick Tracy. In Kramsky's and Mattotti's *Dr. Jekyll and Mr. Hyde* we find references to the works of Edvard Munch, Otto Dix or George Grosz, and the story is thus transported from British late Victorianism to the 1920s of continental Europe – instead of the post-Darwinian aspect of bestiality in mankind we thus find a the inherent but submerged violence of bourgeois decadence ultimately leading to the horrors of fascism.

In the adaptation of Proust, the imagery occasionally presents the reader with the background information which a written text cannot or will not offer. In a famous passage in which the pregnant housemaid is compared to Giotto's *Charity*, we are shown a comic book rendering of that fresco. As most of us probably cannot immediately recall Giotto's fresco – and I wonder how many readers actually could when the *Recherche* was first published – the adaptation now serves as a commentary or even hypertext, but with the twist that in the image Giotto's charity is presented with a face somewhere between the original and the housemaid.

In adaptations of Tolkien texts the problem of intertextuality is, of course, of supreme importance. As we all know, Tolkien preferred the scoop to the spoon when he supped from the cauldron of stories. And thus we may well expect the adaptation also to introduce some intertextual references to take this aspect of the original work into account. The sources of Tolkien's mythological world are predominantly medieval with a strong touch of the heroic revisions of medieval literature and myth from the 19th century. In consequence, an imagery that employs allusions to medieval paintings or illustrations or to 19th century art with its medievalism or fake medievalism would not be out of place. For example the imagery of nature could have included a few nods to the pre-Raphaelite artists. I am not an art critic, but I found nothing of this kind in the graphic novel. The images are generally rather traditional, and in particular Gandalf and the dwarves are exactly what we can expect them to be from innumerable picture books or animated movies for a younger readership. The typology can hardly be ignored, and Gandalf is only a slightly more serious version of Disney's Merlin from *The Sword in the Stone*. In addition, the hoods of the dwarves have been replaced by the more familiar pointy caps, and their first entrance – or the march through the forest – cannot fail to evoke a strong feeling of disneyfication.

And then there are the monsters. They were dear to Tolkien who called for a serious appreciation of their significance in his essay *The Monsters and the Critics*. Unsurprisingly, the spiders are not particularly striking – ever since *Tarantula* we know what an oversized spider looks like. The goblins are more interesting. According to a letter by Tolkien, the goblins of *The Hobbit* "owe a great deal to the goblin tradition ... especially as it appears in George McDonald, except for the soft feet" (quoted from *The Annotated Hobbit*, 108). So, what does McDonald say about goblins in *The Princess and the Goblin*?

> There was a legend current in the country that at one time they lived above ground, and were very like other people... Those who had caught sight of any of them said that they had greatly

altered in the course of generations; and no wonder, seeing they lived away from the sun, in cold and wet and dark places. They were now, not ordinarily ugly, but either absolutely hideous, or ludicrously grotesque both in face and form. (McDonald, n.p.)

However, the narrator then claims that "The goblins themselves were not so far removed from the human as such a description would imply" (ibid). So one might expect something humanoid, but rather misshapen and ugly. In the adaptation, the goblins in some way resemble green hairless monkeys, but actually they are rather reptilian or amphibian, a little reminiscent of turtles. But most of all they have a touch of the various brands of green evil aliens from the Marvel Comics universe, the Badoon, appearing first in the *Silver Surfer* in 1968, or the Skrull who have been around since 1962 in *The Fantastic Four*.

Of course, these creatures are not inhabitants of Middle-earth but aliens, but as we all know, the various monsters of science fiction are all descendants of the ancient bestiarium and so some cross fertilization between fantasy comics and science fiction is nothing exceptional. But no matter what our associations may be, the goblins are certainly beastly instead of merely ugly. As David Wenzel worked for the Marvel Comics series *The Avengers* which occasionally featured the Skrulls, this is not fully surprising, but it marks a departure from Tolkien that the authors elsewhere shied away from. This, of course, makes it easier visually to define the goblins as the Other, as incorrigible enemies who have to be killed without mercy or remorse.

The image of Gollum was, as far as I could see resemblances, inspired by the first animated *Lord of the Rings* movie, and once more there is some similarity with the Badoon from Marvel Comics. In particular the pointed ears are interesting, as they have for some time been a marker of almost every kind of supernatural being from pixies or fairies to leprechauns. In Science Fiction they have been adapted for Mr. Spock from *Star Trek*, and lately Peter Jackson used them for the Elves. Here the elves cannot be distinguished from the humans, unless by their green clothes, and the goblins as well as Gollum have pointed ears as markers of a kind of sub-humanity. The Elves themselves are in some frames reminiscent of quite another tradition, i.e. Robin Hood and his merry men, but the connection, if it is supposed to mean anything, is not quite clear to me.

And then there is Smaug. Predictably, the image is derivative of Tolkien's own picture of the dragon. Both dragons are, of course, red – even though not really golden red as the text prescribes. And both are rolled up, as a curved dragon can in any given panel be π-times longer than a straight one. Wenzel also emphasises the cup and thus the allusion to *Beowulf*.

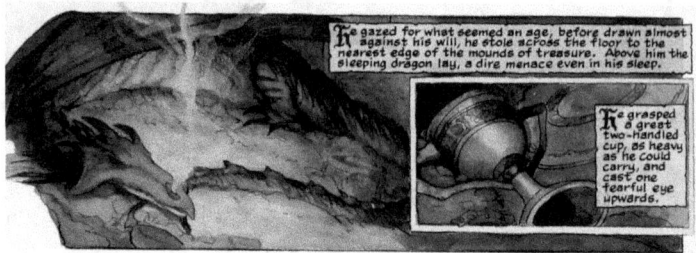

But there is one difference between Tolkien's dragon and the picture in Wenzel's adaptation. The body of Tolkien's Smaug forms a spiral and thus the earliest form of the labyrinth. It is a fitting allusion, as Smaug will at least momentarily try to bring Bilbo under the dragon spell and to draw him in.

Wenzel's dragon (p. 108), however, forms a complete circle and thus alludes to Ouroboros, the eternal snake and symbol of infinity. Of course, the Nordic version of Ouroboros is the Midgard Serpent which will play an instrumental role at Ragnarök. This allusion stresses the destructive aspect, but Smaug is hardly a particularly good symbol for infinity and/or cosmic doom.

Conclusion

Two major aspects seem to govern the comic book adaptation of Tolkien's *The Hobbit*. On the one hand there is the attempt to change as little as possible. In consequence the artistic enterprise is at least to some extent sacrificed and the creative input reduced in favour of more verbatim passages from the original text. This tendency leads almost automatically to a perpetual redundancy, not only between text and image but also between repetitive pictures. The possible motivation for the close link between the imagery and the words, i.e. the reinforcement used to help a young audience in the reading process, can hardly work here, as the understanding is not facilitated by the pictures.

I would tend to diagnose a kind of inferiority complex here which is also occasionally noticeable in Tolkien criticism in claims that Tolkien's work is clearly at the centre of twentieth-century literature (cf. the advertisement for Martin Simonson's book *The Lord of the Rings and the Western Narrative Tradition*), or that Tolkien's achievement actually surpasses everything else written in this era. In consequence, the text must be raised on a pedestal, and that is always an awkward place for a book you want to work on.

The wish to accommodate a young audience may also be at the root of some of the images, in particular the pictures of the dwarves, the magician, and monsters like the goblins and the dragon. However, this imagery turns the comic book into a collection of stereotypes, most of which Tolkien would have

regarded with distinct distaste – I cannot imagine him to be particularly fond of Walt Disney's comic figures or his movies and even less that he would have appreciated the evil aliens from the Marvel universe.
The two aspects counteract each other. The imagery addresses comic book readers of an age group which does not really relish the reading of long texts and demands a little more action, while the comparatively strong adherence to Tolkien's text kowtows to a fan community which presumably expects more of Faërie than a few stereotypes.

Bibliography

Auster, Paul. *The New York Trilogy*. London: Faber and Faber, 1987
---. *City of Glass*. Adaptation by Paul Karasik and David Mazzuchelli. New York: Picador, 2004
Melville, Herman. *Moby Dick*. Adaptation by Bill Sienkiewicz. New York: Classics Illustrated, 1990
McCloud, Scott. *Understanding Comics*. New York: HarperPerennial, 1994
Proust, Marcel. *Remembrance of Things Past (Á la recherche du temps perdu)*. Adaptation by Stéphane Heuet, Translation by Joe Johnson. New York: Nantier, Beall, Minoustchine, 2001
Saraceni, Mario. *The Language of Comics*. London and New York: Routledge, 2003
Stevenson, Robert Louis. *Doktor Jekyll & Mister Hyde*. Adaptation by Lorenzo Mattotti and Jerry Kramsky. Translation by Rossi Schreiber. Hamburg: Carlsen, 2001
Tolkien, J.R.R. *The Annotated Hobbit*. Edited and annotated by Douglas A. Anderson. Boston and New York, Houghton Mifflin, revised and expanded edition 2002
---. *The Hobbit*. Adaptation by Charles Dixon and David Wenzel. London: HarperCollins, revised edition 2006
---. "The Monsters and the Critics" [1936]. *The Monsters and the Critics and other essays*. London: HarperCollins, 2006, 5-48

Schwarz und unheimlich wirkte das Wasser. Und gefährlich ist seine Wirkung auf alle Lebewesen, sobald sie mit ihm in Berührung kommen...

Eine Neubewertung der theoretischen Konzeption von ›Faërie‹ und ›fairy-story‹ auf Basis der 2008 erschienenen erweiterten Ausgabe *Tolkien On Fairy-stories*

Heidi Krüger (Hamburg)

1 Hinführung zum Thema

Über den Begriff ›Faërie‹ schreiben Flieger/Anderson[1]: »Possibly the single most important term in Tolkien's critical lexikon, with a complex of referents« (FA 85). Ich möchte hinzufügen: Die Auseinandersetzung mit ›Faërie‹ ist das unsichtbare, aber steuernde Zentrum des fiktionalen Gesamtwerkes Tolkiens. Der Nachweis dazu kann allerdings nur mittels Analyse der einzelnen fiktionalen Werke erbracht und inhaltlich bestimmt werden[2].

In meinem Essay geht es nicht im engen Sinn um das fiktionale Werk, sondern um die theoretischen Erörterungen Tolkiens zu diesem Themenkomplex. Die Frage, ob diese seine theoretischen Bestimmungen dann in der Tat in seinem fiktionalen Werk umgesetzt wurden, muss hier in extenso undiskutiert bleiben; einige Überlegungen dazu werden aber nicht fehlen.

In einem weiten Sinn allerdings zielt die hier geführte Erörterung dann doch auf das fiktionale Werk, denn Tolkien ist hauptsächlich Dichter, hat sein Leben lang darum gerungen, mittels Dichtung sein Anliegen auszudrücken. Der Vergleich zwischen Theorie und Praxis wäre schon allein deshalb von Bedeutung, weil allzu häufig einfach vorausgesetzt - oder unzulänglich überprüft - wird, dass und ob die literarischen Werke Tolkiens eine 1:1-Umsetzung seiner theoretischen Faërie-Konzeption seien.

Die wichtigste Anlaufstelle für die Frage nach dieser Konzeption war natürlich stets sein Essay *On Fairy-Stories*. Der Punkt ist nur: Es ist nicht einfach, diesen Essay zu verstehen. Unklare oder gar verschwimmende Bestimmungen lassen eigentlich gar nicht zu, eine klare Konzeption von ›Faërie‹ und damit auch von ›fairy-story‹ zu bekommen. Dies soll in Kapitel 3 illustriert und meine Sicht diesbezüglich auf den Punkt gebracht werden.

Das allein wird freilich nicht sehr viel weiter führen, denn die Unklarheiten müssen ja nicht nur beschrieben und klassifiziert, sondern auch beseitigt wer-

---

1 Die beiden Autoren des Buches *On Fairy-stories*, Verlyn Flieger und Douglas A. Anderson, werden von mir im Folgenden mit FA bezeichnet.
2 Solch ein Nachweis kann naturgemäß nur nach und nach erstellt werden. Ansätze dazu sind von der Verfasserin dieses Artikels bisher bezüglich *The Lord of the Rings*, *The Notion Club Papers* und *Leaf by Niggle* vorhanden.

den. Tolkiens Aufsatz kann das nicht schaffen, denn dort sind diese Probleme ja entstanden. Man half sich mit Mutmaßungen oder Einfühlung aus, aber man bekam letztlich keinen wirklichen Grund unter die Füße.

Das ist seit Juli 2008 anders. Die sehnlichst erwartete ›Expanded Edition‹ ist nun endlich erschienen, und das uns erstmalig zur Verfügung gestellte Zusatzmaterial klärt viel, sehr viel.

In welchem Ausmaß dies die Erkenntnisse über Tolkiens literaturtheoretisches und auch weltanschauliches Ringen insgesamt erweitern oder verändern wird, werden wir in den nächsten Jahren sehen. Einige mögliche Aspekte werde ich in meinem Essay andeuten. Konkret aber geht es hier – indem das neue Material einbezogen wird – um eine Beschreibung dessen, was Tolkien, meinem Verständnis nach, mit ›Faërie‹ meint und in welchem Verhältnis die ›fairy-story‹ dazu steht (Kapitel 4 wertet dieses Material aus, Kapitel 5 zieht die Schlussfolgerungen). Damit wird dann eine Grundlage – und eine viel bessere als bislang möglich – geschaffen, um die fiktionalen Werke Tolkiens daraufhin zu beurteilen, ob – oder in welcher Art oder in welcher Art nicht – sie eine Umsetzung der Faërie-Konzeption sind. Zunächst aber soll in Kapitel 2 kurz das neue Material gesichtet werden.

2 Kurzcharakterisierung des neuen Materials

2.1 Historischer Exkurs: Von der Lesung bis zum Essay[3]

Das Werk *On Fairy-Stories*, das wir in den Buchhandlungen kaufen können, ist eine mehrfach überarbeite Version der ursprünglichen Lesung vom 8. März 1939. Wie groß der Unterschied zwischen der Lesung und der Essay-Fassung letztlich ist, wird durch die Neuausgabe erst klar. Zwar ist das Skript der Lesung verloren gegangen, aber FA legen in ihrem Buch einen (wahrscheinlich großen) Teil der Entwürfe dazu vor. Diese publizierten Entwürfe werden von FA als *Manuskript A* bezeichnet und sind wahrscheinlich zwischen 1938 und März 1939 entstanden.

Veröffentlicht wurde *On Fairy-Stories* erstmals 1947[4]. Mit einer Überarbeitung seiner Lesung hat Tolkien eventuell direkt nach dem Vortrag, also 1939, begonnen. 1943 erstellte er aus nicht ganz geklärtem Grund davon ein Schreibmaschinenskript. Eine Auswahl aus seinen Entwürfen bis zu diesem Skript 1943 ist in dem neuen Buch als *Manuskript B* veröffentlicht.

Das Schreibmaschinenskript selbst wird von FA *Manuskript C* genannt. Das *Manuskript C* ist in dem neuen Buch nicht enthalten, weicht aber laut FA nicht

---

3 Insgesamt zu dem kurzen Überblick in Kapitel 2.1 vergleiche FA 122-158.
4 Der Ausbruch des Zweiten Weltkrieges hat verhindert, dass die Lesung wie die früheren Andrew Lang Lectures ein oder zwei Jahre nach der Lesung im Druck erschien.

stark von der ersten Publikation 1947 ab. Nun ist freilich auch die Publikation von 1947 nicht mehr im Handel, sodass der Leser die beiden Fassungen nicht so ohne weiteres vergleichen kann.

Die Edition von 1947 war relativ bald vergriffen. Erst der Sammelband *Tree and Leaf* von 1964, in dem *On Fairy-Stories*, nun erneut von Tolkien überarbeitet, neben der Erzählung *Leaf by Niggle* enthalten war, machte dem ein Ende. Die wichtigsten Änderungen zwischen den beiden Ausgaben – 1947 und 1964 – sind von FA in ihrem Buch aufgelistet, spielen für die Thematik dieses Artikels aber keine Rolle.

2.2 Die Miszellen: besonders ergiebig für die Themenstellung

Das oben genannte *Manuskript B* ist zweigeteilt: Der zweite Teil enthält Miszellen (miscellaneous pages), also Beiträge verschiedener Art. Während der erste Teil und die zweite Hälfte der Miszellen etwa den gleichen Aufbau haben wie der publizierte Essay und – wenn auch sehr lückenhafte – Varianten einzelner Abschnitte davon sind, enthalten die Miszellen in der ersten Hälfte Überlegungen und Ausführungen, die komplett neu sind und das Anliegen Tolkiens auf verblüffende Weise beleuchten. Und es sind diese Passagen, die den publizierten Aufsatz *On Fairy-Stories* in einen ganz anderen Zusammenhang zu stellen vermögen, die dort festgestellten Ungenauigkeiten und Widersprüchlichkeiten teils auflösen, teils klären, teils als notwendig erscheinen lassen.

3 Die Unklarheiten in *On Fairy-Stories*

3.1 Beschreibung der Schwierigkeit anhand Abschnitt 2 und 3[5]

Das Gedankengut der Abschnitte 2 und 3 ist bereits in der Lesung vom 8. März 1939 enthalten. Auch wenn das Skript dazu verloren ist, können zumindest diese beiden Abschnitte rekonstruiert werden: Sie sind als Entwurf in *Manuskript B* enthalten, und dieser Entwurf kann abgeglichen werden mit einer Zeitungsbesprechung vom 9. März 1939 (FA 164-169), in der der Inhalt des Vortrages mehr zitiert oder paraphrasiert als besprochen wird. Der Wortlaut ist fast völlig identisch.

---

[5] FA haben in ihrer Ausgabe die Abschnitte des veröffentlichten Essays durchnummeriert. Ich benutze im Folgenden diese Nummern. Im Anhang habe ich als Service eine Liste erstellt, in der die Nummern aufgeführt und ihnen die ersten Wörter des jeweiligen Absatzes beigefügt sind, sowohl des englischen Originals als auch der Krege-Übersetzung. Ich empfehle den Lesern, diese Nummern in ihre Ausgaben einzutragen. Wenn ich im laufenden Text z.B. FS A 17 schreibe, steht FS für den veröffentlichten Aufsatz, A für Abschnitt.

Ich zitiere die beiden Abschnitte (leicht gekürzt) aus *Manuskript B*:

> The Land of Fairy Story is wide and deep and high, and is filled with many kings[6] and all manner of men, and beasts, and birds; its seas are shoreless and its stars uncounted, its beauty an enchantment and its peril ever-present; both its joy and sorrow are poignant as a sword. In that land a man may (perhaps) count himself fortunate to have wandered, but its very mystery and wealth made dumb the traveller who would report. And while he is there it is dangerous for him to ask too many questions, lest the gates shut and the keys be lost. The fairy gold (too often) turns to withered leaves when it was brought away...
> But there are some questions that one who is to speak about fairy-stories cannot help asking, whatever the folk of Faery may think of him or do to him. What are fairy-stories? What is their origin? What is the use of them? Now, today? (FA 207f)

Die Argumentationslinie in dem Text ist klar: Tolkien spricht – vor Publikum – von Faery, einem geheimnisvollen, aber auch hochgefährlichen Land. Gefährlich ist ebenfalls, während eines Aufenthaltes dort vor Ort Fragen zu stellen, weil man dann dieses Land verliert.

Wenn jemand aber über fairy-*stories* eine Rede halten wolle, dann habe er keine Wahl, er müsse trotzdem Fragen stellen, egal, was die Bewohner jenes Landes von ihm denken und ihm dafür antun werden.

Die Grundproblematik und die Schwierigkeit des Aufsatzes liegen bereits hier offen auf dem Tisch: Ein Professor des Angelsächsischen hält einen Vortrag über Märchen und sagt, er gehe das Risiko dabei ein, dass die Bewohner des Märchenreiches ihm deshalb vielleicht etwas antun werden oder er nie wieder das Märchenreich werde betreten dürfen.

Der erste Selbstschutz beim Hören oder Lesen wird wohl sein: Der Professor spricht symbolisch, bildhaft. Immerhin hat er ja vom Land der Märchen*erzählung* gesprochen, also – in Begriffen der Poetik ausgedrückt – vom *Schauplatz* der Erzählungen. Was aber ist an diesem Schauplatz so gefährlich, und vor allem: für wen? Der Satz: »its perils [are] ever present« findet sich ganz ähnlich in der publizierten Fassung: »all manner of beasts and birds are found there; ... beauty that is an enchantment, and an ever-present peril« (FS A 2).

Die Vernunft würde antworten: Für die fiktiven Märchenfiguren ist der fiktive Schauplatz gefährlich, da dort plötzlich eine böse Fee auftauchen kann,

---

6   In den früheren Fassungen steht da tatsächlich ›kings‹ und nicht ›things‹ wie in der veröffentlichten Fassung.

die Macht hat und einen verhexen kann. Aber so kann es nicht gemeint sein, oder nicht nur, denn: »In that land man may, perhaps, count himself fortunate to have wandered, but its very mystery and wealth made dumb the traveller who would report.« Hier ist nicht von fiktiven Märchenfiguren die Rede, sondern von Reisenden, die sich an diesen geheimnisvollen Orten aufhalten und später versuchen, davon zu berichten, aber vergeblich.

Nun könnte man noch immer glauben, der Vortragende spreche von Erzählungen über Menschen, die in die Faery reisten, so wie es später Smith of Wootton Major[7] tut. Dann wäre auch der hier erwähnte Reisende eine fiktive Figur. Dem entgegen aber spricht wiederum, dass ja just dieser Reisende hier am Rednerpult steht und sich entschieden hat, trotz aller Gefahr die Märchen zu analysieren.

Wovon also wollte der Vortragende sprechen?

3.2. Faërie innerliterarisch oder außerliterarisch?

Ja, wovon wollte Tolkien sprechen. Von der Faërie, das ist klar: »fairy-stories are not in normal English usage stories *about* fairies or elves, but stories about Fairy, that is *Faërie*, the realm or state in which fairies have their being« (FS A 10).

Aber hier ist die alles entscheidende Frage: Wird die Faërie mittels der fairy-story hergestellt, ist also ein innerliterarisches Produkt? Oder befindet sie sich außerhalb der Erzählung, und die fairy-story ist eine Art ›Sachbericht‹ über Außerliterarisches?

Es gibt für beides Belege sowohl in der Lesung als auch in dem Essay, und noch mehr Belege gibt es dafür, dass Tolkien das Phänomen verschwimmen lässt und dazu keine klare Stellung bezogen hat.

3.2.1 Ein wenig Materialsammlung

3.2.1.1 Der Titel der Lesung (*Fairy Stories*[8]) und der Anfang obigen Zitates lassen die Vermutung zu, dass Tolkien die Schauplätze, die Artefakte und das Flair der Märchen als Kunstform durchsucht und gegliedert hat, um das typische Equipment von Märchen darzulegen. Der ›Wanderer‹ ist dann nur eine poetische Umschreibung des Märchenforschers, der sich nicht als Volkskundler, sondern als Literaturfreund und -theoretiker versteht.

---

[7] In Tolkiens gleichnamiger Erzählung von 1967.
[8] Der Titel der Lesung hatte nicht die Präposition ›On‹.

3.2.1.2 Dem widerspricht aber Tolkiens Hinweis auf das in der Faërie lebende Volk, das sich so seine Gedanken macht über die Märchenforscher. Will Tolkien damit sagen, dass das Märchenreich mitsamt seinen (intelligenten) Bewohnern wirklich existiert? Sodass sein Wissen darüber nicht nur aus den tradierten Märchen stammt, sondern – ja, woher?

3.2.1.3 Diese Zweideutigkeit durchzieht den ganzen (veröffentlichten) Aufsatz, durchzog schon die Lesung, soweit wir sie rekonstruieren können. Hier ein paar der markantesten Beispiele, die den Anschein erwecken, als würden das elbische Reich und die elbischen Wesen tatsächlich vorhanden sein:

> For the trouble with the real folk of Faërie is that they do not always look like what they are (FS A 9).

> ... for if elves are true, and really exist independently of our tales about them, then this also is certainly true: elves are not primarily concerned with us, nor we with them. Our fates are sundered, and our paths seldom meet. Even upon the borders of Faërie we encounter them only at some chance crossing of the ways. (FS A 11)
> This is true also, even if they are only creations of Man's mind, "true" only as reflecting in a particular way one of Man's visions of Truth. (FS A 11 Anmerkung)

Tolkien setzt zwar die Existenz der elbischen Wesen in einen Konditionalsatz, aber dies kann auch eine Vorsichtsmaßnahme sein. In Kapitel 3.3 (Thema ›Faërian Drama‹) wird sich zeigen, dass Tolkien nicht immer so vorsichtig ist.

3.2.1.4 Und nun ein Beispiel, wo Tolkien auf der Basis der *Literaturanalyse* ein formales Element der fairy-story bestimmt: »Most good ›fairy-stories‹ are about the *aventures* of men in the Perilous Realm« (FS A 11).

Dieser Satz, so kurz er ist, hat es in sich. Ob die Faërie hier rein literarisch gemeint ist oder dann doch mitschwingt, dass literarische Figuren in einer realen Faërie umhergehen, ist aus diesem Satz nicht zu erschließen. Nimmt man diesen Satz hinzu – »a ›fairy-story‹ is one which touches on or uses Faërie, whatever its own main purpose may be: satire, adventure, morality, fantasy« (FS A 12) –, wird es leider noch uneindeutiger. Denn gemeint sein kann, dass die Erzählung die ›Faërie außerhalb der Erzählung‹ berührt, aber es kann auch gemeint sein, dass sie im Werk selbst thematisiert wird (und dadurch automatisch literarisiert ist).

Aber wenn man von der Vagheit der Faërie absieht, ist das, was Tolkien unter einer fairy-story versteht, oder vor allem versteht, hier literarisch-strukturell bestimmt: *Menschen geraten in die Faërie*. Und da die Faërie gefährlich ist, geschieht mit den Menschen durch diese Begegnung etwas, das offenbar an die Substanz geht.

Interessant – und folgenschwer für die Untersuchung der dichterischen Werke Tolkiens – ist, dass das Genre oder die Gattung durchaus mehr oder weniger beliebig sein kann. ›Fairy-story‹ ist nach obiger Bestimmung keine eigene Gattungsbezeichnung, sondern kann sich in anderen Gattungen verbergen. Der entscheidende Punkt ist, dass dort Menschen in die Faërie geraten.

3.2.1.5 Noch verwirrender wird es, wenn Tolkien einmal sehr konkret ist und sich gänzlich auf den machbaren Teil einer Erzählung konzentriert, also auf die Frage: Mit welchen literarischen Mitteln erzeugt man einen bestimmten Effekt? Wir bekommen hier die verblüffende Antwort: Die Faërie wird mittels klugen Gebrauchs des Adjektivs hergestellt. Ja, die Faërie sei überhaupt erst entstanden, als das Adjektiv in der Genese der Sprache entstanden ist:

> The human mind, endowed with the powers of generalisation and abstraction, sees not only *green-grass* ... but sees that it is *green* as well as being *grass*. But how powerful, how stimulating to the very faculty that produced it, was the invention of the adjective: no spell or incantation in Faërie is more potent... When we can take green from grass, blue from heaven, and red from blood, we have already an enchanter's power... We may put a deadly green upon a man's face and produce a horror... But in such 'fantasy', as it is called, new form is made; Faërie begins; Man becomes a sub-creator. (FS A 27)

3.2.2 Zwischenfazit und -ausblick

Die bisherigen Belege finden sich bereits im Frühstadium des Lesungsentwurfes oder wurzeln zumindest darin. Die Frage, ob Faërie eine innerliterarische oder außerliterarische Entität ist, bleibt unklar. Ja, diese Frage erschöpft noch nicht einmal die wirkliche Problematik, wie schon die Bedeutsamkeit, die Tolkien dem Adjektiv zuweist, umreißt: Faërie sei Ergebnis einer sprachlichen Schöpfung. Falls Faërie nur innerliterarisch vorkommen kann, ist dies weiter nicht brisant. Denn Kunst ist seit jeher dadurch charakterisiert, dass sie neue Formen schafft. Brisant wird es dadurch, dass die Möglichkeit besteht, dass die Faërie auch außerhalb der Kunst existiert. Denn wie kann etwas außerhalb der Kunst existieren, wenn es überhaupt erst durch die Kunst erzeugt wird?

Diesen komplizierten Sachverhalt in seiner ganzen Spannweite hat Tolkien für seine Lesung im März 1939 noch nicht entwickelt. In dem veröffentlichten

Essay hingegen finden wir dafür reichlich Hinweise. Dazu dann im nächsten Kapitel.

3.3 Schöpfung und Realität in Faërie und fairy-story

3.3.1 Vertiefende Überarbeitungen

Es gibt einige Abschnitte in der veröffentlichten Fassung, die wie sperrige Brocken den Fluss des Gedankengangs hemmen und die Lektüre sehr erschweren. Vergleicht man nun mit *Manuskript A* und *B*, stellt man fest, dass genau diese ›Brocken‹ in der ursprünglichen Fassung fehlen und Tolkien sie erst nach der Lesung in sein Konzept eingefügt haben muss. Löst man sie heraus, ist der Gedankengang wieder flüssig.

Das wirklich Interessante aber ist, dass diese herauslösbaren Teile – sie betreffen die Abschnitte 17/18, 28 und 50/51 – in sich selbst zusammenhängen und ihrerseits ein bestimmtes Thema verfolgen. Und nicht nur diese. Das ganze Kapitel ›Fantasy‹ – in dem so wesentliche Termini wie Primary World/Secondary World, Secondary Belief, inner consistency of Reality, Faërian Drama abgehandelt werden - ist nachträglich zwischen die Abschnitte über die Kinder und über Recovery/Escape/Consolation geschoben worden. Und just dieses Kapitel ›Fantasy‹ – das so ganz nicht dazwischen passt – setzt fast nahtlos die Thematik der erwähnten und später eingefügten Abschnitte fort.

Aber es geht noch weiter. Auch der ursprünglich nicht enthaltene Epilog setzt den Gedankengang, der mit den Abschnitten 17/18, 28, 50/51 begann und in dem Kapitel ›Fantasy‹ weiterentwickelt wurde, fort und krönt ihn.

All diese Teile und Kapitel sollen nun insgesamt betrachtet und in ihrer Relevanz für das Thema ausgewertet werden.

3.3.2 Zunächst: Die gleichen Antinomien auf höherer Ebene

Die Grundfrage lautete bisher: Ist Faërie ein innerliterarisches oder ein außerliterarisches Phänomen?

3.3.2.1 Die in der endgültigen Fassung nachgetragenen Texte akzentuieren und vertiefen dabei nun zusätzlich den Gedanken des Schöpferischen, des Kreativen mittels der für Tolkien so bedeutsamen Phantasie. Dichtung ist *Kunst*, und phantastische Dichtung sei es erst recht. Tolkien führt die Begriffe Primary World/Secondary World ein, um die beiden Welten voneinander zu scheiden – die vom Menschen geschaffene künstlerische Welt und die normale Welt, die jeder Mensch und auch der Künstler vorfindet, nicht erschafft. Der Künstler ist sub-creator, er baut mit an einer neuen (Sekundär-)Welt. Faërie wäre danach ein *innerliterarisches* Produkt.

3.3.2.2 Aber dies ist nur ein Teil der Wahrheit. Denn die wahren Künstler seien gar nicht die Menschen, sondern die fairies (oder elves). Eines der Produkte, das sie herstellen, ist das – von Tolkien so genannte – Faërian Drama:

> This is for them [the elves] a form of Art... They do not live in it, though they can, perhaps, afford to spend more time at it than human artists can. The Primary World, Reality, of elves and men is the same, if differently valued and perceived. (FS A 74)

Der Leser, der vielleicht wirklich immer ratloser wird und nicht mehr begreifen kann, wie solche Aussagen zum Verständnis dessen beitragen, was in einer fairy-story die Faërie ist oder wie sie hergestellt wird und vor allem von wem, sieht vielleicht wieder etwas Land bei folgender Aussage:

> At the heart of many man-made stories of the elves lies, open or concealed, pure or alloyed, the desire for a living, realised sub-creative art... Of this desire the elves, in their better (but still perilous) part, are largely made. (FS A 76)

Also sind die elbischen Wesen doch nur Verkörperungen unserer Sehnsüchte, künstlerische Verkörperungen? Aber noch im selben Satz lesen wir:

> and it is from them that we may learn what is the central desire and aspiration of human Fantasy – even if the elves are, all the more in so far as they are, only a product of Fantasy itself.
> (FS A 76)

Also sie sind *nicht immer* ein Produkt unserer Phantasie (vgl. auch den letzten Zitatsatz oben in 3.2.1.3). Die elbische Kunst ist kein Produkt *unserer* Phantasie. Faërie wäre in dem Fall ein *außerliterarisches* Produkt.

Das Problem ist formuliert und noch zugespitzt: Wer genau stellt die Faërie denn nun her, und auf welche Weise? Geht es hier wirklich um Kunst oder um ganz andere Fragen?

3.3.3 Und dann: Ein neuer Aspekt wird sichtbar

Lassen wir die gestellten Fragen an dieser Stelle notgedrungen offen. Im vorletzten Zitat ist durch die Formulierung »the desire for a living, realised sub-creative art« ein neuer Aspekt am Horizont erschienen, der die Problematik noch einmal verkompliziert, aber vermutlich das Zentrum des ganzen Essays *On Fairy-Stories* bedeutet und nur aus diesem Punkt heraus die Problematik lösbar macht. Die entscheidenden Stichworte sind dabei ›living‹ und ›realised‹. Tolkien beschreibt dieses Phänomen in seinen Ausführungen über das *Faërian Drama*.

> Now ›Faërian Drama‹ – those plays which according to abundant records the elves have often presented to men – can produce Fantasy with a realism and immediacy beyond the compass of any human mechanism. As a result their usual effect (upon a man) is to go beyond Secondary Belief. If you are present at a Faërian drama you yourself are, or think that you are, bodily inside its Secondary World... To experience *directly* a Secondary World: the potion is too strong, and you give to it Primary Belief, however marvellous the events. (FS A 74)

Was immer Tolkien unter dem Faërian Drama versteht – es wird hier in seiner Wirkung auf die *Menschen* untersucht. Aber wovon genau spricht er? Selbst FA müssen konstatieren, dass Tolkien nirgendwo Erläuterungen oder gar Definitionen vorlegt (vgl. FA 112).

Besonders interessant (und schwierig) ist die Aussage, dass der Mensch, dem dergleichen widerfährt, diesem Geschehen primären Glauben schenken muss, es mit der Primärwelt verwechselt. FA schreiben direkt zu obigem Zitat:

> So vivid and immediate is Tolkien's report on these extraordinary conditions that readers may find it hard to believe he was not speaking out of his own encounter with the phenomena he describes (FA 138).

Der Eindruck, dass Tolkien von Selbsterlebtem spricht, kann tatsächlich entstehen. Im Moment ist nur wichtig, was genau dieser ›Trank‹ im Menschen bewirkt: nämlich das Gefühl (oder die Gewissheit) von Unmittelbarkeit und Realismus einer nicht-realen Welt. Das bedeutet *nicht* einfach nur, dass man eine Geschichte vollkommen mitlebt und mitfiebert – denn da weiß man dennoch immer, dass man sich in einer Phantasiewelt befindet -, sondern eindeutig, dass man sich als Teil der Geschichte empfindet, als Körper mit enthalten ist und sie mit der Primärwelt verwechselt.

Diese Aussage ist darum so zentral, weil Tolkien daraus eine Bestimmung ableitet, die auf den Punkt bringt, was für ihn der menschliche Zweck des Phantasierens und des Verfassens von fairy-stories ist (vgl. die drei Zitate aus

A 76 in 3.3.2.2): Das Herz der menschlichen Phantasie und der menschlichen fairy-stories sei das Verlangen, eine Sekundärwelt zu erstellen, in der der Mensch sich quasi bewegen kann wie in der normalen Welt.

Diese – befremdlich wirkende – Bestimmung möchte ich der ersten Bestimmung, die ich in 3.2.1.4 aus Tolkiens Texten abgeleitet habe, folgen lassen.

a. *In einer fairy-story geraten Menschen in die (gefährliche) Faërie.*

b. *Die fairy-story wie die menschliche Phantasie überhaupt wurzeln in dem Verlangen, unmittelbar und leibhaftig in der geschaffenen Sekundärwelt anwesend zu sein.*

Die erste Bestimmung ist eine literaturtheoretische und betrifft die fairy-story. Die zweite Bestimmung bezeichne ich in diesem Aufsatz als eine philosophisch-existentielle, und sie betrifft die Faërie.

Auf welche Weise und ob überhaupt diese beiden Bestimmungen zusammenhängen, wird in den nächsten beiden Kapiteln diskutiert.

3.3.4 Secondary Belief in der fairy-story

Im Faërian Drama, hieß es oben, ist der Sekundärglaube so heftig, dass der Erlebende dem Geschehen zwanghaft primäre Realität zuspricht. In einer literarischen Erzählung ist dies in diesem Ausmaß natürlich nicht der Fall. Es sei nur wünschenswert – und in einer phantastischen Erzählung besonders schwer zu erreichen –, dass die fairy-story den Leser so verzaubert, dass ihm auch das Wunderbare innerhalb der Erzählung real erscheint. Da Tolkien ›Unmittelbarkeit‹ und ›Realitätsempfinden‹ als Eigenschaften der direkt erlebten Faërie (und des Faërian Dramas) versteht, muss – so offenbar der Zusammenhang für Tolkien – das Wundersame der fairy-story auf den Leser ebenfalls realistisch und glaubwürdig wirken, denn sonst verfehle das Wundersame seine Wirkung auf den Leser. Deshalb sortiert Tolkien alle die Erzählungen aus dem Bereich fairy-story aus, die dem Leser erklären, dass das geschilderte wundersame Geschehen rational erklärbar (oder nur geträumt) sei, in der erfundenen Welt also gar nicht stattgefunden hat.

3.3.5 Die Eukatastrophe

Die Eukatastrophe ist neben der Anwendung des Adjektivs fast das einzige konkrete *literarische* Mittel, das Tolkien erwähnt, um gute fairy-stories erkennen oder schreiben zu können. Warum *Machandelboom* (vgl. FS A 40) für ihn ein hervorragendes Beispiel einer fairy-story, die an die Faërie rührt, ist, präzisiert er nicht – außer dass es ihm die Tür in ein Jenseits der Zeit öffnet. Für die

Eukatastrophe aber bringt er sogar Beispiele. Und diese machen sinnfällig, wie Tolkien es sich vorstellte, wenn am Ende einer fairy-story die Faërie durch die Realität blitzen soll. In einem Märchen von Andrew Lang z.b. stehen am Ende alle erschlagenen Ritter wieder auf, klirren mit den Schwertern und rufen: ›Lang lebe Prinz Prigio!‹ Und Tolkien kommentiert:

> In such stories when the sudden 'turn' comes we get a piercing glimpse of joy, and heart's desire, that for a moment passes outside the frame, rends indeed the very web of story, and lets a gleam come through. (FS A 101)

Hier, fast am Ende des veröffentlichten Aufsatzes, finden wir endlich einen deutlichen Hinweis, was die Erzählung leisten soll, um eine Anderwelt (Faërie) spürbar zu machen. Der Schlüsselsatz dabei ist: Das Gewebe der Erzählung als solches reißt. Die Erzählung wird *als* Erzählung sichtbar. Das wäre die erzähltechnische Seite.

Die philosophisch-existentielle Seite dabei ist: Eine Realitätsebene, mitsamt ihren (schrecklichen) Bedingungen, wird als nur *eine* Realitätsebene erkannt. Diese Erkenntnis schließt Tolkien aus dem Bereich des Eskapismus ausdrücklich aus (FS A 99). Um die Freude, die laut Tolkien bei diesem wenn auch noch so flüchtigen Erkennen entspringt, durch eine natürlich sehr viel schwächere Analogie erahnbar zu machen, wähle ich einen beliebten Dialog aus dem Alltag:

Jemand erzählt dir, dass dein Lieblingsprojekt zerschlagen worden ist, und du bist traurig. Und dann sagt dieser Jemand ›April, April‹. Diese Erleichterung ist – vom Effekt her – vergleichbar mit der Eukatastrophe. Die Ausweglosigkeit einer Realität erweist sich als Irrtum.

Neben die ersten beiden Bestimmungen, die die Beziehung zwischen Faërie und fairy-story beschreiben, kann ich nun also eine dritte stellen.

a. *In einer fairy-story geraten Menschen in die (gefährliche) Faërie.*
-> literatur-theoretisch
b. *Die fairy-story wie die menschliche Phantasie überhaupt wurzeln in dem Verlangen, unmittelbar und leibhaftig in der geschaffenen Sekundärwelt anwesend zu sein.*
-> philosophisch-existentiell
c. *Das Gewebe der Erzählung/Das Gewebe der Realität reißt.*
-> literatur-theoretisch und philosophisch-existentiell

Hiermit ist nun die ›Sammel- und Ordnungsphase‹ der schwierigsten und problematischsten Erläuterungen Tolkiens beendet.

4 Die Miszellen

4.1 Zwei Vorbemerkungen

4.1.1 Die gedankliche Anordnung innerhalb meiner ersten drei Kapitel stand unter dem Eindruck der schon gelesenen Miszellen, das konnte ich nicht verhindern. Was mir durch die Miszellen klarer geworden war, hat mich die Abschnitte des veröffentlichten Aufsatzes wie Fragmente eines größeren Zusammenhanges, in den ich nun eingeweiht war, sehen gelehrt. Vieles an den Antworten hatte ich schon früher vermutet, aber nun besteht mehr Gewissheit.

4.1.2 Grundsätzlich ist über die folgenden Zitate zu sagen: Es sind Privatnotizen, keine von Tolkien autorisierten Aussagen. Diese Notizen existieren häufig in verschiedenen, auch widersprüchlichen Varianten. Welche davon Tolkiens innerstem Fühlen, innerster Überzeugung entsprechen, welche mehr aus taktischen Gründen (in Anbetracht einer Veröffentlichung) formuliert wurden, ist nicht allein mit dem Buch von FA zu erörtern, und darum geschieht dies hier auch nicht.

4.2 Ein beeindruckender Text

Die Unterteilung in a-d stammt von mir, der originale Text hat keine Absatztrennung mit Ausnahme an dem Ort c. Ich habe ihn am Stück zitiert, um zumindest im Ansatz die Wucht und die Bedeutsamkeit der Aussage zu transportieren. Hier könnte der Ausgangspunkt für ein revidiertes Tolkienbild liegen, mit vielerlei Konsequenzen für die Erörterung der Intentionen seiner literarischen Werke.

> (a) Leaving aside the Question of the Real (objective) existence of Fairies, I will tell you what I think about that. If Fairies really exist – independently of Men – then very few of our 'Fairy-stories' have any relation to them: as little, or less than our ghost-stories have to the real events that may befall human personality (or form) after death.
>
> (b) If Fairies exist they are bound by the Moral Law as is all the created Universe; but their duties and functions are not ours. They are not spirits of the dead, nor a branch of the human race, nor devils in fair shapes whose chief object is our deception and ruin. These are either human ideas out of which the Elf-idea has

been separated, or if Elves really exist mere human hypotheses (or confusions). They are a quite separate creation living in another mode. They appear to us in human form (with hands, faces, voices and language similar to our own): this may be their real form and their difference reside in something other than form, or it may be (probably is) only the way in which their presence affects us. Rabbits and eagles may be aware of them quite otherwise.

(c) For lack of a better word they may be called spirits, daemons; inherent powers of the created world, deriving more directly and 'earlier' (in terrestrial history) from the creating will of God, but nonetheless created, subject to Moral Law, capable of good and evil, and possibly (in this fallen world) actually sometimes evil. They are in fact non-incarnate minds (or souls) of a stature and even nature more near to that of Man (in some cases possibly less, in many maybe greater) than any other rational creatures, known or guessed by us. They can take form at will, or they could do so: they have or had a choice.

(d) Thus a tree-fairy (or a dryad) is, or was, a minor spirit in the process of creation who aided as 'agent' in the making effective of the divine Tree-idea or some part of it, or of even of some one particular example: some tree. He is therefore now bound by use and love to Trees (or a tree), immortal while the world (and trees) last – never to escape, until the End. It is a dreadful Doom (to human minds if they are wise) in exchange for a splendid power. What fate awaits him beyond the Confines of the World, we cannot know. It is likely that the Fairy does not know himself. It is possible that nothing awaits him – outside the World and the Cycle of Story and of Time. (FA 254f)

4.3 Auswertung des Textes

4.3.1 Beziehung der fairy-stories zu den fairies (Text a)

Tolkien setzt hier die Aussagekraft der Märchen bezüglich der fairies fast auf den Nullpunkt: Sie haben praktisch nichts miteinander zu tun. Genauso wenig wie die Spukgeschichten etwas über unser wahres Dasein nach dem Tod erzählen, genauso wenig sagen unsere Märchen etwas über den wahren Zustand der fairies.

4.3.2 Beziehung der fairies zu den Menschen (Text b)

Tolkien setzt zwar wie in dem veröffentlichten Aufsatz auch hier die Information in einen Konditionalsatz (vergleiche oben 3.2.1.3), aber die Beschreibung der fairies wirkt dermaßen exakt, kundig und detailliert, dass fast kein Zweifel übrig sein mag, dass hier nicht nur Buchwissen vorliegt. Seine Bestimmung der fairies beläuft sich auf:
- fairies sind keine Totengeister
- sie sind nicht verwandt mit den Menschen
- sie sind keine verkappten Teufel, die uns betrügen und verderben wollen
- fairies leben in einem anderen Modus als die Menschen
- sie sind eine gesonderte Schöpfung
- sie erscheinen den Menschen in menschlicher Form
- Kaninchen und Adlern erscheinen sie vermutlich in anderer Form

Interessant an dieser Aufstellung ist Folgendes:

4.3.2.1 Tolkien trennt das reale Sein der fairies von den Ideen und Vorstellungen der Menschen über sie (Weiteres dazu Kapitel 5.2.2).

4.3.2.2 Dass die fairies böse seien und uns verführen, sei nur eine menschliche Vorstellung (Weiteres dazu Kapitel 5.2.2).

4.3.3 Das Wesen der fairies (Text c)

Weitere Bestimmungen der fairies, meist unabhängig von dem Vergleich mit den Menschen, lassen sich aus Text c ableiten:
- die fairies können als Geister oder Dämonen bezeichnet werden
- sie sind nicht-inkarnierte ›minds‹ oder Seelen, aber geschaffene Wesen
- sie sind unmittelbarer dran an dem schöpferischen Willen Gottes
- Es reicht (bzw. reichte) ihr Wille, um Form anzunehmen

4.3.4 Beispiel für eine Fairy-Art (Text d)

Wohl kaum ohne eine gewisse Erschütterung kann man besonders diesen Text des Zitates daraufhin lesen – falls man Tolkien lange kennt –, wie genau er zu wissen scheint, dass Baumelben – in der realen Existenz des 20. Jahrhunderts – bis an das Ende der Welt an ihren Baum gebunden sind, da sie ihn realiter mit aufgebaut hätten: »never to escape«. Solche Ideen mögen in der Esoterik oder der

Theosophie zu Hause sein, aber Tolkien hat sie sich offenbar zu eigen gemacht, als habe er es selbst beobachtet. Diese Dinge sind anscheinend Teil seiner lebendigen Weltsicht gewesen.

4.3.5 Zwischenfazit

Dass Tolkien sich ausgiebig mit esoterischer oder theosophischer Literatur, auch mit außersinnlichen Wahrnehmungen auseinandergesetzt hat, war auch schon aufgrund der *Notion Club Papers* zu vermuten. Aber es ist ein anderes, Grübeleien über andere Dimensionen, die der normal Sterbliche nicht wahrnehme, in fiktionaler Form vorzufinden als sie direkt als Tolkiens eigene Erkenntnisse und Sichtweisen zu hören. Sicher bleibt ein Zweifel übrig, ob Tolkien dies alles nur als hypothetisch, als Basisstudium für die fairy-stories erforscht hat. Aber die Eindringlichkeit, mit der er die Existenzform der fairies schildert, ja, so sehr darum bemüht ist, die Meinungen der Menschen über sie von ihrer wahren Existenz zu unterscheiden, machen anscheinend doch klar, dass diese ›andere Dimension‹ für Tolkien eine Realität war, aus der heraus er arbeitete.

5 Schlussfolgerungen und Lösungsansätze

Wie ich in 4.1.2 schon schrieb, ist auf der Basis von FA allein das eben Gesagte in *weltanschaulicher* Hinsicht kaum weiter vertiefbar. Dennoch ist für das Thema meines Artikels von höchster Bedeutung, aus den Miszellen herausgefiltert zu haben, wie Tolkien das Verhältnis zwischen der ›echten‹ Faërie und der fairy-story gewichtet. Diese Gewichtung ist der Angelpunkt, aus dem heraus die in Kapitel drei dargelegten Schwierigkeiten des veröffentlichten Aufsatzes eine neue Wertung und Erklärung bekommen. Dazu im nächsten Kapitel.

5.1 Faërie contra fairy-stories

Das große Thema Tolkiens ist die existentielle und für ihn erkennbare oder erahnbare Faërie. Sie studierte er, und sie suchte er in den fairy-stories. Die fairy-story an sich, die Gattung selbst, ihr formaler Aufbau interessierten ihn nur in soweit, als sie seiner Vorstellung von Faërie nachkamen oder nicht nachkamen. In der Regel kamen sie ihr nicht nach. Dennoch hatte er diesen Maßstab, und dieser ist klar ein außerliterarischer, eine weltanschauliche Forderung an eine Literaturgattung.

Dies verlangt zum einen eine im hier möglichen Rahmen abschließende Betrachtung über die Weltsicht, die Tolkien zu vermitteln für zentral hielt, zum anderen eine im gleichen Sinne abschließende Betrachtung darüber, ob Dichtung – auch seine eigene – diesen Anspruch überhaupt erfüllen kann, erfüllen will oder erfüllt hat.

5.2 Weltsicht

5.2.1 Realisierung der visions of fantasy

Wie schon erläutert, ist das Lebendigwerden der durch die Phantasie erzeugten Produkte für Tolkien der Nerv seiner Faërie-Konzeption. Dieses Zitat: »An essential power of Faërie is thus the power of making immediately effective by the will the visions of ›fantasy‹« (FS A 28) wird in den Miszellen vielfach variiert, und das früher erwähnte Faërian Drama lässt sich vielleicht als eine besondere Form der (mystischen) Vision betrachten. Diese Visionen wurzeln – siehe Bestimmung b in 3.3.3 und 3.3.5 – nach Tolkien in dem Verlangen, in der geschaffenen Sekundärwelt leibhaftig und unmittelbar anwesend zu sein.
Und woher kommt dieses seltsame Bedürfnis?

5.2.2 Utopie

Antwort: aus der Natur des Menschen, die zum einen an dem status quo kein Genüge findet, zum anderen nicht nur das Verlangen, sondern auch die Fähigkeit besitzt, diesen status quo zu überwinden. Siehe dazu folgende drei Zitate aus den Miszellen:

> ... faierie is a power drawn from the same reservoir as that from which the vision and the desire proceed.   (FA 256)

> I think, that when we cross the borders of Faeirie we believe ... that the scientific, measurable, facts and 'laws' of the relationship of things and events are only one aspect of the world.   (FA 257)

> What is this faierie? It reposes (for us now) in a view that the normal world, tangible visible audible, is only an appearance. Behind it is a reservoir of power which is manifested in these forms. If we can drive a well down to this reservoir we shall tap a

power that can not only change the visible forms of things already existent, but spout up with a boundless wealth forms of things never before known – potential but unrealized. (FA 270)

Das zweite Zitat betont die vermutete Erkenntnis: Jenseits der rationalen Grenze stehen die Dinge dieser Welt in einer anderen Beziehung zueinander.

Das dritte Zitat geht einen entscheidenden Schritt weiter: der ›Brunnen‹, aus dem die Visionen stammen, enthält nicht nur die Kraft zu einer neuen Perspektive, sondern auch dazu, bisher nur potentiell Vorhandenes in die *Realität* zu heben.

Damit wird der Faërie eine geradezu revolutionäre Macht zugeordnet, die Tolkien in den Miszellen nicht genauer bestimmt, wohl aber im fiktiven ›Notion-Club‹ seiner *Notion Club Papers* ausführlich diskutieren lässt. Dort lösen vereinte imaginative Kräfte heftige Detonationen in der Oxforder Realität aus. Auch in dem Roman selbst unterscheiden die Protagonisten zwischen dichterischen Schöpfungen einerseits, realen ›Schöpfungen‹ mittels geschulter psychischer Kräfte andererseits. Die eigentliche Faërie betrifft letzteres. Und dass diese ein ›Reich voller Gefahren‹ ist, wird allmählich plausibel. Die Utopie ist zweischneidig.

Das nächste Kapitel deutet eine weitere Gefahr an.

5.2.3 Betrug

»It is often reported of fairies (truly or lyingly, I do not know) that they are workers of illusion, that they are cheaters of men by ›fantasy‹« (FS A 17). So losgelöst im veröffentlichten Aufsatz ist dies irritierend, man weiß nicht, was damit gemeint ist. Selbst das Faërian Drama bezeichnet Tolkien als Täuschung. In den Miszellen aber löst er das auf (siehe oben 4.2, Text b, 4.3.2.1 und 4.3.2.2). Es sind nicht die fairies selbst, die Täuschung ausüben, sondern die von den Menschen *korrumpierten* fairies. Das vielleicht am meisten Überraschende dabei ist aber die Herkunft des Phänomens:

> It is philosophical and theological suspicion that has presented faierie as a deception... This 'doubt' at first makes 'fairies' all take on a devilish aspect. (FA 256)

Es ist also – nach Tolkien – unter anderem die Theologie, die Religion, die die fairies verdorben hat.

Damit verlasse ich den Bereich der Faërie im philosophisch-existentiellen Sinn und wende mich der Frage zu, wie und ob die Gattung ›Märchen‹ diesem hohen Anspruch gerecht werden kann.

Heidi Krüger

5.3 Faërie inner- oder außerhalb der fairy-story?

Tolkien hat mehr als deutlich gemacht – vgl. oben 4.3.1 –, dass die fairy-story nicht im Geringsten das Sein der fairies zu veranschaulichen vermag. Ich folgere z.b. aus 5.2.1, dass dies auch von dem Sein der Faërie gilt. Das wirkt tatsächlich deprimierend und scheint mir eine wesentliche Aussage zu sein. Da er sich aber trotzdem viel mit der fairy-story befasst, auch selbst ja literarisch produziert hat, wird es Zeit, zwei wesentliche Dinge zu unterscheiden: den stofflichen und den literarisch-strukturellen Aspekt.

5.3.1 Der stoffliche Aspekt

5.3.1.1 Der Schauplatz

Wenn Smith of Wootton Major in den Wald geht, wo er Zugang zu den elves finden kann, mit denen er gelegentlich tanzt, dann ist das ein stoffliches Merkmal, gehört zum plot der Geschichte. Smith begegnet der Faërie, ja, aber es ist nicht die Faërie Tolkiens und auch nicht die Faërie, von deren Existenz Tolkien die Leser überzeugen möchte. Analoges gilt für den Schauplatz in *The Lord of the Rings* oder *The Hobbit*. Mittelerde ist keine uns dargestellte Faërie. Die Art der existentiellen Begegnung der Protagonisten mit der Faërie gilt nur für diese. Der Leser kann lesen, wie jemand seiner Faërie begegnet, aber nicht, wie es ›in der Faërie‹ aussieht.[9]

5.3.1.2 Die fairies

Es ist zu konstatieren, dass Tolkien die fairies so, wie er sie in ihrer existentiellen Entität wahrnahm, wahrscheinlich nirgends gestaltet hat, es wohl auch als menschenunmöglich ansah, wie das Zitat in 3.1 schon zeigte: »The fairy gold too often turns to withered leaves when it was brought away.«

Die elves im *Silmarillion*, auch die Ainur tragen Züge der echten fairies, aber insgesamt sind beide Gruppen Teil eines Romangefüges mit roman-immanenten Handlungsentwicklungen.

---

9 Siehe dazu meine Analysen der verschiedenen Erzählebenen in *The Lord of the Rings* (Krüger, *Autor*) und *The Notation Club Papers* (Krüger, *Romanfragmente*): ›Otherworld‹ (Faërie) als lebendige Erfahrung erscheint stets auf einer Erzählebene *über* derjenigen Erzählebene, auf der sie nur erzählte Sage ist. Lebendig ist sie nur für den, der sich auf der gleichen Erzählebene befindet.

5.3.2 Der literarisch-strukturelle Aspekt

Trotz des letztlich geringen Zutrauens zu der modernen fairy-story stellte Tolkien die Forderung auf, dass die fairy-stories den Lesern das Tor in ein Jenseits der Zeit oder des Raums öffnen sollen, und sei es nur für kurz.
Dass dies nicht primär durch eine stoffliche Veranschaulichung geschieht, sollte 5.3.1 zeigen. Wenn das genannte Ziel überhaupt erreicht werden kann, dann durch künstlerische Mittel, wie zum Beispiel das sprachschöpferisch eingesetzte Adjektiv oder die Eukatastrophe. Weitere literarische oder literarisch-strukturelle Mittel nennt er nicht. Aber er entwickelt sie in seinen Werken! Seine Bestimmung *In einer fairy-story geraten Menschen in die (gefährliche) Faërie* trifft vermutlich auf die meisten seiner Werke zu – zu fragen wäre lediglich, ob der Begriff ›fairy-story‹ überhaupt das ausdrückt, was Tolkien innerlich vorschwebte, und ob es nicht tatsächlich notwendig wäre, hierfür eine neue Genrebezeichnung zu wählen.

Ob der Begriff ›Fantasy‹ den Kern trifft (ich denke: nein), müsste diskutiert werden. Auf jeden Fall ist festzuhalten, dass aus den einzelnen Werken Tolkiens teilweise eine sehr komplexe Erzählstruktur herausgearbeitet werden kann, die den Weg der Suche nach der Faërie durch viele Dimensionen der Realität beschreibt.

5.4 Stellungnahme und Ausblick

Am Ende von Kapitel 3 hatte ich drei Bestimmungen, die die Beziehung zwischen Faërie und fairy-story beschreiben, genannt:
a. In einer fairy-story geraten Menschen in die (gefährliche) Faërie.
-> literatur-theoretisch
b. Die fairy-story wie die menschliche Phantasie überhaupt wurzeln in dem Verlangen, unmittelbar und leibhaftig in der geschaffenen Sekundärwelt anwesend zu sein.
-> philosophisch-existentiell
c. Das Gewebe der Erzählung/Das Gewebe der Realität reißt.
-> literatur-theoretisch und philosophisch-existentiell

Dahinter steht nun die Frage: Kann überhaupt eine Literaturgattung einen weltanschaulichen Anspruch erfüllen? Nein, das kann sie nicht!
Dem steht mindestens zweierlei entgegen: die Gesetze des Mediums und die Souveränität des Rezipienten. In *The Notion Club Papers* kann noch so sehr mittels mentalen Trainings einiger Protagonisten eine mythische Insel leibhaftig

betretbar werden: es ist und bleibt innerliterarisch; der Leser kann das dadurch nicht auch. Und ein Autor kann noch so geschickt eine bestimmte Weltsicht vermitteln wollen: der Leser liest das heraus, was er herauslesen will oder kann. Was der Autor wörtlich gemeint hat, liest der Rezipient vielleicht symbolisch, vielleicht psychologisiert er es. Und auch der Autor kann sich seiner eigenen Weltanschauung gar nicht so sicher sein: er kann in seinem Unterbewusstsein eine ganz andere haben als im Bewusstsein, und beim Schreiben arbeitet er eventuell die unbewusste hinein.

Was vielleicht mit Sicherheit übrig bleibt: die Konfrontation mit der Faërie. Sie wird gesucht, oder vor ihr wird geflüchtet. Sie ist das Andere, das Subreale[10], das Unkontrollierbare. Diese formale Bestimmung kann ein Genre definieren. Aber dafür fehlt noch eine Benennung.

Und abschließend: Die Faërie ist immer verloren bei Tolkien, immer schon Legende, und zwar innerhalb der Erzählungen. Das heißt: Es wird innerhalb der Geschichten über verlorene Geschichten reflektiert und wie man sie wiedergewinnen kann. Anders ausgedrückt: Dichtung ist sich selber fragwürdig, muss sich selber suchen und konstituieren, muss sich sogar selber erfinden, um sich zu finden. Das weist in die Postmoderne mit ihren großen Meta-Fragen. Und entzieht sich der Marschrichtung, die der Autor seinen Lesern – vielleicht – vorgeben wollte.

---

10 Zu dem Begriff ‚subreal' siehe Krüger, Shaping 242-247.

Anhang

Nummerierung der Abschnitte nach FA (Die deutschen Angaben beziehen sich auf die Krege-Ausgabe.)

1 I propose *Ich gedenke*	41 If we pause *Wenn wir nun*	81 As for old *Was das fort...*
2 The realm *In seiner ganzen*	42 I will now turn *Ich komme nun auf*	82 We do not *Wir verlieren nicht*
3 There are *Auf manche Fragen*	43 Among those *Unter denjenigen*	83 Recovery *Wiederherstellung*
4 What is a *Was ist ein Märchen?*	44 Actually *Tatsächlich ist es*	84 Of course *Märchen sind*
5 The last *Mit den beiden*	45 It is true *Richtig ist freilich*	85 The ›fantastic‹ *Die »phantastischen«*
6 Supernatural *»Übernatürlich«*	46 The value *Der Wert*	86 And actually *Und tatsächlich*
7 As for *diminutive* *Was die*	47 Andrew Lang's *Andrew Langs*	87 I will now *Ich will nun*
8 But the business *Aber, wie schon*	48 The introduction *Die Einleitung*	88 I have claimed *Ich habe behauptet*
9 Fairy, as *Fairy, als*	49 I suspect *Ich fürchte*	89 For a trifling *Als Beispiel*
10 Now, though I have *Obwohl ich die Elben*	50 Children are *Kinder sind natürlich*	90 Not long ago *Vor noch nicht langer*
11 Stories that *Geschichten, die*	51 A real *Der echte*	91 For my part *Meinerseits*
12 The definition *Die Definition*	52 Now if Lang *Hätte nun Lang*	92 Much that *Vieles von dem*
13 But even if we *Doch selbst wenn*	53 »Is it true?« *»Ist es wahr?«*	93 And if we *Und wenn wir*
14 I will give *Ich will ein oder zwei*	54 Now I was *Nun bin ich*	94 ›The rawness...‹ *»Die Roheit...«*
15 The number of *Märchensammlungen*	55 And as for *Und was die Kinder*	95 This, however *Dies jedoch*
16 But what is *Was sill man aber*	56 All the same *Desungeachtet*	96 But there are *Doch es gibt*
17 Next, after *Gleich nach den*	57 I have said *Ich habe zu diesem*	97 And lastly *Und zuletzt*
18 It is at any rate *Für das echte*	58 It is true *Es ist nun richtig*	98 But the ›consolation‹ *Doch der Trost*
19 There is another *Es gibt noch eine*	59 Dasent *Dasent*	99 The consolation of *Der Trost*
20 The beast-fable *Die Tierfabel*	60 I do not deny *Ich leugne nicht*	100 It is the mark *Es ist das Wahr...*

21 Now *The Monkey's* Auch *The Monkey's*	61 Andrew Lang was Andrew Lang sah	101 Even modern Sogar moderne
22 But that point Doch dieser	62 If we use *child* Wenn wir das Wort	102 This ›joy‹ Diese Freude
23 Actually the question Tatsächlich	63 Let us not Teilen wir	103 Probably every Wohl jeder
24 Statements Aussagen wie	64 Very well So weit	104 I would venture Ich stehe nicht an
25 Of course Natürlich	65 The human mind Der menschliche Geist	105 It is not difficult Es ist nicht schwer
26 I shall therefore Ich werde daher	66 Ridiculous So lächerlich	106 But in God's In Gottes Reich
27 Philology Die Philologie	67 Fantasy Die Phantasie hat	107 The very root Ihre »Wunder«
28 An essential Eine wesentliche	68 But the error Doch Irrtum	108 Of course Natürlich
29 At one time Früher herrschte	69 To make a Um eine Sekundärwelt	109 I say only Ich habe nur gesagt
30 That would seem Die Wahrheit	70 In human art In der Kunst	110 As far as So viel ich weiß
31 Let us take Betrachten wir	71 In *Macbeth* Im *Macbeth*	111 I was introduced Ich wurde ebenso
32 Thórr Thórr	72 A reason Noch wichtiger	112 There is Zum Beispiel
33 Something really Manchmal schimmert	73 For this precise Aus ebendiesem	113 I am speaking Ich spreche hier
34 Yet these things Doch diese	74 Now ›Faërian Drama‹ Das »elbische Theater«	114 I am referring Ich spreche natürlich
35 For a moment Kehren wir	75 We need a Für diese Elbenkunst	115 The absence Daß den Menschen
36 But what of Aber was ist	76 To the elvish Nach dem Elben…	116 The verbal ending Die letzten Worte
37 It seems Ziemlich klar	77 To many Vielen ist sie	117 Endings of Schlüsse
38 The great enemy König Hrothgars	78 Fantasy is a Phantasieren	118 As for the beginnings Was den Anfang
39 But when we Doch wenn wir	79 For creative Denn die schöpferische	
40 For one thing Denn alt	80 Fantasy can Natürlich kann	

Bibliographie

Krüger, Heidi. »Der Autor als Chronist«. *Das Dritte Zeitalter*. Hg. Thomas Le Blanc und Bettina Twrsnick. Wetzlar: Phantastische Bibliothek, 2006, 68-96

---. »Die Romanfragmente *The Lost Road* und *The Notion Club Papers*: Zu ihrer literarisch-konzeptionellen Stellung innerhalb des literarisch-fiktionalen Gesamtwerkes«. *Hither Shore* 3 (2006): 165-179

---. "The Shaping of ,Reality' in Tolkien's Works. An Aspect of Tolkien and Modernity". *Tolkien and Modernity 2*, Hg. Thomas Honegger und Frank Weinreich. Walking Tree Publishers, 2006, 233-272

---. »Leaf by Niggle/Blatt von Tüftler: eine literaturkritische Untersuchung«. *Hither Shore* 4 (2007): 89-107

Tolkien, John Ronald Reuel. »Über Märchen«. *Gute Drachen sind rar: Drei Aufsätze. Aus dem Englischen von Wolfgang Krege*. Stuttgart: Klett-Cotta, ³2002, 51-140

---. *Smith of Wootton Major: Extended Edition*. Hg. Verlyn Flieger. London: HarperCollins, 2005

---. *Tolkien On Fairy-stories: Expanded edition with Commentary and Notes*. Hg. Verlyn Flieger und Douglas A. Anderson. London: HarperCollins, 2008

Als besonders schrecklich empfand ich
die tiefschwarze Nacht. Aber nicht
minder furchterregend waren die riesigen
Spinnweben zwischen den Bäumen.

Ist das des Hobbits Kern?
Essentielle Stellen im *Hobbit*

Christian Weichmann (Braunschweig)

Schon bei den Vorträgen des 2008er Seminars und den begleitenden Diskussionen fiel auf, dass bestimmte Stellen des *Hobbit* sehr oft zitiert, während große Teile des Textes gar nicht erwähnt wurden (was nicht heißt, dass sie nicht berücksichtigt wurden, aber offensichtlich trugen sie nicht so viel Neues dazu bei, dass es sich gelohnt hätte, sie zu zitieren).

Also untersuchte ich daraufhin die Artikel des entstandenen *Hither-Shore*-Bandes, ob sich diese Tendenz auch in den dort verwendeten Zitaten widerspiegelt. Tatsächlich entsprach das Ergebnis (speziell in Bezug auf die Zitierhäufigkeit) nicht ganz meinen Erwartungen. Aber trotzdem zeigte sich eines deutlich: Ausgehend davon, dass die häufig zitierten Stellen die für ein tieferes Verständnis des Buches wichtigsten Stellen sind, ergibt sich, dass diese weitgehend nicht identisch sind mit den bekanntesten (d.h. ohne einen wissenschaftlichen Hintergrund gerne zitierten) Stellen.

Von diesen wurde der Anfangssatz »In a hole in the ground there lived a Hobbit« (H 29) nur von Vanderbeke (HS5 186f) ausführlich behandelt, da er gerade die Umsetzung des Anfangs in Form des Comics besonders untersuchte. Die Good-morning-Diskussion wird gelegentlich erwähnt, aber insgesamt nur selten[1] (HS5 27, 176). Die Rätsel im Dunklen (H 121 ff) waren nur für Weichmann (HS5 163) aufgrund seines speziellen Themas erwähnenswert. Die ›deathbed conversation‹ zwischen Thorin und Bilbo (H 348) gehört immerhin zu den mehr zitierten Stellen (wenn auch nicht so oft, wie ich nach dem Seminar vermutet hätte, doch dazu im Folgenden mehr). Und das Ende wird kaum zitiert[2]:

> "Mr. Baggins, and I am very fond of you; but you are only quite a little fellow in a wide world after all!"
> "Thank goodness!" said Bilbo laughing, and handed him the tobacco-jar. (H 364)

---

1 Chen allerdings geht sogar ausführlich darauf ein (HS5 27).
2 Wenn auch Fornet-Ponse (HS5 117) die direkt vorangehenden Bemerkungen zitiert und Triebel diese und den Anfang des angegebenen Zitats bringt (HS5 69). Eigentlich würde man das auch bei Slack erwarten, aber hier findet es sich nicht.

Wirkung der Musik

Die schon während des Seminars und auch im Buch am meisten zitierte Stelle ist das Lied *Far over the misty mountains* und Bilbos Reaktion darauf (H 44-45). Natürlich wird das Lied in Eilmanns Artikel über die Lieder und Gedichte zitiert und die Reaktion darauf in jenen Aufsätzen (Sternberg, Turner, Fornet-Ponse), die einen besonderen Schwerpunkt auf die Bedeutung von Begehren und der Verehrung der Schönheit von geschaffenen Dingen legen. Fornet-Ponse geht an anderer Stelle auch noch auf das Lied (HS5 109) ein. Interessanterweise zitiert Steimels Text, der weitgehend auf diesem Lied und den Begleitumständen basiert, weder den Titel noch den Text des Liedes, wohl aber Bilbos Gefühle dabei (HS5 139).

Aber auch ansonsten kommen die meisten Autoren dieses Bandes nicht an dieser Stelle vorbei: Bei der Untersuchung der Tugend Tapferkeit braucht Grzegorczyk (HS5 96-98) Bilbos Reaktion. Genauso Klinger (HS5 30-45) und Slack (HS5 180ff), um zu zeigen, wo Bilbo sich das erste Mal als kein gewöhnlicher Hobbit zeigt. Chen hingegen nutzt das Lied, um die Zwerge zu charakterisieren (HS5 18f). Weichmann zitiert hingegen nur die Begleitumstände des Singens, nicht aber das Lied oder die Reaktion. Und Triebel erwähnt die aus Thorins Wiederholung des Liedes folgenden schlechten Träume Bilbos, ohne auf diesen Zusammenhang einzugehen.

Insgesamt ist eine so starke Betonung dieser einen Textpassage ein klarer Hinweis, dass es sich hierbei um eine mehrfach wesentliche Stelle des Romans handelt (und eine eindrucksvolle Unterstützung von Eilmanns These und der von ihm zitierten Briefstelle von Tolkien (L 396) über die Bedeutung der Lyrik in Tolkiens Prosa). Aus den verschiedenen Ansätzen kann man entnehmen, dass dieses Lied gleichzeitig die Handlung vorwegnimmt, sie von der Jedermann-Hobbit-Ebene in die Abenteuer-Helden-Ebene bringt und Bilbo und die Zwerge charakterisiert. Keine andere Passage im gesamten *Hobbit* kommt dieser in Bezug auf die Anzahl der Zitate und vielleicht auch in der Bedeutung für das gesamte Buch auch nur nahe.

Die Übergabe des Arkensteins

Eine zweite häufiger zitierte *Hobbit*-Passage (bei Slack, Fornet-Ponse und Sternberg: HS5 182f, 108f, 125-128) ist die Übergabe des Arkensteins durch Bilbo an Bard und den Elbenkönig und die Reaktionen der beiden Empfänger (H 331). Was diese Stelle mit der ersten gemeinsam hat, ist die Tatsache, dass sie zur Charakterisierung mehrerer Personen beiträgt.

Die deutlich niedrigere Zitatdichte erklärt sich sicherlich daraus, dass die Stelle einerseits nicht in den speziellen Blickwinkel so vieler Texte fällt wie das Zwergenlied. Andererseits hat sie zwar im Buch und im Handlungsablauf eine nicht unbedeutende Funktion, aber diese deckt keineswegs so sehr das ganze Werk ab, wie es die Vorausschau in *Far over the misty mountains* tut.

Die ›deathbed conversation‹

Auch die dritte ausführlich behandelte[3] Szene, zu finden bei Slack, Grzegorczyk, Fornet-Ponse und Turner (HS5 182f, 104, 112f, 86f), zeichnet sich durch einen Beitrag zur Charakterisierung von Personen (in diesem Falle Bilbo und Thorin) aus: die ›deathbed conversation‹ zwischen dem sterbenden und seine Handlungen bereuenden Thorin und dem aus der Schlacht zurückgekehrten und trauernden Bilbo (H 348).

Doch hier werden andere Aspekte mehr in den Vordergrund gerückt: Denn neben dem oben zitierten Ende des Buches zeigt diese Szene am ehesten eine Moral der Geschichte, indem Thorin in Erkenntnis seiner Fehler Bilbo als Vorbild für die idealen Bewohner einer idealen Welt charakterisiert. Außerdem bildet die Stelle in gewissem Sinne eben auch eine Zusammenfassung wesentlicher Teile nicht der Handlung, aber der zugrunde liegenden Motivationen der Personen.

Fazit

Legt man die in diesem Band versammelten Artikel zugrunde, zeigt sich, dass sich ein großer Teil der Aussagen im *Hobbit* in einigen wenigen Schlüsselszenen findet. Natürlich nicht alle Aussagen und nicht nur in diesen Szenen, aber diese Passagen lassen sich kaum übergehen, wenn man sich allgemein oder zumindest unter bestimmten, für die Beiträger wichtigen, Aspekten mit dem *Hobbit* auseinandersetzen will.

Diese Stellen sind alle keine handlungsstarken, sondern dia- oder sogar monologische bzw. gedankliche Äußerungen. Die wichtigste und am häufigsten zitierte Stelle ist sogar eine, die in einer inhaltlichen Zusammenfassung des Buches wahrscheinlich übersprungen oder zumindest zur Unkenntlichkeit gekürzt würde: das Lied *Far over the misty mountains*. Die beiden anderen leisten zwar einen wichtigen Beitrag zur Geschichte und können, ohne dass Teile für das Verständnis fehlen, auch aus einer Nacherzählung nicht weggelassen werden,

---

[3] Wenn auch meinem Eindruck nach keineswegs so ausführlich wie in den Vorträgen und Diskussionen auf dem Seminar.

aber sie liegen beide nach dem Höhe- und Schlusspunkt der klassischen Heldenerzählung, nämlich der Tötung des Drachen. Ja, dieser trägt selbst relativ wenig zu den Auswertungen bei, wenn man vom Begriff der Drachenkrankheit absieht, der mit unterschiedlichen Zitaten über einigen Artikeln schwebt.

Es zeigt sich also, dass die vordergründige Geschichte und die wesentlichen Aussagen des Buches nicht unbedingt zusammenfallen. Dass dies aber einer Analyse bedarf und nicht beim einfachen Lesen auffällt, zeigt die Kunst Tolkiens bei der Konstruktion seines Werks.

Bibliographie

Chen, Fanfan. "The Eucharistic Poetics of *The Hobbit*". *Hither Shore 5 (2009)*: 9-29

Eilmann, Julian Tim Morton. »Singen oder nicht singen: Lieder und Gedichte in J.R.R. olkiens *Der Hobbit*«. *Hither Shore 5 (2009)*: 142-159

Fornet-Ponse, Thomas. »Der Zwerg lebt nicht vom Gold allein – Vom Umgang mit Reichtum im *Hobbit*«. *Hither Shore 5 (2009)*: 106-120

Grzegorczyk, Blanka. "'Some courage and some wisdom, blended in measure': On Moral Imagination in J.R.R. Tolkien's *The Hobbit*". *Hither Shore 5 (2009)*: 93-105

Klinger, Judith. "Changing Perspectives: Secret Doors and Narrative Thresholds in *The Hobbit*". *Hither Shore 5 (2009)*: 30-45

Slack, Anna E. "Seeing Fire and Sword, or Refining Hobbits". *Hither Shore 5 (2009)*: 174-185

Steimel, Heidi. "The Dwarven Philharmonic Orchestra". *Hither Shore 5 (2009)*: 135-141

Sternberg, Martin G. E. "The Treasure of my House – The Arkenstone as Symbol of Kingship and Seat of Royal Luck in *The Hobbit*". *Hither Shore 5 (2009)*: 121-133

Tolkien, John Ronald Reuel. *The annotated Hobbit*. Hg. Douglas A. Anderson. Boston, New York: Houghton Mifflin, 2002.

---. *The Letters of J.R.R. Tolkien*. Hg. Humphrey Carpenter. London: HarperCollins, 1981

Turner, Allan. "*The Hobbit* and Desire". *Hither Shore 5 (2009)*: 83-92

Vanderbeke, Dirk. "The not-quite-moving-pictures: The comic-book adaptation of *The Hobbit*". *Hither Shore 5 (2009)*: 186-195

Weichmann, Dr. Christian. »Sehen und (nicht) gesehen werden – Augen als Schutz und Bedrohung im *Hobbit*«. *Hither Shore 5 (2009)*: 161-173

Die Strömung trug die Fässer fort, durch das Wassertor in Richtung Freiheit. Der Waldfluss führte zur Ostgrenze des Düsterwaldes und weiter zum Langen See...

Zusammenfassungen der englischen Beiträge

Die eucharistische Poesie von *The Hobbit or There and Back Again*
Fanfan Chen

Dieser Beiträgt versucht, Jean-Luc Marions Philosophie einer eucharistischen Hermeneutik auf eine phänomenologische Lektüre des *Hobbit* anzuwenden. Die eucharistische Poesie beinhaltet durch passive Rezeption und den Wiedergewinn ikonischer Sprache angereicherte Phänomene der Sprache. Poetische Diktion und narrativer Fluss werden als Substanzen betrachtet, die eine eucharistische Transsubstantiation ermöglichen. Bachelards auf den vier klassischen Elementen basierende Poesie der Materie hilft dabei, Wörter und Bilder als Substanzpartikel tragend zu analysieren; Ricoeurs Texttheorie von Narrative und Zeit verbindet die räumliche Poesie mit zeitlicher Musikalität und dem Erzählen von Geschichten.

Eine genaue stilistische Analyse der Form erklärt ferner den in Tolkiens Zweitschöpfung erzeugten eucharistischen Effekt. Durch die Kommunion zwischen Autor, Text und Leser entfaltet sich eine imaginäre Textwelt vor den Augen des Lesers. Wie Tolkien behauptete, handelt es sich dabei um eine Welt der Sprache.

Nach einer Darlegung des Wesens der eucharistischen Poesie in der Konstruktion einer imaginären Textwelt von Sprache wird eine Untersuchung der Metapoesie des Elements ‚Erde' Bilbos ‚down-to-earth'-Heldentum und den Sprachstil und -charakter der Zwerge aufdecken. Der horizontale Archaismus des Labyrinths als einem universalen nostalgischen Ort der Erde hallt in den verschiedenen Sprachen der Geschöpfe als Symphonie der Natur wider.

Vom Raum zur Zeit übergehend, ergibt eine Analyse der Narrative als einer mythologischen Brücke zwischen Vergangenheit und Gegenwart das Thema der narrativen Autorität. Der Erzähler nimmt eine vertikale Position an und übt herrschende Autorität über das Geschichtenerzählen aus. Schließlich endet der Artikel mit einer Untersuchung des stilistischen Diskurses des Erzählers mit rhetorischen Figuren und phonologischen Parallelismen.

Wechselnde Perspektiven: Geheime Türen und Narrative Türschwellen in *The Hobbit*

Judith Klinger

Nicht allein Bilbo lässt sich im *Hobbit* auf ein unabsehbares Abenteuer ein: Mit ihm wagt sich auch der Erzähler auf unbekanntes Terrain vor. Gemeinsam überschreiten sie die Grenze, die Bilbos wohl märchenhafte, aber sichere und vertraute Welt vom Bereich des ›Legendären‹ und der epischen Geschichte scheidet, den der Drache beherrscht. Um diese ganz andere Welt real werden zu lassen, eröffnet Tolkiens *Hobbit* nicht nur neue Erfahrungen für seine Protagonisten, sondern bringt diese auch in der Textur der Erzählung selbst zum Vorschein.

Mein Beitrag untersucht anhand exemplarischer Textpassagen, wie sich der Übergang in die fremde Wirklichkeit vollzieht und mithilfe welcher narrativer Strategien der Erzähler an dieser Grenzüberschreitung beteiligt ist. Während der Erzähler zuerst in der Rolle eines Vermittlers zwischen der Realität seines Publikums und jener der erzählten Welt auftritt, treten im Verlauf der Geschichte Perspektivwechsel und -verschiebungen zutage, die mit dem narratologischen Konzept der Fokalisierung (Genette, Jahn) genauer beschrieben werden können. Vermittels variabler Fokalisierungen, die – insbesondere durch Bilbos Träume – eine fremde, ›magische‹ Realität sichtbar machen, entwickelt der Text eine Mehrstimmigkeit, die die entscheidende Grenzüberschreitung vorbereitet.

Die Entdeckung der verborgenen Tür an Durins Tag erweist sich nun in mehrfacher Hinsicht als Schwellenmoment. Zum einen kommt es mit der an Bilbo gebundenen Fokalisierung zur Verschmelzung subjektiver und objektiver Faktoren, so dass kosmische Konstellation und individuelle Erfahrung in einem Moment ›mythischer‹ Weltwahrnehmung den Sinn der Ereignisse erzeugen. Zum anderen dringt auch die Erzählung selbst in einen neuen Raum vor. Markiert durch Referenzbrüche sowie abrupte Tempus- und Perspektivwechsel öffnet sich die Geschichte selbst der ›mythischen‹ (oder – in der Terminologie des *Hobbit* – ›magischen‹) Wirklichkeit. Damit stellt sich zugleich ein Übergang zum ›epischen Erzählstil‹ her, der wesentliche Züge des *Herrn der Ringe* vorwegnimmt.

Insgesamt zeigt sich, dass die vermeintlich so schlichte Erzählung mit komplexen Strategien an der Realisierung dessen arbeitet, was Tolkien andernorts als Einblicke in die Welt des Faërie beschrieben hat: Der ›mythische Effekt‹ solcher Geschichten besteht darin, dass sie eine ›Tür in die andere Zeit‹ aufzustoßen vermögen. Anders als Tolkiens übrige Mittelerde-Schriften eröffnet sein *Hobbit* diese veränderte Wahrnehmung auch auf der Ebene des Erzählens selbst.

Wölfe, Raben und Adler: Eine mythische Präsenz in einer Hobbitsage

Guglielmo Spirito

Mythen, Legenden, Geschichten und Sagen, die Wölfe – und Werwölfe –, Raben und Adler beinhalten, sind in der ganzen antiken Welt bekannt. In *The Hobbit* treffen wir sie mit vermischten Eigenschaften von verschiedenen Echos aus antiken Traditionen, aus Nord und Süd und West. Wölfe und Adler sind zudem im größten Teil von Tolkiens zweitschöpferischem Mittelerde-Werk präsent, im Gegensatz zu Raben, die nur in *The Hobbit* gefunden werden. Die in diesem Buch erkennbaren Züge von Wolf und Adler stehen dagegen in Kontinuität zu den späteren und größeren Werken.

Irgendwie nehmen wir eine Faszination sowohl im Autoren als auch im Leser war: Wie kommt das? Warum werden wir von ihnen angezogen, sowohl mit Bewunderung als auch mit Furcht, mit Sympathie und Misstrauen? Wie ist ihr unbekanntes und unsere normalen Grenzen überschreitendes Sein relevant für diese Wahrnehmung? Sind sie Verbündete, Feinde oder was, für die Hobbits und für uns selbst?

›Sing we now softly, and dreams let us weave him!‹: Träume und Traumvisionen in J.R.R. Tolkiens *The Hobbit*

Doreen Triebel

Zahlreiche Überlieferungen und Manuskripte belegen, dass die Menschen im Mittelalter, genau wie heute, fasziniert waren vom Phänomen prophetischer Träume, und aus der Beschäftigung mit deren Analyse und Interpretation erwuchs die literarische Form der Traumvision. Jedoch war die zeitgenössische Traumlehre, die ihren Weg in die Werke von Chaucer, William Langland, dem Pearl Poeten oder das *Mabinogion* fand, aufgrund des Einflusses zahlreicher sehr unterschiedlicher Theorien teilweise gegenläufig und diente recht unterschiedlichen Funktionen.

Die Darstellung dieser nächtlichen Visionen in Tolkiens literarischem Werk folgt weitestgehend mittelalterlichen Konventionen, was besonders in der Beziehung zwischen Traum und Realität deutlich wird. Tolkien schätzte dieses Motiv, denn er glaubte, dass Träume in Verbindung stehen mit Faery und dass sie ebenso fähig sind, »strange powers of the mind« (FS 14) zu erwecken. Jedoch widerstrebte es ihm, diese als ein Mittel zur rationalen Erklärung von wundersamen Ereignissen oder Wesen in einer Geschichte zu verwenden, als eine Möglichkeit »[to cheat] deliberately the primal desire at the heart of Faërie: the realisation, independent of the conceiving mind, of imaged wonder« (ibid.).

Das Motiv der prophetischen Visionen wurde im *Hobbit* zwar subtiler realisiert als in *The Lord of the Rings*, *The Lost Road* oder *The Notion Club Papers*. Aber die unterschiedlichen Träume decken nichtsdestotrotz das komplette Spektrum von weniger bedeutungsvollen Visionen bis hin zu solchen, die ganz klar prophetisch sind, ab. Diese visuellen Erscheinungen jedoch können nicht nur mögliche zukünftige Ereignisse vorhersagen, sie bieten darüber hinaus aufschlussreiche Einsichten in die seelischen Zustände der Figuren. Von besonderer Wichtigkeit sind in diesem Zusammenhang die Träume, welche von den Elben bzw. Faery induziert werden. Sie gleichen dem, was Tolkien als ›Faërian Drama‹ bezeichnete und zeigen somit die gefährliche Seite der elbischen Verzauberung.

Dieser Artikel untersucht die verschiedenen Beispiele von Träumen und Visionen in *The Hobbit*, analysiert diese im weiteren Kontext mittelalterlicher Literatur, die vergleichbare Elemente enthält, und zeigt, wie dieses gemeinsame Motiv das Buch mit den darauffolgenden Werken, im Besonderen *The Lord of the Rings*, verbindet, aber gleichzeitig auch davon abgrenzt.

Der Hobbit und Begehren
Allan Turner

Eine bemerkenswerte Passage in *The Hobbit* findet sich im ersten Kapitel, als die Zwerge ihr Lied über den Einsamen Berg und den verlorenen Schatz singen, der Bilbo für die Möglichkeiten eines Abenteuers weckt. Tolkien verwendet es, um sowohl die Attraktion durch schöne Objekte als auch die durch Kunst auf die Imagination ausgeübte Macht in der Erweckung des Begehrens zu thematisieren.

Dieser Beitrag untersucht, wie Tolkien diese beiden Konzepte des Begehrens entwickelt. Auf der einen Seite wird nachverfolgt, wie sich seine Charakterisierung der Zwerge während der Entstehung von *The Hobbit* gewandelt hat und wie exzessive Gier nun eher als persönliche psychologische Eigenschaft gezeichnet wird denn als innere Qualität wie in den früheren Versionen des *Silmarillion*. Auf der anderen Seite wird die Beziehung zwischen Begehren und Kunst durch Tolkiens Ausarbeitung dieses Gedankens in *On Fairy-Stories* nachverfolgt, wobei Parallelen zu einigen seiner Motive des Begehrens in den Werken der deutschen Romantiker gefunden werden können.

Über Moralische Imagination in J.R.R. Tolkien's *The Hobbit*

Blanka Grzegorczyk

Moralische Erziehung wurde eher überraschend berichtenswert. Sogar noch unerwarteter war, dass sie nicht wenig gelehrte Reflexion entfachte. Die Sorge darum, geistliches Bewusstsein, auch in der Literatur zu nähren, wurde ein Teil von Erziehungsdebatten, die die Notwendigkeit einer Narratisierung betonen, die geeignet ist, um der *Angst* der gegenwärtigen Zeit zu begegnen. Verbunden mit diesen Trends entstand ein neues Interesse am Konzept der moralischen Imagination.

Obwohl moralische Imagination in der Forschung sehr unterschiedlich definiert wird, betrachten die meisten den auf gesundem Menschenverstand basierenden Zugang Aristoteles' zur Ethik als ein sehr geeignetes Werkzeug, um sie zu untersuchen. Die Frage nach dem Was, Warum und Wie der moralischen Imagination deutet daraufhin, dass eine ausgewogene Erziehung einen gewissen kontemplativen Geist benötigt und dass Erziehung durch Geschichten eine Person auf das vorbereiten können, was Aristoteles »die Praxis und Übung der Tugend« nennt.

In der jüngeren Forschung, die dem wachsenden Bewusstsein einer engen Verbindung zwischen Spiritualität und ethischem Verhalten Rechnung trägt, nimmt Fantasy als eine literarische Art, die in der Lage ist, moralische Imagination zu fördern, eine besondere Stellung ein.

Dieser Beitrag untersucht den *Hobbit* im Kontext der komplexen Beziehung zwischen Literatur und Ethik. Näherhin argumentiert er, eine aristotelische Tugendtheorie könne Arbeitsweisen und Funktion moralischer Imagination erhellen, was fruchtbar für die Analyse des *Hobbit* ist.

Das Interesse dieses Beitrags liegt in den Repräsentationen der menschlichen Werterfahrungen. Eine genaue Lektüre des Romans zeigt, wie mit Ethik und Spiritualität verbundene Themen in moderner mythopoetischer Fantasy ausgedrückt sein können und warum eine solche narrative Artikulation wichtig ist.

Der Schatz meines Hauses
Der Arkenstein als Symbol von Königtum und Sitz des Königsheils in *The Hobbit*
Martin G.E. Sternberg (Bonn)

Einzigartige Edelsteine wie der Arkenstein stehen bei Tolkien regelmäßig in Verbindung mit Königtum und Machtansprüchen. Ziel des Artikels ist, die historischen Quellen und Parallelen dieser Idee des Leitsteins herauszuarbeiten und für die Interpretation des *Hobbit* nutzbar zu machen. Dabei zeigt sich, dass Tolkiens Arkenstein in einer Tradition steht, die vom frühen Mittelalter bis in die Gegenwart reicht. Sie speist sich aus der germanischen Vorstellung von bestimmten Gegenständen als Verkörperungen des Sippenheils, der Verbindung zwischen bestimmten Edelsteinen und Dynastien als deren Leitstein. Hinzu kommen Vorstellungen und Legenden, die sich mit indischen Diamanten wie dem Koh-i-noor verbinden. Sie waren gerade in der Kolonialmacht Großbritannien sehr präsent, und Tolkiens Bezugnahme auf sie lässt sich detailliert nachweisen.

Der Arkenstein ist vor diesem Hintergrund nicht nur ein kostbares Juwel, sondern Sitz von Thorins Königsheil und seines Herrscherprestiges sowie Kristallisationspunkt der Erinnerung seiner Familie und der Zwerge von Erebor. Das wird auch in der Bezeichnung des Arkensteins als heirloom, Erbstück, sichtbar.

Der Verlust des Arkensteins bedeutet daher eine Minderung und Gefährdung von Thorins Königtum, und seine Eigenschaft als heirloom lässt es zweifelhaft erscheinen, dass Thorin den Arkenstein an Bilbo überhaupt hätte übertragen können. Bilbos Übergabe des Arkensteins an Bard, um Thorin zur Herausgabe des von Bard beanspruchten Anteils am Schatz zu zwingen, erinnert damit an altnordische Sagas, in denen der Träger des Sippenheils gegen ein Mitglied der jeweiligen Familie eingesetzt wird. Der vorgesehene Rückkauf des Arkensteins von Bard hätte für Thorin Kosten nicht nur an Gold, sondern vor allem an Herrscherprestige und Königsheil und kann daher den Konflikt nicht lösen.

Durch die Heranziehung der Vorstellung des königlichen Leitsteins und Heilsträgers entsteht so eine zweite Wertungsebene, die im Widerspruch zur moralisierenden Erzählerstimme steht, aber dadurch gestützt wird, dass sie das wörtliche Verständnis einiger Textstellen erlaubt. Der Konflikt um den Arkenstein speist sich so weniger aus Gier als vielmehr aus einem Konflikt unterschiedlicher kultureller Konzepte, in dem die Akzeptanz echter kultureller Vielfalt die im *Hobbit* von der Erzählerstimme suggerierte moralische Eindeutigkeit konterkariert.

Die Zwergenphilharmonie
Heidi Steimel

Bilbos Abenteuer beginnt mit unerwarteten Gästen, die ihre Musikinstrumente mitbringen und durch ihr Spielen sein Herz für ihre Sache gewinnen. Sechs verschiedene Instrumente werden erwähnt: Blas- und Saiteninstrumente sowie ein Schlaginstrument. Die miteinander verwandten Zwerge spielen die gleichen Instrumente.

Da ich davon ausgehe, dass die Musik in Mittelerde in der Vorstellung des Autors der Musik unseres Mittelalters ähnlich ist, vermute ich auch, dass die Instrumente den damaligen ähneln. Die Musik war wahrscheinlich einfacher als unsere heutige, einstimmig oder mit einfachen Harmonien versehen.

Ursprünglich hatte Tolkien gedacht, dass die Zwerge ihre Instrumente herbeizaubern würden. Dies wurde später geändert. Es gibt keine Erklärung dafür, wieso sie auf die Reise genommen wurden, auch keinen klaren Hinweis auf ihr Schicksal; allem Anschein nach wurden sie ein Opfer der Goblins bei der Gefangennahme in der Höhle.

Der Bericht über das ungeplante Konzert ist ungewöhnlich in Tolkiens Werken; Gesang ist meistens wichtiger für ihn als rein instrumentales Musizieren. Doch wird im Buch klar gesagt, dass die Instrumente nicht nur lange ohne Gesang zusammen spielten, sondern auch, dass sie den Gesang weiter begleiteten. Allerdings verstärkte das einsetzende Singen die Wirkung auf Bilbo, den Zuhörer: Er fing an, die Zwerge zu verstehen und ihr Anliegen zu begreifen, auch wenn er die Worte zunächst nicht bewusst verstand.

Nach seiner Rückkehr in das Auenland war Bilbo verändert; im späteren Buch *Der Herr der Ringe* lesen wir von den Liedern, die er dichtete und komponierte, obwohl er selbst anscheinend kein Instrument spielte. So wurde sein Leben auch durch Musik verändert – wie das vieler Leser, die selbst inspiriert wurden, Mittelerde musikalisch nachzuempfinden.

Seeing Fire and Sword, or Refining Hobbits
Anna E. Slack

»My dear Bilbo!« he [Gandalf] said. »Something is the matter with you! You are not the hobbit that you were« (H 270). Die meisten Leser würden nach der Lektüre von Tolkiens Geschichte in weiser Übereinstimmung mit Gandalfs Diagnose nicken. Denn im *Hobbit* sehen wir Bilbo Baggins, einen unbeholfenen Jedermann aus dem Auenland, in eine von Zwergen, Zauberern,

Goblins, Spinnen und nicht zuletzt einem sehr großen und prächtigen Drachen bevölkerte Welt eintreten. Auf der letzten Seite angelangt, erscheint es angemessen zu sagen, unser Held sei ›dort und wieder zurück‹ gewesen und er habe auf diesem Weg seinen Eifer mehr als zur Genüge bewiesen. Wir könnten dies die konventionelle Heldenreise eines konventionellen Jedermann-Helden nennen. Aber diese Beschreibung würde weder Bilbos Abenteuer noch seinem Charakter gerecht.

Dieser Beitrag untersucht Bilbos Rolle als Protagonist hinsichtlich der Frage, was für eine Art Hobbit er geworden ist – oder offenbart hat zu sein – in einer Erzählung, die die Grenzen zwischen Legenden, Sagen, Faërie und gewöhnlichem Leben erforscht und verhandelt. Indem Bilbo vor allem Thorin gegenübergestellt wird, will dieser Beitrag Bilbos zentrale Natur als Protagonist erhellen, der das Reich von Feuer und Schwert sowohl interpretiert als auch beeinflusst – ein Charakterzug, der in Tolkiens Werken unverändert Hobbits zukommt.

Die Comic-Adaption von *Der Hobbit*
Dirk Vanderbeke

Neuere Adaptationsstudien haben sich von der früher häufig bestimmenden Frage nach der Werktreue von Adaptationen abgewandt und ihr Interesse eher auf medientheoretische Aspekte gerichtet. Der vorliegende Artikel trägt dem Rechnung und beschäftigt sich mit ästhetischen Problemen in Charles Dixons und David Wenzels Adaptation von J.R.R. Tolkiens *The Hobbit*.

Besonders auffällige Aspekte sind dabei die erheblichen Redundanzen, einerseits als Folge einer weitgehenden Übereinstimmung von Bild und Text und andererseits durch immer wieder ähnliche Bilder, da die Autoren offensichtlich versucht haben, so viel wie möglich von Tolkiens Roman zu erhalten, und sich die beträchtliche Textmenge nur durch viele Panels bewältigen lässt, auch wenn dies aus medienästhetischen Gesichtspunkten nicht erforderlich wäre. Der Versuch, eine möglichst große Werktreue zu erhalten, führt hier gerade dazu, dass die Adaptation die Möglichkeiten des eigenen Mediums viel zu wenig ausschöpft.

Ein weiteres Thema ist die stilistische Bearbeitung, die das eigentlich nahe liegende intertextuelle Potential von Tolkiens Werk wie z.B. Zitate aus mittelalterlichem Bildmaterial oder Mythenillustrationen weitgehend ungenutzt lässt und sich statt dessen eher an klischeehaften Bildern von Zwergen und Zauberern aus Kinderbüchern oder sogar den filmischen Umsetzungen á la Walt Disney orientiert.

Insgesamt wird deutlich, dass die Adaptation aus medientheoretischer Sicht gescheitert ist, da die Autoren den Möglichkeiten des eigenen Mediums nicht ausreichend vertrauen und daher auch keine eigene künstlerische Vision entwickeln. Für die Argumentation werden dabei auch andere Romanadaptionen herangezogen, z.B. Stéphane Heuets *A la recherche du temps perdu*, Bill Sienkiewiczs *Moby Dick*, Lorenzo Mattottis und Jerry Kramskys *Doktor Jekyll & Mister Hyde* sowie Paul Karasiks and David Mazzuchellis *City of Glass*, bei denen bewusste Differenzen zum Original zu kreativen und überraschenden Ansätzen und Lesarten geführt haben – und gerade dadurch die Romanvorlagen in ihrer spezifischen Eigenart besser erfasst, aber auch neu gesehen werden können.

Summaries of the German Essays

Dwarves Do Not Live on Gold Alone – Dealing with Wealth in *The Hobbit*
Thomas Fornet-Ponse

This paper analyses the hierarchy of values and the question of the right and wrong handling of material and immaterial values in *The Hobbit*, first with regard to the protagonists and second concerning the critique of wealth (and possessiveness, respectively) as a recurring motif.

A comparison of Bilbo, Thorin, the Master of Lake-town, Bard and the Elven-king with their different respective attitudes to wealth and treasure leads to a coherent picture of the depiction of a good life as it is propagated in *The Hobbit*. A peaceful living together of Elves, Men, Dwarves (and Hobbits), combined with hedonic elements, is regarded more highly than the possession of treasure. This can be summed up in Thorin's last words to Bilbo: "If more of us valued food and cheer and song above hoarded gold, it would be a merrier world" (H 348).

Bilbo's (and the Elven-king's) attitude and his priorities serves as a prime example of this depiction of a good life, while Bard emphasises the dimension of justified claims. Thorin's and the Master's attitudes are explained by the 'dragon-sickness' and thus characterised as pathological.

This conception is supported by an analysis of the comparison of bread and gold as nourishment, which is a recurring motif. Many times, the protagonists suffer from lack of food and are dependent on the hospitality of others. Thus, the starving of the Master in the desert and Thorin's behaviour stress the insufficiency of gold for survival.

The Hobbit shows a clear conception of a good life: A person who is able to renounce gold for peace and friendship is rewarded; gold is to be used instead of hoarded to make the world a better place. Food, revelry and song are important elements of a good life, but not as simple nourishment, laughter and singing but rather as a means of stressing the social meaning of festivities and strengthening social bonds. Furthermore, music has an important function for commemorating legends and prophecies.

To sing or not to sing: Songs and poems in J.R.R. Tolkien's *The Hobbit*

Julian Eilmann

The subject matter of Tolkien poetry and song is a research topic of great relevance for our understanding of Tolkien as an author and poet. Until now, we have been lacking a comprehensive monograph on Tolkien's poetry, a study with the aim of interpreting Tolkien's entire lyrical work, including those poems with no connection to the Middle-earth mythology, to arrive at a far-reaching understanding of Tolkien as a lyricist.

This essay analyses the poetry in *The Hobbit* with regard to its meaning and its functions in the prose text, thereby establishing the basis for a deeper understanding of song and poetry in Tolkien's mythology. The wide range of characters that act as poets or singers in *The Hobbit* is striking. In contrast to *The Lord of the Rings*, not only Elves, Men, Dwarves and Hobbits, but even Goblins are presented as authors of poetry, the latter singing three songs in the novel. Furthermore, some protagonists, such as the Elves, sing in an unexpected manner, contradicting the noble image we get from their characterization in *The Lord of the Rings*.

However, during the extensive analysis my working hypothesis that the usages of verse in both hobbit novels deviate from each other had to be revised. The tension between a dominant collective song culture and the individual artistic creation, which is significant for the Middle-earth legendarium, is equally effective in *The Hobbit*. The contradicting mythological context and the genre character of a children's novel explain the irritation in respect of song usage.

The Dwarven songs in the *The Hobbit* demonstrate a consistent folk song structure and thus refer to an underlying common song tradition. Furthermore, songs are used in terms of occasional poetry and can be adopted by the protagonists for present situations by means of a literary technique called contrafacture.

Additionally, the Lake-town song and the Dwarven song *Under the Mountain dark and tall* (H 235f) show that poetry in *The Hobbit* is an integral part of social and political communication and can be used for political, panegyrical and economic purposes. By having characters from *The Lord of the Rings* adopt verses from *The Hobbit*, Tolkien creates intertextual connections between his two hobbit novels.

Over and above that, poetry in *The Hobbit* fulfils narrative functions in the text. The songs of the Rivendell Elves act as a narrative framework and the Dwarven song *Far over the misty mountains cold* (H14f) has crucial expository qualities.

Seeing and (Not) Being Seen
Christian Weichmann

Originating from the conclusion that the Dwarves are justified in calling their operation a "dark business" since a large part of the plot of *The Hobbit* is set in the dark, this article investigates how Tolkien describes this, and which consequences there are for the story and its protagonists

In this context, the Ring is seen as some kind of "equalizer" for Bilbo, but not regarding his companions but in regard to his environment and the dangers lurking therein. For the Ring now allows the Hobbit, who is very often not able to see much himself since it is so dark, to remain unseen himself. However, more often than not this is a psychological advantage rather than a direct aid in his quest: It provides some protection against danger and thus allows him to risk just a little bit more, thus becoming the actual decisive factor for his increasing success throughout the book.

The alternative aspect to not being able to see well and trying not to be seen are eyes, especially those of Gollum, the spiders, and of Smaug, that are able to see in the dark and even glow strongly enough to strike fear into the hearts of Bilbo, the Dwarves, and the reader.

Finally, the article has some comments on why it might be that these eyes actually glow. Is this some artistic rendition of ancient theories on active seeing, or is it based on the depiction of light as some workable and storable substance that is so typical of Tolkien's mythology?

A Reassessment of the Theoretical Concept of 'Faërie' and 'fairy story' based on the Expanded Edition of *Tolkien On Fairy-stories*, published in 2008
Heidi Krüger

The *Expanded Edition* of the famous essay *On Fairy-Stories*, published in 2008, is likely to cause quite a stir, as it has the potential of causing a big gallimaufry, or at least revising, existing views on Tolkien.

This edition provides the reader with many manuscripts that document Tolkien's preliminary work for his lecture from 8 March 1939 and his subsequent – and thorough – revisions up until 1943.

It is especially the first part (the first 19 pages) of his 'miscellanies' – which were of course, never intended for publication in this form – that Tolkien expands upon about his views on the topics of Faërie und fairies in a liberality sure to open the eyes of many a reader regarding Tolkien's views on the visible and the invisible world.

In my paper, I have analysed how this fact influences the understanding of Tolkien's poetology. I have concentrated on the key terms 'Faërie' and 'fairy story,' both of which Tolkien treated extensively in his published essay.

Based on this essay, I have first extracted the substantial difficulties and contradictions found therein. I have then structured, described and defined them, if possible, by means of theoretical categories.

Building upon this, I draw upon those 'miscellanies' that put the still open questions, problems and contradictions of the essay in a surprisingly new light. Both 'Faërie' and 'fairy story' are given a significance, individually as well as in their relation to one another, that is likely to astonish some, and to validate others. All questions, contradictions and problems are resolved, but this can only be the start of a new discourse. We need to re-evaluate whether Tolkien's own works meet his demands – and, even, whether he wanted them to. The new material has challenged our old findings.

Endlich lag das Ufer des riesigen Sees vor uns. Nicht weit von der Mündung des Waldflusses: die seltsame Stadt, die auf Pfählen ins Wasser gebaut war.

Rezensionen

Judith E. Tonning & Brendan N. Wolfe (Eds.): The Chronicle of the Oxford University C.S. Lewis Society.

Oxford: The Oxford C.S. Lewis Society

Much of Tolkien scholarship before the launch of *Tolkien Studies* in 2004 was published in the form of monographs, collections of papers or, on a more regular basis, in journals such as *Mallorn, Mythlore, Anor, Amon Hen* etc. The latter publications could not (and probably would not) always deny their roots in Tolkien fandom and thus the (rather malicious) question has been raised whether these journals should be considered 'proper scholarly journals' or rather tail-ends of fanzines (cf. the often colourful illustrations of varying degrees of artistry next to pieces of fan-fiction).

C.S. Lewis scholarship, by contrast, has (as far as I know) never attracted a similar mix of popular enthusiasm and scholarly acumen – or at least this has not found expression in fanzine/journal publications. Yet there exists also no internationally acknowledged flagship comparable to *Tolkien Studies*. The journal of the Oxford University C.S. Lewis Society thus fills a gap and functions as a regular platform for the publication of new research.

As the editors write, *The Chronicle* "provides a forum for rigorous academic engagement with the thoughts of C.S. Lewis and his intellectual and literary peers and forebears." It is published three times a year, peer-reviewed, and indexed in the MLA. Although most of the papers and book-reviews centre around C.S. Lewis and his work, Tolkien scholars often find articles that compare the two Inklings-authors explicitly, such as John Robinson's 'Faerie in J.R.R. Tolkien and C.S. Lewis: Escape vs. Recovery' (in volume 5, issue 2, May 2008), while others, focussing solely on Lewis, may be of interest to people researching similar themes in Tolkien's work (e.g. their concepts of gender).

All in all, Tolkien scholars with a healthy general interest in the work of his friend and fellow-Inkling will find *The Chronicle* worth studying. Further information can be found at www.cslewischronicle.org

Thomas Honegger

Anne Besson: D'Asimov à Tolkien. Cycles et séries dans la littérature de genre.

Paris: CNRS Editions, 2004, 250 pp., Softcover

Mit vorliegender aufschlussreicher Studie untersucht die Autorin eine Fragestellung, die gerade für die Fantasy- und Science-Fiction-Literatur von großer Bedeutung ist, aber dennoch bislang kaum näher betrachtet wurde: Charakteristika, Eigenart und Funktion eines (Roman-)Zyklus. Anne Besson nähert sich ihr in zwei Teilen von je zwei Kapiteln, die von Einleitung und Schluss gerahmt sind.

Der erste Teil bezieht sich auf allgemeine Charakteristika des Romanzyklus und erläutert im ersten Kapitel die Differenzen zwischen einem Zyklus und einer Serie, deren Ähnlichkeit sie unter Rekurs auf die Entstehungsgeschichte aus Fortsetzungsromanen vor allem im gleichen (kommerziellen) Interesse ausmacht, deren Hauptunterschied aber in der Abhängigkeit bzw. Unabhängigkeit der einzelnen Romane von den früheren besteht. Weiterhin erläutert sie die jeweiligen Hauptrichtungen – sentimentale und Polizeiromane als Serien; Fantasy und Science Fiction als Zyklen – und geht abschließend auch auf andere Medien ein.

Das zweite Kapitel analysiert die Einheit und Diskontinuität sowie die Kriterien der Definition eines Romanzyklus. Als Zeichen der Einheit dient neben dem Paratext die ›intrigue‹ (nach Ricoeur), was sie u.a. am Beispiel Tolkiens darlegt, Namen und wiederholtes Auftreten der Personen sowie Analepsen und Prolepsen. Die Diskontinuität kann sich in einer relativen Autonomie der einzelnen Bände niederschlagen, wobei dem ersten und letzten noch eine besondere Rolle zukommt, aber auch in der Produktion von Fortsetzungen (da Zyklen nicht notwendig geschlossen sein müssen) – als Beispiel kann sie auf Tolkien verweisen. Schließlich erläutert sie anhand verschiedener Beispiele (Zyklen von Isaac Asimov, Kim Stanley Robinson, Ursula Le Guin) den offenen Charakter eines Zyklus mit seiner Tendenz zur Expansion.

Der zweite Teil nimmt den zeitlichen Aspekt eines Zyklus in den Blick, wozu Besson im dritten Kapitel sich der Chronologie eines Zyklus, den Anleihen aus der Realgeschichte, den Evidenzen für ein Vergehen der Zeit und den Schwierigkeiten und Inkohärenzen chronologischer Freiheit zuwendet, bevor sie auch auf die Seite des Rezipienten mit den verschiedenen Möglichkeiten der Lektüre, der Wiederholung und dem Spannungsaufbau sowie auf das Gleichgewicht zwischen Text und Leser eingeht.

Das letzte Kapitel bespricht das Thema der Zeit und der Erinnerung zunächst unter individuellem Aspekt beim Leser, beim Umgang mit Vergessen oder ungenauen Erinnerungen der Protagonisten. Ferner wird das Verhältnis von Gesellschaft und geschichtlicher Zeit anhand verwendeter Kalender, der Generationenfolge sowie von Archiven und Dokumenten untersucht. Das Kapitel abschließend wendet sich Besson den für eine Zivilisation wichtigen Legenden zu, geht dabei zunächst auf das für ›primitive‹ Gesellschaften zentrale Verständnis der ewigen Wiederkehr ein, um sodann die Mythologie des Zyklus und den Zyklus als Mythologie zu untersuchen.

Zum Schluss schlägt sie als Antwort auf die Frage, weshalb Zyklen gelesen würden, vor: Dies hinge mit tiefen und weitgehend unformulierten Sehnsüchten der Leser nach Identität und Ewigkeit zusammen.

Thomas Fornet-Ponse

Lucie Armitt: Fantasy Fiction: An Introduction.
London: Continuum, 2005, 229 + x pp., Hardcover

It is over a quarter of a century since the publication of Rosemary Jackson's well-known book *Fantasy: The Literature of Subversion*, and although this is still a standard introductory text, it is beginning to show signs of age, not least because perceptions of fantasy have changed in the intervening period. In the afterglow of 1960s iconoclasm, Jackson concentrated on the side of the fantastic that challenges and undermines accepted notions of reality, while largely dismissing as reactionary entertainment the Tolkienian secondary world fantasy. However, the upsurge of public interest and the rapid growth of Tolkien criticism during the last ten years have made such a position untenable. This more balanced approach by Lucie Armitt may be seen as a bid to offer a contemporary alternative.

Armitt does not attempt a precise definition of what she understands by fantasy, although she gives a number of examples which suggest that she includes all kinds of non-realistic fiction. What unites her examples is an underlying metaphor for all fantasy, taken from an article on utopias by Louis Marin, namely a horizon, which is a "symbol of simultaneous limit and infinity" (4). On the one hand, it symbolises an unending desire, since the horizon constantly retreats as one tries to approach. On the other, as the hazy boundary between earth and sky, it is a "fraying edge" (7) which promises a glimpse of something that is neither but lies beyond. This allows her to integrate Todorov's theory by regarding the fantastic not as a genre in itself but as another, similar borderline, that between the uncanny and the marvellous. Fantasy, then, in the Tolkienian sense, remains on one side of the dividing line, whereas the literary fantastic makes use of the haze to move between different realities.

The two long chapters of detailed readings range from *Utopia* and *Gulliver's Travels* to *Harry Potter* and Yann Martel's *Life of Pi*, taking in such standards as Mary Shelley, Lewis Carroll, H.G. Wells and George Orwell. There is a significant section on *The Lord of the Rings*, although Armitt does not escape from the blindness that so often plagues critics when commenting on Tolkien. She mistakenly claims Pippin's memory of the food provided by Gildor to be an immature recollection of Lórien (62). More seriously, she misinterprets Frodo's dream in the house of Tom Bombadil as a prefiguring of Gandalf's rescue from the peak after his battle with the Balrog (36), in spite of the clear reference at the Council of Elrond to Orthanc and the treachery of Saruman. This seriously undermines the point she is trying to make, that it belongs to the type of the medieval dream vision.

Nevertheless, the book presents a useful overview of the broad range of non-realistic literature. The author's task is assisted by the common basic structure for all the volumes in the series, as listed on the back cover. This includes such features as a broad definition of the genre, critical concerns to bear in mind while reading, detailed readings of key texts, and a summary of the most important criticism in the field, together with an annotated reading list. Although it is characterised by the subtitle as "an introduction", readers should be aware that it presupposes a considerable familiarity with concepts and vocabulary of literary criticism, so it is not always an easy read for the non-specialist.

Allan Turner

Fanfan Chen: Fantasticism. Poetics of Fantastic Literature.
(Arbeiten zur Literarischen Phantastik 1)
Berlin: Peter Lang, 2007, 376 pp., Paperback

We cannot complain about a lack of books on fantasy literature – or, to use the more general term, 'literature of the fantastic'. There are the important classics, dating mostly to the 1980s and often written in response to Todorov's seminal study.[1] More recently, we have seen, next to a plethora of

---

1   See Tzvetan Todorov, *The Fantastic: A Structural Approach to a Genre*, Ithaca: Cornell University Press 1973/1975, Rosemary Jackson, *The Literature of Subversion*, London: Methuen 1981, Kathryn Hume, *Fantasy and Mimesis; Responses to Reality in Western*

specialised studies on individual authors, the publication of some new approaches to the topic such as Farah Mendlesohn's *The Rhetorics of Fantasy* (2008), Frank Weinreich's *Fantasy. Einführung* (2007), Lucie Armitt's *Fantasy: An Introduction* (2005), Richard Mathews's *Fantasy: The Liberation of Imagination* (2002), and Colin Manlove's *The Fantasy Literature of England* (1999).[2] Fanfan Chen's book is different from all of these. First of all, it is written from a truly comparatistic perspective. Chen, born and raised in Taiwan, spent her post-graduate years in Europe and received her doctoral degree from the University of Poitiers. She is one of the few scholars interested in the literature of the fantastic who are able to straddle the great divide between East and West – and her book is a testimony to this.

Fantasticism is not an easy book. Whereas many of her predecessors in the field dealt with the theoretical aspects of fantastic literature with a light touch (see, for example, Manlove's truly minimalist and catholic definition of fantasy as "a fiction involving the supernatural or impossible" p. 3), Chen spends exactly half of her study (188 out of 376 pages) on laying the theoretical foundations. The starting point is, as with so many studies before, Todorov's concept of the fantastic as being grounded in the reader's hesitation of how to classify a 'fantastic' phenomenon. Chen gives it short shrift by showing its utter inadequacy for Chinese literature, which often shows no absolute division between the 'real' and the 'unreal' and thus does usually not evoke any hesitation on the reader's part.

This observation is programmatic: Chen, as a trained comparatist, uses not only English, French, German and South-American literature as touchstones, but also Chinese literary works. Her choice of theoretical texts is equally wide: Plato, Aristotle, the philosophy of Daoism and Lao Zi's *Dao De Jing*, Carl Gustav Jung, Owen Barfield, the French literary theorists Jean Genette and Tzvetan Todorov and the French critics Jean-Luc Marion, Gaston Bachelard and Gilbert Durand are the pillars on which she erects her elaborate critical framework. The intricate and involved argument may be summarized as follows (running the unavoidable risk of being a 'simplificateur terrible'): fantastic literature (and myth) comprises the transitional realm between the realm of the unknown (Plato's *Ideal Forms*, Lao Zi's *Being*) and the realm of the known (the manifestations of the Ideal Forms/Being in the physical world). Chen thus defines fantastic literature "as

---

Literature, New York: Methuen 1984, Christine Brook-Rose, *A Rhetoric of the Unreal: Studies in Narrative and Structure, especially of the Fantastic*, Cambridge: Cambridge University Press 1981, Brian Attebery, *The Fantasy Tradition in American Literature*, Bloomington: Indiana University Press 1980, and his *Strategies of Fantasy*, Bloomington: Indiana University Press 1992.

2   Farah Mendlesohn, *The Rhetorics of Fantasy*, Middletown: Wesleyan University Press 2008, Frank Weinreich's *Fantasy. Einführung*, Oldenburg: Oldib 2007, Lucie Armitt's *Fantasy: An Introduction*, New York: Continuum 2005, Richard Mathews's *Fantasy: The Liberation of Imagination*, New York and London: Routledge 2002, and Colin Manlove's *The Fantasy Literature of England*, Basingstoke: Palgrave 1999.

literary narratives or poeticized storytelling about the imaginary unknown" (p. 38). Just as science explores the physical world by means of experiments, fantastic literature explores the realm of the unknown by means of storytelling. As a consequence, fantastic literature is not only a universal phenomenon of humanity, but also extant from the very inception of the human race, though represented differently according to the evolutionary and cultural phases. Based on Barfield's concept of the development of the human mind, Chen presents a categorisation of fantastic literature and relates the literary 'phenotypes' to the historical and cultural background (e.g. that a strong centralistic power is not conducive to fantastic writings, p. 103). Such (necessarily) sweeping statements may not stand up to close scrutiny in their generalisations, but they certainly ask for more research along the lines indicated.

The second part of the study presents three concepts by means of which fantastic literature can be characterised and thus categorised: the dream discourse, the mirror discourse, and the magician's hat discourse. The dream discourse presents the unknown as a second reality. The reader finds him/herself immersed in the secondary world of the tale. J.R.R. Tolkien's epic *The Lord of the Rings* or the Chinese classic *Journey to the West* would be typical representatives of this type. The mirror discourse, by contrast, is grounded in the primary reality of the physical world; yet by 'reflecting' images of this primary reality it renders them uncanny and causes an estrangement. It is thus closer to the nightmare than to the dream. Oscar Wilde's *The Picture of Dorian Gray* may be seen as a typical story illustrating the characteristics of the mirror discourse. The magician's hat discourse, finally, baffles readers by including strange and bizarre elements within a realistic framework (e.g. Gogol's *The Nose*).

Chen analyses some of these works in depth (e.g. Goethe's *Faust* as an example of the dream-discourse) next to sketching possible interpretations for a plethora of additional texts. The focus is mainly on the textual analysis of canonical authors from the period of Romanticism, the 19th and early 20th centuries, such as Hoffmann, Kafka, Maupassant, Poe, Stoker, Dunsany, Wells, Orwell, Cortazar, and Bulgakov, and recent 'fantasy' authors are missing. They are, however, taken into consideration in Chen's discussion of periodisation and themes. Chen does not merely analyse the imagery and motifs of the fantastic, but also pays close attention to the language used. She postulates, in accordance with Barfield and Tolkien, a meaningful unity of form and content – which is also reflected in the narrative quality of fantastic literature.

As I warned, *Fantasticism. Poetics of Fantastic Literature* is not an easy book to read – and even less easy to summarize, so that I have only touched upon a fraction of its themes. Its wide scope in space and time, spanning Western as well as Eastern literature, literary criticism and philosophy, renders it a treasure-trove for highly original, sometimes even (from a Western point of view) bizarre ideas and insights. *Fantasticism* provides new impulses to the study of fantastic literature in general and fantasy in particular and deserves a prolonged and more detailed examination than I have been able to give within the limited space of a short review.

Thomas Honegger

Eduardo Segura & Thomas Honegger (eds.): Myth and Magic. Art according to the Inklings.

Zürich/Jena: Walking Tree Publishers, 2007. iii + 337 pp., Paperback

Dem Titel des Bandes nach zu urteilen, widmet er sich primär dem Kunstverständnis der Inklings; ein Blick ins Inhaltsverzeichnis ergibt aber ein etwas anderes Bild, das nicht ohne Weiteres auf einen Nenner zu bringen ist. So untersucht Tom Shippey, wie die Differenzierung zwischen ›magia‹ und ›goeteia‹ bei Tolkien, Lewis und Williams eine große Rolle spielt, analysiert Dieter Bachmann drei von Tolkien für Magie verwendete Wörter (goetia, gûl und lúth), widmet sich Miryam Librán-Morena der Frage, wie Tolkiens Geschichte von Beren und Lúthien von zwei griechischen Mythen beeinflusst ist (von Orpheus und Eurydike sowie von Protesilaos und Laodameia) oder geht Eugenio M. Olivares-Merino sehr ausführlich auf Tolkiens Verständnis von Grendel ein. Eduardo Segura schließlich bespricht auf der Grundlage von *Leaf by Niggle* Tolkiens Verständnis von Kunst.

Trotz dieser Disparität liegt ein gewisser Schwerpunkt des Bandes bei Mythen und Magie, und auch wenn der Großteil der Beiträge sich ausschließlich mit Tolkien auseinandersetzt, kommt daneben vor allem Lewis zur Sprache – besonders bei Colin Duriez, der sich mit dem Verhältnis von Mythos, Tatsachen und Inkarnation vor allem bei ihm auseinandersetzt, und im Beitrag von Devin Brown, der dessen Sicht eines literarischen Mythos als Träger tieferer, fundamentaler Wahrheiten untersucht. Aber auch in der Auseinandersetzung von Margarita Carretero-González mit der besonderen Stellung und Funktion von Liebe und Opfer in den Werken von Tolkien, Lewis und Rowling oder in der Analyse des Namens ›Ransom‹ in der Perelandra-Trilogie durch Fernando J. Soto und Marta García de la Puerta.

Zum Teil wird dieser disparate Eindruck dadurch erklärt, dass Segura und Honegger in diesem Band auch mehreren spanischen Forschern die Gelegenheit geben wollten, ihre Arbeiten einem breiteren Publikum vorzustellen, auch wenn diese vielleicht nicht direkt zum Oberthema passten.

Ferner widmet sich Martin Simonson dem Aspekt der ›Recovery‹ bei Tolkien vor dem Hintergrund der bis dato kaum untersuchten Beziehung zwischen Tolkiens Vorstellungen und amerikanischem Transzendentalismus (Emerson und Thoreau), geht Verlyn Flieger in *Smith of Wootton Major* der Frage nach, wann eine Fairy-story eine Faërie-Story ist, d.h. im ›Perilous Realm‹ spielt, wofür dieses Werk Tolkiens paradigmatisch stehen kann. Darüber hinaus zeigt Patrick Curry auf der Basis einer begrifflichen und symbolisch-mythologischen hermeneutischen Analyse interessante Ähnlichkeiten zwischen Tolkiens und Max Webers Sicht der Moderne auf. Des Weiteren untersucht Thomas Honegger die Geschichte der meta-fiktionellen Elemente, die Tolkien einsetzte, um die (vor allem elbischen) Legenden und seine menschliche Leserschaft in Beziehung zu setzen, und John Garth argumentiert in seiner detaillierten Analyse des Kapitels »The Passage of the Marshes« aus *The Lord of the Rings* für eine Lektüre auf der Basis der Kriegserfahrungen Tolkiens, wozu er auch andere Kriegsschriftsteller heranzieht.

Auch wenn man angesichts des Titels eine etwas breitere Berücksichtigung der Inklings – vor allem über Tolkien und Lewis hinaus – und eine etwas größere inhaltliche Geschlossenheit erwartet hätte, tut dies den einzelnen Beiträgen keinen Abbruch, denn auch diejenigen, die nicht aus der Feder bekannter Tolkienforscher stammen, sind durchaus lesenswert.

Thomas Fornet-Ponse

Verlyn Flieger & Douglas A. Anderson (Eds.): J.R.R. Tolkien: On Fairy-stories.

London: HarperCollins 2008, 320 pp., Hardcover

Over the years, *On Fairy-Stories* (OFS) has become one of the canonical theoretical texts on fantastic literature. This is not only due to the fact that Tolkien has become one of the most successful authors of fantastic literature in English, but also to the relative dearth of academic studies in this field. The influence of OFS has been mostly indirect.

Tolkien's ideas, first presented to a wider audience in his Andrew Lang Lecture at the University of St Andrews on 8 March 1939, have been seen as directly relevant to his own writings (i.e. *The Hobbit* and *The Lord of the Rings*, but also *Farmer Giles of Ham* and *Smith of Wootton Major*) of which *The Lord of the Rings*, in turn, would serve as models for many of the later works in the genre. OFS has thus become the theoretical cornerstone for the 'secondary world' tradition within fantasy (vs. the Todorovian framework). Reason enough, one may think, to provide a critical edition of the text, which was first published in 1947 in Essays Presented to Charles Williams and subsequently went out of print, but was then made available (in a slightly revised version) in *Tree and Leaf* (1964) and again in *The Monsters and the Critics* (1985). The handwritten manuscript drafts and individual notes as well as the typed and corrected versions have been available for research in the Bodleian for many years.

Verlyn Flieger and Douglas A. Anderson have taken upon themselves the arduous task of arranging, deciphering and transcribing the extant material (having done some research on Tolkien's manuscripts myself and, by chance, having worked alongside Verlyn Flieger in the Bodleian in August 2006, I can personally testify to the challenging nature of the undertaking). The results of their labour are now available in a handsomely produced volume that comprises the original text of the essay as published in 1947, and a transcription of two early manuscripts (MSS A and B) as well as the typed text (MS C) that served as the proof text for the printers. Although the original text of Tolkien's Lang Lecture cannot be identified and reconstructed with any certainty, we get a fairly good idea of what he said on that Wednesday in March 1939 thanks to the rather detailed newspaper reports of the event, which are also reproduced in the volume.

It is of interest that some key-concepts such as 'sub-creation' or the specific connection between the happy ending of the fairy story and the Christian gospel were not yet in existence in the original lecture and the early drafts. Also, we can see how Tolkien was developing and refining his critical vocabulary and concepts which, in the end, would comprise the central terms Fantasy, Enchantment, Escape, Recovery, and Consolation. And, as Heidi Krüger's discussion of the development of *On Fairy-Stories* in this issue of *Hither Shore* makes clear, the documents show that the 'final product', i.e. the 1947 essay and its later reprints, was not so much a harmoniously unified whole, but rather a text that still harboured many of the contradictions, tensions and unresolved issues as the heritage of its long germination and diversified scope.

The editorial notes and the introduction to the manuscripts are, as may be expected from such old hands, highly relevant, illuminating, informative and a testimony to their erudition. Unfortunately, a slight shift in page-numeration in the final stages of the production rendered the references on pages 195ff all off the mark by two pages – something that can be easily corrected in a new printing.

Due to the different nature of the primary text, OFS is less 'academic' than Michael Drout's edition of Tolkien's lecture *Beowulf: The Monsters and the Critics* and thus more easily accessible to the general reader. I'm sure that it will not only renew the interest of a wider public in this central theoretical text, but also that it is going to provide important impulses for the discussion of the foundations of Tolkienian fantasy. *Thomas Honegger*

Das einst so liebliche Tal lag schon lange öde da und mit Ruinen übersät – überschattet vom Einsamen Berg, wo der Drache immer noch hauste...

Lynn Forrest-Hill (ed.): The Mirror Crack'd. Fear and Horror in J.R.R. Tolkien's Major Works.

Cambridge: Cambridge Scholars Publishing, 2008, 246 pp., Hardcover

The idea that elements of horror and fear play an important role in Tolkien's (major) works has not yet received much attention. The volume edited by Lynn Forest-Hill endeavours to close this gap in the critical reception and presents a selection of ten papers focussing in varying degrees on horror, fear, and related topics such as monstrosity or evil.

Maria Rafaella Benvenuto opens the collection with a short piece on the medieval roots of Tolkien's monsters and outlines several of the themes dealt with in greater detail in the following chapters.

Jessica Burke, then, attempts a definition of the central term 'fear' and related ones such as 'horror' and 'terror' and their connection to monstrosity and evil. Overall, Burke provides some stimulating ideas on monsters and monstrosity, yet the relevance of her discussion for Tolkien's work is not always clear.

A similar criticism may be also applied to Reno E. Lauro's paper on medieval aesthetics. He outlines the tradition of linking light, order and harmony with our aesthetic predilections, and discusses Barfield's influence on Tolkien's conception of evil. He also analyses the use of terms such as 'magic' and 'goetia' and draws some interesting parallels to Heidegger's understanding of 'technology'.

All these elements are applied to his discussion of Shelob – who is (next to spiders in general) also the topic of Rainer Nagel's paper. Nagel's delineation of the religious and secular traditions of the spider is comparatively brief, to the point and a model in clarity and first-hand acquaintance with the sources quoted.

Next in line is Shandi Stevenson who looks at the pre-Christian literature (or, in the case of Beowulf, at literature set in a pre-Christian era) of Northern Europe and compares this pre-Christian view of the world with the Christian depiction of evil. She has a point when she highlights the fact that Tolkien's innovative addition to this pre-Christian scenario is the danger (and thus the horror) of the realisation that even good people are never safe from the transforming power of evil.

Michael Cunningham, then, locates horror in liminal situations, i.e. in situations of 'crossing borders' (be they spiritual or geographical) and Amy

Amendt-Raduege contributes an informative and engaging exploration of the medieval (mostly Old Norse) sources and analogues of Tolkien's 'revenants' such as barrow-wights, black riders etc.

The development of dragons in Tolkien is competently traced by Romuald Lakowski, who focuses on the figure of Glorund/Glaurung in the various textual variants of Tolkien's legendarium. He discusses the medieval parallels and analogues, notably Fafnir in the *Völsunga Saga* and the anonymous Beowulf-dragon, but also the dragon in Spenser's Renaissance epic *The Faerie Queen* – yet does not mention any of the rather numerous dragons in Middle English romances.

Kristine Larsen applies geomythology in order to trace myths of horror back to cataclystic events such as meteors, solar and lunar eclipses, earthquakes etc. She demonstrates that Tolkien, as so often, provided his secondary world with a complex background comparable to ours.

Finally, Julie Pridmore takes a closer look at wolves in medieval history, literature and in Tolkien's works and analyses the development of the 'canine' wolf-opponent that replaces the originally feline protagonists of the earlier texts (Tevildo, Oikeroi in *Lost Tales 2*).

The overall presentation of the volume is appealing, though the choice of the cover picture is, to me, somewhat mystifying (it shows a rolling rural landscape under a lowering sky – slightly off-colour. The closest feelings of 'horror' I get is due to the fact that it reminds me of similar pictures seen in the movie *The Ring*). The content of the book is somewhat mixed. Without wanting to be overly or destructively critical, I would like to point out and discuss some of the shortcomings.

Firstly, there are (as I know from experience) the almost inevitable typos, misplacements, and omissions. Thus, we find an enigmatic sentence such as "Even the O have a complex history" (p. 24 – 'O' should be 'Orcs' and not the heroine of the erotic novel *Histoire d'O*), Thum 2004, quoted in Pridmore's essay, is not listed in the bibliography, and several entries in the bibliography of Amendt-Raduege's paper are not in correct alphabetical order (at least not if listed by editor) etc.

Secondly, we have at least one translation mistake (which may go back to a typo?) from Old English. Thus, Burke translates 'deofla hryre' (p. 43) as 'the devil's fall', after quoting the correct rendering by Chickering ('the fall of devils'). 'deofla', however, is genitive plural of 'deofl', so it should be 'the devils's (or demons's) fall' – which could include the Devil himself, of course, but theologically there is a difference. The same translation problem occurs with the genitive plural form 'wundor-smitha', which should be rendered as 'from/of wondrous smiths' and not 'of [a] wondrous smith'. Minor points, you may think, but it is exactly to such 'minor points' that philologists like Tolkien paid close attention and were often able to prove major points.

Thirdly, some (per se correct) interpretations and observations do not give the complete picture since specific key-elements have not been taken into consideration. Pridmore, for example, points out the prominence of the wolf in contexts of battle, yet she does not identify it as one of the three 'beasts of battle' (wolf, raven, eagle), a literary-poetic motif which occurs in almost all instances of large-scale conflict in Anglo-Saxon (and also in Old Norse) poetry. This is of relevance since the only 'positive' example of a wolf she quotes – the beast has been guarding the head of the martyr-king Edmund – is a deliberate inversion of this traditional 'beast of battle' motif in order to demonstrate God's power.

Fourthly, some of the papers would have profited from taking into consideration recent publications on their topics. Lauro's discussion of 'magic' and 'goetia' could be complemented by Tom Shippey's 'New Learning and New Ignorance: Magia, Goetia, and the Inklings' and Dieter Bachmann's 'Words for Magic: goetia, gûl and lúth' (both in Eduardo Segura and Thomas Honegger, eds., *Myth and Magic: Art according to the Inklings*, Walking Tree Publishers 2007 – maybe published too late for inclusion in Lauro's paper). His analysis of Shelob would find further inspiration in Judith Klinger's 'Hidden Paths of Time: March 13th and the Riddles of Shelob's Lair' (in Thomas Honegger and Frank Weinreich, eds., *Tolkien and Modernity 2*, Walking Tree Publisher, 2006 – see also the detailed review of Klinger's paper in *Tolkien Studies 5*, pp. 252-255).

Fifthly, quite a few of the essays give the impression that knowledge about matters medieval comes exclusively (or at least predominantly) from secondary literature, and the Middle Ages get a very summary treatment (see, for example, pp. 27, 57-58). As a medievalist, I want to point out that the period of a thousand years usually labelled 'the Middle Ages' is as diversified as any other period and a hundred years during the Middle Ages still lasted a hundred years. Generalisations about 'the Middle Ages' must be therefore viewed with a healthy dose of suspicion.

Sixthly, the use of specific terminology is sometimes neither correct nor helpful to the understanding of the issue. A sentence such as "Frodo is presumably so burdened by the gravitas of the Ring that its consuming shadow is beginning to manifest ontological effects by negating the effects of light". (Lauro, p. 69) is neither correct ('gravitas' is a Roman virtue and not the same as 'gravity') nor clearly understandable. What is wrong with 'Frodo is so weighed down by the burden of the Ring that its consuming shadow is beginning to show concrete effects on his personality by negating the effects of light'? Less jargon would be preferable in such a context. Problems with the correct use of specific terminology can also be found in Burke's discussion of the (admittedly thorny) problem of evil. Thus, she misapplies or misunderstands Thomas Aquinas' category of 'ens'/'being' as applying to everything in existence and thus comes to such conclusions as: "Can we then say that because murder exists, it is to some extent good?" (p. 29). Aquinas' basic idea is that since creation (and thus everything created) was originally good, all things that exist (even in a fallen state of being) partake in this original 'goodness' because the devil can only pervert, but not create. Thus, to answer her rhetorical question, even murder may still keep a tiny share in this original goodness, most likely in form of a twisted and perverted, yet originally 'good' motivation. I don't have the space to go into a discussion of medieval theology and philosophy, but I would like to emphasise that it is quite complex, sophisticated, and important for the deeper understanding of Tolkien's work. Burke furthermore argues that Augustine's view of the nature of evil is (fundamentally) different from that of Boethius, which is not quite the case: both see evil as a perversion of something originally 'good' or as an absence of 'good'. Finally, the inclusion of Nietzschean ideas in order to 'reconstruct' Tolkien's concept of 'complete evil' is neither justified nor even helpful.

Seventhly, and lastly, a point that also applies to many other studies on Tolkien: the non-inclusion of current theoretical concepts. A colleague of mine (rightly) commented that Tolkien studies seem often to take place in a self-sufficient universe with Tolkien scholars quoting other Tolkien scholars but without much input from other fields of study and without a deeper engagement with current literary theories. I gave him a few counter-examples, but had to admit that, on the whole, his point is a valid one. So here, too. I would have expected (or wished) a longish introductory overview-essay on current theories on fear and horror in literature together with an attempt towards a definition of the key terms.

I hope to have given the reader a fair idea about the strengths, weak points and shortcomings of this volume. The fact that criticism has taken up more space than praise is, on the one hand, due to the fact that there are several debatable points which I felt could not go unchallenged, but also, on the other, to the text-type of 'critical review'.

It should not be forgotten that the collection contains several well-written and well-researched papers and thus makes a brave (though in places somewhat flawed) beginning in an area little researched.

Thomas Honegger

Christian Kölzer:
›Fairy tales are more than true‹.
Das mythische und neomythische Weltdeutungspotential der Fantasy am Beispiel von J.R.R. Tolkiens *The Lord of the Rings* und Philip Pullmans *His Dark Materials*.
(SALS 32) Trier: WVT 2008, 364 Seiten, Paperback

In dieser in Gießen entstandenen Dissertation widmet sich Christian Kölzer dem Weltdeutungspotential der Fantasy anhand zweier ausgewählter und – wie im Verlauf der Arbeit deutlich wird – sehr unterschiedlich angelegter bedeutender Werke der von ihm so genannten ›existentiellen Fantasy‹: Tolkiens *The Lord of the Rings* und Pullmans *His Dark Materials*. Unter ›existentieller Fantasy‹ versteht er dabei unter Rekurs auf Linus Hausers Forschungen zur neomythischen Vernunft diejenige Art von Fantasy, die große Nähe zur mythischen Erzählweise und ähnliches Weltdeutungspotential aufweist. Sie bewegt sich zwischen dem klassischen Mythos und religionsförmigem Neomythos. Den Unterschied bestimmt er wie folgt: »Texte mit ernstzunehmenden weltanschaulichen Grundpositionen erkennen die Endlichkeit des Menschen als radikal an, während neomythisch ausgerichtete Texte mit den Möglichkeiten der Überwindung der Endlichkeit mit eigenen Mitteln und somit mit dem Traum der Autotheosis spielen.« (104)

Bevor sich Kölzer aber den beiden zur Debatte stehenden Werken als idealtypischen Vertretern je einer Seite des Spektrums – Tolkiens Werk als in der Tradition des klassischen Mythos stehend und Pullman als Beispiel einer neomythischen, da naturwissenschaftlich-materialistischen Weltsicht – zuwendet, erläutert er nach einer kurzen einleitenden Standortbestimmung zunächst das Rezeptionsproblem der Fantasy. Schon in diesen beiden Kapiteln kritisiert er deutlich eine Annexion der Anderwelt, indem er die Unabhängigkeit der textinternen Realität von der extrafiktionalen Wirklichkeit unterstreicht.

Anschließend formuliert er unter Rekurs auf Linus Hauser einen ›Befreiungsversuch‹, wozu er zunächst Tolkiens Konzeption der Fantasy anhand von *On Fairy-Stories* darlegt. Anschließend gibt er eine nähere Bestimmung des Begriffs ›existentielle Fantasy‹, zu deren Abschluss er die angemessene Rezeptionshaltung ihr gegenüber darin sieht, den Sinn nicht hinter den Geschichten zu suchen, sondern dieser »muss als Anwendung der in den Geschichten vermittelten textintern-realen Inhalte erschlossen werden« (103). Damit kritisiert er grundsätzlich gelegentliche Versuche der Historisierung oder Politisierung der phantastischen Anderwelt (explizit bezieht er sich vor allem auf van de Bergh, *Mittelerde und das 21. Jahrhundert* (Trier 2005), nennt aber auch Schneidewinds *Untersuchungen zur Biologie Mittelerdes*). Dies erlaubt ihm auch, z.B. den Vorwurf des Rassismus an Tolkiens Werk oder des Genozids an den Orks nach der Ringzerstörung – wie z.b. von Alexander van de Bergh – als unzutreffend zu kritisieren. Denn in der Sekundärwelt seien die Unterschiede der Rassen ein Fakt und keine Ideologie; ferner gehöre es zur Eigenart dieser Art Fantasy, eine klare Unterscheidung zwischen Gut und Böse zu propagieren, zu der dann auch die gewaltsame Vernichtung der der bösen Seite zuzurechnenden Kreaturen gehört (vgl. 164).

Nach diesen theoretischen und durchaus erhellenden Ausführungen bespricht er zunächst Tolkiens Werk, wozu er mit ausgewählten narratologischen Aspekten beginnt – der Funktion des Erzählers, der Historisierung und Authentisierung, der Nostalgie und Melancholie und schließlich dem Verhältnis von Sekundärwelt und Primärwelt –, um anschließend drei Grundprinzipien näher zu entfalten. Zunächst legt er unter Rekurs auf *The Silmarillion* die göttlich gestiftete Wohlordnung alles Seienden dar, anschließend bespricht er Tolkiens Plädoyer zur Rückkehr zur Natur und schließlich erläutert er den Primat des Guten. Abgesehen von einzelnen Kleinigkeiten sind seine Ausführungen dabei durchaus korrekt und im Sinne seiner Absichten auch zielführend, ergeben allerdings auch nichts eigentlich Neues, zudem gibt es eine Auseinandersetzung mit der zur Verfügung stehenden Sekundärliteratur nur in sehr begrenztem Maße, d.h. abgesehen von Veldmans Fantasy nur in der Form der oben schon genannten Kritik (das hat der Autor indes auch zu Beginn angekündigt, vgl. 8).

Das gleiche Vorgehen wählt er bei Pullmann: Hier bespricht er das Genre und den Erzählverlauf bzw. -horizont als ausgewählte narratologische Aspekte; die drei besprochenen Grundprinzipien sind das kreative der Parallel- und Alternativwelten, das philosophische des naturwissenschaftlichen Materialismus und das ideologische mit dem ›Sündenfall‹ als Selbsterlösung des Menschen. Wiederum sind seine Ausführungen durchweg korrekt und im Sinne seines Argumentationszieles auch sehr plausibel.

Anschließend wird in einer kurzen Synopse die jeweils vertretene Position zur Stellung des Menschen, zur Stellung der Transzendenz und zur Stellung des Mythos zusammengefasst; ein Fazit und ein Epilog schließen die Studie ab.

Während der Autor sicherlich seine gesetzten Ziele erreicht, d.h. die Besonderheit der ›existentiellen Fantasy‹ als Vermittlungsweise weltanschaulicher Grundpositionen herausgestellt und an zwei idealtypischen Vertretern konkretisiert hat, ist zu konstatieren, dass gerade bei der Untersuchung von Tolkiens Werk eine gründlichere Auseinandersetzung mit der Sekundärliteratur dem Unterfangen nicht geschadet hätte. Sie hätte dem Autor ermöglicht, einiges allgemein Bekannte knapper zu fassen und dafür bei anderen Themen detaillierter und differenzierter argumentieren zu können.

Thomas Fornet-Ponse

Martin Simonson: *The Lord of the Rings* and the Western Narrative Tradition.
Zürich/Jena: Walking Tree Publishers, 2008, 250 Seiten, Paperback

Mit dieser Studie legt der in Spanien lebende Martin Simonson eine englische Übersetzung bzw. Überarbeitung seiner Dissertation vor, was – dies sei schon zu Beginn gesagt – sehr zu begrüßen ist, da dieser Arbeit eine gründliche und aufmerksame Rezeption nur gewünscht werden kann. Denn ich stimme Thomas Honegger in seinem Geleitwort völlig zu: Diese Arbeit »is going to provide a new impulse to Tolkien studies and that his theory will prove able to develop and evolve by means of incorporating new insights and discoveries« (5).

Simonson hat sich keine geringere Frage vorgenommen als diejenige nach dem Genre des *Lord of the Rings*, wobei er zwei Forschungsrichtungen kombinieren möchte, nämlich diejenige nach den von Tolkien verwendeten Quellen und diejenige nach der ›applicability‹ in den geschichtlichen und kulturellen Bedingungen des 20. Jahrhunderts.

Seine Arbeitshypothese lautet, die Originalität des *Lord of the Rings* bestehe in seiner Fähigkeit, eine große Zahl literarischer Traditionen in Dialog miteinander zu bringen, wobei dies immer in einem konkreten literarischen Kontext geschehe.

Zur Erläuterung dieser These beginnt Simonson zunächst nach einer kurzen Einführung mit den vier hauptsächlichen Genres in der westlichen narrativen Tradition: Epos (von Homer bis Beowulf), Romanze (vom Mittelalter bis zum 19. Jahrhundert), moderner Roman (von gothic novel bis hin zu fantasy novels) und Mythos. Dies bildet auch den Ausgangs- und Referenzpunkt für die Vergleiche der verschiedenen Traditionen im *Lord of the Rings* im vierten Kapitel. Anschließend widmet er sich den Ähnlichkeiten und Unterschieden zwischen

Tolkiens Werk und dem von Kriegsautoren wie Owen, Sassoon, Thomas, Gurney oder Graves als auch von modernen Autoren wie Eliot, Pound und Joyce vertretenen ›Ironic Myth‹. Tolkien unterscheide sich von ihnen vor allem durch die Leichtigkeit und Beweglichkeit der Interaktion der verschiedenen Traditionen sowie durch die dauernde Erkundung ihrer Begrenzungen. Mittelerde könne als künstliche Konstruktion eines neuen Chronotop angesehen werden, was eben erst einen so dynamischen intertraditionellen Dialog erlaube.

Simonsons Ausführungen hierzu sind schon sehr klar und überzeugend. Das eigentliche Potential seiner Arbeit liegt aber im vierten Kapitel, in dem er detailliert und kenntnisreich die Dynamik des intertraditionellen literarischen Dialogs in *The Lord of the Rings* untersucht und aufschlussreiche Schlussfolgerungen anbietet. Ich nenne nur zwei Beispiele:

In den ersten Kapiteln bestätigen die Charaktere Bilbo, Gandalf, Frodo und Sam die Möglichkeit von Abenteuern und den Einschluss dunkler, fantastischer Elemente in ein Narrativ, das als eine Mischung aus bürgerlichem Märchen und humoristischem bzw. bäuerlichem Roman aus dem 19. Jhd. beginnt. Ein solcher Dialog der Traditionen wird beim Erscheinen der Schwarzen Reiter im Shire sowie bei der Begegnung mit den Elben besonders deutlich. Während Frodo bei letzterer in der Lage ist, sich an die nun eher Züge einer Romanze tragende Situation anzupassen, fällt dies Sam und Pippin, die deutlich dem Roman verhaftet sind, wesentlich schwerer, was sich schon an ihrer Sprache zeigt.

Bei der Analyse der Entwicklung Aragorns zeigen sich zahlreiche Traditionen: In Bree hat er Züge einer Figur sowohl aus einem Epos als auch aus einem Abenteuerroman, in Rivendell verbindet er vor allem die Traditionen der Romanze und des Epos, was in Lórien weitgehend auf die der Romanze konzentriert wird, wohingegen er auf der Verfolgungsjagd durch Rohan Charakteristika aller drei Traditionen aufweist. Bei den Schlachten in Rohan erscheint er als ein epischer Held, in Isengard wechselt er zum Abenteuerroman, während er in Minas Tirith wieder als Held einer Romanze bzw. eines Epos erscheint. Schließlich aber endet er mit der Romanze, vermutlich weil er als König Verantwortlichkeit und Stabilität zeigen muss, was grundlegenden Zügen eines epischen Helden widerspricht.

Darüber hinaus bespricht Simonson die Episode mit Tom Bombadil, Rivendell, die Minen von Moria, wo sich an der Brücke von Khazad-dûm christliche und pagane Tradition begegnen, Gandalf als Botschafter der Valar sowie Frodo und Sam. Der Dialog zwischen den Traditionen endet am Feld von Cormallen, was ganz deutlich bei den Protagonisten Frodo, Aragorn und Gandalf zu sehen ist. Die weitgehend in der sehr flexiblen Tradition der Romanze stehende Heimreise der Hobbits soll daher auch sukzessive abbauen und zugleich die Entwicklung dieser Tradition illustrieren – beginnend in der mittelalterlichen Tradition und immer schwächer werdend, je näher sie Bree kommen –, bis sie im Shire mit dem Roman des 19. Jahrhunderts verschmilzt.

Im Schlusskapitel seiner Arbeit nennt Simonson die Hauptzüge jeder Tradition im *Lord of the Rings* und unterstreicht somit die Unmöglichkeit einer eindeutigen Genre-Zuschreibung: »The result is a narrative that transmits, while updating and renewing, the narrative legacy of our own past« (224). Damit ähnele er zwar Modernisten wie Eliot, Pound und Joyce, unterscheide sich von diesen aber durch die kohärenten und gut kontextualisierten Bezüge zur inneren Geschichte seiner Sekundärwelt wie auch durch den Wunsch, eine Hoffnungsbotschaft der modernen Welt durch eine in entfernter Vergangenheit spielende Legende zu vermitteln; es entsteht eine »meta-narrative of hope for the twentieth century« (225).

Thomas Fornet-Ponse

Tolkien Studies. An Annual Scholarly Review. Volume V. 2008

Morgantown: West Virginia University Press, 310 pp., Hardcover

The fifth volume of *Tolkien Studies* presents, on 310 pages, feature articles, Tolkien's academic essay on and his 'edition' of Chaucer's *Reeve's Tale*, notes, reviews, and the annotated bibliography.

The volume's (invited) opening essay is by Brian Rosebury, who is best known for his study *Tolkien: A Cultural Phenomenon* (2003). Starting from the (I think correct) premises that Tolkien is not essentially a theorist, he takes an informed and detailed look at the concept of 'revenge' by means of an analysis of its occurrences in Tolkien's work. Rosebury observes, among other things, that good emotions are usually consonant with reason. Furthermore, he points out that we often encounter actions that, even if they cannot be approved of from a modern Christian point of view, are often respected (e.g. Beorn's killing of the captured orc and warg). After looking at 'revenge' in many and different cases (the dwarves, Turin, Sauron, Melkor etc.), he comes (rather unsurprisingly) to the conclusion that the treatment of revenge in the Professor's work is "complex and subtle".

Carl Phelpstead's and Corey Olsen's papers may be seen as two complementary pieces. Phelpstead gives an illuminating discussion of the role and function of the poetic passages inserted into the main prose narrative. He acknowledges the influence of William Morris's work but stresses the even more important model function of the original Old Norse saga-literature itself. There we find basically two categories of verse: 'authenticating verse', cited by the narrator as corroboration of the narrative, and 'situational verse', spoken by a character within the narrative. Tolkien, then, adds to this 'situational authenticating verse', where a character recites a verse as authority for information given (we may think of Bilbo's verse on Strider/Aragorn). In general, Tolkien uses verse to give depth and to vary the pace of the narrative, to further characterisation, and to provide a heightened discourse for the expression of emotions.

Olsen's discussion of the elvish song of the ent and the entwife (recited by Treebeard in *The Two Towers*) may be seen as an in-depth and applied illustration of Phelpstead's 'theoretical prolegomena'. His close and careful reading of the song (including a study of the earlier drafts) brings out the multiple points of view that are inherent in it. Composed by the elves, recited and commented on by Treebeard, it presents the ents as basically passive and the entwives as active agents. Both, however, have allowed their love for their lands to skew their priorities (a typically 'Boethian' problem) and a common shared life seems only possible in an 'apocalyptic' end-time. Olsen's discussion of the song has wider implications for the interpretation of the ents and entwives and his analysis is an important contribution to the current debate on Tolkien's ecocriticism.

The 'tree-motif' re-occurs in James C. Davis article, which provides a contrastive analysis of (basically) how Saruman is presented in the movies and in the book. Jackson's treatment (and visually prominent presentation) of the wizard as the creator of an industrial complex, together with his omission of the Old Forest episode, is seen as simplifying the ecological theme so that, provocatively speaking, Saruman seems evil because he destroys the trees. This stands in contrast to Tolkien's approach. He foregrounds the pastoral (see his prolonged and extensive description of the Shire) and in general presents the interaction between man/hobbit and nature as a more complex issue. Davis's discussion of the theme in the movie(s) and book contributes, as he intended, to a greater understanding of the literary text. However, his use of the concept of 'nature' could have profited from the inclusion of the historical perspective. Seeing 'nature' as an (almost) purely positive thing is largely an achievement of the Romantic movement, although it is likely that Tolkien's conception is more complex and influenced by the medieval tradition(s).

Lynn Forest-Hill, in her fine paper, looks at the thematic connection between *Homecoming*, the Old English *Battle of Maldon* and the 15th century biography of the French knight Pierre Terrail, Seigneur de Bayard (1473-1524) on the one hand, and the depiction of Boromir in *The Lord of the Rings* on the other. After a competent summary of the scholarship devoted to the *Battle of Maldon* and Homecoming, she convincingly argues how the figure of Beorhtnoth/Byrhtnoth is taken up and modified in Boromir. Whereas the former dies without repenting of his 'ofermod' (which may be translated as 'overweening pride'), Boromir overcomes his self-delusion and through a process of self-awareness, contrition and confession, gains forgiveness. His heroic death shows parallels to that of the model-knight Bayard and thus, so Forest-Hill, we have a shift towards the concept of the 'Christian hero'. Although I find her argument lucid and convincing, I would have wished her to include the figure of Roland in the discussion. This may have complicated matters, but it would also have taken into account one obvious analogue and helped to work out Boromir's development even better.

Lastly, Jason Fisher provides a straightforward study of the origin of the three elven rings. He points out that the final names and attributions to their wearers were given relatively late (first galley proofs). He establishes likely reasons for Tolkien allocating the ring of fire to Gandalf, the ring of air to Elrond, and the ring of water to Galadriel and shows how he strengthens the bond between wearer and ring by means of textual allusions. Finally, Fisher unearths a nice piece of 'Tolkienian depth' by paralleling the fate of the three silmarils – which find their final resting-places in the sky, the ocean, and the fires of the earth, respectively – with the three elven rings, so that it may indeed be not surprising that Elrond, the descendant of Eärendil who 'carries' one of the silmarils across the sky each night, is given the ring of air.

The "Notes and Documents" are more and more dominated by (most welcome) reprints of Tolkien's own work. They start off with the Professor's paper on Chaucer's use of northern dialect features in the *Reeve's Tale*, which is followed by Tolkien's own edition of the *Reeve's Tale*, and concluded by Ross Smith's commented translation of George Steiner's 1973 obituary of Tolkien. Reprinting Tolkien's hard-to-get (academic) articles or making accessible unpublished work is a laudable enterprise – and though Michael Drout and, earlier on, Tom Shippey have given us authoritative assessments of Tolkien's influence as a medievalist, it may be worth thinking about adding a brief comment on the status of the republished essays within current academic discourse. Thus, a reference to Simon C.P. Horobin's 2001 essay 'J.R.R. Tolkien as a Philologist: A Reconsideration of the Northernisms in Chaucer's *Reeve's Tale*, published in *English Studies* 82.2:97-105, would help to put Tolkien's particular achievement in his paper into perspective. The rest of the book is taken up by 120 pages of in-depth reviews, the annotated Year's Work in *Tolkien Studies*, and the compiled bibliography for 2006.

The fifth volume of TS offers thus once more a rich and varied selection of excellent articles and keeps up the laudable work of making accessible hard-to-get Tolkienian texts and of 'cartographing' the current research.

Thomas Honegger

Die Suche hatte begonnen.
Verborgene Pfade führen manchmal zu geheimen Pforten. Und schlafende Drachen zu wecken, ist nur selten eine gute Idee...

Rezensionen

Allan Turner (ed.): *The Silmarillion* – Thirty Years On.
Zürich/Jena: Walking Tree Publishers, 2008, 163 pp., Paperback

Diese Aufsatzsammlung ist anlässlich des 30-jährigen Jubiläums des *Silmarillion* von Allan Turner herausgegeben worden. Der Akzent liegt daher tatsächlich auf dem 1977 erschienenen und von Christopher Tolkien zusammengestellten und bearbeiteten Buch und nicht auf dem in der *History of Middle-earth* in seinen verschiedenen Entstehungsschichten zu findenden *Silmarillion*-Komplex.

Der erste der sechs Beiträge von Rhona Beare ist zwar schon seit längerer Zeit bekannt, aber eigens für diese Publikation neu bearbeitet worden. Darin setzt sie sich mit dem nordischen (primär angelsächsischen, aber auch keltischen) Charakter der Mythologie auseinander und kann neue Einsichten vor allem hinsichtlich des Wortes earendel im Sinne seiner Verwendung in den Blickling homilies, d.h. als Johannes der Täufer, vermitteln.

Der zweite Beitrag von Michael Drout ist sehr autobiographisch geprägt. Auf der Basis seiner eigenen Leseerfahrung mit dem *Silmarillion* hebt er dessen ›nostalgischen‹ Charakter hervor – wie es gerade aufgrund seines wesentlich pessimistischeren Grundzugs und des sehr seltenen Trostes durch eine Eukatastrophe Trauer und Verlusterfahrungen in Ordnung und Schönheit formt.

Eine einzelne Geschichte greift Anna Slack in ihren Ausführungen zu Tolkiens Konzept der sub-creation in der Geschichte von Beren und Lúthien auf, wobei sie diese Geschichte als eine Debatte über die Natur der sub-creation und der möglichen Aufnahme in die Primärwelt liest. Die Geschichte kulminiert in Lúthiens Gesang vor Mandos, der in die eukatastrophische Rückkehr der Liebenden mündet.

Michaël Devaux widmet sich der Ainulindalë und der gegenwärtigen Forschungslage. Dazu bespricht er zunächst die Entstehungsgeschichte des Textes und anschließend die vorliegenden Versionen und ihre Grundzüge unter der Fragestellung, ob diese ursprünglich, später, einzig oder fundamental sind. Schließlich diskutiert er katholische Elemente, d.h. er stellt die Übereinstimmungen zur biblischen Schöpfungsvorstellung sowie die Rolle der Ainur und Melkors als geschaffener Wesen bei der Schöpfung der Welt heraus.

Eine ganz andere Fragestellung geht Jason Fisher an, der einerseits nach inhaltlichen Übereinstimmungen oder Strukturanalogien zwischen Elias Lönnrot, Tolkien und Hieronymus fragt, insofern alle drei ähnliche, nämlich mythopoetische Aufgaben in ihrer jeweiligen Sammlung und Kompilation von Texten durchgeführt hätten. Andererseits widmet er sich auch der Rolle Christopher Tolkiens, die in ihrer mythographischen Dimension ebenfalls große Ähnlichkeiten zu derjenigen Lönnrots und Hieronymus' aufweise.

Der letzte Beitrag des Bandes von Nils Ivar Agøy untersucht die Frage nach den Gesichtspunkten, Hörerschaften und den verlorenen Texten im *Silmarillion*. Er widerspricht der weit verbreiteten Ansicht, das *Silmarillion* sei ein Teil von Bilbos »Übersetzungen aus dem Elbischen«, denn dies funktioniere für das 1977 erschienene Werk nicht gut, weil mindestens zwei verschiedene Erzählerstimmen präsent seien: Zum einen eine allwissende und zum anderen eine von elbischen Traditionen abhängige. Daher sei das *Silmarillion* als Träger der »großen Legenden«, als deren Hintergrund und Umriss zu verstehen.

Wie bei den beteiligten Personen nicht anders zu erwarten, sind die Beiträge durchgängig von hoher Qualität und versprechen sowohl dem schon gut informierten Leser einige interessante Einblicke als auch dem weniger gut informierten (dem allerdings wohl noch einige mehr).

Thomas Fornet-Ponse

Sarah Wells (ed.): The Ring Goes Ever On.
Proceedings of the Tolkien 2005 Conference: 50 Years of *The Lord of the Rings*. 2 Vols.
Coventry: The Tolkien Society, 2008, 421 + 414 pp., Paperback

Da eine ausführliche Besprechung dieser beiden voluminösen Bände angesichts des zu bearbeitenden Umfangs für diese Ausgabe von *Hither Shore* nicht möglich war, sei hier nur eine kurze Information gegeben, die im nächsten Jahr ergänzt werden soll.

Es handelt sich bei diesen Bänden um die Veröffentlichung sämtlicher zur Publikation eingereichter Beiträge und damit so gut wie aller gehaltenen Vorträge der großen Tolkien Konferenz vom August 2005 in Birmingham. Die insgesamt 97 Beiträge von z.T. sehr unterschiedlicher Länge stammen von Autoren aus der ganzen Welt (unter ihnen sehr bekannte Tolkienforscher wie auch junge Nachwuchsforscher).

Sie sind in elf Sektionen gegliedert, die folgende Themenbereiche abdecken: 1) Tolkiens Leben; 2) Tolkiens literarische Leistung; 3) Tolkien in anderen Ländern; 4) Andere Stimmen: 5) Das Erzählen von Legenden: Mythos und

Geschichtenerzählen; 6) Tolkiens Personen; 7) Tolkiens Vermächtnis; 8) Theologie und die Natur von Gut und Böse; 9) Tolkiens Quellen; 10) Mittelerde in den Filmen; 11) Tolkiens Welt.

Vermittelt dies schon einen Eindruck der enormen Fülle an abgedeckten Aspekten, wird dieser bei einem Blick in die einzelnen Sektionen noch weiter verstärkt.

Zu 1) gibt es z.b. einen Beitrag zur Copyright-Diskussion mit Ace Books, zwei zu Tolkiens Verhältnis zu Charles Williams, und verständlicherweise bleiben auch die Weltkriege nicht unbeachtet.

Zu 2) geht es von Realitätskonzeptionen über Träume, Visionen und Prophezeiungen zum Naturverständnis und zum Verhältnis zur Postmoderne.

Die anderen Länder (3) decken Brasilien, Polen, Spanien, Katalonien, Italien und Russland ab, während sich Sektion 4 vor allem mit dem Verhältnis zu anderen (Fantasy-)Autoren beschäftigt.

In Sektion 5 werden so unterschiedliche Aspekte beachtet wie die hethitische Mythologie (ein Beitrag mit eher peripherer Relevanz für die Tolkienforschung), Tolkiens Konzeption von Universalität oder der Paratext.

Ähnlich vielfältig ist das Bild in Teil 6, wo sich der Bogen von der Männlichkeitskonzeption über Aragorns Beziehungen zu Éowyn und Arwen zu Frodos Widerstand gegen den Ring und zum Mut spannt.

Der erste Band schließt mit Sektion 7, die sich der Popularität Tolkiens ebenso widmet wie seiner Behandlung in Schule und Universität oder dem Fantasy-Genre.

Der zweite Band beginnt mit der theologischen Sektion (8), die mehrere Beiträge zum Problem des Bösen enthält, darüber aber auch Fragen der Vorsehung, des Paganismus oder der Sterblichkeit thematisiert.

Bei den Quellen (9) werden u.a. George MacDonald, Simone de Beauvoir, altgermanische Sprachen oder William Morris besprochen und bei den Filmen (10) zwar ausschließlich die Adaption Peter Jacksons, aber unter so verschiedenen Gesichtspunkten wie Tolkiens Katholizismus, der Umsetzung von Macht und Überwachung oder der Bedeutung des Wortes in Buch und Film.

Mit der ausführlichen Sektion 11 enden die Proceedings mit 17 Beiträgen u.a. zu Sprichwörtern bei Tolkien, seinem Verhältnis zur Technologie oder Ökologie, aber auch zu Zahlen, Gärten oder Mondschöpfungsmythen.

Wie kaum anders zu erwarten bei einer solchen Fülle an Themen und Autoren und der großen Unterschiede an wissenschaftlicher Ausbildung, Erfahrung und Reputation ist der wissenschaftliche Ertrag der einzelnen Beiträge sehr unterschiedlich. Bei einigen ist es sehr zu bedauern, dass sie nicht früher der weiteren Diskussion anheim gestellt worden waren, bei anderen handelt es sich weniger um Forschungsbeiträge als vielmehr um eher assoziativ ausgeführte und nicht immer detailliert belegte Gedankengänge. In einem Fall (Greg Wright) sogar um die Wiedergabe einer E-Mail-Korrespondenz zwischen einem Protestanten und einer Katholikin.

Im Großen und Ganzen kann sich die Qualität der Beiträge aber durchaus sehen lassen, und gerade die enorme Vielfalt lädt dazu ein, einfach in diesen Bänden zu schmökern und sich gelegentlich mit Aspekten auseinanderzusetzen, die man bisher entweder gar nicht oder zumindest nicht so gesehen hatte. Darüber hinaus ist die Aufsatzsammlung gerade mit diesen Unterschieden in Thema und Herangehensweise ein gutes Zeugnis der Unterschiede der weltweiten Auseinandersetzung mit Tolkien – schließlich ist die streng rationale, den Gesetzen der (deutschen) Wissenschaftslandschaft folgende Analyse der Werke bei weitem nicht die einzige Möglichkeit!

Thomas Fornet-Ponse

Dimitra Fimi: Tolkien, Race and Cultural History. From Fairies to Hobbits.

New York/London: Palgrave Macmillan 2009, 240 pp., Hardcover[3]

Tolkien, Race and Cultural History: From Fairies to Hobbits is a book that accomplishes three things. Firstly, it closes some gaps in Tolkien studies by gathering earlier research, supplementing it with new information and, most prominently, linking it to the socio-cultural background of the time. Thus, in the first part of the book, Fimi provides a coherent and sustained discussion of the origin and contemporary inspiration(s) or analogues of Tolkien's fairies/ elves. Secondly, her study dares, in the second part, to venture into little-known territory, such as the theories of linguistic aesthetics and Tolkien's concept of 'native language'.[4] The third part, finally, is devoted to a discussion of the effects

---

[3] A more detailed and longer review of Fimi's book: in *Tolkien Studies* 6.
[4] There is, however, a deplorable gap in Fimi's coverage of the relevant secondary literature on this very topic – which is to be blamed on the lengthy production process at the publisher's. Many of the topics Fimi covered in her chapter on 'linguistis aesthetic' have also been discussed by Ross Smith – once in his 2007 book *Inside Language. Linguistic and Aesthetic Theory in Tolkien* and earlier on in his article 'Fitting Sense to Sound: Linguistic Aesthetics and Phonosemantics in the Work of J.R.R. Tolkien' (*Tolkien Studies* 3, 2006). Fimi's typescript had been submitted before Smith's book was published and it has, unfortunately, not been possible to change the chapter in question so as to take into consideration Smith's ideas.

of the publication of *The Hobbit* (and, later on, *The Lord of the Rings*) on the development of the legendarium. The fluid and changing matter of the *Legendarium* now has to be brought into accordance with the published narrative fiction and the 'novelistic' style of *The Lord of the Rings* heralds the transition from the mythological to a 'historical' discourse.

This new focus on 'history' brings to the fore questions concerning the origin of Men, their subdivisions and racial specification that, as Fimi knowledgeably demonstrates, very much reflect theories on race current in the late Victorian and the Edwardian times – and which Tolkien started to question under the impact of the rising Nazi-ideology.

The basic approach of the study, as has become clear, is biographical-historical. Fimi links events from the professor's life and times with the growth and transformation of Tolkien's *Legendarium*. Her study is well worth reading – for the specialist as well as (or even more so) for the general reader. She brings together – often for the first time – relevant research from cultural history and lays out her arguments 'fair and square'.

The Tolkien scholar may miss some of the more 'exotic' publications on some of the topics discussed, but this can be seen as part of the overall strength of the book: it keeps to the middle road of academia and loses itself neither in a wild-goose chase for comprehensiveness, nor does it try to push any 'monomythic' interpretation of Tolkien's work. Fimi's approach is subtler, and yet it forces us to reconsider some well-beloved clichés. Thus, it will not be possible to go on talking naïvely about the 'linguistic inspiration' of Tolkien's fiction without adding at least some qualifying remarks.

Whether Tolkien really intended to use his (artistically and commercially) successful literary output for a post festum justification of his work on invented languages may have to be investigated further – Fimi's book has given us some answers but also has opened up some avenues for future research.

Thomas Honegger

Vom Nebelgebirge blickten wir zurück nach Osten – bis zu dem Berg, den auch der Frühling nicht ganz von Eis und Schnee befreien kann.

Unsere Autoren und Autorinnen

Fanfan Chen, Prof. Dr. phil, hat in Poitiers in französischer und komparativer Literaturwissenschaft promotivert, ist gegenwärtig Professorin für europäische und komparative Literaturwissenschaft an der National Dong Hwa University in Taiwan und hat an mehreren europäischen Universitäten gelehrt. Sie kann zahlreiche Publikationen über phantastische Literatur vorweisen und ist Mitherausgeberin der neu gegründeten Zeitschrift des Phantastischen *Fastitocalon* und hat jüngst eine Monographie *Fantasticsm: Poetics of Fantastic Literature* publiziert.
chenfantasticism@gmail.com   ffchen@mail.ndhu.edu.tw

Julian Tim Morton Eilmann studierte in Aachen und Nottingham Geschichte, Germanistik und Kunstgeschichte und ist gegenwärtig Lehrer für Deutsch und Geschichte an einem Aachener Gymnasium. Vor seiner Berufung ins Schulwesen war er mehrere Jahre Redakteur und Autor bei einer Filmproduktion. Er ist Preisträger des Deutschen Jugendvideopreises. Weiterhin ist er als Galerist und Konservator einer Künstlerstiftung tätig. Sein Forschungsschwerpunkt bei Tolkien liegt im Bereich Tolkien-Lyrik.
julianeilmann@web.de

Thomas Fornet-Ponse studierte Katholische Theologie, Philosophie und Alte Geschichte in Bonn und Jerusalem, war 2006/07 Studienleiter beim Theologischen Studienjahr in Jerusalem und promoviert gegenwärtig in Katholischer Theologie. Er veröffentlichte zahlreiche Aufsätze zu Tolkien, Pratchett und Lewis und ist Beisitzer im Vorstand der Deutschen Tolkien Gesellschaft und inhaltlicher Koordinator des Tolkien Seminars wie von *Hither Shore*.
hither-shore@tolkiengesellschaft.de

Blanka Grzegorczyk studierte Englische Literatur an der Universität Breslau und promoviert dort derzeit im selben Fach. Ihre akademischen Interessen liegen bei moderner mythopoetischer Fantasy, Volkssagen, Erzählstudien und Kulturtheorie. Ihre Forschungsinteresse liegt im Feld der modernen mythopoetischen Fantasy für Kinder und junge Erwachsene mit einem speziellen Akzent darauf, wie diese Texte auf die kulturellen, politischen und wirtschaftlichen Bewegungen der letzten fünfzehn Jahre reagieren und wie sie im Blick auf die Gestaltung gesellschaftlichen Verständnisses und Zukunftsaspirationen eingesetzt werden.
blanka.grzegorczyk@gmail.com

Thomas Honegger, Prof. Dr. phil, hat in Zürich promoviert und zahlreiche Bände zu Tolkien, mittelalterlicher Sprache und Literatur herausgegeben und verschiedene Beiträge zu Chaucer, Shakespeare und mittelalterlichen Romanzen publiziert. Seit 2002 lehrt er als Professor für Mediävistik an der Friedrich-Schiller-Universität Jena.
Homepage: www2.uni-jena.de/fsu/anglistik/homepage/Honegger3.htm

Judith Klinger, Dr. Phil., studierte Germanistik und Anglistik an der Universität Hamburg sowie Dokumentarfilm und Fernsehpublizistik an der Hochschule für Fernsehen und Film, München. Promotion über Identitätskonzeptionen im Prosa-*Lancelot*. Nach einer Lehrtätigkeit an der Universität Bayreuth ist sie seit 1995 am Lehrstuhl für Germanistische Mediävistik der Universität Potsdam beschäftigt, Habilitationsprojekt im Bereich der Gender Studies.
jklinger@rz.uni-potsdam.de

Heidi Krüger, war nach einem Studium der Germanistik und Philosophie in Tübingen und Zürich Dozentin an der Universität Växjö (Schweden). Danach absolvierte sie eine Zweitausbildung zur Regisseurin in Musik- und Sprechtheater. Übersetzungen aus dem Schwedischen und Finnischen; zahlreiche Literatur- und Philosophieseminare.
kuenstlertheater@gmx.de

Anna Slack studierte in Cambridge Englische Literatur und ist gegenwärtig Lehrerin für Englische Sprache an einer privaten Sprachschule in Palermo. In Cambridge war sie Sekretärin der Cambridge Tolkien Society und veröffentlichte in Aufsatzbänden von Walking Tree Publishers.
AnnaSlack@cantab.net

Guglielmo Spirito OFM Conv., Prof. Dr. theol., studierte vor seinem Eintritt in den Franziskanerorden Philosophie und Ägyptologie, erwarb in Rom sein theologisches Lizenziat am Camillianum und sein Doktorat (mit der Spezialisierung in Spiritualität) am Antonianum. Seit 1994 ist er Professor für Patristik, Franziskanische Spiritualität und Literatur (vor allem Tolkien) am Theologischen Institut Assisi und an der Päpstlichen Fakultät des Heiligen Bonaventura in Rom. Er lehrte auch in Kroatien, Rumänien, Russland, Mexiko, England, Kanada, Armenien und Ägypten. Über Tolkien hat er verschiedene Essays, Aufsätze und Bücher publiziert; er ist auch Mitglied der Italienischen Tolkien Gesellschaft.
fraguspi@gmail.com

Autoren

Heidi Steimel ist in den USA geboren und aufgewachsen und hat einen Bachelor of Music von der Grace University, Omaha, Nebraska. Gegenwärtig ist sie in Deutschland als Kirchenmusikerin, Klavierlehrerin und Übersetzerin tätig.
heidisteimel@web.de

Martin Sternberg hat in Münster 1990-1996 Alte Geschichte, Mittlere Geschichte, Kunstgeschichte sowie Rechtswissenschaft studiert und arbeitet als Referent bei einer Bundesbehörde. Bei seinem Geschichts- und Philosophiestudium lag ein Schwerpunkt auf Spätantike und frühem Christentum.
lasgalen@web.de

Doreen Triebel studierte Anglistik, Psychologie und Deutsch als Fremdsprache in Jena und Nottingham. Der Titel ihrer Masterarbeit von 2008 lautet *Journeys in Faery: The Representation of a Perilous Otherworld in the Faery-stories of J.R.R. Tolkien*. Derzeit ist sie Fulbright Stipendiatin an der Illinois State University, USA, und arbeitet dort auch als Foreign Language Teaching Assistant.
doreen-t@gmx.de

Allan Turner, Ph.D., studierte Germanistik, Mediävistik und allgemeine Linguistik. Seine Dissertation, auf dem Gebiet der Übersetzungswissenschaft, untersucht die Probleme in der Übersetzung der philologischen Elemente im *Herr der Ringe*. Er interessiert sich derzeit hauptsächlich für die Stilistik von Tolkiens Werken. Er unterrichtet englische Sprachpraxis und British Cultural Studies an der Universität Marburg.
allangturner@aol.com

Christian Weichmann, Dr. rer. nat., promovierte in Physik an der Rheinischen Friedrich-Wilhelms-Universität Bonn und ist 2. Vorsitzender der Deutschen Tolkien Gesellschaft.
maksatan@gmx.de

Dirk Vanderbeke, Prof. Dr. phil., studierte Germanistik und Anglistik/Amerikanistik in Frankfurt und Wisconsin (Milwaukee) und publizierte zu verschiedensten Themen, z.B. Wissenschaft und Literatur, Joyce, Pynchon, Comics, Selbstähnlichkeiten und Vampire. Zusätzlich hat er eine kommentierte Edition einer deutschen Übersetzung von James Joyces *Ulysses* herausgegeben. Gegenwärtig lehrt er an der Universität Jena und als Gastprofessor an der Universität Zielona Góra.
vanderbeke@t-online.de

Our Authors

Fanfan Chen is Professor of European and Comparative Literature at the National Dong Hwa University in Taiwan and has lectured and taught at several European universities. She received her PhD in French and Comparative Literature from the University of Poitiers and has published widely on fantastic literature in various academic journals. Her most recent study is *Fantasticsm: Poetics of Fantastic Literature* (Lang, 2007) and she is co-editor of the newly founded Journal of the fantastic *Fastitocalon* (WVT Trier). chenfantasticism@gmail.com   ffchen@mail.ndhu.edu.tw

Julian Tim Morton Eilmann studied History, German Philology, and History of Arts at Aachen and Nottingham and is currently working as a grammar school teacher for German and History in Aachen. Before that he worked as a journalist and author for a film production company. He is winner of the German Youth Video Award. In addition, he is fulfilling the functions of gallery owner and conservator for an artists foundation. His research on Tolkien focuses on Tolkien poetry.   julianeilmann@web.de

Thomas Fornet-Ponse studied Catholic theology, philosophy, and ancient history at Bonn and Jerusalem. He worked as an inspector of Studies at Theologisches Studienjahr Jerusalem. He is a committee member of the German Tolkien Society and has been charged with conceptually coordinating the Tolkien Seminars as well as *Hither Shore*.   hither-shore@tolkiengesellschaft.de

Blanka Grzegorczyk, a graduate of the Institute of English Studies, University of Wrocław, is currently pursuing a Ph.D. in English literature at the same university. Her academic interests include modern mythopoetic fantasy, folktales and storytelling, narrative studies, and cultural theory. Her research interest is in the field of modern mythopoetic fantasy for children and young adults, with a particular focus on the way these texts have responded to the cultural, political and economic movements of the last fifteen years and how they are implicated in shaping social understanding and aspirations for the future. blanka.grzegorczyk@gmail.com

Thomas Honegger holds a Ph.D. from the University of Zurich. He edited several volumes on Tolkien, medieval language and literature, and published papers on Chaucer, Shakespeare, and mediaeval romance. He teaches, since 2002, as Professor for Mediaeval Studies at Friedrich-Schiller-University Jena (Germany). Homepage:
www2.uni-jena.de/fsu/anglistik/homepage/Honegger3.htm

Authors   *Hither Shore 5 (2008)*   273

Judith Klinger, Dr. Phil., studied German philology and English philology at the University of Hamburg, then studied documentary filming and TV media studies at the university of TV and film at Munich. PhD thesis on concepts of identity in the prose *Lancelot*. Taught at Bayreuth University and has been employed at the chair of German Mediaeval Studies at Potsdam University since 1995. She is currently working on a post-doctoral thesis in the field of gender studies.
jklinger@rz.uni-potsdam.de

Heidi Krüger, studied German philology and philosophy in Tübingen and Zurich, later lecturer at Växjö University (Sweden). Afterwards, she received training as a director for musical theatre and drama. Translations from Swedish and Finnish; has given many seminars on literature as well as philosophy.
kuenstlertheater@gmx.de

Anna Slack graduated with a first class degree in English Literature from the University of Cambridge in 2005 and is a teacher of English Language at a private language school in Palermo, Sicily. She edited the tri-annual journal of the Cambridge Tolkien Society and was for one year the society secretary. She helped pioneer and partook in the acclaimed performance of the BBC Radio Adaptation of *The Lord of the Rings* in aid of the National Trust. Furthermore, she delivered a lecture at the Tolkien 2005 conference and contributed to volumes by Walking Tree Publishers.
AnnaSlack@cantab.net

Guglielmo Spirito OFM Conv., Prof. Dr. theol., studied philosophy and egyptology before joining the Order of Saint Francis in the 1980s. In Rome he obtained the Degree (Licenza) in Pastoral Theology of Health Care at the Camillianum and the Doctorate in Theology with specialitation in Spirituality at the Pontifical Ateneum Antonianum. Since 1994 he is professor of Patristic and Franciscan Spirituality and of Theology and Literature (especially J.R.R. Tolkien) at the Theological Institute of Assisi and at the Pontifical Faculty of Saint Bonaventure in Rome. He gave courses in Croazia, Romania, Russia and Mexico, and lectures in England and Canada, Armenia and Egypt. On Tolkien he had published essays, articles and books. He is also a member of the Società Tolkieniana Italiana.
fraguspi@gmail.com

Heidi Steimel was born and educated in the U.S.A., holds a Bachelor of Mucis from Grace University, Omaha, Nebraska and is currently working in Germany as church musician, piano teacher, translator and interpreter.
heidisteimel@web.de

Martin Sternberg studied Ancient History, Mediaeval History, History of Arts, and Law at Münster (1990-1996). He is currently working as a jurist in the field of telecommunications. During his studies, he specialised in Late Antiquity and Early Christianity.
lasgalen@web.de

Doreen Triebel studied English and American language and literatures, Psychology and German as a Foreign Language at Jena and Nottingham. In 2008 she graduated from the former with *Journeys in Faery: The Representation of a Perilous Otherworld in the Faery-stories of J.R.R. Tolkien* being the title of her Master's thesis. She currently holds a Fulbright scholarship and works as a Foreign Language Teaching Assistant at Illinois State University, USA.
doreen-t@gmx.de

Allan Turner, Ph.D., studied German philology, Mediaeval studies, and General linguistics. His PhD thesis in translation studies examines the problems inherent in translating the philological elements in *The Lord of the Rings*. His main focus of interest is currently on the stylistics of Tolkien's works. He has been teaching English language skills and British Cultural Studies at the University of Marburg.
vallangturner@aol.com

Christian Weichmann, Dr. rer. nat., PhD in Physics at Rheinische Friedrich-Wilhelms-University Bonn; he is vice chairman of the German Tolkien Society.
maksatan@gmx.de

Dirk Vanderbeke, Prof. Dr. phil., studied German and English Literature at the University of Frankfurt/Main and at the Universtiy of Wisconsin – Milwaukee. He has published on a variety of topics, e.g. Science and Literature, Joyce, Pynchon, comics, self-similarity and vampires. In addition he has co-edited an annotated edition of the German translation of James Joyce's *Ulysses*, published in celebration of the Bloomsday centenary. At present he teaches at the University of Jena and, as a guest-professor, at the University of Zielona Góra.
vanderbeke@t-online.de

Die Blumen in Beorns Garten waren für mich wie Vorboten des blühenden Auenlandes, und ich konnte sein dichtes Gras förmlich unter den Füßen spüren.

Endlich wieder zurück!

Siglenverzeichnis

Die Schriften von J.R.R. Tolkien werden im Text jeweils ohne Angabe des Verfassernamens mit den folgenden Siglen zitiert. Die jeweils benutzte Ausgabe findet sich im Literaturverzeichnis.

AI:	The Lay of Aotrou and Itroun
ATB:	The Adventures of Tom Bombadil and other Verses from the Red Book / Die Abenteuer des Tom Bombadil und andere Gedichte aus dem Roten Buch
AW:	Ancrene Wisse and Hali Meiðhad
B:	Die Briefe von J.R.R. Tolkien
BA:	Bilbos Abschiedslied
BB:	Baum und Blatt
BGH:	Bauer Giles von Ham
BLS:	Bilbo's Last Song
BMC:	Beowulf: The Monster and the Critics
BT:	Blatt von Tüftler
BUK:	Beowulf: Die Ungeheuer und ihre Kritiker
BW:	Die Briefe vom Weihnachtsmann
CH:	The Children of Húrin
CP:	Chaucer as a Philologist
EA:	The End of the Third Age (History of Middle-earth 9). Auszug
EW:	English and Welsh / Englisch und Walisisch
FC:	Letters from Father Christmas
FGH:	Farmer Giles of Ham
FH:	Finn and Hengest
FS:	On Fairy-Stories
GD:	Gute Drachen sind rar
GN:	Guide to the Names in the Lord of the Rings
GPO:	Sir Gawain and the Green Knight, Pearl, and Sir Orfeo
H:	The Hobbit / Der Hobbit / Der kleine Hobbit
HB:	The Homecoming of Beorhtnoth Beorhthelm's Son
HdR:	Der Herr der Ringe
HdR I:	Der Herr der Ringe. Bd. 1. Die Gefährten
HdR II:	Der Herr der Ringe. Bd. 2. Die Zwei Türme
HdR III:	Der Herr der Ringe. Bd. 3. Die Rückkehr des Königs / Die Wiederkehr des Königs
HdR A:	Der Herr der Ringe. Anhänge
HG:	Herr Glück
HH I/II:	The History of the Hobbit
HL:	Ein heimliches Laster
KH:	Die Kinder Húrins
L:	The Letters of J.R.R. Tolkien
LB:	The Lays of Beleriand (History of Middle-earth 3)
LN:	Leaf by Niggle
LotR:	The Lord of the Rings
LotR I:	The Fellowship of the Ring. Being the first part of The Lord of the Rings

Siglenverzeichnis

LotR II:	The Two Towers. Being the second part of The Lord of the Rings
LotR III:	The Return of the King. Being the third part of The Lord of the Rings
LotR A:	The Lord of the Rings. Appendices
LR:	The Lost Road and other Writings (History of Middle-earth 5)
LT 1:	The Book of Lost Tales 1 (History of Middle-earth 1)
LT 2:	The Book of Lost Tales 2 (History of Middle-earth 2)
MB:	Mr. Bliss
MC:	The Monsters and the Critics and Other Essays
ME:	A Middle English Vocabulary
MR:	Morgoth's Ring (History of Middle-earth 10)
My:	Mythopoeia
NM:	Nachrichten aus Mittelerde
OE:	The Old English Exodus
OK:	Ósanwe-Kenta
P:	Pictures by J.R.R. Tolkien
PM:	The Peoples of Middle-earth (History of Middle-earth 12)
R:	Roverandom
RBG:	The Rivers and Beacon-hills of Gondor
RGEO:	The Road Goes Ever On (with Donald Swann)
RS:	The Return of the Shadow (History of Middle-earth 6)
S:	Silmarillion
SD:	The Sauron Defeated (History of Middle-earth 9)
SG:	Der Schmied von Großholzingen
SGG:	Sir Gawain and the Green Knight / Sir Gawain und der Grüne Ritter (Essay)
SM:	The Shaping of Middle-earth (History of Middle-earth 4)
SP:	Songs for the Philologists
TB:	On Translating Beowulf
TI:	The Treason of Isengard (History of Middle-earth 7)
TL:	Tree and Leaf
ÜB:	Zur Übersetzung des Beowulf
ÜM:	Über Märchen
UK:	Die Ungeheuer und ihre Kritiker. Gesammelte Aufsätze
UT:	Unfinished Tales
VG 1:	Das Buch der Verschollenen Geschichten 1
VG 2:	Das Buch der Verschollenen Geschichten 2
WJ:	The War of the Jewels (History of Middle-earth 11)
SV:	A Secret Vice
SWM:	Smith of Wootton Major
VA:	Valedictory Address
WR:	The War of the Ring (History of Middle-earth 8)

Zum 10-jährigen Jubiläum der DTG ...

... auch und gerade als Hausverlag der DTG einen Beitrag zu leisten, ist für das Team im Scriptorium Oxoniae eine Selbstverständlichkeit. Schnell waren wir uns einig: Dieses Jubiläumsjahrbuch braucht eine besondere Optik. Anke Eißmann erlaubte uns, ohne zu zögern, das von ihr gestaltete Jubiläumslogo zu verwenden. Auch an dieser Stelle noch einmal Dank dafür! Und das Thema des 2008er Seminars »*Der Hobbit*« gibt – aus unserer Sicht fast schon zwingend – die Farbgestaltung des Jahrbuches vor: Und nun haben wir also

das »rote Buch« der DTG, den *Hither Shore* 2008.

Unser Brainstorming brachte aber noch eine andere Idee: das nüchterne Erscheinungsbild im Innern des *Hither Shore* ein wenig aufzulockern. Zum Beispiel durch grafische Elemente und etwas Farbe (die zusätzlichen Druckkosten hierfür trägt der Verlag). Und weil wir gerade Kontakt zu einem jungen Fotografen haben, wollten wir den Versuch wagen: Wir geben einem Nachwuchskünstler die Chance, sich einem breiteren Tolkien-Publikum bekannt zu machen – und falls das Wagnis gelingt und unsere Herausgeber zustimmen, könnten sich möglicherweise andere junge Künstler an der Mitgestaltung späterer Jahrbücher versuchen.

An unserem »roten Buch« hat Bo Gröper, 18, mitgewirkt. Er ist Schüler des Kreativzweigs eines Berufskollegs nahe Düsseldorf und seit Jahren schon begeisterter Hobbyfotograf. Natürlich hat er zuallererst den *Hobbit* noch einmal gelesen, bevor er sich an unsere Aufgabe gemacht hat: Wie könnte die nüchterne Innengestaltung unseres »roten Buches« aufgelockert werden?

Seine Antwort: »Meine Suche nach schönen Naturmotiven führt mich sowieso immer wieder in die nähere und weitere Umgebung von Düsseldorf. Auf meinen Streifzügen habe ich nun bewusst Ausschau gehalten nach Motiven, die Assoziationen mit Mittelerde bzw. dem Hobbit in mir auslösen. Dabei ging es mir nicht um eindeutige oder gar 1:1-Abbildungen von Mittelerde-Szenarien, sondern rein um spontane Gedan-kenblitze. Du kommst z.B. beim Spazierengehen auf eine Lichtung, siehst dort Pilze wachsen und denkst automatisch: Auenland!«

Mit dieser associativen Vorgehensweise sind Bo Gröper, wie wir meinen, eine Reihe schöner Motive gelungen. Daraus entstanden sind einzelne Seiten eines fiktiven Reisetagebuches, das sich in etwa an dem Weg »hin und wieder zurück« aus dem *Hobbit* orientiert.

Wir hoffen, dass die Kombination aus Fachtexten und Fiktion, aus Nüchternheit und Auflockerung zu einem erhöhten Lesevergnügen führt. Wir wünschen allen eine angenehme Lektüre und gratulieren der DTG von hier aus noch einmal herzlich. SuR

Index

Adler, Eagles	15, 20, 23, 30, 42f, 47-49, 54-57, 61-64, 74, 163, 180, 210, 211, 229
Anderson, Douglas A.	6-7, 55, 144, 197, 248f
Aristoteles, Aristotle	11, 28, 69f, 72, 93-98, 100-105, 231, 245
Arkenstein, Arkenstone	73, 97, 104, 107-109, 111-117, 121-132, 172, 182f, 223, 232
Art	9, 14, 16, 22, 28, 59, 67, 84, 92, 95, 98, 101, 135, 137, 139, 144, 176, 186-188, 191-192, 194, 205-206, 219, 237-238, 241, 247, 253, 267
Bachelard, Gaston	14f, 19f, 227, 245
Bard	20, 73, 79, 99, 108f, 111-117, 119, 122, 126f, 130-132, 166, 182f, 223, 232, 236
Barfield, Owen	11, 13, 23f, 41, 245f, 251
Beorn	21f, 37f, 72, 74, 108, 118, 180, 259
Beowulf	44, 49, 58, 75, 97f, 123, 127, 174, 193, 249, 251f, 257
Bilbo	9, 12f, 15-28, 30-45, 48, 52f, 62-64, 69, 72-79, 83, 86-90, 96-101, 104, 106-112, 115-119, 125-132, 135, 139-141, 148, 150, 153-155, 161-173, 174-184, 189, 194, 222-224, 227, 228, 230, 232, 233, 234, 236, 238, 258, 260, 264
Bombur	76-78, 109, 135, 138
Bruchtal, Rivendell	33f, 36, 39, 76, 109, 153-155, 237, 258
Chaucer, Geoffrey	58, 67, 70, 229, 259, 261, 270
Courage	s. *Tapferkeit*
Dain	54, 87, 102, 111f, 114-117, 131
Dale	20, 79, 102, 114f, 119, 141
‚deathbed conversation'	87, 222, 224
Desire	16, 22f, 44, 50, 71, 83-92, 99, 107, 111, 126, 128, 176-178, 205f, 208, 213, 230, 243
Disney, Walt	83, 192, 195, 234
Drachenkrankheit, Dragon-Sickness	85, 99, 106, 108f, 111-118, 131f, 225, 236
Drama, dramatisch, dramatic	31, 37, 39, 43f, 78, 93, 139, 152, 175, 202, 204-207, 213f, 219, 230
Dream	s. *Traum*
Düsterwald, Mirkwood	15, 20, 22, 26, 38, 43, 72f, 76-78, 96, 109, 118f, 164, 167, 170f, 181
Dwarved	s. *Zwerge*
Eagles	s. *Adler*
Elben, Elves (Elf)	21, 27, 30, 33, 43, 45, 58, 62, 76-78, 85f, 88, 98f, 101f, 107, 108-111, 116-118, 126, 132, 136, 142, 144, 152, 154f, 158, 164f, 167f, 170, 183, 193, 201, 202, 205f, 209, 211, 215, 218, 219, 230, 236, 237, 258, 260, 266
Elbenkönig, Elvenking (Elf-Lord)	15, 20, 26, 73, 96f, 99, 101f, 108-111, 114-118, 130, 165, 183, 223, 236
Eliade, Mircea	11f, 16
Elrond	18, 33, 39, 76, 184, 244, 261
Elves	s. *Elben*
Elvenking	s. *Elbenkönig*
Erebor	83, 86, 110, 122, 126, 131, 232

Erzähler, Narrator('s voice)	13, 15-17, 19, 21f, 24, 25-27, 30f, 34-38, 40-45, 74, 88f, 107, 110f, 114, 116, 132, 138, 145f, 149, 153f, 166-169, 176-181, 183, 189, 193, 227, 228, 232, 256, 259, 264
Esgaroth	s. Seestadt
Faërie	41, 44, 71, 76, 89, 195, 197-208, 212-217, 228, 230, 234, 238f, 241, 247, 252
Fantasy (Genre)	9, 12, 16, 28, 44, 53, 89, 91, 93, 97, 100f, 104f, 139, 193, 202, 203, 204, 205, 206, 216, 231, 242, 243, 244, 245, 248f, 255f, 257, 265
Far over the misty mountains	18, 109, 140, 146-148, 155f, 223, 224, 237
Fili	15, 110, 131, 135f, 140
Flieger, Verlyn	6f, 23f, 197, 247, 248f
Focalization	34-45
Frodo	23, 30, 49, 62, 73, 75f, 140, 244, 253, 258, 265
Galadriel	76, 88, 261
Gandalf	17-19, 21, 23, 25, 27, 30, 32-34, 36-38, 43, 55, 62-64, 69, 73, 78-80, 97, 108, 112, 117f, 126, 162f, 167, 172, 176-180, 182, 192, 244, 258, 261
Ganymede	56-62, 64
Gerechtigkeit, Justice	96f, 100-104, 114f
Gesellschaft, society, social	12, 94, 99, 100-103, 122, 145, 147-150, 155, 175f, 236, 237, 243
Gimli	17, 88
Girion	20, 115, 117, 125-128, 132
Goblins, Orks	15, 21, 24, 26, 30, 33, 36f, 43, 52, 62f, 73, 96f, 118, 131, 140, 142, 144, 152, 154, 162f, 166f, 178, 180, 192f, 195, 233f, 237, 252, 256
Gold, Hort, Schatz, Hoard, Treasure	17f, 53, 73, 83-86, 88, 91, 96f, 99f, 102f, 106-120, 121-126, 129f, 132, 138, 140, 148, 151, 156f, 161, 168, 182f, 200, 215, 230, 232, 236, 246
Gollum	15f, 26, 85, 91, 109, 162f, 169-171, 180, 193, 238
Hedonistisch, hedonisch	107, 117
Hero, Heroism (heroic)	9, 12, 16f, 20, 28, 30, 39, 43, 49, 54f, 62f, 72f, 78f, 87f, 96-98, 108, 110, 113, 119, 123, 131, 149, 174-184, 192, 252, 261
Der Herr der Ringe, The Lord of the Rings	9, 31, 39, 40, 51f, 55, 61f, 71-76, 80, 85, 88, 92, 97, 99, 116, 132, 135, 139f, 142-145, 147f, 151f, 157, 170, 177, 183, 193f, 197, 215, 228, 230, 233, 237, 244, 246, 248, 249, 255, 257-259, 260, 264, 267
History (epic)	25, 27f, 30-33, 44, 50f, 53, 55, 58, 102, 113, 121f, 127, 132, 137-139, 179, 210, 252, 266f
Hort, Hoard	s. Gold
Der Hobbit, The Hobbit	9, 27, 30-32, 34f, 39-45, 47, 51, 53-57, 61f, 67, 69, 71-73, 75-80, 83-92, 93, 95-105, 106, 112, 116f, 119, 121f, 125, 127f, 132, 139, 142-158, 161f, 166, 169, 173, 176, 183, 186f, 189-192, 194, 215, 222-224, 227, 228, 229, 230, 231, 232, 233, 234, 236, 237, 238, 248, 267
Imagination, Imaginary	9-15, 19f, 28, 31f, 35, 41f, 44f, 48, 50, 52, 63, 68, 89, 92, 93-95, 99, 102, 105, 121, 124, 128, 214, 231, 246
Justice	s. Gerechtigkeit
Kili	15, 77, 110, 131, 135f, 140
Kingship	114, 121, 123f, 128, 131

Kunst(schöpfung)	145, 149, 157, 203-205, 219, 225, 230, 247
Lake-town	s. Seestadt
Legenden, legends, legendary	28, 30-36, 44f, 53f, 76, 86, 113, 115-117, 124, 178-184, 192, 217, 228, 229, 232, 234, 236, 243, 248, 259, 264
Lied, Song	18, 30, 32f, 38, 44, 60, 69, 83, 86, 89f, 97, 99, 106, 107, 109f, 113, 117, 119, 126, 139f, 142-158, 177, 183, 223f, 230, 233, 236, 237, 260
The Lord of the Rings	s. Der Herr der Ringe
Lyrik, Poetics, Poem	9, 13f, 16, 18, 20, 28, 60, 70, 85, 90, 97, 124, 139f, 142-146, 148, 150, 151, 152-157, 191, 200, 223, 237, 244, 246
Macrobius	68, 70, 72, 74f
Marion, Jean-Luc	10, 12f, 227, 245
Master of Lake-town	96, 99f, 110, 112-115, 117-119, 236
Mirkwood	s. Düsterwald
The Monster and the Critics	192, 249
Moral(philosophie), Morality, moral	69, 72, 93-105, 108, 112, 115, 122, 130, 175, 202, 209f, 224, 231f
Musik, Music, musical	14, 18, 20, 26, 89, 109, 120, 135-141, 143, 146, 147, 155, 175, 184, 223, 233, 236
Mythos, Myth	11f, 16, 20, 23, 28, 41, 44, 48f, 54-56, 58, 61, 101, 192, 229, 245, 247, 252f, 255, 256-258, 264, 267
Mythologie, Mythology	9, 28, 41, 54, 76, 85f, 105, 122, 148, 153, 156f, 173, 237, 238, 243, 252, 263, 265
Narration	9, 12, 14, 24, 31f, 36, 38, 40, 42f, 189
Narrator('s voice)	s. Erzähler
The Nauglafrin	84-87, 89,
Necromancer	55, 80, 179
On Fairy-Stories	9, 27, 44, 71, 78, 89, 91, 99, 101, 197-199, 206, 230, 238, 248f, 255
Orks	s. Goblins
Panegyrik	146, 150, 151, 158, 237
Poetics, Poem	s. Lyrik
Poesie, Poetry	45, 57, 80, 84, 97, 140, 143, 145, 148, 152, 154f, 158, 227, 237, 253
Politik, politisch, Politics, political	55, 99, 102f, 122, 142, 145, 148-151, 158, 237
possessiveness	84-91, 99, 132, 236
Rateliff, John	40, 56, 62, 77f, 84-87, 113, 116, 121, 138f, 143f, 154, 161
Reichtum, Wohlstand	106-108, 112, 116, 118, 150
Ricoeur, Paul	11f, 25, 28, 227, 242
Ring	74, 76-78, 85, 87, 91, 96, 161-163, 166-173, 180-182, 238, 253f, 256, 261, 264f
Rivendell	s. Bruchtal
Roac, Roäc	53-55, 109, 111
Romantik, Romanticism	70, 90-92, 137, 230, 246, 260
Sam, Samwise	30, 49, 62, 76, 181, 258
Schatz	s. Gold
Seestadt, Lake-town, Esgaroth	40, 42f, 79, 96, 99, 102f, 110, 113-116, 118, 123, 148-151, 158, 168, 236f
Shippey, Tom	84, 97, 112, 122, 166, 247, 253, 261

Smaug	15, 17, 22f, 30f, 39, 42-44, 54, 78f, 87, 89, 96f, 104, 107f, 110f, 113f, 118f, 125f, 128, 140, 154, 156f, 161, 165-169, 171, 181f, 193f, 238
Society, social	s. Gesellschaft
Song	s. Lied
Spinnen, Spiders	22, 33, 73, 78, 97, 109, 118, 153, 167f, 170, 181, 192, 234, 238, 251
Tapferkeit, Courage	16, 78, 93, 95-98, 105, 112, 125, 183f, 223
Thingol	85, 116, 156
Thorin	15, 17-19, 21, 39, 53f, 73, 77f, 84, 86-88, 92, 99, 104, 106-120, 121-123, 126-132, 135, 138f, 145, 147f, 151, 157, 163, 165, 168, 178f, 181-183, 222-224, 232-234, 236
Thrain	123, 127
Thror	32-34, 53f, 102, 116, 123, 149, 179
Traum, Dream	16, 19, 24f, 37f, 41, 50, 55, 67-80, 111, 180, 182, 223, 228, 229f, 244, 246, 255, 265
Treasure	s. Gold
Tugend, virtue	60, 93-105, 131, 177, 223, 231, 253
Unexpected Party	17, 107, 109, 118, 135, 162, 171
Zwerge, Dwarves	9, 14-20, 26, 32f, 37-39, 41f, 44, 54, 62f, 72-74, 76, 80, 83-91, 96-100, 107-119, 122, 125-127, 130f, 135-140, 142, 145-157, 161f, 164-169, 171, 176-182, 189, 192, 194, 223f, 227, 230, 232, 233f, 236, 237, 238, 259

www.ingramcontent.com/pod-product-compliance
Lightning Source LLC
Chambersburg PA
CBHW051631230426
43669CB00013B/2258